THE COMPLETE GUIDE TO STOICISM

SENECA

EPICTETUS

MARCUS AURELIUS

FP CLASSICS

First Published 2024

FiNGERPRINT! CLASSICS
An imprint of Prakash Books India Pvt. Ltd

113/A, Darya Ganj,
New Delhi-110 002
Email: info@prakashbooks.com/sales@prakashbooks.com

Fingerprint Publishing
@FingerprintP
@fingerprintpublishingbooks
www.fingerprintpublishing.com

ISBN: 978 93 6214 427 0

"Remember then, that if you think the things which are by nature slavish to be free, and the things which are in the power of others to be your own, you will be hindered, you will lament, you will be disturbed, you will blame both gods and men; but if you think that only which is your own to be your own, and if you think that what is another's, as it really is, belongs to another, no man will ever compel you, no man will hinder you, you will never blame any man, you will accuse no man, you will do nothing involuntarily (against your will), no man will harm you, you will have no enemy, for you will not suffer any harm."

About the Edition

This edition brings together foundational texts of Stoic philosophy, offering a comprehensive resource for both newcomers and seasoned practitioners. It includes 'The Enchiridion' and 'Discourses' by Epictetus provide practical guidance on how to live in accordance with nature and reason; Seneca's 'Letters from a Stoic' offers personal reflections and moral exhortations, addressing a wide range of human experiences and challenges; and Marcus Aurelius' 'Meditations' explore the inner thoughts of a philosopher-king striving to align his actions with his Stoic beliefs. Together, these works present a complete and accessible introduction to Stoic thought, emphasizing virtue, self-control, and rationality.

CONTENTS

1. How to Live: Discourses and The Enchiridion 9

2. Letters from a Stoic 173

3. Meditations 413

HOW TO LIVE

Discourses and The Enchiridion

Translated by

GEORGE LONG

Very little is known of the life of Epictetus. It is said that he was a native of Hierapolis in Phrygia, a town between the Maeander and a branch of the Maeander named the Lycus. Hierapolis is mentioned in the epistle of Paul to the people of Colossae (Coloss. iv., 13); from which it has been concluded that there was a Christian church in Hierapolis in the time of the apostle. The date of the birth of Epictetus is unknown. The only recorded fact of his early life is that he was a slave in Rome, and his master was Epaphroditus, a profligate freedman of the Emperor Nero. There is a story that the master broke his slave's leg by torturing him; but it is better to trust to the evidence of Simplicius, the commentator on the *Enchiridion*, or Manual, who says that Epictetus was weak in body and lame from an early age. It is not said how he became a slave; but it has been asserted in modern times that the parents sold the child. I have not, however, found any authority for this statement.

It may be supposed that the young slave showed intelligence, for his master sent or permitted him to attend the lectures of C. Musonius Rufus, an eminent Stoic philosopher. It may seem strange that such a master should have wished to have his slave made into a philosopher; but Garnier, the author of a *Mémoire sur les Ouvrages d'Epictète*, explains this matter very well in a communication to Schweighaeuser. Garnier says: "Epictetus, born at Hierapolis of Phrygia of poor parents, was indebted apparently for the advantages of a good education to the whim, which was common at the end of the Republic and under the first emperors, among the great of Rome to reckon among their numerous slaves grammarians, poets, rhetoricians, and philosophers, in the same way as rich financiers in these later ages have been led to form at a great cost rich and numerous libraries. This supposition is the only one which can explain to us how a wretched child, born as poor as Irus, had received a good education, and how a rigid Stoic was the slave of Epaphroditus, one of the officers of the imperial guard. For we cannot suspect that it was through predilection for the Stoic doctrine, and for his own use, that the confidant and the minister of the debaucheries of Nero would have desired to possess such a slave."

Some writers assume that Epictetus was manumitted by his master, but I can find no evidence for this statement. Epaphroditus accompanied Nero when he fled from Rome before his enemies, and he aided the miserable tyrant in killing himself. Domitian (Sueton., Domit. 14), afterwards put Epaphroditus to death for this service to Nero. We may conclude that Epictetus in some way obtained his freedom, and that he began to teach at Rome; but after the expulsion of the philosophers from Rome by Domitian, A.D. 89, he retired to Nicopolis in Epirus, a city built by Augustus to commemorate the victory at Actium. Epictetus opened a school or lecture room at Nicopolis, where he taught till he was an old man. The time of his death is unknown. Epictetus was never married, as we learn from Lucian (Demonax, c. 55, torn, ii., ed. Hemsterh., p. 393). When Epictetus was finding fault with Demonax, and advising him to take a wife and beget children, for this also, as Epictetus said, was a philosopher's duty, to leave in place of himself another in the universe, Demonax refuted the doctrine by answering: Give me then, Epictetus, one of your own daughters. Simplicius says (Comment., c. 46, p. 432, ed. Schweigh.) that Epictetus lived alone a long time. At last he took a woman into his house as a nurse for a child, which one of Epictetus' friends was going to expose on account of his poverty, but Epictetus took the child and brought it up.

Photius (Biblioth., 58) mentions among Arrian's works *Conversations with Epictetus*, (Greek: *Homiliai Epichtaeton*), in twelve books. Upton thinks that this work is only another name for the Discourses, and that Photius has made the mistake of taking the Conversations to be a different work from the Discourses.

Yet Photius has enumerated eight books of the Discourses and twelve books of the Conversations. Schweighaeuser observes that Photius had not seen these works of Arrian on Epictetus, for so he concludes from the brief notice of these works by Photius. The fact is that Photius does not say that he had read these books, as he generally does when he is speaking of the books which he enumerates in his Bibliotheca. The conclusion is that we are not certain that there was a work of Arrian entitled, *The Conversations of Epictetus.*

Upton remarks in a note on iii., 23 (p. 184, Trans.), that "there are many passages in these dissertations which are ambiguous or rather confused on account of the small questions, and because the matter is not expanded by oratorical copiousness, not to mention other causes." The discourses of Epictetus, it is supposed, were spoken extempore, and so one thing after another would come into the thoughts of the speaker (Wolf). Schweighaeuser also observes in a note (ii., 336 of his edition) that the connection of the discourse is sometimes obscure through the omission of some words which are necessary to indicate the connection of the thoughts. The reader then will find that he cannot always understand Epictetus, if he does not read him very carefully, and some passages more than once. He must also think and reflect, or he will miss the meaning. I do not say that the book is worth all this trouble. Every man must judge for himself. But I should not have translated the book, if I had not thought it worth study; and I think that all books of this kind require careful reading, if they are worth reading at all.

G.L.

DISCOURSES

Of The Things Which Are In Our Power And Not In Our Power

Of all the faculties (except that which I shall soon mention), you will find not one which is capable of contemplating itself, and, consequently, not capable either of approving or disapproving. How far does the grammatic art possess the contemplating power? As far as forming a judgment about what is written and spoken. And how far music? As far as judging about melody. Does either of them then contemplate itself? By no means. But when you must write something to your friend, grammar will tell you what words you should write; but whether you should write or not, grammar will not tell you. And so it is with music as to musical sounds; but whether you should sing at the present time and play on the lute, or do neither, music will not tell you. What faculty then will tell you? That which contemplates both itself and all other things. And what is this faculty? The rational faculty; for this is the only faculty that we have received which examines itself, what it is, and what power it has, and what is the value of this gift, and examines all other faculties: for what else is there which tells us that golden things are beautiful, for they do not say so themselves? Evidently it is the faculty which is capable of judging of appearances. What else judges of music, grammar, and the other faculties, proves their uses, and points out the occasions for using them? Nothing else.

What then should a man have in readiness in such circumstances? What else than this? What is mine, and what is not mine; and what is permitted to me, and what is not permitted to me. I must die. Must I then die lamenting? I must be put in chains. Must I then also lament? I must go into exile. Does any man then hinder me from going with smiles and cheerfulness and contentment? Tell me the secret which you possess. I will not, for this is in my power. But I will put you in chains. Man, what are you talking about? Me, in chains? You may fetter my leg, but my will not even Zeus himself can overpower. I will throw you into prison. My poor body, you mean. I will cut your head off. When then have I told you that my head alone cannot be cut off? These are the things which philosophers should meditate on, which they should write daily, in which they should exercise themselves.

What then did Agrippinus say? He said, "I am not a hindrance to myself." When it was reported to him that his trial was going on in the Senate, he said: "I hope it may turn out well; but it is the fifth hour of the day"—this was the time when he was used to exercise himself and then take the cold bath—"let us go and take our exercise." After he had taken his exercise, one comes and tells him, "You have been condemned." "To banishment," he replies, "or to death?" "To banishment." "What about my property?" "It is not taken from you." "Let us go to Aricia then," he said, "and dine."

How A Man On Every Occasion Can Maintain His Proper Character

To the rational animal only is the irrational intolerable; but that which is rational is tolerable. Blows are not naturally intolerable. How is that? See how the Lacedaemonians endure whipping when they have learned that whipping is consistent with reason. To hang yourself is not intolerable. When then you have the opinion that it is rational, you go and hang yourself. In short, if we observe, we shall find that the animal man is pained by nothing so much as by that which is irrational; and, on the contrary, attracted to nothing so much as to that which is rational.

Only consider at what price you sell your own will: if for no other reason, at least for this, that you sell it not for a small sum. But that which is great and superior perhaps belongs to Socrates and such as are like him. Why then, if we are naturally such, are not a very great number of us like him? Is it true then that all horses become swift, that all dogs are skilled in tracking footprints? What then, since I am naturally dull, shall I, for this reason, take no pains? I hope not. Epictetus is not superior to Socrates; but if he is not inferior, this is enough for me; for I shall never be a Milo, and yet I do not neglect my body; nor shall I be a Croesus, and yet I do not neglect my property; nor, in a word, do we neglect looking after anything because we despair of reaching the highest degree.

How A Man Should Proceed From The Principle Of God Being The Father Of All Men To The Rest

If a man should be able to assent to this doctrine as he ought, that we are all sprung from God in an especial manner, and that God is the father both of men and of gods, I suppose that he would never have any ignoble or mean thoughts about himself. But if Caesar (the emperor) should adopt you, no one could endure your arrogance; and if you know that you are the son of Zeus, will you not be elated? Yet we do not so; but since these two things are mingled in the generation of man, body in common with the animals, and reason and intelligence in common with the gods, many incline to this kinship, which is miserable and mortal; and some few to that which is divine and happy. Since then it is of necessity that every man uses everything according to the opinion which he has about it, those, the few, who think that they are formed for fidelity and modesty and a sure use of appearances have no mean or ignoble thoughts about themselves; but with the many it is quite the contrary. For they say, What am I? A poor, miserable man, with my wretched bit of flesh. Wretched, indeed; but you possess something better than your bit of flesh. Why then do you neglect that which is better, and why do you attach yourself to this?

Through this kinship with the flesh, some of us inclining to it become like wolves, faithless and treacherous and mischievous; some become like lions, savage and bestial and untamed; but the greater part of us become foxes, and other worse animals. For what else is a slanderer and malignant man than a fox, or some other more wretched and meaner animal? See then and take care that you do not become some one of these miserable things.

Of Progress Or Improvement

He who is making progress, having learned from philosophers that desire means the desire of good things, and aversion means aversion from bad things; having learned too that happiness and tranquillity are not attainable by man otherwise than by not failing to obtain what he desires, and not falling into that which he would avoid; such a man takes from himself desire altogether and confers it, but he employs his aversion only on things which are dependent on his will. For if he attempts to avoid anything independent of his will, he knows that sometimes he will fall in with something which he wishes to avoid, and he will be unhappy. Now if virtue promises good fortune and tranquillity and happiness, certainly also the progress towards virtue is progress towards each of these things. For it is always true that to whatever point the perfecting of anything leads us, progress is an approach towards this point.

How then do we admit that virtue is such as I have said, and yet seek progress in other things and make a display of it? What is the product of virtue? Tranquillity. Who then makes improvement? Is it he who has read many books of Chrysippus? But does virtue consist in having understood Chrysippus? If this is so, progress is clearly nothing else than knowing a great deal of Chrysippus. But now we admit that virtue produces one thing, and we declare that approaching near to it is another thing, namely, progress or improvement. Such a person, says one, is already able to read Chrysippus by himself. Indeed, sir, you are making great progress. What kind of progress? But why do you mock the man? Why do you draw him away from the perception of his own misfortunes? Will you not show him the effect of virtue that he may learn where to look for improvement? Seek it there, wretch, where your work lies. And where is your work? In desire and in aversion, that you may not be disappointed in your desire, and that you may not fall into that which you would avoid; in your pursuit and avoiding, that you commit no error; in assent and suspension of assent, that you be not deceived. The first things, and the most necessary are those which I have named. But if with trembling and lamentation you seek not to fall into that which you avoid, tell me how you are improving.

Do you then show me your improvement in these things? If I were talking to an athlete, I should say, Show me your shoulders; and then he might say, Here are my Halteres. You and your Halteres look to that. I should reply, I wish to see the effect of the Halteres. So, when you say: Take the treatise on the active powers (Greek: *hormea*), and see how I have studied it, I reply: Slave, I am not inquiring about this, but how you exercise pursuit and avoidance, desire and aversion, how you design and purpose and prepare yourself, whether conformably to nature or not. If conformably, give me evidence of it, and I will say that you are making progress; but if not conformably, be gone, and not only expound your books, but write such books yourself; and what will you gain by it? Do you not know that the whole book costs only five denarii? Does then the expounder seem to be worth more than five denarii? Never then look for the matter itself in one place, and progress towards it in another. Where then is progress? If any of you, withdrawing himself from externals, turns to his own will (Greek: *proairesis*) to exercise it and to improve it by labor, so as to make it conformable to nature, elevated, free, unrestrained, unimpeded, faithful, modest; and if he has learned that he who desires or avoids the things which are not in his power can neither be faithful nor free, but of necessity he must change with them and be tossed about with them as in a tempest, and of necessity must subject himself to others who have the power to procure or prevent what lie desires or would avoid; finally, when he rises in the morning, if he observes and keeps these rules, bathes as a man of fidelity, eats as a modest man; in like manner, if in every matter that occurs he works out his chief principles (Greek: *ta proaegoumena*) as the runner does with reference to running, and the trainer of the voice with reference to the voice—this is the man who truly makes progress, and this is the man who has not travelled in vain. But if he has strained his efforts to the practice of reading books, and labors only at this, and has travelled for this, I tell him to return home immediately, and not to neglect his affairs there; for this for which he has travelled is nothing. But the other thing is something, to study how a man can rid his life of lamentation and groaning, and saying, Woe to me, and wretched that I am, and to rid it also of misfortune and disappointment, and to learn what death is, and exile, and prison, and poison, that he may be able to say when he is in fetters, Dear Crito, if it is the will of the gods that it be so, let it be so; and not to say, Wretched am I, an old man: have I kept my gray hairs for this? Who is it that speaks thus? Do you think that I shall name some man of no repute and of low condition? Does not Priam say this? Does not Oedipus say this? Nay, all kings say it! For what else is tragedy than the perturbations (Greek: *pathae*) of men who value externals exhibited in this kind of poetry? But if a man must learn by fiction that no external things which are independent of the will concern us, for my part I should like this fiction, by the aid of which I should live happily and undisturbed. But you must consider for yourselves what you wish.

What then does Chrysippus teach us? The reply is, to know that these things are not false, from which happiness comes and tranquillity arises. Take my books, and you will learn how true and conformable to nature are the things which make me free from perturbations. O great good fortune! O the great benefactor who points out the way! To Triptolemus all men have erected temples and altars, because he gave us food by cultivation; but to him who discovered truth and brought it to light and communicated it to all, not the truth which shows us how to live, but how to live well, who of you for this reason has built an altar, or a temple, or has dedicated a statue, or who worships God for this? Because the gods have given the vine, or wheat, we sacrifice to them; but because they have produced in the human mind that fruit by which they designed to show us the truth which relates to happiness, shall we not thank God for this?

Against The Academics

If a man, said Epictetus, opposes evident truths, it is not easy to find arguments by which we shall make him change his opinion. But this does not arise either from the man's strength or the teacher's weakness; for when the man, though he has been confuted, is hardened like a stone, how shall we then be able to deal with him by argument?

Now there are two kinds of hardening, one of the understanding, the other of the sense of shame, when a man is resolved not to assent to what is manifest nor to desist from contradictions. Most of us are afraid of mortification of the body, and would contrive all means to avoid such a thing, but we care not about the soul's mortification. And indeed with regard to the soul, if a man be in such a state as not to apprehend anything, or understand at all, we think that he is in a bad condition; but if the sense of shame and modesty are deadened, this we call even power (or strength).

Of Providence

From everything, which is or happens in the world, it is easy to praise Providence, if a man possesses these two qualities: the faculty of seeing what belongs and happens to all persons and things, and a grateful disposition. If he does not possess these two qualities, one man will not see the use of things which are and which happen: another will not be thankful for them, even if he does know them. If God had made colors, but had not made the faculty of seeing them, what would have been their use? None at all. On the other hand, if he had made the faculty of vision, but had not made objects such as to fall under the faculty, what in that case also would have been the use of it? None at all. Well, suppose that he had made both, but had not made light? In that case, also, they would have been of no use. Who is it then who has fitted this to that and that to this?

What, then, are these things done in us only? Many, indeed, in us only, of which the rational animal had peculiar need; but you will find many common to us with irrational animals. Do they then understand what is done? By no means. For use is one thing, and understanding is another; God had need of irrational animals to make use of appearances, but of us to understand the use of appearances. It is therefore enough for them to eat and to drink, and to copulate, and to do all the other things which they severally do. But for us, to whom he has given also the intellectual faculty, these things are not sufficient; for unless we act in a proper and orderly manner, and conformably to the nature and constitution of each thing, we shall never attain our true end. For where the constitutions of living beings are different, there also the acts and the ends are different. In those animals then whose constitution is adapted only to use, use alone is enough; but in an animal (man), which has also the power of understanding the use, unless there be the due exercise of the understanding, he will never attain his proper end. Well then God constitutes every animal, one to be eaten, another to serve for agriculture, another to supply cheese, and another for some like use; for which purposes what need is there to understand appearances and to be able to distinguish them? But God has introduced man to be a spectator of God and of his works; and not only a spectator of them, but an interpreter. For this reason it is shameful for man to begin and to end where irrational animals do; but rather he ought to begin where they begin, and to end where nature ends in us; and nature ends in contemplation and understanding, and in a way of life conformable to nature. Take care then not to die without having been spectators of these things.

But you take a journey to Olympia to see the work of Phidias, and all of you think it a misfortune to die without having seen such things. But when there is no need to take a journey, and where a man is, there he has the works (of God) before him, will you not desire to see and understand them? Will you not perceive either what you are, or what you were born for, or what this is for which you have received the faculty of sight? But you may say, There are some things disagreeable and troublesome in life. And are there none at Olympia? Are you not scorched? Are you not pressed by a crowd? Are you not without comfortable means of bathing? Are you not wet when it rains? Have you not abundance of noise, clamor, and other disagreeable things? But I suppose that setting all these things off against the magnificence of the spectacle, you bear and endure. Well then and have you not received faculties by which you will be able to bear all that happens? Have you not received greatness of soul? Have you not received manliness? Have you not received endurance? And why do I trouble myself about anything that can happen if I possess greatness of soul? What shall distract my mind, or disturb me, or appear painful? Shall I not use the power for the purposes for which I received it, and shall I grieve and lament over what happens?

Come, then, do you also having observed these things look to the faculties which you have, and when you have looked at them, say: Bring now, O Zeus, any difficulty that thou pleasest, for I have means given to me by thee and powers for honoring myself through the things which happen. You do not so; but you sit still, trembling for fear that some things will happen, and weeping, and lamenting, and groaning for what does happen; and then you blame the gods. For what is the consequence of such meanness of spirit but impiety? And yet God has not only given us these faculties, by which we shall be able to bear everything that happens without being depressed or broken by it; but, like a good king and a true father, He has given us these faculties free from hindrance, subject to no compulsion, unimpeded, and has put them entirely in our own power, without even having reserved to Himself any power of hindering or impeding. You, who have received these powers free and as your own, use them not; you do not even see what you have received, and from whom; some of you being blinded to the giver, and not even acknowledging your benefactor, and others, through meanness of spirit, betaking yourselves to fault-finding and making charges against God. Yet I will show to you that you have powers and means for greatness of soul and manliness; but what powers you have for finding fault making accusations, do you show me.

How From The Fact That We Are Akin To God A Man May Proceed To The Consequences

I indeed think that the old man ought to be sitting here, not to contrive how you may have no mean thoughts nor mean and ignoble talk about yourselves, but to take care that there be not among us any young men of such a mind, that when they have recognized their kinship to God, and that we are fettered by these bonds, the body, I mean, and its possessions, and whatever else on account of them is necessary to us for the economy and commerce of life, they should intend to throw off these things as if they were burdens painful and intolerable, and to depart to their kinsmen. But this is the labor that your teacher and instructor ought to be employed upon, if he really were what he should be. You should come to him and say: Epictetus, we can no longer endure being bound to this poor body, and feeding it, and giving it drink and rest, and cleaning it, and for the sake of the body complying with the wishes of these and of those. Are not these things indifferent and nothing to us; and is not death no evil? And are we not in a manner kinsmen of God, and did we not come from him? Allow us to depart to the place from which we came; allow us to be released at last from these bonds by which we are bound and weighed down. Here there are robbers and thieves and courts of justice, and those who are named tyrants, and think that they have some power over us by means of the body and its possessions. Permit us to show them that they have no power over any man. And I on my part would say: Friends, wait for God: when he shall give the signal and release you from this service, then go to him; but for the present endure to dwell in this place where he has put you. Short indeed is this time of your dwelling here, and easy to bear for those who are so disposed; for what tyrant, or what thief, or what courts of justice are formidable to those who have thus considered as things of no value the body and the possessions of the body? Wait then, do not depart without a reason.

Of Contentment

With respect to gods, there are some who say that a divine being does not exist; others say that it exists, but is inactive and careless, and takes no forethought about anything; a third class say that such a being exists and exercises forethought, but only about great things and heavenly things, and about nothing on the earth; a fourth class say that a divine being exercises forethought both about things on the earth and heavenly things, but in a general way only, and not about things severally. There is a fifth class to whom Ulysses and Socrates belong, who say:

> I move not without thy knowledge.—*Iliad*, x., 278.

Before all other things then it is necessary to inquire about each of these opinions, whether it is affirmed truly or not truly. For if there are no gods, how is it our proper end to follow them? And if they exist, but take no care of anything, in this case also how will it be right to follow them? But if indeed they do exist and look after things, still if there is nothing communicated from them to men, nor in fact to myself, how even so is it right (to follow them)? The wise and good man then, after considering all these things, submits his own mind to him who administers the whole, as good citizens do to the law of the state. He who is receiving instruction ought to come to be instructed with this intention, How shall I follow the gods in all things, how shall I be contented with the divine administration, and how can I become free? For he is free to whom everything happens according to his will, and whom no man can hinder. What then, is freedom madness? Certainly not; for madness and freedom do not consist. But, you say, I would have everything result just as I like, and in whatever way I like. You are mad, you are beside yourself. Do you not know that freedom is a noble and valuable thing? But for me inconsiderately to wish for things to happen as I inconsiderately like, this appears to be not only not noble, but even most base. For how do we proceed in the matter of writing? Do I wish to write the name of Dion as I choose? No, but I am taught to choose to write it as it ought to be written. And how with respect to music? In the same manner. And what universally in every art or science? Just the same. If it were not so, it would be of no value to know anything, if knowledge were adapted to every man's whim. Is it then in this alone, in this which is the greatest and the chief thing, I mean freedom, that I am permitted to will inconsiderately? By no means; but to be instructed is this, to learn to wish that everything may happen as it does. And how do things happen? As the disposer has disposed them? And he has appointed summer and winter, and abundance and scarcity, and virtue and vice, and all such opposites for the harmony of the whole; and to each of us he has given a body, and parts of the body, and possessions, and companions.

What then remains, or what method is discovered of holding commerce with them? Is there such a method by which they shall do what seems fit to them, and we not the less shall be in a mood which is conformable to nature? But you are unwilling to endure, and are discontented; and if you are alone, you call it solitude; and if you are with men, you call them knaves and robbers; and you find fault with your own parents and children, and brothers and neighbors. But you ought when you are alone to call this condition by the name of tranquillity and freedom, and to think yourself like to the gods; and when you are with many, you ought not to call it crowd, nor trouble, nor uneasiness, but festival and assembly, and so accept all contentedly.

What then is the punishment of those who do not accept? It is to be what they are. Is any person dissatisfied with being alone? Let him be alone. Is a man dissatisfied with his parents? Let him be a bad son, and lament. Is he dissatisfied with his children? Let him be a bad father. Cast him into prison. What prison? Where he is already, for he is there against his will; and where a man is against his will, there he is in prison. So Socrates was not in prison, for he was there willingly. Must my leg then be lamed? Wretch, do you then on account of one poor leg find fault with the world? Will you not willingly surrender it for the whole? Will you not withdraw from it? Will you not gladly part with it to him who gave it? And will you be vexed and discontented with the things established by Zeus, which he, with the Moirae (fates) who were present and spinning the thread of your generation, defined and put in order? Know you not how small a part you are compared with the whole. I mean with respect to the body, for as to intelligence you are not inferior to the gods nor less; for the magnitude of intelligence is not measured by length nor yet by height, but by thoughts.

How Everything May Be Done Acceptably To The Gods

When some one asked, How may a man eat acceptably to the gods, he answered: If he can eat justly and contentedly, and with equanimity, and temperately, and orderly, will it not be also acceptable to the gods? But when you have asked for warm water and the slave has not heard, or if he did hear has brought only tepid water, or he is not even found to be in the house, then not to be vexed or to burst with passion, is not this acceptable to the gods? How then shall a man endure such persons as this slave? Slave yourself, will you not bear with your own brother, who has Zeus for his progenitor, and is like a son from the same seeds and of the same descent from above? But if you have been put in any such higher place, will you immediately make yourself a tyrant? Will you not remember who you are, and whom you rule? That they are kinsmen, that they are brethren by nature, that they are the offspring of Zeus? But I have purchased them, and they have not purchased me. Do you see in what direction you are looking, that it is towards the earth, towards the pit, that it is towards these wretched laws of dead men? but towards the laws of the gods you are not looking.

What Philosophy Promises

When a man was consulting him how he should persuade his brother to cease being angry with him, Epictetus replied: Philosophy does not propose to secure for a man any external thing. If it did (or if it were not, as I say), philosophy would be allowing something which is not within its province. For as the carpenter's material is wood, and that of the statuary is copper, so the matter of the art of living is each man's life. When then is my brother's? That again belongs to his own art; but with respect to yours, it is one of the external things, like a piece of land, like health, like reputation. But Philosophy promises none of these. In every circumstance I will maintain, she says, the governing part conformable to nature. Whose governing part? His in whom I am, she says.

How then shall my brother cease to be angry with me? Bring him to me and I will tell him. But I have nothing to say to you about his anger.

When the man who was consulting him said, I seek to know this, How, even if my brother is not reconciled to me, shall I maintain myself in a state conformable to nature? Nothing great, said Epictetus, is produced suddenly, since not even the grape or the fig is. If you say to me now that you want a fig, I will answer to you that it requires time: let it flower first, then put forth fruit, and then ripen. Is then the fruit of a fig-tree not perfected suddenly and in one hour, and would you possess the fruit of a man's mind in so short a time and so easily? Do not expect it, even if I tell you.

That We Ought Not To Be Angry With The Errors (Faults) Of Others

Ought not then this robber and this adulterer to be destroyed? By no means say so, but speak rather in this way: This man who has been mistaken and deceived about the most important things, and blinded, not in the faculty of vision which distinguishes white and black, but in the faculty which distinguishes good and bad, should we not destroy him? If you speak thus you will see how inhuman this is which you say, and that it is just as if you would say, Ought we not to destroy this blind and deaf man? But if the greatest harm is the privation of the greatest things, and the greatest thing in every man is the will or choice such as it ought to be, and a man is deprived of this will, why are you also angry with him? Man, you ought not to be affected contrary to nature by the bad things of another. Pity him rather; drop this readiness to be offended and to hate, and these words which the many utter: "These accursed and odious fellows." How have you been made so wise at once? and how are you so peevish? Why then are we angry? Is it because we value so much the things of which these men rob us? Do not admire your clothes, and then you will not be angry with the thief. Consider this matter thus: you have fine clothes; your neighbor has not; you have a window; you wish to air the clothes. The thief does not know wherein man's good consists, but he thinks that it consist in having fine clothes, the very thing which you also think. Must he not then come and take them away? When you show a cake to greedy persons, and swallow it all yourself, do you expect them not to snatch it from you? Do not provoke them; do not have a window; do not air your clothes. I also lately had an iron lamp placed by the side of my household gods; hearing a noise at the door, I ran down, and found that the lamp had been carried off. I reflected that he who had taken the lamp had done nothing strange. What then? To-morrow, I said, you will find an earthen lamp; for a man only loses that which he has. I have lost my garment. The reason is that you had a garment. I have a pain in my head. Have you any pain in your horns? Why then are you troubled? For we only lose those things, we have only pains about those things, which we possess.

But the tyrant will chain—what? The leg. He will take away—what? The neck. What then will he not chain and not take away? The will. This is why the ancients taught the maxim, Know thyself. Therefore we ought to exercise ourselves in small things, and beginning with them to proceed to the greater. I have pain in the head. Do not say, Alas! I have pain in the ear. Do not say alas! And I do not say that you are not allowed to groan, but do not groan inwardly; and if your slave is slow in bringing a bandage, do not cry out and torment yourself, and say, Every body hates me; for who would not hate such a man? For the future, relying on these opinions, walk about upright, free; not trusting to the size of your body, as an athlete, for a man ought not to be invincible in the way that an ass is.

How We Should Behave To Tyrants

If a man possesses any superiority, or thinks that he does when he does not, such a man, if he is uninstructed, will of necessity be puffed up through it. For instance, the tyrant says, I am master of all! And what can you do for me? Can you give me desire which shall have no hindrance? How can you? Have you the infallible power of avoiding what you would avoid? Have you the power of moving towards an object without error? And how do you possess this power? Come, when you are in a ship, do you trust to yourself or to the helmsman? And when you are in a chariot, to whom do you trust but to the driver? And how is it in all other arts? Just the same. In what, then, lies your power? All men pay respect to me. Well, I also pay respect to my platter, and I wash it and wipe it; and for the sake of my oil-flask, I drive a peg into the wall. Well, then, are these things superior to me? No, but they supply some of my wants, and for this reason I take care of them. Well, do I not attend to my ass? Do I not wash his feet? Do I not clean him? Do you not know that every man has regard to himself, and to you just the same as he has regard to his ass? For who has regard to you as a man? Show me. Who wishes to become like you? Who imitates you, as he imitates Socrates? But I can cut off your head. You say right. I had forgotten that I must have regard to you, as I would to a fever and the bile, and raise an altar to you, as there is at Rome an altar to fever.

What is it then that disturbs and terrifies the multitude? Is it the tyrant and his guards? (By no means.) I hope that it is not so. It is not possible that what is by nature free can be disturbed by anything else, or hindered by any other thing than by itself. But it is a man's own opinions which disturb him. For when the tyrant says to a man, I will chain your leg, he who values his leg says, Do not; have pity. But he who values his own will says, If it appears more advantageous to you, chain it. Do you not care? I do not care. I will show you that I am master. You cannot do that. Zeus has set me free; do you think that he intended to allow his own son to be enslaved? But you are master of my carcase; take it. So when you approach me, you have no regard to me? No, but I have regard to myself; and if you wish me to say that I have regard to you also, I tell you that I have the same regard to you that I have to my pipkin.

What then? When absurd notions about things independent of our will, as if they were good and (or) bad, lie at the bottom of our opinions, we must of necessity pay regard to tyrants: for I wish that men would pay regard to tyrants only, and not also to the bedchamber men. How is it that the man becomes all at once wise, when Caesar has made him superintendent of the close stool? How is it that we say immediately, Felicion spoke sensibly to me? I wish he were ejected from the bedchamber, that he might again appear to you to be a fool.

Has a man been exalted to the tribuneship? All who meet him offer their congratulations; one kisses his eyes, another the neck, and the slaves kiss his hands. He goes to his house, he finds torches lighted. He ascends the Capitol; he offers a sacrifice on the occasion. Now who ever sacrificed for having had good desires? for having acted conformably to nature? For in fact we thank the gods for those things in which we place our good.

A person was talking to me to-day about the priesthood of Augustus. I say to him: Man, let the thing alone; you will spend much for no purpose. But he replies, Those who draw up agreements will write my name. Do you then stand by those who read them, and say to such persons, It is I whose name is written there? And if you can now be present on ail such occasions, what will you do when you are dead? My name will remain. Write it on a stone, and it will remain. But come, what remembrance of you will there be beyond Nicopolis? But I shall wear a crown of gold. If you desire a crown at all, take a crown of roses and put it on, for it will be more elegant in appearance.

Against Those Who Wish To Be Admired

When a man holds his proper station in life, he does not gape after things beyond it. Man, what do you wish to happen to you? I am satisfied if I desire and avoid conformably to nature, if I employ movements towards and from an object as I am by nature formed to do, and purpose and design and assent. Why then do you strut before us as if you had swallowed a spit? My wish has always been that those who meet me should admire me, and those who follow me should exclaim, O the great philosopher! Who are they by whom you wish to be admired? Are they not those of whom you are used to say that they are mad? Well, then, do you wish to be admired by madmen?

On Praecognitions

Praecognitions are common to all men, and praecognition is not contradictory to praecognition. For who of us does not assume that Good is useful and eligible, and in all circumstances that we ought to follow and pursue it? And who of us does not assume that Justice is beautiful and becoming? When then does the contradiction arise? It arises in the adaptation of the praecognitions to the particular cases. When one man says, "He has done well; he is a brave man," and another says, "Not so; but he has acted foolishly," then the disputes arise among men. This is the dispute among the Jews and the Syrians and the Egyptians and the Romans; not whether holiness should be preferred to all things and in all cases should be pursued, but whether it is holy to eat pig's flesh or not holy. You will find this dispute also between Agamemnon and Achilles; for call them forth. What do you say, Agamemnon? ought not that to be done which is proper and right? "Certainly." Well, what do you say, Achilles? do you not admit that what is good ought to be done? "I do most certainly." Adapt your praecognitions then to the present matter. Here the dispute begins. Agamemnon says, "I ought not to give up Chryseis to her father." Achilles says, "You ought." It is certain that one of the two makes a wrong adaptation of the praecognition of "ought" or "duty." Further, Agamemnon says, "Then if I ought to restore Chryseis, it is fit that I take his prize from some of you." Achilles replies, "Would you then take her whom I love?" "Yes, her whom you love." "Must I then be the only man who goes without a prize? and must I be the only man who has no prize?" Thus the dispute begins.

What then is education? Education is the learning how to adapt the natural praecognitions to the particular things conformably to nature; and then to distinguish that of things some are in our power, but others are not. In our power are will and all acts which depend on the will; things not in our power are the body, the parts of the body, possessions, parents, brothers, children, country, and, generally, all with whom we live in society. In what then should we place the good? To what kind of things (Greek: *ousia*) shall we adapt it? To the things which are in our power? Is not health then a good thing, and soundness of limb, and life, and are not children and parents and country? Who will tolerate you if you deny this?

Let us then transfer the notion of good to these things. Is it possible, then, when a man sustains damage and does not obtain good things, that he can be happy? It is not possible. And can he maintain towards society a proper behavior? He can not. For I am naturally formed to look after my own interest. If it is my interest to have an estate in land, it is my interest also to take it from my neighbor. If it is my interest to have a garment, it is my interest also to steal it from the bath. This is the origin of wars, civil commotions, tyrannies, conspiracies. And how shall I be still able to maintain my duty towards Zeus? For if I sustain damage and am unlucky, he takes no care of me. And what is he to me if he cannot help me? And further, what is he to me if he allows me to be in the condition in which I am? I now begin to hate him. Why then do we build temples, why setup statues to Zeus, as well as to evil demons, such as to Fever; and how is Zeus the Saviour, and how the giver of rain, and the giver of fruits? And in truth if we place the nature of Good in any such things, all this follows.

What should we do then? This is the inquiry of the true philosopher who is in labor. Now I do not see what the good is nor the bad. Am I not mad? Yes. But suppose that I place the good somewhere among the things which depend on the will; all will laugh at me. There will come some greyhead wearing many gold rings on his fingers, and he will shake his head and say: "Hear, my child. It is right that you should philosophize; but you ought to have some brains also; all this that you are doing is silly. You learn the syllogism from philosophers; but you know how to act better than philosophers do." Man why then do you blame me, if I know? What shall I say to this slave? If I am silent, he will burst. I must speak in this way: "Excuse me, as you would excuse lovers; I am not my own master; I am mad."

How We Should Struggle With Circumstances

It is circumstances (difficulties) which show what men are. Therefore when a difficulty falls upon you, remember that God, like a trainer of wrestlers, has matched you with a rough young man. For what purpose? you may say. Why, that you may become an Olympic conqueror; but it is not accomplished without sweat. In my opinion no man has had a more profitable difficulty than you have had, if you choose to make use of it as an athlete would deal with a young antagonist. We are now sending a scout to Rome; but no man sends a cowardly scout, who, if he only hears a noise and sees a shadow anywhere, comes running back in terror and reports that the enemy is close at hand. So now if you should come and tell us: "Fearful is the state of affairs at Rome; terrible is death; terrible is exile; terrible is calumny; terrible is poverty; fly, my friends, the enemy is near," we shall answer: "Begone, prophesy for yourself; we have committed only one fault, that we sent such a scout."

Diogenes, who was sent as a scout before you, made a different report to us. He says that death is no evil, for neither is it base; he says that fame (reputation) is the noise of madmen. And what has this spy said about pain, about pleasure, and about poverty? He says that to be naked is better than any purple robe, and to sleep on the bare ground is the softest bed; and he gives as a proof of each thing that he affirms his own courage, his tranquillity, his freedom, and the healthy appearance and compactness of his body. There is no enemy near, he says; all is peace. How so, Diogenes? "See," he replies, "if I am struck, if I have been wounded, if I have fled from any man." This is what a scout ought to be. But you come to us and tell us one thing after another. Will you not go back, and you will see clearer when you have laid aside fear?

On The Same

If these things are true, and if we are not silly, and are not acting hypocritically when we say that the good of man is in the will, and the evil too, and that everything else does not concern us, why are we still disturbed, why are we still afraid? The things about which we have been busied are in no man's power; and the things which are in the power of others, we care not for. What kind of trouble have we still?

But give me directions. Why should I give you directions? Has not Zeus given you directions? Has he not given to you what is your own free from hindrance and free from impediment, and what is not your own subject to hindrance and impediment? What directions then, what kind of orders did you bring when you came from him? Keep by every means what is your own; do not desire what belongs to others. Fidelity (integrity) is your own, virtuous shame is your own; who then can take these things from you? who else than yourself will hinder you from using them? But how do you act? When you seek what is not your own, you lose that which is your own. Having such promptings and commands from Zeus, what kind do you still ask from me? Am I more powerful than he, am I more worthy of confidence? But if you observe these, do you want any others besides? "Well, but he has not given these orders," you will say. Produce your praecognitions (Greek: *prolaepseis*), produce these proofs of philosophers, produce what you have often heard, and produce what you have said yourself, produce what you have read, produce what you have meditated on; and you will then see that all these things are from God.

If I have set my admiration on the poor body, I have given myself up to be a slave; if on my poor possessions, I also make myself a slave. For I immediately make it plain with what I may be caught; as if the snake draws in his head, I tell you to strike that part of him which he guards; and do you be assured that whatever part you choose to guard, that part your master will attack. Remembering this, whom will you still flatter or fear?

But I should like to sit where the Senators sit. Do you see that you are putting yourself in straits, you are squeezing yourself? How then shall I see well in any other way in the amphitheatre? Man, do not be a spectator at all, and you will not be squeezed. Why do you give yourself trouble? Or wait a little, and when the spectacle is over, seat yourself in the place reserved for the Senators and sun yourself. For remember this general truth, that it is we who squeeze ourselves, who put ourselves in straits; that is, our opinions squeeze us and put us in straits. For what is it to be reviled? Stand by a stone and revile it, and what will you gain? If then a man listens like a stone, what profit is there to the reviler? But if the reviler has as a stepping-stone (or ladder) the weakness of him who is reviled, then he accomplishes something. Strip him. What do you mean by him? Lay hold of his garment, strip it off. I have insulted you. Much good may it do you.

This was the practice of Socrates; this was the reason why he always had one face. But we choose to practise and study anything rather than the means by which we shall be unimpeded and free. You say: "Philosophers talk paradoxes." But are there no paradoxes in the other arts? And what is more paradoxical than to puncture a man's eye in order that he may see? If any one said this to a man ignorant of the surgical art, would he not ridicule the speaker? Where is the wonder, then, if in philosophy also many things which are true appear paradoxical to the inexperienced?

In How Many Ways Appearances Exist, And What Aids We Should Provide Against Them

Appearances are to us in four ways. For either things appear as they are; or they are not, and do not even appear to be; or they are, and do not appear to be; or they are not, and yet appear to be. Further, in all these cases to form a right judgment (to hit the mark) is the office of an educated man. But whatever it is that annoys (troubles) us, to that we ought to apply a remedy. If the sophisms of Pyrrho and of the Academics are what annoys (troubles), we must apply the remedy to them. If it is the persuasion of appearances, by which some things appear to be good, when they are not good, let us seek a remedy for this. If it is habit which annoys us, we must try to seek aid against habit. What aid, then, can we find against habit? The contrary habit. You hear the ignorant say: "That unfortunate person is dead; his father and mother are overpowered with sorrow; he was cut off by an untimely death and in a foreign land." Hear the contrary way of speaking. Tear yourself from these expressions; oppose to one habit the contrary habit; to sophistry oppose reason, and the exercise and discipline of reason; against persuasive (deceitful) appearances we ought to have manifest praecognitions (Greek: *prolaepseis*), cleared of all impurities and ready to hand.

When death appears an evil, we ought to have this rule in readiness, that it is fit to avoid evil things, and that death is a necessary thing. For what shall I do, and where shall I escape it? Suppose that I am not Sarpedon, the son of Zeus, nor able to speak in this noble way. I will go and I am resolved either to behave bravely myself or to give to another the opportunity of doing so; if I cannot succeed in doing anything myself, I will not grudge another the doing of something noble. Suppose that it is above our power to act thus; is it not in our power to reason thus? Tell me where I can escape death; discover for me the country, show me the men to whom I must go, whom death does not visit. Discover to me a charm against death. If I have not one, what do you wish me to do? I cannot escape from death. Shall I not escape from the fear of death, but shall I die lamenting and trembling? For the origin of perturbation is this, to wish for something, and that this should not happen. Therefore if I am able to change externals according to my wish, I change them; but if I cannot, I am ready to tear out the eyes of him who hinders me. For the nature of man is not to endure to be deprived of the good, and not to endure the falling into the evil. Then at last, when I am neither able to change circumstances nor to tear out the eyes of him who hinders me, I sit down and groan, and abuse whom I can, Zeus and the rest of the gods. For if they do not care for me, what are they to me? Yes, but you will be an impious man. In what respect, then, will it be worse for me than it is now? To sum up, remember that unless piety and your interest be in the same thing, piety cannot be maintained in any man. Do not these things seem necessary (true)?

That We Ought Not To Be Angry With Men; And What Are The Small And The Great Things Among Men

What is the cause of assenting to anything? The fact that it appears to be true. It is not possible then to assent to that which appears not to be true. Why? Because this is the nature of the understanding, to incline to the true, to be dissatisfied with the false, and in matters uncertain to withhold assent. What is the proof of this? Imagine (persuade yourself), if you can, that it is now night. It is not possible. Take away your persuasion that it is day. It is not possible. Persuade yourself or take away your persuasion that the stars are even in number. It is impossible. When then any man assents to that which is false, be assured that he did not intend to assent to it as false, for every soul is unwillingly deprived of the truth, as Plato says; but the falsity seemed to him to be true. Well, in acts what have we of the like kind as we have here truth or falsehood? We have the fit and the not fit (duty and not duty), the profitable and the unprofitable, that which is suitable to a person and that which is not, and whatever is like these. Can then a man think that a thing is useful to him and not choose it? He cannot. How says Medea?

"'Tis true I know what evil I shall do,
But passion overpowers the better counsel."

She thought that to indulge her passion and take vengeance on her husband was more profitable than to spare her children. It was so; but she was deceived. Show her plainly that she is deceived, and she will not do it; but so long as you do not show it, what can she follow except that which appears to herself (her opinion)? Nothing else. Why then are you angry with the unhappy woman that she has been bewildered about the most important things, and is become a viper instead of a human creature? And why not, if it is possible, rather pity, as we pity the blind and the lame, so those who are blinded and maimed in the faculties which are supreme?

Whoever then clearly remembers this, that to man the measure of every act is the appearance (the opinion), whether the thing appears good or bad. If good, he is free from blame; if bad, himself suffers the penalty, for it is impossible that he who is deceived can be one person, and he who suffers another person—whoever remembers this will not be angry with any man, will not be vexed at any man, will not revile or blame any man, nor hate, nor quarrel with any man.

Does a man then differ in no respect from a stork? Don't suppose that I say so; but there is no difference in these matters (which I have mentioned). In what then is the difference? Seek and you will find that there is a difference in another matter. See whether it is not in a man the understanding of what he does, see if it is not in social community, in fidelity, in modesty, in steadfastness, in intelligence. Where then is the great good and evil in men? It is where the difference is. If the difference is preserved and remains fenced round, and neither modesty is destroyed, nor fidelity, nor intelligence, then the man also is preserved; but if any of these things is destroyed and stormed like a city, then the man too perishes: and in this consist the great things. Alexander, you say, sustained great damage then when the Hellenes invaded and when they ravaged Troy, and when his brothers perished. By no means; for no man is damaged by an action which is not his own; but what happened at that time was only the destruction of stork's nests. Now the ruin of Alexander was when he lost the character of modesty, fidelity, regard to hospitality, and to decency. When was Achilles ruined? Was it when Patroclus died? Not so. But it happened when he began to be angry, when he wept for a girl, when he forgot that he was at Troy not to get mistresses, but to fight. These things are the ruin of men, this is being besieged, this is the destruction of cities, when right opinions are destroyed, when they are corrupted.

On Constancy (Or Firmness)

The being (nature) of the good is a certain will; the being of the bad is a certain kind of will. What, then, are externals? Materials for the will, about which the will being conversant shall obtain its own good or evil. How shall it obtain the good? If it does not admire (over-value) the materials; for the opinions about the materials, if the opinions are right, make the will good: but perverse and distorted opinions make the will bad. God has fixed this law, and says, "If you would have anything good, receive it from yourself." You say, No, but I will have it from another. Do not so: but receive it from yourself. Therefore when the tyrant threatens and calls me, I say, Whom do you threaten? If he says, I will put you in chains, I say, You threaten my hands and my feet. If he says, I will cut off your head, I reply, You threaten my head. If he says, I will throw you into prison, I say, You threaten the whole of this poor body. If he threatens me with banishment, I say the same. Does he then not threaten you at all? If I feel that all these things do not concern me, he does not threaten me at all; but if I fear any of them, it is I whom he threatens. Whom then do I fear? the master of what? The master of things which are in my own power? There is no such master. Do I fear the master of things which are not in my power? And what are these things to me?

Do you philosophers then teach us to despise kings? I hope not. Who among us teaches to claim against them the power over things which they possess? Take my poor body, take my property, take my reputation, take those who are about me. If I advise any persons to claim these things, they may truly accuse me. Yes, but I intend to command your opinions also. And who has given you this power? How can you conquer the opinion of another man? By applying terror to it, he replies, I will conquer it. Do you not know that opinion conquers itself, and is not conquered by another? But nothing else can conquer will except the will itself. For this reason too the law of God is most powerful and most just, which is this: Let the stronger always be superior to the weaker. Ten are stronger than one. For what? For putting in chains, for killing, for dragging whither they choose, for taking away what a man has. The ten therefore conquer the one in this in which they are stronger. In what then are the ten weaker? If the one possesses right opinions and the others do not. Well then, can the ten conquer in this matter? How is it possible? If we were placed in the scales, must not the heavier draw down the scale in which it is.

How strange then that Socrates should have been so treated by the Athenians. Slave, why do you say Socrates? Speak of the thing as it is: how strange that the poor body of Socrates should have been carried off and dragged to prison by stronger men, and that anyone should have given hemlock to the poor body of Socrates, and that it should breathe out the life. Do these things seem strange, do they seem unjust, do you on account of these things blame God? Had Socrates then no equivalent for these things? Where then for him was the nature of good? Whom shall we listen to, you or him? And what does Socrates say? "Anytus and Melitus can kill me, but they cannot hurt me." And further, he says, "If it so pleases God, so let it be."

But show me that he who has the inferior principles overpowers him who is superior in principles. You will never show this, nor come near showing it; for this is the law of nature and of God that the superior shall always overpower the inferior. In what? In that in which it is superior. One body is stronger than another: many are stronger than one: the thief is stronger than he who is not a thief. This is the reason why I also lost my lamp, because in wakefulness the thief was superior to me. But the man bought the lamp at this price: for a lamp he became a thief, a faithless fellow, and like a wild beast. This seemed to him a good bargain. Be it so. But a man has seized me by the cloak, and is drawing me to the public place: then others bawl out, Philosopher, what has been the use of your opinions? see, you are dragged to prison, you are going to be beheaded. And what system of philosophy (Greek: *eisagogaen*) could I have made so that, if a stronger man should have laid hold of my cloak, I should not be dragged off; that if ten men should have laid hold of me and cast me into prison, I should not be cast in? Have I learned nothing else then? I have learned to see that everything which happens, if it be independent of my will, is nothing to me. I may ask, if you have not gained by this. Why then do you seek advantage in anything else than in that in which you have learned that advantage is?

Will you not leave the small arguments (Greek: *logaria*) about these matters to others, to lazy fellows, that they may sit in a corner and receive their sorry pay, or grumble that no one gives them anything; and will you not come forward and make use of what you have learned? For it is not these small arguments that are wanted now; the writings of the Stoics are full of them. What then is the thing which is wanted? A man who shall apply them, one who by his acts shall bear testimony to his words. Assume, I intreat you, this character, that we may no longer use in the schools the examples of the ancients, but may have some example of our own.

To whom then does the contemplation of these matters (philosophical inquiries) belong? To him who has leisure, for man is an animal that loves contemplation. But it is shameful to contemplate these things as runaway slaves do; we should sit, as in a theatre, free from distraction, and listen at one time to the tragic actor, at another time to the lute-player; and not do as slaves do. As soon as thc slavc has taken his station he praises the actor and at the same time looks round; then if any one calls out his master's name, the slave is immediately frightened and disturbed. It is shameful for philosophers thus to contemplate the works of nature. For what is a master? Man is not the master of man; but death is, and life and pleasure and pain; for if he comes without these things, bring Caesar to me and you will see how firm I am. But when he shall come with these things, thundering and lightning, and when I am afraid of them, what do I do then except to recognize my master like the runaway slave? But so long as I have any respite from these terrors, as a runaway slave stands in the theatre, so do I. I bathe, I drink, I sing; but all this I do with terror and uneasiness. But if I shall release myself from my masters, that is from those things by means of which masters are formidable, what further trouble have I, what master have I still?

What then, ought we to publish these things to all men? No, but we ought to accommodate ourselves to the ignorant (Greek: *tois idiotais*) and to say: "This man recommends to me that which he thinks good for himself. I excuse him." For Socrates also excused the jailer who had the charge of him in prison and was weeping when Socrates was going to drink the poison, and said, "How generously he laments over us." Does he then say to the jailer that for this reason we have sent away the women? No, but he says it to his friends who were able to hear (understand) it; and he treats the jailer as a child.

That Confidence (Courage) Is Not Inconsistent With Caution

The opinion of the philosophers perhaps seem to some to be a paradox; but still let us examine as well as we can, if it is true that it is possible to do everything both with caution and with confidence. For caution seems to be in a manner contrary to confidence, and contraries are in no way consistent. That which seems to many to be a paradox in the matter under consideration in my opinion is of this kind; if we asserted that we ought to employ caution and confidence in the same things, men might justly accuse us of bringing together things which cannot be united. But now where is the difficulty in what is said? for if these things are true, which have been often said and often proved, that the nature of good is in the use of appearances, and the nature of evil likewise, and that things independent of our will do not admit either the nature of evil or of good, what paradox do the philosophers assert if they say that where things are not dependent on the will, there you should employ confidence, but where they are dependent on the will, there you should employ caution? For if the bad consists in the bad exercise of the will, caution ought only to be used where things are dependent on the will. But if things independent of the will and not in our power are nothing to us, with respect to these we must employ confidence; and thus we shall both be cautious and confident, and indeed confident because of our caution. For by employing caution towards things which are really bad, it will result that we shall have confidence with respect to things which are not so.

We are then in the condition of deer; when they flee from the huntsmen's feathers in fright, whither do they turn and in what do they seek refuge as safe? They turn to the nets, and thus they perish by confounding things which are objects of fear with things that they ought not to fear. Thus we also act: in what cases do we fear? In things which are independent of the will. In what cases on the contrary do we behave with confidence, as if there were no danger? In things dependent on the will. To be deceived then, or to act rashly, or shamelessly, or with base desire to seek something, does not concern us at all, if we only hit the mark in things which are independent of our will. But where there is death or exile or pain or infamy, there we attempt to run away, there we are struck with terror. Therefore, as we may expect it to happen with those who err in the greatest matters, we convert natural confidence (that is, according to nature) into audacity, desperation, rashness, shamelessness; and we convert natural caution and modesty into cowardice and meanness, which are full of fear and confusion. For if a man should transfer caution to those things in which the will may be exercised and the acts of the will, he will immediately by willing to be cautious have also the power of avoiding what he chooses; but if he transfer it to the things which are not in his power and will, and attempt to avoid the things which are in the power of others, he will of necessity fear, he will be unstable, he will be disturbed; for death or pain is not formidable, but the fear of pain or death. For this reason we commend the poet, who said:

"Not death is evil, but a shameful death."

Confidence (courage) then ought to be employed against death, and caution against the fear of death. But now we do the contrary, and employ against death the attempt to escape; and to our opinion about it we employ carelessness, rashness, and indifference. These things Socrates properly used to call tragic masks; for as to children masks appear terrible and fearful from inexperience, we also are affected in like manner by events (the things which happen in life) for no other reason than children are by masks. For what is a child? Ignorance. What is a child? Want of knowledge. For when a child knows these things, he is in no way inferior to us. What is death? A tragic mask. Turn it and examine it. See, it does not bite. The poor body must be separated from the spirit either now or later as it was separated from it before. Why then are you troubled if it be separated now? for if it is not separated now, it will be separated afterwards. Why? That the period of the universe may be completed, for it has need of the present, and of the future, and of the past. What is pain? A mask. Turn it and examine it. The poor flesh is moved roughly, then on the contrary smoothly. If this does not satisfy (please) you, the door is open; if it does, bear (with things). For the door ought to be open for all occasions; and so we have no trouble.

What then is the fruit of these opinions? It is that which ought to be the most noble and the most becoming to those who are really educated, release from perturbation, release from fear. Freedom. For in these matters we must not believe the many, who say that free persons only ought to be educated, but we should rather believe the philosophers who say that the educated only are free. How is this? In this manner: Is freedom anything else than the power of living as we choose? Nothing else. Tell me then, ye men, do you wish to live in error? We do not. No one then who lives in error is free. Do you wish to live in fear? Do you wish to live in sorrow? Do you wish to live in perturbation? By no means. No one then who is in a state of fear or sorrow or perturbation is free; but whoever is delivered from sorrows and fears and perturbations, he is at the same time also delivered from servitude. How then can we continue to believe you, most dear legislators, when you say, We only allow free persons to be educated? For philosophers say we allow none to be free except the educated; that is, God does not allow it. When then a man has turned round before the praetor his own slave, has he done nothing? He has done something. What? He has turned round his own slave before the praetor. Has he done nothing more? Yes: he is also bound to pay for him the tax called the twentieth. Well then, is not the man who has gone through this ceremony become free? No more than he is become free from perturbations. Have you who are able to turn round (free) others no master? is not money your master, or a girl or a boy, or some tyrant or some friend of the tyrant? Why do you trouble then when you are going off to any trial (danger) of this kind? It is for this reason that I often say, study and hold in readiness these principles by which you may determine what those things are with reference to which you ought to be cautious, courageous in that which does not depend on your will, cautious in that which does depend on it.

Of Tranquillity (Freedom From Perturbation)

Consider, you who are going into court, what you wish to maintain and what you wish to succeed in. For if you wish to maintain a will conformable to nature, you have every security, every facility, you have no troubles. For if you wish to maintain what is in your own power and is naturally free, and if you are content with these, what else do you care for? For who is the master of such things? Who can take them away? If you choose to be modest and faithful, who shall not allow you to be so? If you choose not to be restrained or compelled, who shall compel you to desire what you think that you ought not to desire? who shall compel you to avoid what you do not think fit to avoid? But what do you say? The judge will determine against you something that appears formidable; but that you should also suffer in trying to avoid it, how can he do that? When then the pursuit of objects and the avoiding of them are in your power, what else do you care for? Let this be your preface, this your narrative, this your confirmation, this your victory, this your peroration, this your applause (or the approbation which you will receive).

Therefore Socrates said to one who was reminding him to prepare for his trial, Do you not think then that I have been preparing for it all my life? By what kind of preparation? I have maintained that which was in my own power. How then? I have never done anything unjust either in my private or in my public life.

But if you wish to maintain externals also, your poor body, your little property, and your little estimation, I advise you to make from this moment all possible preparation, and then consider both the nature of your judge and your adversary. If it is necessary to embrace his knees, embrace his knees; if to weep, weep; if to groan, groan. For when you have subjected to externals what is your own, then be a slave and do not resist, and do not sometimes choose to be a slave, and sometimes not choose, but with all your mind be one or the other, either free or a slave, either instructed or uninstructed, either a well-bred cock or a mean one, either endure to be beaten until you die or yield at once; and let it not happen to you to receive many stripes and then to yield. But if these things are base, determine immediately. Where is the nature of evil and good? It is where truth is: where truth is and where nature is, there is caution: where truth is, there is courage where nature is.

For this reason also it is ridiculous to say, Suggest something to me (tell me what to do). What should I suggest to you? Well, form my mind so as to accommodate itself to any event. Why that is just the same as if a man who is ignorant of letters should say, Tell me what to write when any name is proposed to me. For if I should tell him to write Dion, and then another should come and propose to him not the name of Dion but that of Theon, what will be done? what will he write? But if you have practised writing, you are also prepared to write (or to do) anything that is required. If you are not, what can I now suggest? For if circumstances require something else, what will you say, or what will you do? Remember then this general precept and you will need no suggestion. But if you gape after externals, you must of necessity ramble up and down in obedience to the will of your master. And who is the master? He who has the power over the things which you seek to gain or try to avoid.

How Magnanimity Is Consistent With Care

Things themselves (materials) are indifferent; but the use of them is not indifferent. How then shall a man preserve firmness and tranquillity, and at the same time be careful and neither rash nor negligent? If he imitates those who play at dice. The counters are indifferent; the dice are indifferent. How do I know what the cast will be? But to use carefully and dexterously the cast of the dice, this is my business. Thus then in life also the chief business is this: distinguish and separate things, and say: Externals are not in my power: will is in my power. Where shall I seek the good and the bad? Within, in the things which are my own. But in what does not belong to you call nothing either good or bad, or profit or damage or anything of the kind.

What then? Should we use such things carelessly? In no way: for this on the other hand is bad for the faculty of the will, and consequently against nature; but we should act carefully because the use is not indifferent, and we should also act with firmness and freedom from perturbations because the material is indifferent. For where the material is not indifferent, there no man can hinder me or compel me. Where I can be hindered and compelled, the obtaining of those things is not in my power, nor is it good or bad; but the use is either bad or good, and the use is in my power. But it is difficult to mingle and to bring together these two things—the carefulness of him who is affected by the matter (or things about him), and the firmness of him who has no regard for it; but it is not impossible: and if it is, happiness is impossible. But we should act as we do in the case of a voyage. What can I do? I can choose the master of the ship, the sailors, the day, the opportunity. Then comes a storm. What more have I to care for? for my part is done. The business belongs to another, the master. But the ship is sinking—what then have I to do? I do the only thing that I can, not to be drowned full of fear, nor screaming nor blaming God, but knowing that what has been produced must also perish: for I am not an immortal being, but a man, a part of the whole, as an hour is a part of the day: I must be present like the hour, and past like the hour. What difference then does it make to me how I pass away, whether by being suffocated or by a fever, for I must pass through some such means.

How then is it said that some external things are according to nature and others contrary to nature? It is said as it might be said if we were separated from union (or society): for to the foot I shall say that it is according to nature for it to be clean; but if you take it as a foot and as a thing not detached (independent), it will befit it both to step into the mud and tread on thorns, and sometimes to be cut off for the good of the whole body; otherwise it is no longer a foot. We should think in some such way about ourselves also. What are you? A man. If you consider yourself as detached from other men, it is according to nature to live to old age, to be rich, to be healthy. But if you consider yourself as a man and a part of a certain whole, it is for the sake of that whole that at one time you should be sick, at another time take a voyage and run into danger, and at another time be in want, and in some cases die prematurely. Why then are you troubled? Do you not know, that as a foot is no longer a foot if it is detached from the body, so you are no longer a man if you are separated from other men. For what is a man? A part of a state, of that first which consists of gods and of men; then of that which is called next to it, which is a small image of the universal state. What then must I be brought to trial; must another have a fever, another sail on the sea, another die, and another be condemned? Yes, for it is impossible in such a universe of things, among so many living together, that such things should not happen, some to one and others to others. It is your duty then since you are come here, to say what you ought, to arrange these things as it is fit. Then some one says, "I shall charge you with doing me wrong." Much good may it do you: I have done my part; but whether you also have done yours, you must look to that; for there is some danger of this too, that it may escape your notice.

Of Indifference

The hypothetical proposition is indifferent: the judgment about it is not indifferent, but it is either knowledge or opinion or error. Thus life is indifferent: the use is not indifferent. When any man then tells you that these things also are indifferent, do not become negligent; and when a man invites you to be careful (about such things), do not become abject and struck with admiration of material things. And it is good for you to know your own preparation and power, that in those matters where you have not been prepared, you may keep quiet, and not be vexed, if others have the advantage over you. For you too in syllogisms will claim to have the advantage over them; and if others should be vexed at this, you will console them by saying, "I have learned them, and you have not." Thus also where there is need of any practice, seek not that which is acquired from the need (of such practice), but yield in that matter to those who have had practice, and be yourself content with firmness of mind.

Go and salute a certain person. How? Not meanly. But I have been shut out, for I have not learned to make my way through the window; and when I have found the door shut, I must either come back or enter through the window. But still speak to him. In what way? Not meanly. But suppose that you have not got what you wanted. Was this your business, and not his? Why then do you claim that which belongs to another? Always remember what is your own, and what belongs to another; and you will not be disturbed. Chrysippus therefore said well, So long as future things are uncertain, I always cling to those which are more adapted to the conservation of that which is according to nature; for God himself has given me the faculty of such choice. But if I knew that it was fated (in the order of things) for me to be sick, I would even move towards it; for the foot also, if it had intelligence, would move to go into the mud. For why are ears of corn produced? Is it not that they may become dry? And do they not become dry that they may be reaped? for they are not separated from communion with other things. If then they had perception, ought they to wish never to be reaped? But this is a curse upon ears of corn to be never reaped. So we must know that in the case of men too it is a curse not to die, just the same as not to be ripened and not to be reaped. But since we must be reaped, and we also know that we are reaped, we are vexed at it; for we neither know what we are nor have we studied what belongs to man, as those who have studied horses know what belongs to horses. But Chrysantas when he was going to strike the enemy checked himself when he heard the trumpet sounding a retreat: so it seemed better to him to obey the general's command than to follow his own inclination. But not one of us chooses, even when necessity summons, readily to obey it, but weeping and groaning we suffer what we do suffer, and we call them "circumstances." What kind of circumstances, man? If you give the name of circumstances to the things which are around you, all things are circumstances; but if you call hardships by this name, what hardship is there in the dying of that which has been produced? But that which destroys is either a sword, or a wheel, or the sea, or a tile, or a tyrant. Why do you care about the way of going down to Hades? All ways are equal. But if you will listen to the truth, the way which the tyrant sends you is shorter. A tyrant never killed a man in six months: but a fever is often a year about it. All these things are only sound and the noise of empty names.

How We Ought To Use Divination

Through an unreasonable regard to divination many of us omit many duties. For what more can the diviner see than death or danger or disease, or generally things of that kind? If then I must expose myself to danger for a friend, and if it is my duty even to die for him, what need have I then for divination? Have I not within me a diviner who has told me the nature of good and of evil, and has explained to me the signs (or marks) of both? What need have I then to consult the viscera of victims or the flight of birds, and why do I submit when he says, It is for your interest? For does he know what is for my interest, does he know what is good; and as he has learned the signs of the viscera, has he also learned the signs of good and evil? For if he knows the signs of these, he knows the signs both of the beautiful and of the ugly, and of the just and of the unjust. Do you tell me, man, what is the thing which is signified for me: is it life or death, poverty or wealth? But whether these things are for my interest or whether they are not, I do not intend to ask you. Why don't you give your opinion on matters of grammar, and why do you give it here about things on which we are all in error and disputing with one another?

What then leads us to frequent use of divination? Cowardice, the dread of what will happen. This is the reason why we flatter the diviners. Pray, master, shall I succeed to the property of my father? Let us see: let us sacrifice on the occasion. Yes, master, as fortune chooses. When he has said, You shall succeed to the inheritance, we thank him as if we received the inheritance from him. The consequence is that they play upon us.

Will you not then seek the nature of good in the rational animal? for if it is not there, you will not choose to say that it exists in any other thing (plant or animal). What then? are not plants and animals also the works of God? They are; but they are not superior things, nor yet parts of the gods. But you are a superior thing; you are a portion separated from the Deity; you have in yourself a certain portion of him. Why then are you ignorant of your own noble descent? Why do you not know whence you came? will you not remember when you are eating who you are who eat and whom you feed? When you are in social intercourse, when you are exercising yourself, when you are engaged in discussion, know you not that you are nourishing a god, that you are exercising a god? Wretch, you are carrying about a god with you, and you know it not. Do you think that I mean some god of silver or of gold, and external? You carry him within yourself, and you perceive not that you are polluting him by impure thoughts and dirty deeds. And if an image of God were present, you would not dare to do any of the things which you are doing; but when God himself is present within and sees all and hears all, you are not ashamed of thinking such things and doing such things, ignorant as you are of your own nature and subject to the anger of God. Then why do we fear when we are sending a young man from the school into active life, lest he should do anything improperly, eat improperly, have improper intercourse with women; and lest the rags in which he is wrapped should debase him, lest fine garments should make him proud. This youth (if he acts thus) does not know his own God; he knows not with whom he sets out (into the world). But can we endure when he says, "I wish I had you (God) with me." Have you not God with you? and do you seek for any other when you have him? or will God tell you anything else than this? If you were a statue of Phidias, either Athena or Zeus, you would think both of yourself and of the artist, and if you had any understanding (power of perception) you would try to do nothing unworthy of him who made you or of yourself, and try not to appear in an unbecoming dress (attitude) to those who look upon you. But now because Zeus has made you, for this reason do you care not how you shall appear? And yet is the artist (in the one case) like the artist in the other? or the work in the one case like the other? And what work of an artist, for instance, has in itself the faculties, which the artist shows in making it? Is it not marble or bronze, or gold or ivory? and the Athena of Phidias, when she has once extended the hand and received in it the figure of Victory, stands in that attitude for ever. But the works of God have power of motion, they breathe, they have the faculty of using the appearances of things and the power of examining them. Being the work of such an artist do you dishonor him? And what shall I say, not only that he made you, but also entrusted you to yourself and made you a deposit to yourself? Will you not think of this too, but do you also dishonor your guardianship? But if God had entrusted an orphan to you, would you thus neglect him? He has delivered yourself to your own care, and says: "I had no one fitter to entrust him to than yourself; keep him for me such as he is by nature, modest, faithful, erect, unterrified, free from passion and perturbation." And then you do not keep him such.

But some will say, Whence has this fellow got the arrogance which he displays and these supercilious looks? I have not yet so much gravity as befits a philosopher; for I do not yet feel confidence in what I have learned and in what I have assented to. I still fear my own weakness. Let me get confidence and then you shall see a countenance such as I ought to have and an attitude such as I ought to have; then I will show to you the statue, when it is perfected, when it is polished. What do you expect?

a supercilious countenance? Does the Zeus at Olympia lift up his brow? No, his look is fixed as becomes him who is ready to say:

> Irrevocable is my word and shall not fail.
>
> *Iliad*, i., 526.

Such will I show myself to you, faithful, modest, noble, free from perturbation. What, and immortal, too, except from old age, and from sickness? No, but dying as becomes a god, sickening as becomes a god. This power I possess; this I can do. But the rest I do not possess, nor can I do. I will show the nerves (strength) of a philosopher. What nerves are these? A desire never disappointed, an aversion which never falls on that which it would avoid, a proper pursuit (Greek: *hormaen*), a diligent purpose, an assent which is not rash. These you shall see.

That When We Cannot Fulfil That Which The Character Of A Man Promises, We Assume The Character Of A Philosopher

It is no common (easy) thing to do this only, to fulfil the promise of a man's nature. For what is a man? The answer is, A rational and mortal being. Then by the rational faculty from whom are we separated? From wild beasts. And from what others? From sheep and like animals. Take care then to do nothing like a wild beast; but if you do, you have lost the character of a man; you have not fulfilled your promise. See that you do nothing like a sheep; but if you do, in this case also the man is lost. What then do we do as sheep? When we act gluttonously, when we act lewdly, when we act rashly, filthily, inconsiderately, to what have we declined? To sheep. What have we lost? The rational faculty. When we act contentiously and harmfully and passionately and violently, to what have we declined? To wild beasts. Consequently some of us are great wild beasts, and others little beasts, of a bad disposition and small, whence we may say, Let me be eaten by a lion. But in all these ways the promise of a man acting as a man is destroyed. For when is a conjunctive (complex) proposition maintained? When it fulfils what its nature promises; so that the preservation of a complex proposition is when it is a conjunction of truths. When is a disjunctive maintained? When it fulfils what it promises. When are flutes, a lyre, a horse, a dog, preserved? (When they severally keep their promise.) What is the wonder then if man also in like manner is preserved, and in like manner is lost? Each man is improved and preserved by corresponding acts, the carpenter by acts of carpentry, the grammarian by acts of grammar. But if a man accustoms himself to write ungrammatically, of necessity his art will be corrupted and destroyed. Thus modest actions preserve the modest man, and immodest actions destroy him; and actions of fidelity preserve the faithful man, and the contrary actions destroy him. And on the other hand contrary actions strengthen contrary characters: shamelessness strengthens the shameless man, faithlessness the faithless man, abusive words the abusive man, anger the man of an angry temper, and unequal receiving and giving make the avaricious man more avaricious.

For this reason philosophers admonish us not to be satisfied with learning only, but also to add study, and then practice. For we have long been accustomed to do contrary things, and we put in practice opinions which are contrary to true opinions. If then we shall not also put in practice right opinions, we shall be nothing more than the expositors of the opinions of others. For now who among us is not able to discourse according to the rules of art about good and evil things (in this fashion)? That of things some are good, and some are bad, and some are indifferent: the good then are virtues, and the things which participate in virtues; and the bad are the contrary; and the indifferent are wealth, health, reputation. Then, if in the midst of our talk there should happen some greater noise than usual, or some of those who are present should laugh at us, we are disturbed. Philosopher, where are the things which you were talking about?

Whence did you produce and utter them? From the lips, and thence only. Why then do you corrupt the aids provided by others? Why do you treat the weightiest matters as if you were playing a game of dice? For it is one thing to lay up bread and wine as in a storehouse, and another thing to eat. That which has been eaten, is digested, distributed, and is become sinews, flesh, bones, blood, healthy color, healthy breath. Whatever is stored up, when you choose you can readily take and show it; but you have no other advantage from it except so far as to appear to possess it. For what is the difference between explaining these doctrines and those of men who have different opinions? Sit down now and explain according to the rules of art the opinions of Epicurus, and perhaps you will explain his opinions in a more useful manner than Epicurus himself. Why then do you call yourself a Stoic? Why do you deceive the many? Why do you act the part of a Jew, when you are a Greek? Do you not see how (why) each is called a Jew, or a Syrian, or an Egyptian? and when we see a man inclining to two sides, we are accustomed to say, This man is not a Jew, but he acts as one. But when he has assumed the affects of one who has been imbued with Jewish doctrine and has adopted that sect, then he is in fact and he is named a Jew.

How We May Discover The Duties Of Life From Names

Consider who you are. In the first place, you are a man; and this is one who has nothing superior to the faculty of the will, but all other things subjected to it; and the faculty itself he possesses unenslaved and free from subjection. Consider then from what things you have been separated by reason. You have been separated from wild beasts; you have been separated from domestic animals (Greek: *probaton*). Further, you are a citizen of the world, and a part of it, not one of the subservient (serving), but one of the principal (ruling) parts, for you are capable of comprehending the divine administration and of considering the connection of things. What then does the character of a citizen promise (profess)? To hold nothing as profitable to himself; to deliberate about nothing as if he were detached from the community, but to act as the hand or foot would do, if they had reason and understood the constitution of nature, for they would never put themselves in motion nor desire anything otherwise than with reference to the whole. Therefore, the philosophers say well, that if the good man had foreknowledge of what would happen, he would co-operate towards his own sickness and death and mutilation, since he knows that these things are assigned to him according to the universal arrangement, and that the whole is superior to the part, and the state to the citizen. But now because we do not know the future, it is our duty to stick to the things which are in their nature more suitable for our choice, for we were made among other things for this.

After this, remember that you are a son. What does this character promise? To consider that everything which is the son's belongs to the father, to obey him in all things, never to blame him to another, nor to say or do anything which does him injury, to yield to him in all things and give way, co-operating with him as far as you can. After this know that you are a brother also, and that to this character it is due to make concessions; to be easily persuaded, to speak good of your brother, never to claim in opposition to him any of the things which are independent of the will, but readily to give them up, that you may have the larger share in what is dependent on the will. For see what a thing it is, in place of a lettuce, if it should so happen, or a seat, to gain for yourself goodness of disposition. How great is the advantage.

Next to this, if you are a senator of any state, remember that you are a senator; if a youth, that you are a youth; if an old man, that you are an old man; for each of such names, if it comes to be examined, marks out the proper duties. But if you go and blame your brother, I say to you, You have forgotten who you are and what is your name. In the next place, if you were a smith and made a wrong use of the hammer, you would have forgotten the smith; and if you have forgotten the brother and instead of a brother have become an enemy, would you appear not to have changed one thing for another in that case? And if instead of a man, who is a tame animal and social, you are become a mischievous wild beast, treacherous, and biting, have you lost nothing? But (I suppose) you must lose a bit of money that you may suffer damage? And does the loss of nothing else do a man damage? If you had lost the art of grammar or music, would you think the loss of it a damage? and if you shall lose modesty, moderation (*Greek: chtastolaen*) and gentleness, do you think the loss nothing? And yet the things first mentioned are lost by some cause external and independent of the will, and the second by our own fault; and as to the first neither to have them nor to lose them is shameful; but as to the second, not to have them and to lose them is shameful and matter of reproach and a misfortune.

What then? shall I not hurt him who has hurt me? In the first place consider what hurt (Greek: *blabae*) is, and remember what you have heard from the philosophers. For if the good consists in the will (purpose, intention, Greek: *proaireeis*), and the evil also in the will, see if what you say is not this: What then, since that man has hurt himself by doing an unjust act to me, shall I not hurt myself by doing some unjust act to him? Why do we not imagine to ourselves (mentally think of) something of this kind? But where there is any detriment to the body or to our possession, there is harm there; and where the same thing happens to the faculty of the will, there is (you suppose) no harm; for he who has been deceived or he who has done an unjust act neither suffers in the head nor in the eye nor in the hip, nor does he lose his estate; and we wish for nothing else than (security to) these things. But whether we shall have the will modest and faithful or shameless and faithless, we care not the least, except only in the school so far as a few words are concerned. Therefore our proficiency is limited to these few words; but beyond them it does not exist even in the slightest degree.

What The Beginning Of Philosophy Is

The beginning of philosophy, to him at least who enters on it in the right way and by the door is a consciousness of his own weakness and inability about necessary things; for we come into the world with no natural notion of a right-angled triangle, or of a diesis (a quarter tone), or of a half-tone; but we learn each of these things by a certain transmission according to art; and for this reason those who do not know them do not think that they know them. But as to good and evil, and beautiful and ugly, and becoming and unbecoming, and happiness and misfortune, and proper and improper, and what we ought to do and what we ought not to do, who ever came into the world without having an innate idea of them? Wherefore we all use these names, and we endeavor to fit the preconceptions to the several cases (things) thus: he has done well; he has not done well; he has done as he ought, not as he ought; he has been unfortunate, he has been fortunate; he is unjust, he is just; who does not use these names? who among us defers the use of them till he has learned them, as he defers the use of the words about lines (geometrical figures) or sounds? And the cause of this is that we come into the world already taught as it were by nature some things on this matter (Greek: *topon*), and proceeding from these we have added to them self-conceit (Greek: *oiaesin*). For why, a man says, do I not know the beautiful and the ugly? Have I not the notion of it? You have. Do I not adapt it to particulars? You do. Do I not then adapt it properly? In that lies the whole question; and conceit is added here; for beginning from these things which are admitted men proceed to that which is matter of dispute by means of unsuitable adaptation; for if they possessed this power of adaptation in addition to those things, what would hinder them from being perfect? But now since you think that you properly adapt the preconceptions to the particulars, tell me whence you derive this (assume that you do so). Because I think so. But it does not seem so to another, and he thinks that he also makes a proper adaptation;

or does he not think so? He does think so. Is it possible then that both of you can properly apply the preconceptions to things about which you have contrary opinions? It is not possible. Can you then show us anything better towards adapting the preconceptions beyond your thinking that you do? Does the madman do any other things than the things which seem to him right? Is then this criterion sufficient for him also? It is not sufficient. Come then to something which is superior to seeming (Greek: *tou dochein*). What is this?

Observe, this is the beginning of philosophy, a perception of the disagreement of men with one another, and an inquiry into the cause of the disagreement, and a condemnation and distrust of that which only "seems," and a certain investigation of that which "seems" whether it "seems" rightly, and a discovery of some rule (Greek: *chanonos*), as we have discovered a balance in the determination of weights, and a carpenter's rule (or square) in the case of straight and crooked things.—This is the beginning of philosophy. Must we say that all things are right which seem so to all? And how is it possible that contradictions can be right?—Not all then, but all which seem to us to be right.—How more to you than those which seem right to the Syrians? why more than what seem right to the Egyptians? why more than what seems right to me or to any other man? Not at all more. What then "seems" to every man is not sufficient for determining what "is"; for neither in the case of weights nor measures are we satisfied with the bare appearance, but in each case we have discovered a certain rule. In this matter then is there no rule superior to what "seems"? And how is it possible that the most necessary things among men should have no sign (mark), and be incapable of being discovered? There is then some rule. And why then do we not seek the rule and discover it, and afterwards use it without varying from it, not even stretching out the finger without it? For this, I think, is that which when it is discovered cures of their madness those who use mere "seeming" as a measure, and misuse it; so that for the future proceeding from certain things (principles) known and made clear we may use in the case of particular things the preconceptions which are distinctly fixed.

What is the matter presented to us about which we are inquiring? Pleasure (for example). Subject it to the rule, throw it into the balance. Ought the good to be such a thing that it is fit that we have confidence in it? Yes. And in which we ought to confide? It ought to be. Is it fit to trust to anything which is insecure? No. Is then pleasure anything secure? No. Take it then and throw it out of the scale, and drive it far away from the place of good things. But if you are not sharp-sighted, and one balance is not enough for you, bring another. Is it fit to be elated over what is good? Yes. Is it proper then to be elated over present pleasure? See that you do not say that it is proper; but if you do, I shall then not think you worthy even of the balance. Thus things are tested and weighed when the rules are ready. And to philosophize is this, to examine and confirm the rules; and then to use them when they are known is the act of a wise and good man.

Of Disputation Or Discussion

What things a man must learn in order to be able to apply the art of disputation, has been accurately shown by our philosophers (the Stoics); but with respect to the proper use of the things, we are entirely without practice. Only give to any of us, whom you please, an illiterate man to discuss with, and he cannot discover how to deal with the man. But when he has moved the man a little, if he answers beside the purpose, he does not know how to treat him, but he then either abuses or ridicules him, and says, He is an illiterate man; it is not possible to do anything with him. Now a guide, when he has found a man out of the road, leads him into the right way; he does not ridicule or abuse him and then leave him. Do you also show the illiterate man the truth, and you will see that he follows. But so long as you do not show him the truth, do not ridicule him, but rather feel your own incapacity.

Now this was the first and chief peculiarity of Socrates, never to be irritated in argument, never to utter anything abusive, anything insulting, but to bear with abusive persons and to put an end to the quarrel. If you would know what great power he had in this way, read the Symposium of Xenophon, and you will see how many quarrels he put an end to. Hence with good reason in the poets also this power is most highly praised:

> Quickly with skill he settles great disputes.
> Hesiod, *Theogony*, v. 87.

On Anxiety (Solicitude)

When I see a man anxious, I say, What does this man want? If he did not want something which is not in his power, how could he be anxious? For this reason a lute player when he is singing by himself has no anxiety, but when he enters the theatre, he is anxious, even if he has a good voice and plays well on the lute; for he not only wishes to sing well, but also to obtain applause: but this is not in his power. Accordingly, where he has skill, there he has confidence. Bring any single person who knows nothing of music, and the musician does not care for him. But in the matter where a man knows nothing and has not been practised, there he is anxious. What matter is this? He knows not what a crowd is or what the praise of a crowd is. However, he has learned to strike the lowest chord and the highest; but what the praise of the many is, and what power it has in life, he neither knows nor has he thought about it. Hence he must of necessity tremble and grow pale. Is any man then afraid about things which are not evils? No. Is he afraid about things which are evils, but still so far within his power that they may not happen? Certainly he is not. If then the things which are independent of the will are neither good nor bad, and all things which do depend on the will are within our power, and no man can either take them from us or give them to us, if we do not choose, where is room left for anxiety? But we are anxious about our poor body, our little property, about the will of Caesar; but not anxious about things internal. Are we anxious about not forming a false opinion? No, for this is in my power. About not exerting our movements contrary to nature? No, not even about this. When then you see a man pale, as the physician says, judging from the complexion, this man's spleen is disordered, that man's liver; so also say, this man's desire and aversion are disordered, he is not in the right way, he is in a fever. For nothing else changes the color, or causes trembling or chattering of the teeth, or causes a man to

Sink in his knees and shift from foot to foot.
Iliad, xiii., 281.

For this reason, when Zeno was going to meet Antigonus, he was not anxious, for Antigonus had no power over any of the things which Zeno admired; and Zeno did not care for those things over which Antigonus had power. But Antigonus was anxious when he was going to meet Zeno, for he wished to please Zeno; but this was a thing external (out of his power). But Zeno did not want to please Antigonus; for no man who is skilled in any art wishes to please one who has no such skill.

Should I try to please you? Why? I suppose, you know the measure by which one man is estimated by another. Have you taken pains to learn what is a good man and what is a bad man, and how a man becomes one or the other? Why then are you not good yourself? How, he replies, am I not good? Because no good man laments or groans or weeps, no good man is pale and trembles, or says, How will he receive me, how will he listen to me? Slave, just as it pleases him. Why do you care about what belongs to others? Is it now his fault if he receives badly what proceeds from you? Certainly. And is it possible that a fault should be one man's, and the evil in another? No. Why then are you anxious about that which belongs to others? Your question is reasonable; but I am anxious how I shall speak to him. Cannot you then speak to him as you choose? But I fear that I may be disconcerted? If you are going to write the name of Dion, are you afraid that you would be disconcerted? By no means. Why? is it not because you have practised writing the name? Certainly. Well, if you were going to read the name, would you not feel the same? and why? Because every art has a certain strength and confidence in the things which belong to it. Have you then not practised speaking? and what else did you learn in the school? Syllogisms and sophistical propositions? For what purpose? was it not for the purpose of discoursing skilfully? and is not discoursing skilfully the same as discoursing seasonably and cautiously and with intelligence, and also without making mistakes and without hindrance, and besides all this with confidence? Yes. When then you are mounted on a horse and go into a plain, are you anxious at being matched against a man who is on foot, and anxious in a matter in which you are practised, and he is not? Yes, but that person (to whom I am going to speak) has power to kill me. Speak the truth, then, unhappy man, and do not brag, nor claim to be a philosopher, nor refuse to acknowledge your masters, but so long as you present this handle in your body, follow every man who is stronger than yourself. Socrates used to practice speaking, he who talked as he did to the tyrants, to the dicasts (judges), he who talked in his prison. Diogenes had practised speaking, he who spoke as he did to Alexander, to the pirates, to the person who bought him. These men were confident in the things which they practised. But do you walk off to your own affairs and never leave them: go and sit in a corner, and weave syllogisms, and propose them to another. There is not in you the man who can rule a state.

To Naso

When a certain Roman entered with his son and listened to one reading, Epictetus said, This is the method of instruction; and he stopped. When the Roman asked him to go on, Epictetus said, Every art when it is taught causes labor to him who is unacquainted with it and is unskilled in it, and indeed the things which proceed from the arts immediately show their use in the purpose for which they were made; and most of them contain something attractive and pleasing. For indeed to be present and to observe how a shoemaker learns is not a pleasant thing; but the shoe is useful and also not disagreeable to look at. And the discipline of a smith when he is learning is very disagreeable to one who chances to be present and is a stranger to the art: but the work shows the use of the art. But you will see this much more in music; for if you are present while a person is learning, the discipline will appear most disagreeable; and yet the results of music are pleasing and delightful to those who know nothing of music. And here we conceive the work of a philosopher to be something of this kind: he must adapt his wish (Greek: *boulaesin*) to what is going on, so that neither any of the things which are taking place shall take place contrary to our wish, nor any of the things which do not take place shall not take place when we wish that they should. From this the result is to those who have so arranged the work of philosophy, not to fail in the desire, nor to fall in with that which they would avoid; without uneasiness, without fear, without perturbation to pass through life themselves, together with their associates maintaining the relations both natural and acquired, as the relation of son, of father, of brother, of citizen, of man, of wife, of neighbor, of fellow-traveller, of ruler, of ruled. The work of a philosopher we conceive to be something like this. It remains next to inquire how this must be accomplished.

We see then that the carpenter (Greek: *techton*) when he has learned certain things becomes a carpenter; the pilot by learning certain things becomes a pilot. May it not then in philosophy also not be sufficient to wish to be wise and good, and that there is also a necessity to learn certain things? We inquire then what these things are. The philosophers say that we ought first to learn that there is a God and that he provides for all things; also that it is not possible to conceal from him our acts, or even our intentions and thoughts. The next thing is to learn what is the nature of the gods; for such as they are discovered to be, he, who would please and obey them, must try with all his power to be like them. If the divine is faithful, man also must be faithful; if it is free, man also must be free; if beneficent, man also must be beneficent; if magnanimous, man also must be magnanimous; as being then an imitator of God he must do and say everything consistently with this fact.

To Or Against Those Who Obstinately Persist In What They Have Determined

When some persons have heard these words, that a man ought to be constant (firm), and that the will is naturally free and not subject to compulsion, but that all other things are subject to hindrance, to slavery, and are in the power of others, they suppose that they ought without deviation to abide by everything which they have determined. But in the first place that which has been determined ought to be sound (true). I require tone (sinews) in the body, but such as exists in a healthy body, in an athletic body; but if it is plain to me that you have the tone of a frenzied man and you boast of it, I shall say to you, Man, seek the physician; this is not tone, but atony (deficiency in right tone). In a different way something of the same kind is felt by those who listen to these discourses in a wrong manner; which was the case with one of my companions, who for no reason resolved to starve himself to death. I heard of it when it was the third day of his abstinence from food, and I went to inquire what had happened. "I have resolved," he said. "But still tell me what it was which induced you to resolve; for if you have resolved rightly, we shall sit with you and assist you to depart, but if you have made an unreasonable resolution, change your mind." "We ought to keep to our determinations." "What are you doing, man? We ought to keep not to all our determinations, but to those which are right; for if you are now persuaded that it is right, do not change your mind, if you think fit, but persist and say, We ought to abide by our determinations. Will you not make the beginning and lay the foundation in an inquiry whether the determination is sound or not sound, and so then build on it firmness and security? But if you lay a rotten and ruinous foundation, will not your miserable little building fall down the sooner, the more and the stronger are the materials which you shall lay on it? Without any reason would you withdraw from us out of life a man who is a friend and a companion, a citizen of the same city, both the great and the small city? Then while you are committing murder and destroying a man who has done no wrong, do you say that you ought to abide by your determinations? And if it ever in any way came into your head to kill me, ought you to abide by your determinations?"

Now this man was with difficulty persuaded to change his mind. But it is impossible to convince some persons at present; so that I seem now to know what I did not know before, the meaning of the common saying, that you can neither persuade nor break a fool. May it never be my lot to have a wise fool for my friend; nothing is more untractable. "I am determined," the man says. Madmen are also, but the more firmly they form a judgment on things which do not exist, the more hellebore they require. Will you not act like a sick man and call in the physician?—I am sick, master, help me; consider what I must do: it is my duty to obey you. So it is here also: I know not what I ought to do, but I am come to learn.—Not so; but speak to me about other things: upon this I have determined.—What other things? for what is greater and more useful than for you to be persuaded that it is not sufficient to have made your determination and not to change it. This is the tone (energy) of madness, not of health.—I will die, if you compel me to this.—Why, man? What has happened?—I have determined—I have had a lucky escape that you have not determined to kill me—I take no money. Why?—I have determined—Be assured that with the very tone (energy) which you now use in refusing to take, there is nothing to hinder you at some time from inclining without reason to take money, and then saying, I have determined. As in a distempered body, subject to defluxions, the humor inclines sometimes to these parts, and then to those, so too a sickly soul knows not which way to incline; but if to this inclination and movement there is added a tone (obstinate resolution), then the evil becomes past help and cure.

That We Do Not Strive To Use Our Opinions About Good And Evil

Where is the good? In the will. Where is the evil? In the will. Where is neither of them? In those things which are independent of the will. Well then? Does any one among us think of these lessons out of the schools? Does any one meditate (strive) by himself to give an answer to things as in the case of questions?—Is it day?—Yes.—Is it night?—No.—Well, is the number of stars even?—I cannot say.—When money is shown (offered) to you, have you studied to make the proper answer, that money is not a good thing? Have you practised yourself in these answers, or only against sophisms? Why do you wonder then if in the cases which you have studied, in those you have improved; but in those which you have not studied, in those you remain the same? When the rhetorician knows that he has written well, that he has committed to memory what he has written, and brings an agreeable voice, why is he still anxious? Because he is not satisfied with having studied. What then does he want? To be praised by the audience? For the purpose then of being able to practise declamation he has been disciplined; but with respect to praise and blame he has not been disciplined. For when did he hear from any one what praise is, what blame is, what the nature of each is, what kind of praise should be sought, or what kind of blame should be shunned? And when did he practise this discipline which follows these words (things)? Why then do you still wonder, if in the matters which a man has learned, there he surpasses others, and in those in which he has not been disciplined, there he is the same with the many. So the lute player knows how to play, sings well, and has a fine dress, and yet he trembles when he enters on the stage; for these matters he understands, but he does not know what a crowd is, nor the shouts of a crowd, nor what ridicule is. Neither does he know what anxiety is, whether it is our work or the work of another, whether it is possible to stop it or not. For this reason if he has been praised, he leaves the theatre puffed up, but if he has been ridiculed, the swollen bladder has been punctured and subsides.

This is the case also with ourselves. What do we admire? Externals. About what things are we busy? Externals. And have we any doubt then why we fear or why we are anxious? What then happens when we think the things, which are coming on us, to be evils? It is not in our power not to be afraid, it is not in our power not to be anxious. Then we say, Lord God, how shall I not be anxious? Fool, have you not hands, did not God make them for you? Sit down now and pray that your nose may not run. Wipe yourself rather and do not blame him. Well then, has he given to you nothing in the present case? Has he not given to you endurance? Has he not given to you magnanimity? Has he not given to you manliness? When you have such hands do you still look for one who shall wipe your nose? But we neither study these things nor care for them. Give me a man who cares how he shall do anything, not for the obtaining of a thing, but who cares about his own energy. What man, when he is walking about, cares for his own energy? Who, when he is deliberating, cares about his own deliberation, and not about obtaining that about which he deliberates? And if he succeeds, he is elated and says, How well we have deliberated; did I not tell you, brother, that it is impossible, when we have thought about anything, that it should not turn out thus? But if the thing should turn out otherwise, the wretched man is humbled; he knows not even what to say about what has taken place. Who among us for the sake of this matter has consulted a seer? Who among us as to his actions has not slept in indifference? Who? Give (name) to me one that I may see the man whom I have long been looking for, who is truly noble and ingenuous, whether young or old; name him.

What then are the things which are heavy on us and disturb us? What else than opinions? What else than opinions lies heavy upon him who goes away and leaves his companions and friends and places and habits of life? Now little children, for instance, when they cry on the nurse leaving them for a short time, forget their sorrow if they receive a small cake. Do you choose then that we should compare you to little children? No, by Zeus, for I do not wish to be pacified by a small cake, but by right opinions. And what are these? Such as a man ought to study all day, and not to be affected by anything that is not his own, neither by companion nor place nor gymnasia, and not even by his own body, but to remember the law and to have it before his eyes. And what is the divine law? To keep a man's own, not to claim that which belongs to others, but to use what is given, and when it is not given, not to desire it; and when a thing is taken away, to give it up readily and immediately, and to be thankful for the time that a man has had the use of it, if you would not cry for your nurse and mamma. For what matter does it make by what thing a man is subdued, and on what he depends? In what respect are you better than he who cries for a girl, if you grieve for a little gymnasium, and little porticos, and young men, and such places of amusement? Another comes and laments that he shall no longer drink the water of Dirce. Is the Marcian water worse than that of Dirce? But I was used to the water of Dirce. And you in turn will be used to the other. Then if you become attached to this also, cry for this too, and try to make a verse like the verse of Euripides,

The hot baths of Nero and the Marcian water.

See how tragedy is made when common things happen to silly men.

When then shall I see Athens again and the Acropolis? Wretch, are you not content with what you see daily? Have you anything better or greater to see than the sun, the moon, the stars, the whole earth, the sea? But if indeed you comprehend Him who administers the whole, and carry him about in yourself, do you still desire small stones and a beautiful rock?

How We Must Adapt Preconceptions To Particular Cases

What is the first business of him who philosophizes? To throw away self-conceit (Greek: *oiaesis*). For it is impossible for a man to begin to learn that which he thinks that he knows. As to things then which ought to be done and ought not to be done, and good and bad, and beautiful and ugly, all of us talking of them at random go to the philosophers; and on these matters we praise, we censure, we accuse, we blame, we judge and determine about principles honorable and dishonorable. But why do we go to the philosophers? Because we wish to learn what we do not think that we know. And what is this? Theorems. For we wish to learn what philosophers say as being something elegant and acute; and some wish to learn that they may get profit from what they learn. It is ridiculous then to think that a person wishes to learn one thing, and will learn another; or further, that a man will make proficiency in that which he does not learn. But the many are deceived by this which deceived also the rhetorician Theopompus, when he blames even Plato for wishing everything to be defined. For what does he say? Did none of us before you use the words good or just, or do we utter the sounds in an unmeaning and empty way without understanding what they severally signify? Now who tells you, Theopompus, that we had not natural notions of each of these things and preconceptions (Greek: *prolaepseis*)? But it is not possible to adapt preconceptions to their correspondent objects if we have not distinguished (analyzed) them, and inquired what object must be subjected to each preconception. You may make the same charge against physicians also. For who among us did not use the words healthy and unhealthy before Hippocrates lived, or did we utter these words as empty sounds? For we have also a certain preconception of health, but we are not able to adapt it. For this reason one says, Abstain from food; another says, Give food; another says, Bleed;

and another says, Use cupping. What is the reason? is it any other than that a man cannot properly adapt the preconceptions of health to particulars?

How We Should Struggle Against Appearances

Every habit and faculty is maintained and increased by the corresponding actions: the habit of walking by walking, the habit of running by running. If you would be a good reader, read; if a writer, write. But when you shall not have read for thirty days in succession, but have done something else, you will know the consequence. In the same way, if you shall have lain down ten days, get up and attempt to make a long walk, and you will see how your legs are weakened. Generally then if you would make anything a habit, do it; if you would not make it a habit, do not do it, but accustom yourself to do something else in place of it.

So it is with respect to the affections of the soul: when you have been angry, you must know that not only has this evil befallen you, but that you have also increased the habit, and in a manner thrown fuel upon fire.

In this manner certainly, as philosophers say, also diseases of the mind grow up. For when you have once desired money, if reason be applied to lead to a perception of the evil, the desire is stopped, and the ruling faculty of our mind is restored to the original authority. But if you apply no means of cure, it no longer returns to the same state, but being again excited by the corresponding appearance, it is inflamed to desire quicker than before: and when this takes place continually, it is henceforth hardened (made callous), and the disease of the mind confirms the love of money. For he who has had a fever, and has been relieved from it, is not in the same state that he was before, unless he has been completely cured. Something of the kind happens also in diseases of the soul. Certain traces and blisters are left in it, and unless a man shall completely efface them, when he is again lashed on the same places, the lash will produce not blisters (weals) but sores. If then you wish not to be of an angry temper, do not feed the habit: throw nothing on it which will increase it: at first keep quiet, and count the days on which you have not been angry. I used to be in passion every day; now every second day; then every third, then every fourth. But if you have intermitted thirty days, make a sacrifice to God. For the habit at first begins to be weakened, and then is completely destroyed. "I have not been vexed to-day, nor the day after, nor yet on any succeeding day during two or three months; but I took care when some exciting things happened." Be assured that you are in a good way.

How then shall this be done? Be willing at length to be approved by yourself, be willing to appear beautiful to God, desire to be in purity with your own pure self and with God. Then when any such appearance visits you, Plato says, Have recourse to expiations, go a suppliant to the temples of the averting deities. It is even sufficient if you resort to the society of noble and just men, and compare yourself with them, whether you find one who is living or dead.

But in the first place, be not hurried away by the rapidity of the appearance, but say, Appearances, wait for me a little; let me see who you are, and what you are about; let me put you to the test. And then do not allow the appearance to lead you on and draw lively pictures of the things which will follow; for if you do, it will carry you off wherever it pleases. But rather bring in to oppose it some other beautiful and noble appearance, and cast out this base appearance. And if you are accustomed to be exercised in this way, you will see what shoulders, what sinews, what strength you have. But now it is only trifling words, and nothing more.

This is the true athlete, the man who exercises himself against such appearances. Stay, wretch, do not be carried away. Great is the combat, divine is the work; it is for kingship, for freedom, for happiness, for freedom from perturbation. Remember God; call on him as a helper and protector, as men at sea call on the Dioscuri in a storm. For what is a greater storm than that which comes from appearances which are violent and drive away the reason? For the storm itself, what else is it but an appearance? For take away the fear of death, and suppose as many thunders and lightnings as you please, and you will know what calm and serenity there is in the ruling faculty. But if you have once been defeated and say that you will conquer hereafter, and then say the same again, be assured that you will at last be in so wretched a condition and so weak that you will not even know afterwards that you are doing wrong, but you will even begin to make apologies (defences) for your wrong-doing, and then you will confirm the saying of Hesiod to be true,

With constant ills the dilatory strives.

Of Inconsistency

Some things men readily confess, and other things they do not. No one then will confess that he is a fool or without understanding; but quite the contrary you will hear all men saying, I wish that I had fortune equal to my understanding. But men readily confess that they are timid, and they say: I am rather timid, I confess; but as to other respects you will not find me to be foolish. A man will not readily confess that he is intemperate; and that he is unjust, he will not confess at all. He will by no means confess that he is envious or a busybody. Most men will confess that they are compassionate. What then is the reason?

The chief thing (the ruling thing) is inconsistency and confusion in the things which relate to good and evil. But different men have different reasons; and generally what they imagine to be base, they do not confess at all. But they suppose timidity to be a characteristic of a good disposition, and compassion also; but silliness to be the absolute characteristic of a slave. And they do not at all admit (confess) the things which are offences against society. But in the case of most errors for this reason chiefly they are induced to confess them, because they imagine that there is something involuntary in them as in timidity and compassion; and if a man confess that he is in any respect intemperate, he alleges love (or passion) as an excuse for what is involuntary. But men do not imagine injustice to be at all involuntary. There is also in jealousy, as they suppose, something involuntary; and for this reason they confess to jealousy also.

Living then among such men, who are so confused, so ignorant of what they say, and of the evils which they have or have not, and why they have them, or how they shall be relieved of them, I think it is worth the trouble for a man to watch constantly (and to ask) whether I also am one of them, what imagination I have about myself, how I conduct myself, whether I conduct myself as a prudent man, whether I conduct myself as a temperate man, whether I ever say this, that I have been taught to be prepared for everything that may happen. Have I the consciousness, which a man who knows nothing ought to have, that I know nothing? Do I go to my teacher as men go to oracles, prepared to obey? or do I like a snivelling boy go to my school to learn history and understand the books which I did not understand before, and, if it should happen so, to explain them also to others? Man, you have had a fight in the house with a poor slave, you have turned the family upside down, you have frightened the neighbors, and you come to me as if you were a wise man, and you take your seat and judge how I have explained some word, and how I have babbled whatever came into my head. You come full of envy, and humbled, because you bring nothing from home; and you sit during the discussion thinking of nothing else than how your father is disposed towards you and your brother. What are they saying about me there? now they think that I am improving, and are saying, He will return with all knowledge. I wish I could learn everything before I return; but much labor is necessary, and no one sends me anything, and the baths at Nicopolis are dirty; everything is bad at home, and bad here.

On Friendship

What a man applies himself to earnestly, that he naturally loves. Do men then apply themselves earnestly to the things which are bad? By no means. Well, do they apply themselves to things which in no way concern themselves? Not to these either. It remains then that they employ themselves earnestly only about things which are good; and if they are earnestly employed about things, they love such things also. Whoever then understands what is good can also know how to love; but he who cannot distinguish good from bad, and things which are neither good nor bad from both, how can he possess the power of loving? To love, then, is only in the power of the wise.

For universally, be not deceived, every animal is attached to nothing so much as to its own interests. Whatever then appears to it an impediment to this interest, whether this be a brother, or a father, or a child, or beloved, or lover, it hates, spurns, curses; for its nature is to love nothing so much as its own interests: this is father, and brother, and kinsman, and country, and God. When then the gods appear to us to be an impediment to this, we abuse them and throw down their statues and burn their temples, as Alexander ordered the temples of Aesculapius to be burned when his dear friend died.

For this reason, if a man put in the same place his interest, sanctity, goodness, and country, and parents, and friends, all these are secured: but if he puts in one place his interest, in another his friends, and his country and his kinsmen and justice itself, all these give way, being borne down by the weight of interest. For where the I and the Mine are placed, to that place of necessity the animal inclines; if in the flesh, there is the ruling power; if in the will, it is there; and if it is in externals, it is there. If then I am there where my will is, then only shall I be a friend such as I ought to be, and son, and father; for this will be my interest, to maintain the character of fidelity, of modesty, of patience, of abstinence, of active co-operation, of observing my relations (towards all). But if I put myself in one place, and honesty in another, then the doctrine of Epicurus becomes strong, which asserts either that there is no honesty or it is that which opinion holds to be honest (virtuous).

It was through this ignorance that the Athenians and the Lacedaemonians quarrelled, and the Thebans with both; and the great king quarrelled with Hellas, and the Macedonians with both: and the Romans with the Getae. And still earlier the Trojan war happened for these reasons. Alexander was the guest of Menelaus, and if any man had seen their friendly disposition, he would not have believed any one who said that they were not friends. But there was cast between them (as between dogs) a bit of meat, a handsome woman, and about her war arose. And now when you see brothers to be friends appearing to have one mind, do not conclude from this anything about their friendship, not even if they swear it and say that it is impossible for them to be separated from one another. For the ruling principle of a bad man cannot be trusted; it is insecure, has no certain rule by which it is directed, and is overpowered at different times by different appearances. But examine, not what other men examine, if they are born of the same parents and brought up together, and under the same pedagogue; but examine this only, wherein they place their interest, whether in externals or in the will. If in externals, do not name them friends, no more than name them trustworthy or constant, or brave or free; do not name them even men, if you have any judgment. For that is not a principle of human nature which makes them bite one another, and abuse one another, and occupy deserted places or public places, as if they were mountains, and in the courts of justice display the acts of robbers; nor yet that which makes them intemperate and adulterers and corrupters, nor that which makes them do whatever else men do against one another through this one opinion only, that of placing themselves and their interests in the things which are not within the power of their will. But if you hear that in truth these men think the good to be only there, where will is, and where there is a right use of appearances, no longer trouble yourself whether they are father or son, or brothers, or have associated a long time and are companions, but when you have ascertained this only, confidently declare that they are friends, as you declare that they are faithful, that they are just. For where else is friendship than where there is fidelity, and modesty, where there is a communion of honest things and of nothing else.

But you may say, Such a one treated me with regard so long; and did he not love me? How do you know, slave, if he did not regard you in the same way as he wipes his shoes with a sponge, or as he takes care of his beast? How do you know, when you have ceased to be useful as a vessel, he will not throw you away like a broken platter? But this woman is my wife, and we have lived together so long. And how long did Eriphyle live with Amphiaraus, and was the mother of children and of many? But a necklace came between them: and what is a necklace? It is the opinion about such things. That was the bestial principle, that was the thing which broke asunder the friendship between husband and wife, that which did not allow the woman to be a wife nor the mother to be a mother. And let every man among you who has seriously resolved either to be a friend himself or to have another for his friend, cut out these opinions, hate them, drive them from his soul. And thus first of all he will not reproach himself, he will not be at variance with himself, he will not change his mind, he will not torture himself. In the next place, to another also, who is like himself, he will be altogether and completely a friend. But he will bear with the man who is unlike himself, he will be kind to him, gentle, ready to pardon on account of his ignorance, on account of his being mistaken in things of the greatest importance; but he will be harsh to no man, being well convinced of Plato's doctrine that every mind is deprived of truth unwillingly. If you cannot do this, yet you can do in all other respects as friends do, drink together, and lodge together, and sail together, and you may be born of the same parents, for snakes also are: but neither will they be friends, nor you, so long as you retain these bestial and cursed opinions.

On The Power Of Speaking

Every man will read a book with more pleasure or even with more ease, if it is written in fairer characters. Therefore every man will also listen more readily to what is spoken, if it is signified by appropriate and becoming words. We must not say then that there is no faculty of expression: for this affirmation is the characteristic of an impious and also of a timid man. Of an impious man, because he undervalues the gifts which come from God, just as if he would take away the commodity of the power of vision, or hearing, or of seeing. Has then God given you eyes to no purpose? and to no purpose has he infused into them a spirit so strong and of such skilful contrivance as to reach a long way and to fashion the forms of things which are seen? What messenger is so swift and vigilant? And to no purpose has he made the interjacent atmosphere so efficacious and elastic that the vision penetrates through the atmosphere which is in a manner moved? And to no purpose has he made light, without the presence of which there would be no use in any other thing?

Man, be neither ungrateful for these gifts nor yet forget the things which are superior to them. But indeed for the power of seeing and hearing, and indeed for life itself, and for the things which contribute to support it, for the fruits which are dry, and for wine and oil give thanks to God: but remember that he has given you something else better than all these, I mean the power of using them, proving them, and estimating the value of each. For what is that which gives information about each of these powers, what each of them is worth? Is it each faculty itself? Did you ever hear the faculty of vision saying anything about itself? or the faculty of hearing? or wheat, or barley, or a horse, or a dog? No; but they are appointed as ministers and slaves to serve the faculty which has the power of making use of the appearances of things. And if you inquire what is the value of each thing, of whom do you inquire? who answers you? How then can any other faculty be more powerful than this, which uses the rest as ministers and itself proves each and pronounces about them? for which of them knows what itself is, and what is its own value? which of them knows when it ought to employ itself and when not? what faculty is it which opens and closes the eyes, and turns them away from objects to which it ought not to apply them and does apply them to other objects? Is it the faculty of vision? No, but it is the faculty of the will. What is that faculty which closes and opens the ears? what is that by which they are curious and inquisitive, or on the contrary unmoved by what is said? is it the faculty of hearing? It is no other than the faculty of the will. Will this faculty then, seeing that it is amidst all the other faculties which are blind and dumb and unable to see anything else except the very acts for which they are appointed in order to minister to this (faculty) and serve it, but this faculty alone sees sharp and sees what is the value of each of the rest; will this faculty declare to us that anything else is the best, or that itself is? And what else does the eye do when it is opened than see? But whether we ought to look on the wife of a certain person, and in what manner, who tells us? The faculty of the will. And whether we ought to believe what is said or not to believe it, and if we do believe, whether we ought to be moved by it or not, who tells us? Is it not the faculty of the will?

But if you ask me what then is the most excellent of all things, what must I say? I cannot say the power of speaking, but the power of the will, when it is right (Greek: *orthae*). For it is this which uses the other (the power of speaking), and all the other faculties both small and great. For when this faculty of the will is set right, a man who is not good becomes good: but when it fails, a man becomes bad. It is through this that we are unfortunate, that we are fortunate, that we blame one another, are pleased with one another. In a word, it is this which if we neglect it makes unhappiness, and if we carefully look after it, makes happiness.

What then is usually done? Men generally act as a traveller would do on his way to his own country, when he enters a good inn, and being pleased with it should remain there. Man, you have forgotten your purpose: you were not travelling to this inn, but you were passing through it. But this is a pleasant inn. And how many other inns are pleasant? and how many meadows are pleasant? yet only for passing through. But your purpose is this, to return to your country, to relieve your kinsmen of anxiety, to discharge the duties of a citizen, to marry, to beget children, to fill the usual magistracies. For you are not come to select more pleasant places, but to live in these where you were born and of which you were made a citizen. Something of the kind takes place in the matter which we are considering. Since by the aid of speech and such communication as you receive here you must advance to perfection, and purge your will and correct the faculty which makes use of the appearances of things; and since it is necessary also for the teaching (delivery) of theorems to be effected by a certain mode of expression and with a certain variety and sharpness, some persons captivated by these very things abide in them, one captivated by the expression, another by syllogisms, another again by sophisms, and still another by some other inn (Greek: *paudocheiou*) of the kind; and there they stay and waste away as they were among sirens.

Man, your purpose (business) was to make yourself capable of using conformably to nature the appearances presented to you, in your desires not to be frustrated, in your aversion from things not to fall into that which you would avoid, never to have no luck (as one may say), nor ever to have bad luck, to be free, not hindered, not compelled, conforming yourself to the administration of Zeus, obeying it, well satisfied with this, blaming no one, charging no one with fault, able from your whole soul to utter these verses:

Lead me, O Zeus, and thou too Destiny

To (Or Against) A Person Who Was One Of Those Who Were Not Valued (Esteemed) By Him

A certain person said to him (Epictetus): Frequently I desired to hear you and came to you, and you never gave me any answer; and now, if it is possible, I entreat you to say something to me. Do you think, said Epictetus, that as there is an art in anything else, so there is also an art in speaking, and that he who has the art, will speak skilfully, and he who has not, will speak unskilfully?—I do think so.—He then who by speaking receives benefit himself, and is able to benefit others, will speak skilfully; but he who is rather damaged by speaking and does damage to others, will he be unskilled in this art of speaking? And you may find that some are damaged and others benefited by speaking. And are all who hear benefited by what they hear? Or will you find that among them also some are benefited and some damaged? There are both among these also, he said. In this case also then those who hear skilfully are benefited, and those who hear unskilfully are damaged? He admitted this. Is there then a skill in hearing also, as there is in speaking? It seems so. If you choose, consider the matter in this way also. The practice of music, to whom does it belong? To a musician. And the proper making of a statue, to whom do you think that it belongs? To a statuary. And the looking at a statue skilfully, does this appear to you to require the aid of no art? This also requires the aid of art. Then if speaking properly is the business of the skilful man, do you see that to hear also with benefit is the business of the skilful man? Now as to speaking and hearing perfectly, and usefully, let us for the present, if you please, say no more, for both of us are a long way from everything of the kind. But I think that every man will allow this, that he who is going to hear philosophers requires some amount of practice in hearing. Is it not so?

Why then do you say nothing to me? I can only say this to you, that he who knows not who he is, and for what purpose he exists, and what is this world, and with whom he is associated, and what things are the good and the bad, and the beautiful and the ugly, and who neither understands discourse nor demonstration, nor what is true nor what is false, and who is not able to distinguish them, will neither desire according to nature nor turn away nor move towards, nor intend (to act), nor assent, nor dissent, nor suspend his judgment: to say all in a few words, he will go about dumb and blind, thinking that he is somebody, but being nobody. Is this so now for the first time? Is it not the fact that ever since the human race existed, all errors and misfortunes have arisen through this ignorance?

This is all that I have to say to you; and I say even this not willingly. Why? Because you have not roused me. For what must I look to in order to be roused, as men who are expert in riding are roused by generous horses? Must I look to your body? You treat it disgracefully. To your dress? That is luxurious. To your behavior, to your look? That is the same as nothing. When you would listen to a philosopher, do not say to him, You tell me nothing; but only show yourself worthy of hearing or fit for hearing; and you will see how you will move the speaker.

That Logic Is Necessary

When one of those who were present said, Persuade me that logic is necessary, he replied, Do you wish me to prove this to you? The answer was, Yes. Then I must use a demonstrative form of speech. This was granted. How then will you know if I am cheating you by my argument? The man was silent. Do you see, said Epictetus, that you yourself are admitting that logic is necessary, if without it you cannot know so much as this, whether logic is necessary or not necessary?

Of Finery In Dress

A certain young man, a rhetorician, came to see Epictetus, with his hair dressed more carefully than was usual and his attire in an ornamental style; whereupon Epictetus said, Tell me if you do not think that some dogs are beautiful and some horses, and so of all other animals. I do think so, the youth replied. Are not then some men also beautiful and others ugly? Certainly. Do we then for the same reason call each of them in the same kind beautiful, or each beautiful for something peculiar? And you will judge of this matter thus. Since we see a dog naturally formed for one thing, and a horse for another, and for another still, as an example, a nightingale, we may generally and not improperly declare each of them to be beautiful then when it is most excellent according to its nature; but since the nature of each is different, each of them seems to me to be beautiful in a different way. Is it not so? He admitted that it was. That then which makes a dog beautiful, makes a horse ugly; and that which makes a horse beautiful, makes a dog ugly, if it is true that their natures are different. It seems to be so. For I think that what makes a Pancratiast beautiful, makes a wrestler to be not good, and a runner to be most ridiculous; and he who is beautiful for the Pentathlon, is very ugly for wrestling. It is so, said he. What then makes a man beautiful? Is it that which in its kind makes both a dog and a horse beautiful? It is, he said. What then makes a dog beautiful? The possession of the excellence of a dog. And what makes a horse beautiful? The possession of the excellence of a horse. What then makes a man beautiful? Is it not the possession of the excellence of a man? And do you then, if you wish to be beautiful, young man, labor at this, the acquisition of human excellence? But what is this? Observe whom you yourself praise, when you praise many persons without partiality: do you praise the just or the unjust? The just. Whether do you praise the moderate or the immoderate? The moderate. And the temperate or the intemperate? The temperate. If then you make yourself such a person, you will know that you will make yourself beautiful; but so long as you neglect these things, you must be ugly (Greek: *aischron*), even though you contrive all you can to appear beautiful.

In What A Man Ought To Be Exercised Who Has Made Proficiency; And That We Neglect The Chief Things

There are three things (topics, Greek: *topoi*) in which a man ought to exercise himself who would be wise and good. The first concerns the desires and the aversions, that a man may not fail to get what he desires, and that he may not fall into that which he does not desire. The second concerns the movements towards an object and the movements from an object, and generally in doing what a man ought to do, that he may act according to order, to reason, and not carelessly. The third thing concerns freedom from deception and rashness in judgment, and generally it concerns the assents (Greek: *sugchatatheseis*). Of these topics the chief and the most urgent is that which relates to the affects (Greek: *ta pathae*; perturbations); for an affect is produced in no other way than by a failing to obtain that which a man desires or falling into that which a man would wish to avoid. This is that which brings in perturbations, disorders, bad fortune, misfortunes, sorrows, lamentations, and envy; that which makes men envious and jealous; and by these causes we are unable even to listen to the precepts of reason. The second topic concerns the duties of a man; for I ought not to be free from affects (Greek: *apathae*) like a statue, but I ought to maintain the relations (Greek: *scheseis*) natural and acquired, as a pious man, as a son, as a father, as a citizen.

The third topic is that which immediately concerns those who are making proficiency, that which concerns the security of the other two, so that not even in sleep any appearance unexamined may surprise us, nor in intoxication, nor in melancholy. This, it may be said, is above our power. But the present philosophers neglecting the first topic and the second (the affects and duties), employ themselves on the third, using sophistical arguments (Greek: *metapiptontas*), making conclusions from questioning, employing hypotheses, lying. For a man must, it is said, when employed on these matters, take care that he is not deceived. Who must? The wise and good man. This then is all that is wanting to you. Have you successfully worked out the rest? Are you free from deception in the matter of money? If you see a beautiful girl do you resist the appearance? If your neighbor obtains an estate by will, are you not vexed? Now is there nothing else wanting to you except unchangeable firmness of mind (Greek: *ametaptosia*)? Wretch, you hear these very things with fear and anxiety that some person may despise you, and with inquiries about what any person may say about you. And if a man come and tell you that in a certain conversation in which the question was, Who is the best philosopher, a man who was present said that a certain person was the chief philosopher, your little soul which was only a finger's length stretches out to two cubits. But if another who is present says, You are mistaken; it is not worth while to listen to a certain person, for what does he know? he has only the first principles, and no more? then you are confounded, you grow pale, you cry out immediately, I will show him who I am, that I am a great philosopher. It is seen by these very things: why do you wish to show it by others? Do you not know that Diogenes pointed out one of the sophists in this way by stretching out his middle finger? And then when the man was wild with rage, This, he said, is the certain person: I have pointed him out to you. For a man is not shown by the finger, as a stone or a piece of wood; but when any person shows the man's principles, then he shows him as a man.

Let us look at your principles also. For is it not plain that you value not at all your own will (Greek: *proairesis*), but you look externally to things which are independent of your will? For instance, what will a certain person say? and what will people think of you? Will you be considered a man of learning; have you read Chrysippus or Antipater?

for if you have read Archedamus also, you have every thing (that you can desire). Why you are still uneasy lest you should not show us who you are? Would you let me tell you what manner of man you have shown us that you are? You have exhibited yourself to us as a mean fellow, querulous, passionate, cowardly, finding fault with everything, blaming everybody, never quiet, vain: this is what you have exhibited to us. Go away now and read Archedamus; then if a mouse should leap down and make a noise, you are a dead man. For such a death awaits you as it did—what was the man's name—Crinis; and he too was proud, because he understood Archedamus. Wretch, will you not dismiss these things that do not concern you at all? These things are suitable to those who are able to learn them without perturbation, to those who can say: "I am not subject to anger, to grief, to envy: I am not hindered, I am not restrained. What remains for me? I have leisure, I am tranquil: let us see how we must deal with sophistical arguments; let us see how when a man has accepted an hypothesis he shall not be led away to anything absurd." To them such things belong. To those who are happy it is appropriate to light a fire, to dine; if they choose, both to sing and to dance. But when the vessel is sinking, you come to me and hoist the sails.

What Is The Matter On Which A Good Man Should Be Employed, And In What We Ought Chiefly To Practise Ourselves

The material for the wise and good man is his own ruling faculty: and the body is the material for the physician and the aliptes (the man who oils persons); the land is the matter for the husbandman. The business of the wise and good man is to use appearances conformably to nature: and as it is the nature of every soul to assent to the truth, to dissent from the false, and to remain in suspense as to that which is uncertain; so it is its nature to be moved towards the desire for the good, and to aversion from the evil; and with respect to that which is neither good nor bad it feels indifferent. For as the money-changer (banker) is not allowed to reject Caesar's coin, nor the seller of herbs, but if you show the coin, whether he chooses or not, he must give up what is sold for the coin; so it is also in the matter of the soul. When the good appears, it immediately attracts to itself; the evil repels from itself. But the soul will never reject the manifest appearance of the good, any more than persons will reject Caesar's coin. On this principle depends every movement both of man and God.

Against (or with respect to) this kind of thing chiefly a man should exercise himself. As soon as you go out in the morning, examine every man whom you see, every man whom you hear; answer as to a question, What have you seen? A handsome man or woman? Apply the rule. Is this independent of the will, or dependent? Independent. Take it away. What have you seen? A man lamenting over the death of a child. Apply the rule. Death is a thing independent of the will. Take it away. Has the proconsul met you? Apply the rule. What kind of a thing is a proconsul's office? Independent of the will or dependent on it? Independent. Take this away also; it does not stand examination; cast it away; it is nothing to you.

If we practised this and exercised ourselves in it daily from morning to night, something indeed would be done. But now we are forthwith caught half asleep by every appearance, and it is only, if ever, that in the school we are roused a little. Then when we go out, if we see a man lamenting, we say, He is undone. If we see a consul, we say, He is happy. If we see an exiled man, we say, He is miserable. If we see a poor man, we say, He is wretched; he has nothing to eat.

We ought then to eradicate these bad opinions, and to this end we should direct all our efforts. For what is weeping and lamenting? Opinion. What is bad fortune? Opinion. What is civil sedition, what is divided opinion, what is blame, what is accusation, what is impiety, what is trifling? All these things are opinions, and nothing more, and opinions about things independent of the will, as if they were good and bad. Let a man transfer these opinions to things dependent on the will, and I engage for him that he will be firm and constant, whatever may be the state of things around him. Such as is a dish of water, such is the soul. Such as is the ray of light which falls on the water, such are the appearances. When the water is moved, the ray also seems to be moved, yet it is not moved. And when then a man is seized with giddiness, it is not the arts and the virtues which are confounded, but the spirit (the nervous power) on which they are impressed; but if the spirit be restored to its settled state, those things also are restored.

Miscellaneous

When some person asked him how it happened that since reason has been more cultivated by the men of the present age, the progress made in former times was greater. In what respect, he answered, has it been more cultivated now, and in what respect was the progress greater then? For in that in which it has now been more cultivated, in that also the progress will now be found. At present it has been cultivated for the purpose of resolving syllogisms, and progress is made. But in former times it was cultivated for the purpose of maintaining the governing faculty in a condition conformable to nature, and progress was made. Do not then mix things which are different, and do not expect, when you are laboring at one thing to make progress in another. But see if any man among us when he is intent upon this, the keeping himself in a state conformable to nature and living so always, does not make progress. For you will not find such a man.

It is not easy to exhort weak young men; for neither is it easy to hold (soft) cheese with a hook. But those who have a good natural disposition, even if you try to turn them aside, cling still more to reason.

To The Administrator Of The Free Cities Who Was An Epicurean

When the administrator came to visit him, and the man was an Epicurean, Epictetus said, It is proper for us who are not philosophers to inquire of you who are philosophers, as those who come to a strange city inquire of the citizens and those who are acquainted with it, what is the best thing in the world, in order that we also after inquiry may go in quest of that which is best and look at it, as strangers do with the things in cities. For that there are three things which relate to man—soul, body, and things external, scarcely any man denies. It remains for you philosophers to answer what is the best. What shall we say to men? Is the flesh the best? and was it for this that Maximus sailed as far as Cassiope in winter (or bad weather) with his son, and accompanied him that he might be gratified in the flesh? When the man said that it was not, and added, Far be that from him. Is it not fit then, Epictetus said, to be actively employed about the best? It is certainly of all things the most fit. What then do we possess which is better than the flesh? The soul, he replied. And the good things of the best, are they better, or the good things of the worse? The good things of the best. And are the good things of the best within the power of the will or not within the power of the will? They are within the power of the will. Is then the pleasure of the soul a thing within the power of the will? It is, he replied. And on what shall this pleasure depend? On itself? But that cannot be conceived; for there must first exist a certain substance or nature (Greek: *ousia*) of good, by obtaining which we shall have pleasure in the soul. He assented to this also. On what then shall we depend for this pleasure of the soul? for if it shall depend on things of the soul, the substance (nature) of the good is discovered; for good cannot be one thing, and that at which we are rationally delighted another thing; nor if that which precedes is not good, can that which comes after be good, for in order that the thing which comes after may be good, that which precedes must be good. But you would not affirm this, if you are in your right mind, for you would then say what is inconsistent both with Epicurus and the rest of your doctrines. It remains then that the pleasure of the soul is in the pleasure from things of the body; and again that those bodily things must be the things which precede and the substance (nature) of the good.

Seek for doctrines which are consistent with what I say, and by making them your guide you will with pleasure abstain from things which have such persuasive power to lead us and overpower us. But if to the persuasive power of these things, we also devise such a philosophy as this which helps to push us on towards them and strengthens us to this end, what will be the consequence? In a piece of toreutic art which is the best part? the silver or the workmanship? The substance of the hand is the flesh; but the work of the hand is the principal part (that which precedes and leads the rest). The duties then are also three: those which are directed towards the existence of a thing; those which are directed towards its existence in a particular kind; and third, the chief or leading things themselves. So also in man we ought not to value the material, the poor flesh, but the principal (leading things, Greek: *ta proaegoumena*). What are these? Engaging in public business, marrying, begetting children, venerating God, taking care of parents, and generally, having desires, aversions (Greek: *echchlinein*), pursuits of things and avoidances, in the way in which we ought to do these things, and according to our nature. And how are we constituted by nature? Free, noble, modest; for what other animal blushes? what other is capable of receiving the appearance (the impression) of shame? and we are so constituted by nature as to subject pleasure to these things, as a minister, a servant, in order that it may call forth our activity, in order that it may keep us constant in acts which are conformable to nature.

How We Must Exercise Ourselves Against Appearances (Greek: *Phantasias*)

As we exercise ourselves against sophistical questions, so we ought to exercise ourselves daily against appearances; for these appearances also propose questions to us. A certain person's son is dead. Answer; the thing is not within the power of the will: it is not an evil. A father has disinherited a certain son. What do you think of it? It is a thing beyond the power of the will, not an evil. Caesar has condemned a person. It is a thing beyond the power of the will, not an evil. The man is afflicted at this. Affliction is a thing which depends on the will: it is an evil. He has borne the condemnation bravely. That is a thing within the power of the will: it is a good. If we train ourselves in this manner, we shall make progress; for we shall never assent to anything of which there is not an appearance capable of being comprehended. Your son is dead. What has happened? Your son is dead. Nothing more? Nothing. Your ship is lost. What has happened? Your ship is lost. A man has been led to prison. What has happened? He has been led to prison. But that herein he has fared badly, every man adds from his own opinion. But Zeus, you say, does not do right in these matters. Why? because he has made you capable of endurance? because he has made you magnanimous? because he has taken from that which befalls you the power of being evils? because it is in your power to be happy while you are suffering what you suffer? because he has opened the door to you, when things do not please you? Man, go out and do not complain!

Hear how the Romans feel towards philosophers, if you would like to know. Italicus, who was the most in repute of the philosophers, once when I was present, being vexed with his own friends and as if he was suffering something intolerable, said: "I cannot bear it, you are killing me; you will make me such as that man is," pointing to me.

To A Certain Rhetorician Who Was Going Up To Rome On A Suit

When a certain person came to him, who was going up to Rome on account of a suit which had regard to his rank, Epictetus inquired the reason of his going to Rome, and the man then asked what he thought about the matter. Epictetus replied: If you ask me what you will do in Rome, whether you will succeed or fail, I have no rule (Greek: *theoraema*) about this. But if you ask me how you will fare, I can tell you: if you have right opinions (Greek: *dogmata*), you will fare well; if they are false, you will fare ill. For to every man the cause of his acting is opinion. For what is the reason why you desired to be elected governor of the Cnossians? Your opinion. What is the reason that you are now going up to Rome? Your opinion. And going in winter, and with danger and expense? I must go. What tells you this? Your opinion. Then if opinions are the causes of all actions, and a man has bad opinions, such as the cause may be, such also is the effect! Have we then all sound opinions, both you and your adversary? And how do you differ? But have you sounder opinions than your adversary? Why? You think so. And so does he think that his opinions are better; and so do madmen. This is a bad criterion. But show to me that you have made some inquiry into your opinions and have taken some pains about them. And as now you are sailing to Rome in order to become governor of the Cnossians, and you are not content to stay at home with the honors which you had, but you desire something greater and more conspicuous, so when did you ever make a voyage for the purpose of examining your own opinions, and casting them out, if you have any that are bad? Whom have you approached for this purpose? What time have you fixed for it? What age? Go over the times of your life by yourself, if you are ashamed of me (knowing the fact) when you were a boy, did you examine your own opinions?

and did you not then, as you do all things now, do as you did do? and when you were become a youth and attended the rhetoricians, and yourself practised rhetoric, what did you imagine that you were deficient in? And when you were a young man and engaged in public matters, and pleaded causes yourself, and were gaining reputation, who then seemed your equal? And when would you have submitted to any man examining and showing that your opinions are bad? What then do you wish me to say to you? Help me in this matter. I have no theorem (rule) for this. Nor have you, if you came to me for this purpose, come to me as a philosopher, but as to a seller of vegetables or a shoemaker. For what purpose then have philosophers theorems? For this purpose, that whatever may happen, our ruling faculty may be and continue to be conformable to nature. Does this seem to you a small thing? No; but the greatest. What then? does it need only a short time? and is it possible to seize it as you pass by? If you can, seize it.

Then you will say, I met with Epictetus as I should meet with a stone or a statue: for you saw me and nothing more. But he meets with a man as a man, who learns his opinions, and in his turn shows his own. Learn my opinions: show me yours; and then say that you have visited me. Let us examine one another: if I have any bad opinion, take it away; if you have any, show it. This is the meaning of meeting with a philosopher. Not so (you say): but this is only a passing visit, and while we are hiring the vessel, we can also see Epictetus. Let us see what he says. Then you go away and say: Epictetus was nothing; he used solecisms and spoke in a barbarous way. For of what else do you come as judges? Well, but a man may say to me, if I attend to such matters (as you do), I shall have no land as you have none; I shall have no silver cups as you have none, nor fine beasts as you have none. In answer to tins it is perhaps sufficient to say: I have no need of such things; but if you possess many things you have need of others: whether you choose or not, you are poorer than I am. What then have I need of? Of that which you have not? of firmness, of a mind which is conformable to nature, of being free from perturbation.

In What Manner We Ought To Bear Sickness

When the need of each opinion comes, we ought to have it in readiness: on the occasion of breakfast, such opinions as relate to breakfast; in the bath, those that concern the bath; in bed, those that concern bed.

> Let sleep not come upon thy languid eyes Before each daily action thou hast scann'd; What's done amiss, what done, what left undone; From first to last examine all, and then Blame what is wrong, in what is right rejoice.

And we ought to retain these verses in such way that we may use them, not that we may utter them aloud, as when we exclaim, "Paean Apollo." Again in fever we should have ready such opinions as concern a fever; and we ought not, as soon as the fever begins, to lose and forget all. A man who has a fever may say: If I philosophize any longer, may I be hanged: wherever I go, I must take care of the poor body, that a fever may not come. But what is philosophizing? Is it not a preparation against events which may happen? Do you not understand that you are saying something of this kind? "If I shall still prepare myself to bear with patience what happens, may I be hanged." But this is just as if a man after receiving blows should give up the Pancratium. In the Pancratium it is in our power to desist and not to receive blows.

But in the other matter if we give up philosophy, what shall we gain? What then should a man say on the occasion of each painful thing? It was for this that I exercised myself, for this I disciplined myself. God says to you: Give me a proof that you have duly practised athletics, that you have eaten what you ought, that you have been exercised, that you have obeyed the aliptes (the oiler and rubber). Then do you show yourself weak when the time for action comes?

Now is the time for the fever. Let it be borne well. Now is the time for thirst, bear it well. Now is the time for hunger, bear it well. Is it not in your power? Who shall hinder you? The physician will hinder you from drinking; but he cannot prevent you from bearing thirst well: and he will hinder you from eating; but he cannot prevent you from bearing hunger well.

But I cannot attend to my philosophical studies. And for what purpose do you follow them? Slave, is it not that you may be happy, that you may be constant, is it not that you may be in a state conformable to nature and live so? What hinders you when you have a fever from having your ruling faculty conformable to nature? Here is the proof of the thing, here is the test of the philosopher. For this also is a part of life, like walking, like sailing, like journeying by land, so also is fever. Do you read when you are walking? No. Nor do you when you have a fever. But if you walk about well, you have all that belongs to a man who walks. If you bear a fever well, you have all that belongs to a man in a fever. What is it to bear a fever well? Not to blame God or man; not to be afflicted at that which happens, to expect death well and nobly, to do what must be done: when the physician comes in, not to be frightened at what he says; nor if he says you are doing well, to be overjoyed. For what good has he told you? and when you were in health, what good was that to you? And even if he says you are in a bad way, do not despond. For what is it to be ill? is it that you are near the severance of the soul and the body? what harm is there in this? If you are not near now, will you not afterwards be near? Is the world going to be turned upside down when you are dead? Why then do you flatter the physician? Why do you say if you please, master, I shall be well? Why do you give him an opportunity of raising his eyebrows (being proud; or showing his importance)? Do you not value a physician, as you do a shoemaker when he is measuring your foot, or a carpenter when he is building your house, and so treat the physician as to the body which is not yours, but by nature dead? He who has a fever has an opportunity of doing this: if he does these things, he has what belongs to him. For it is not the business of a philosopher to look after these externals, neither his wine nor his oil nor his poor body, but his own ruling power. But as to externals how must he act? so far as not to be careless about them. Where then is there reason for fear? where is there then still reason for anger, and of fear about what belongs to others, about things which are of no value? For we ought to have these two principles in readiness, that except the will nothing is good nor bad; and that we ought not to lead events, but to follow them. My brother ought not to have behaved thus to me. No, but he will see to that; and, however he may behave, I will conduct myself towards him as I ought. For this is my own business; that belongs to another: no man can prevent this, the other thing can be hindered.

About Exercise

We ought not to make our exercises consist in means contrary to nature and adapted to cause admiration, for if we do so, we who call ourselves philosophers, shall not differ at all from jugglers. For it is difficult even to walk on a rope; and not only difficult, but it is also dangerous. Ought we for this reason to practice walking on a rope, or setting up a palm-tree, or embracing statues? By no means. Every thing which is difficult and dangerous is not suitable for practice; but that is suitable which conduces to the working out of that which is proposed to us. And what is that which is proposed to us as a thing to be worked out? To live with desire and aversion (avoidance of certain things) free from restraint. And what is this? Neither to be disappointed in that which you desire, nor to fall into anything which you would avoid. Towards this object then exercise (practice) ought to tend. For since it is not possible to have your desire not disappointed and your aversion free from falling into that which you would avoid, without great and constant practice, you must know that if you allow your desire and aversion to turn to things which are not within the power of the will, you will neither have your desire capable of attaining your object, nor your aversion free from the power of avoiding that which you would avoid. And since strong habit leads (prevails), and we are accustomed to employ desire and aversion only to things which are not within the power of our will, we ought to oppose to this habit a contrary habit, and where there is great slipperiness in the appearances, there to oppose the habit of exercise. Then at last, if occasion presents itself, for the purpose of trying yourself at a proper time you will descend into the arena to know if appearances overpower you as they did formerly. But at first fly far from that which is stronger than yourself; the contest is unequal between a charming young girl and a beginner in philosophy. The earthen pitcher, as the saying is, and the rock do not agree.

What Solitude Is, And What Kind Of Person A Solitary Man Is

Solitude is a certain condition of a helpless man. For because a man is alone, he is not for that reason also solitary; just as though a man is among numbers, he is not therefore not solitary. When then we have lost either a brother, or a son, or a friend on whom we were accustomed to repose, we say that we are left solitary, though we are often in Rome, though such a crowd meet us, though so many live in the same place, and sometimes we have a great number of slaves. For the man who is solitary, as it is conceived, is considered to be a helpless person and exposed to those who wish to harm him. For this reason when we travel, then especially do we say that we are lonely when we fall among robbers, for it is not the sight of a human creature which removes us from solitude, but the sight of one who is faithful and modest and helpful to us. For if being alone is enough to make solitude, you may say that even Zeus is solitary in the conflagration and bewails himself saying, Unhappy that I am who have neither Hera, nor Athena, nor Apollo, nor brother, nor son, nor descendant, nor kinsman. This is what some say that he does when he is alone at the conflagration. For they do not understand how a man passes his life when he is alone, because they set out from a certain natural principle, from the natural desire of community and mutual love and from the pleasure of conversation among men. But none the less a man ought to be prepared in a manner for this also (being alone), to be able to be sufficient for himself and to be his own companion. For as Zeus dwells with himself, and is tranquil by himself, and thinks of his own administration and of its nature, and is employed in thoughts suitable to himself; so ought we also to be able to talk with ourselves, not to feel the want of others also, not to be unprovided with the means of passing our time; to observe the divine administration, and the relation of ourselves to everything else; to consider how we formerly were affected towards things that happened and how at present; what are still the things which give us pain; how these also can be cured and how removed; if any things require improvement, to improve them according to reason.

Well then, if some man should come upon me when I am alone and murder me? Fool, not murder You, but your poor body.

What kind of solitude then remains? what want? why do we make ourselves worse than children; and what do children do when they are left alone? They take up shells and ashes, and they build something, then pull it down, and build something else, and so they never want the means of passing the time. Shall I then, if you sail away, sit down and weep, because I have been left alone and solitary? Shall I then have no shells, no ashes? But children do what they do through want of thought (or deficiency in knowledge), and we through knowledge are unhappy.

Every great power (faculty) is dangerous to beginners. You must then bear such things as you are able, but conformably to nature: but not . . . Practise sometimes a way of living like a person out of health that you may at some time live like a man in health.

Certain Miscellaneous Matters

As bad tragic actors cannot sing alone, but in company with many, so some persons cannot walk about alone. Man, if you are anything, both walk alone and talk to yourself, and do not hide yourself in the chorus. Examine a little at last, look around, stir yourself up, that you may know who you are.

You must root out of men these two things, arrogance (pride) and distrust. Arrogance then is the opinion that you want nothing (are deficient in nothing); but distrust is the opinion that you cannot be happy when so many circumstances surround you. Arrogance is removed by confutation; and Socrates was the first who practised this. And (to know) that the thing is not impossible inquire and seek. This search will do you no harm; and in a manner this is philosophizing, to seek how it is possible to employ desire and aversion (Greek: *echchlisis*) without impediment.

I am superior to you, for my father is a man of consular rank. Another says, I have been a tribune, but you have not. If we were horses, would you say, My father was swifter? I have much barley and fodder, or elegant neck ornaments. If then you were saying this, I said, Be it so: let us run then. Well, is there nothing in a man such as running in a horse, by which it will be known which is superior and inferior? Is there not modesty (Greek: *aidos*), fidelity, justice? Show yourself superior in these, that you may be superior as a man. If you tell me that you can kick violently, I also will say to you, that you are proud of that which is the act of an ass.

That We Ought To Proceed With Circumspection To Everything

In every act consider what precedes and what follows, and then proceed to the act. If you do not consider, you will at first begin with spirit, since you have not thought at all of the things which follow; but afterwards when some consequences have shown themselves, you will basely desist (from that which you have begun).—I wish to conquer at the Olympic games.—(And I too, by the gods; for it is a fine thing.) But consider here what precedes and what follows; and then, if it is for your good, undertake the thing. You must act according to rules, follow strict diet, abstain from delicacies, exercise yourself by compulsion at fixed times, in heat, in cold; drink no cold water, nor wine, when there is opportunity of drinking it. In a word, you must surrender yourself to the trainer, as you do to a physician. Next in the contest, you must be covered with sand, sometimes dislocate a hand, sprain an ankle, swallow a quantity of dust, be scourged with the whip; and after undergoing all this, you must sometimes be conquered. After reckoning all these things, if you have still an inclination, go to the athletic practice. If you do not reckon them, observe you will behave like children who at one time play as wrestlers, then as gladiators, then blow a trumpet, then act a tragedy, when they have seen and admired such things. So you also do: you are at one time a wrestler (athlete), then a gladiator, then a philosopher, then a rhetorician; but with your whole soul you are nothing: like the ape you imitate all that you see; and always one thing after another pleases you, but that which becomes familiar displeases you. For you have never undertaken anything after consideration, nor after having explored the whole matter and put it to a strict examination; but you have undertaken it at hazard and with a cold desire. Thus some persons having seen a philosopher and having heard one speak like Euphrates—and yet who can speak like him?—wish to be philosophers themselves.

Man, consider first what the matter is (which you propose to do), then your own nature also, what it is able to bear. If you are a wrestler, look at your shoulders, your thighs, your loins: for different men are naturally formed for different things. Do you think that, if you do (what you are doing daily), you can be a philosopher? Do you think that you can eat as you do now, drink as you do now, and in the same way be angry and out of humor? You must watch, labor, conquer certain desires, you must depart from your kinsmen, be despised by your slaves, laughed at by those who meet you, in everything you must be in an inferior condition, as to magisterial office, in honors, in courts of justice. When you have considered all these things completely, then, if you think proper, approach to philosophy, if you would gain in exchange for these things freedom from perturbations, liberty, tranquillity. If you have not considered these things, do not approach philosophy: do not act like children, at one time a philosopher, then a tax collector, then a rhetorician, then a procurator (officer) of Caesar. These things are not consistent. You must be one man either good or bad; you must either labor at your own ruling faculty or at external things; you must either labor at things within or at external things; that is, you must either occupy the place of a philosopher or that of one of the vulgar.

A person said to Rufus when Galba was murdered: Is the world now governed by Providence? But Rufus replied: Did I ever incidentally form an argument from Galba that the world is governed by Providence?

That We Ought With Caution To Enter Into Familiar Intercourse With Men

If a man has frequent intercourse with others either for talk, or drinking together, or generally for social purposes, he must either become like them, or change them to his own fashion. For if a man places a piece of quenched charcoal close to a piece that is burning, either the quenched charcoal will quench the other, or the burning charcoal will light that which is quenched. Since then the danger is so great, we must cautiously enter into such intimacies with those of the common sort, and remember that it is impossible that a man can keep company with one who is covered with soot without being partaker of the soot himself. For what will you do if a man speaks about gladiators, about horses, about athletes, or what is worse about men? Such a person is bad, such a person is good; this was well done, this was done badly. Further, if he scoff, or ridicule, or show an ill-natured disposition? Is any man among us prepared like a lute-player when he takes a lute, so that as soon as he has touched the strings, he discovers which are discordant, and tunes the instrument? Such a power as Socrates had who in all his social intercourse could lead his companions to his own purpose? How should you have this power? It is therefore a necessary consequence that you are carried about by the common kind of people.

Why then are they more powerful than you? Because they utter these useless words from their real opinions; but you utter your elegant words only from your lips; for this reason they are without strength and dead, and it is nauseous to listen to your exhortations and your miserable virtue, which is talked of everywhere (up and down). In this way the vulgar have the advantage over you; for every opinion (Greek: *dogma*) is strong and invincible. Until then the good (Greek: *chompsai*) sentiments (Greek: *hupolaepseis*) are fixed in you, and you shall have acquired a certain power for your security, I advise you to be careful in your association with common persons; if you are not, every day like wax in the sun there will be melted away whatever you inscribe on your minds in the school. Withdraw then yourselves far from the sun so long as you have these waxen sentiments. For this reason also philosophers advise men to leave their native country, because ancient habits distract them and do not allow a beginning to be made of a different habit; nor can we tolerate those who meet us and say: See such a one is now a philosopher, who was once so and so. Thus also physicians send those who have lingering diseases to a different country and a different air; and they do right. Do you also introduce other habits than those which you have; fix you opinions and exercise yourselves in them. But you do not so; you go hence to a spectacle, to a show of gladiators, to a place of exercise (Greek: *chuston*), to a circus; then you come back hither, and again from this place you go to those places, and still the same persons. And there is no pleasing (good) habit, nor attention, nor care about self and observation of this kind. How shall I use the appearances presented to me? according to nature, or contrary to nature? how do I answer to them? as I ought, or as I ought not? Do I say to those things which are independent of the will, that they do not concern me? For if you are not yet in this state, fly from your former habits, fly from the common sort, if you intend ever to begin to be something.

On Providence

When you make any charge against Providence, consider, and you will learn that the thing has happened according to reason. Yes, but the unjust man has the advantage. In what? In money. Yes, for he is superior to you in this, that he flatters, is free from shame, and is watchful. What is the wonder? But see if he has the advantage over you in being faithful, in being modest; for you will not find it to be so; but wherein you are superior, there you will find that you have the advantage. And I once said to a man who was vexed because Philostorgus was fortunate: Would you choose to lie with Sura? May it never happen, he replied, that this day should come? Why then are you vexed, if he receives something in return for that which he sells; or how can you consider him happy who acquires those things by such means as you abominate; or what wrong does Providence, if he gives the better things to the better men? Is it not better to be modest than to be rich? He admitted this. Why are you vexed then, man, when you possess the better thing? Remember then always and have in readiness the truth, that this is a law of nature, that the superior has an advantage over the inferior in that in which he is superior; and you will never be vexed.

But my wife treats me badly. Well, if any man asks you what this is, say, my wife treats me badly. Is there then nothing more? Nothing. My father gives me nothing. (What is this? my father gives me nothing. Is there nothing else then? Nothing); but to say that this is an evil is something which must be added to it externally, and falsely added. For this reason we must not get rid of poverty, but of the opinion about poverty, and then we shall be happy.

About Cynicism

When one of his pupils inquired of Epictetus, and he was a person who appeared to be inclined to Cynicism, what kind of person a Cynic ought to be, and what was the notion (Greek: *prolaepsis*) of the thing, we will inquire, said Epictetus, at leisure; but I have so much to say to you that he who without God attempts so great a matter, is hateful to God, and has no other purpose than to act indecently in public.

In the first place, in the things which relate to yourself, you must not be in any respect like what you do now; you must not blame God or man; you must take away desire altogether, you must transfer avoidance (Greek: *echchlisis*) only to the things which are within the power of the will; you must not feel anger nor resentment or envy nor pity; a girl must not appear handsome to you, nor must you love a little reputation, nor be pleased with a boy or a cake. For you ought to know that the rest of men throw walls around them and houses and darkness when they do any such things, and they have many means of concealment. A man shuts the door, he sets somebody before the chamber; if a person comes, say that he is out, he is not at leisure. But the Cynic instead of all these things must use modesty as his protection; if he does not, he will be indecent in his nakedness and under the open sky. This is his house, his door; this is the slave before his bedchamber; this is his darkness. For he ought not to wish to hide anything that he does; and if he does, he is gone, he has lost the character of a Cynic, of a man who lives under the open sky, of a free man; he has begun to fear some external thing, he has begun to have need of concealment, nor can he get concealment when he chooses. For where shall he hide himself and how? And if by chance this public instructor shall be detected, this paedagogue, what kind of things will he be compelled to suffer? when then a man fears these things, is it possible for him to be bold with his whole soul to superintend men? It cannot be: it is impossible.

In the first place then you must make your ruling faculty pure, and this mode of life also. Now (you should say), to me the matter to work on is my understanding, as wood is to the carpenter, as hides to the shoemaker; and my business is the right use of appearances. But the body is nothing to me: the parts of it are nothing to me. Death? Let it come when it chooses, either death of the whole or of a part. Fly, you say. And whither; can any man eject me out of the world? He cannot. But wherever I go, there is the sun, there is the moon, there are the stars, dreams, omens, and the conversation (Greek: *omilia*) with gods.

Then, if he is thus prepared, the true Cynic cannot be satisfied with this; but he must know that he is sent a messenger from Zeus to men about good and bad things, to show them that they have wandered and are seeking the substance of good and evil where it is not, but where it is, they never think; and that he is a spy, as Diogenes was carried off to Philip after the battle of Chaeroneia as a spy. For in fact a Cynic is a spy of the things which are good for men and which are evil, and it is his duty to examine carefully and to come and report truly, and not to be struck with terror so as to point out as enemies those who are not enemies, nor in any other way to be perturbed by appearances nor confounded.

It is his duty then to be able with a loud voice, if the occasion should arise, and appearing on the tragic stage to say like Socrates: Men, whither are you hurrying, what are you doing, wretches? like blind people you are wandering up and down; you are going by another road, and have left the true road; you seek for prosperity and happiness where they are not, and if another shows you where they are, you do not believe him. Why do you seek it without? In the body? It is not there. If you doubt, look at Myro, look at Ophellius. In possessions? It is not there. But if you do not believe me, look at Croesus: look at those who are now rich, with what lamentations their life is filled. In power? It is not there. If it is, those must be happy who have been twice and thrice consuls; but they are not. Whom shall we believe in these matters? You who from without see their affairs and are dazzled by an appearance, or the men themselves? What do they say? Hear them when they groan, when they grieve, when on account of these very consulships and glory and splendor they think that they are more wretched and in greater danger. Is it in royal power? It is not: if it were, Nero would have been happy, and Sardanapalus. But neither was Agamemnon happy, though he was a better man than Sardanapalus and Nero; but while others are snoring, what is he doing?

Much from his head he tore his rooted hair:
Iliad, x., 15.

and what does he say himself?

"I am perplexed," he says, "and
Disturb'd I am," and "my heart out of my bosom
Is leaping."
Iliad, x., 91.

Wretch, which of your affairs goes badly? Your possessions? No. Your body? No. But you are rich in gold and copper. What then is the matter with you? That part of you, whatever it is, has been neglected by you and is corrupted, the part with which we desire, with which we avoid, with which we move towards and move from things. How neglected? He knows not the nature of good for which he is made by nature and the nature of evil; and what is his own, and what belongs to another; and when anything that belongs to others goes badly, he says, Woe to me, for the Hellenes are in danger. Wretched is his ruling faculty, and alone neglected and uncared for. The Hellenes are going to die destroyed by the Trojans. And if the Trojans do not kill them, will they not die? Yes; but not all at once. What difference then does it make? For if death is an evil, whether men die altogether, or if they die singly, it is equally an evil. Is anything else then going to happen than the separation of the soul and the body? Nothing. And if the Hellenes perish, is the door closed, and is it not in your power to die? It is. Why then do you lament (and say), Oh, you are a king and have the sceptre of Zeus? An unhappy king does not exist more than an unhappy god. What then art thou? In truth a shepherd: for you weep as shepherds do, when a wolf has carried off one of their sheep: and these who are governed by you are sheep. And why did you come hither? Was your desire in any danger? was your aversion (Greek: *echchlisis*)? was your movement (pursuits)? was your avoidance of things? He replies, No; but the wife of my brother was carried off. Was it not then a great gain to be deprived of an adulterous wife? Shall we be despised then by the Trojans? What kind of people are the Trojans, wise or foolish? If they are wise, why do you fight with them? If they are fools, why do you care about them?

Do you possess the body then free or is it in servile condition? We do not know. Do you not know that it is the slave of fever, of gout, ophthalmia, dysentery, of a tyrant, of fire, of iron, of everything which is stronger? Yes, it is a slave. How then is it possible that anything which belongs to the body can be free from hindrance? and how is a thing great or valuable which is naturally dead, or earth, or mud? Well then, do you possess nothing which is free? Perhaps nothing. And who is able to compel you to assent to that which appears false? No man. And who can compel you not to assent to that which appears true? No man. By this then you see that there is something in you naturally free. But to desire or to be averse from, or to move towards an object or to move from it, or to prepare yourself, or to propose to do anything, which of you can do this, unless he has received an impression of the appearance of that which is profitable or a duty? No man. You have then in these things also something which is not hindered and is free. Wretched men, work out this, take care of this, seek for good here.

That We Ought Not To Be Moved By A Desire Of Those Things Which Are Not In Our Power

Let not that which in another is contrary to nature be an evil to you; for you are not formed by nature to be depressed with others nor to be unhappy with others, but to be happy with them. If a man is unhappy, remember that his unhappiness is his own fault; for God has made all men to be happy, to be free from perturbations. For this purpose he has given means to them, some things to each person as his own, and other things not as his own; some things subject to hindrance and compulsion and deprivation; and these things are not a man's own; but the things which are not subject to hindrances, are his own; and the nature of good and evil, as it was fit to be done by him who takes care of us and protects us like a father, he has made our own. But you say, I have parted from a certain person, and he is grieved. Why did he consider as his own that which belongs to another? why, when he looked on you and was rejoiced, did he not also reckon that you are a mortal, that it is natural for you to part from him for a foreign country? Therefore he suffers the consequences of his own folly. But why do you or for what purpose bewail yourself? Is it that you also have not thought of these things? but like poor women who are good for nothing, you have enjoyed all things in which you took pleasure, as if you would always enjoy them, both places and men and conversation; and now you sit and weep because you do not see the same persons and do not live in the same places. Indeed you deserve this, to be more wretched than crows and ravens who have the power of flying where they please and changing their nests for others, and crossing the seas without lamenting or regretting their former condition. Yes, but this happens to them because they are irrational creatures. Was reason then given to us by the gods for the purpose of unhappiness and misery, that we may pass our lives in wretchedness and lamentation? Must all persons be immortal and must no man go abroad, and must we ourselves not go abroad, but remain rooted like plants; and if any of our familiar friends goes abroad, must we sit and weep; and on the contrary, when he returns, must we dance and clap our hands like children?

But my mother laments when she does not see me. Why has she not learned these principles? and I do not say this, that we should not take care that she may not lament, but I say that we ought not to desire in every way what is not our own. And the sorrow of another is another's sorrow; but my sorrow is my own. I then will stop my own sorrow by every means, for it is in my power; and the sorrow of another I will endeavor to stop as far as I can; but I will not attempt to do it by every means; for if I do, I shall be fighting against God, I shall be opposing Zeus and shall be placing myself against him in the administration of the universe; and the reward (the punishment) of this fighting against God and of this disobedience not only will the children of my children pay, but I also shall myself, both by day and by night, startled by dreams, perturbed, trembling at every piece of news, and having my tranquillity depending on the letters of others. Some person has arrived from Rome. I only hope there is no harm. But what harm can happen to you, where you are not? From Hellas (Greece) some one is come; I hope that there is no harm. In this way every place may be the cause of misfortune to you. Is it not enough for you to be unfortunate there where you are, and must you be so even beyond sea, and by the report of letters? Is this the way in which your affairs are in a state of security? Well then suppose that my friends have died in the places which are far from me. What else have they suffered than that which is the condition of mortals? Or how are you desirous at the same time to live to old age, and at the same time not to see the death of any person whom you love? Know you not that in the course of a long time many and various kinds of things must happen; that a fever shall overpower one, a robber another, and a third a tyrant? Such is the condition of things around us, such are those who live with us in the world;

cold and heat, and unsuitable ways of living, and journeys by land, and voyages by sea, and winds, and various circumstances which surround us, destroy one man, and banish another, and throw one upon an embassy and another into an army. Sit down then in a flutter at all these things, lamenting, unhappy, unfortunate, dependent on another, and dependent not on one or two, but on ten thousands upon ten thousands.

Did you hear this when you were with the philosophers? did you learn this? do you not know that human life is a warfare? that one man must keep watch, another must go out as a spy, and a third must fight? and it is not possible that all should be in one place, nor is it better that it should be so. But you neglecting to do the commands of the general complain when anything more hard than usual is imposed on you, and you do not observe what you make the army become as far as it is in your power; that if all imitate you, no man will dig a trench, no man will put a rampart round, nor keep watch, nor expose himself to danger, but will appear to be useless for the purposes of an army. Again, in a vessel if you go as a sailor, keep to one place and stick to it. And if you are ordered to climb the mast, refuse; if to run to the head of the ship, refuse; and what master of a ship will endure you? and will he not pitch you overboard as a useless thing, an impediment only and bad example to the other sailors? And so it is here also: every man's life is a kind of warfare, and it is long and diversified. You must observe the duty of a soldier and do every thing at the nod of the general; if it is possible, divining what his wishes are; for there is no resemblance between that general and this, neither in strength nor in superiority of character. Know you not that a good man does nothing for the sake of appearance, but for the sake of doing right? What advantage is it then to him to have done right? And what advantage is it to a man who writes the name of Dion to write it as he ought? The advantage is to have written it. Is there no reward then? Do you seek a reward for a good man greater than doing what is good and just? At Olympia you wish for nothing more, but it seems to you enough to be crowned at the games. Does it seem to you so small and worthless a thing to be good and happy?

For these purposes being introduced by the gods into this city (the world), and it being now your duty to undertake the work of a man, do you still want nurses also and a mamma, and do foolish women by their weeping move you and make you effeminate? Will you thus never cease to be a foolish child? know you not that he who does the acts of a child, the older he is, the more ridiculous he is?

So in this matter also: if you kiss your own child, or your brother or friend, never give full license to the appearance (Greek: *phantasian*), and allow not your pleasure to go as far as it chooses; but check it, and curb it as those who stand behind men in their triumphs and remind them that they are mortal. Do you also remind yourself in like manner, that he whom you love is mortal, and that what you love is nothing of your own; it has been given to you for the present, not that it should not be taken from you, nor has it been given to you for all time, but as a fig is given to you or a bunch of grapes at the appointed season of the year. But if you wish for these things in winter, you are a fool. So if you wish for your son or friend when it is not allowed to you, you must know that you are wishing for a fig in winter. For such as winter is to a fig, such is every event which happens from the universe to the things which are taken away according to its nature. And further, at the times when you are delighted with a thing, place before yourself the contrary appearances. What harm is it while you are kissing your child to say with a lisping voice: To-morrow you will die; and to a friend also: To-morrow you will go away or I shall, and never shall we see one another again? But these are words of bad omen—and some incantations also are of bad omen; but because they are useful, I don't care for this; only let them be useful. But do you call things to be of bad omen except those which are significant of some evil? Cowardice is a word of bad omen, and meanness of spirit, and sorrow, and grief, and shamelessness. These words are of bad omen; and yet we ought not to hesitate to utter them in order to protect ourselves against the things. Do you tell me that a name which is significant of any natural thing is of evil omen? say that even for the ears of corn to be reaped is of bad omen, for it signifies the destruction of the ears, but not of the world. Say that the falling of the leaves also is of bad omen, and for the dried fig to take the place of the green fig, and for raisins to be made from the grapes. For all these things are changes from a former state into other states; not a destruction, but a certain fixed economy and administration. Such is going away from home and a small change: such is death, a greater change, not from the state which now is to that which is not, but to that which is not now. Shall I then no longer exist? You will not exist, but you will be something else, of which the world now has need; for you also came into existence not when you chose, but when the world had need of you.

Let these thoughts be ready to hand by night and by day; these you should write, these you should read; about these you should talk to yourself and to others. Ask a man: Can you help me at all for this purpose? and further, go to another and to another. Then if anything that is said be contrary to your wish, this reflection first will immediately relieve you, that it is not unexpected. For it is a great thing in all cases to say: I knew that I begot a son who is mortal. For so you also will say: I knew that I am mortal, I knew that I may leave my home, I knew that I may be ejected from it, I knew that I may be led to prison. Then if you turn round and look to yourself, and seek the place from which comes that which has happened, you will forthwith recollect that it comes from the place of things which are out of the power of the will, and of things which are not my own. What then is it to me? Then, you will ask, and this is the chief thing: And who is it that sent it? The leader, or the general, the state, the law of the state. Give it me then, for I must always obey the law in everything. Then, when the appearance (of things) pains you, for it is not in your power to prevent this, contend against it by the aid of reason, conquer it: do not allow it to gain strength nor to lead you to the consequences by raising images such as it pleases and as it pleases. If you be in Gyara, do not imagine the mode of living at Rome, and how many pleasures there were for him who lived there and how many there would be for him who returned to Rome; but fix your mind on this matter, how a man who lives in Gyara ought to live in Gyara like a man of courage. And if you be in Rome, do not imagine what the life in Athens is, but think only of the life in Rome.

Then in the place of all other delights substitute this, that of being conscious that you are obeying God, that not in word, but in deed you are performing the acts of a wise and good man. For what a thing it is for a man to be able to say to himself: Now whatever the rest may say in solemn manner in the schools and may be judged to be saying in a way contrary to common opinion (or in a strange way), this I am doing; and they are sitting and are discoursing of my virtues and inquiring about me and praising me; and of this Zeus has willed that I shall receive from myself a demonstration, and shall myself know if he has a soldier such as he ought to have, a citizen such as he ought to have, and if he has chosen to produce me to the rest of mankind as a witness of the things which are independent of the will: See that you fear without reason, that you foolishly desire what you do desire; seek not the good in things external; seek it in yourselves: if you do not, you will not find it. For this purpose he leads me at one time hither, at another time sends me thither, shows me to men as poor, without authority, and sick; sends me to Gyara, leads me into prison, not because he hates me—far from him be such a meaning, for who hates the best of his servants? nor yet because he cares not for me, for he does not neglect any even of the smallest things; but he does this for the purpose of exercising me and making use of me as a witness to others. Being appointed to such a service, do I still care about the place in which I am, or with whom I am, or what men say about me? and do I not entirely direct my thoughts to God and to his instructions and commands?

Having these things (or thoughts) always in hand, and exercising them by yourself, and keeping them in readiness, you will never be in want of one to comfort you and strengthen you. For it is not shameful to be without something to eat, but not to have reason sufficient for keeping away fear and sorrow. But if once you have gained exemption from sorrow and fear, will there any longer be a tyrant for you, or a tyrant's guard, or attendants on Caesar? Or shall any appointment to offices at court cause you pain, or shall those who sacrifice in the Capitol on the occasion of being named to certain functions, cause pain to you who have received so great authority from Zeus? Only do not make a proud display of it, nor boast of it; but show it by your acts; and if no man perceives it, be satisfied that you are yourself in a healthy state and happy.

To Those Who Fall Off (Desist) From Their Purpose

Consider as to the things which you proposed to yourself at first, which you have secured, and which you have not; and how you are pleased when you recall to memory the one, and are pained about the other; and if it is possible, recover the things wherein you failed. For we must not shrink when we are engaged in the greatest combat, but we must even take blows. For the combat before us is not in wrestling and the Pancration, in which both the successful and the unsuccessful may have the greatest merit, or may have little, and in truth may be very fortunate or very unfortunate; but the combat is for good fortune and happiness themselves. Well then, even if we have renounced the contest in this matter (for good fortune and happiness), no man hinders us from renewing the combat again, and we are not compelled to wait for another four years that the games at Olympia may come again; but as soon as you have recovered and restored yourself, and employ the same zeal, you may renew the combat again; and if again you renounce it, you may again renew it; and if you once gain the victory, you are like him who has never renounced the combat. Only do not through a habit of doing the same thing (renouncing the combat), begin to do it with pleasure, and then like a bad athlete go about after being conquered in all the circuit of the games like quails who have run away.

To Those Who Fear Want

Are you not ashamed at being more cowardly and more mean than fugitive slaves? How do they when they run away leave their masters? on what estates do they depend, and what domestics do they rely on? Do they not after stealing a little, which is enough for the first days, then afterwards move on through land or through sea, contriving one method after another for maintaining their lives? And what fugitive slave ever died of hunger? But you are afraid lest necessary things should fail you, and are sleepless by night. Wretch, are you so blind, and don't you see the road to which the want of necessaries leads?—Well, where does it lead?—to the same place to which a fever leads, or a stone that falls on you, to death. Have you not often said this yourself to your companions? have you not read much of this kind, and written much? and how often have you boasted that you were easy as to death?

Learn then first what are the things which are shameful, and then tell us that you are a philosopher: but at present do not, even if any other man calls you so, allow it.

Is that shameful to you which is not your own act, that of which you are not the cause, that which has come to you by accident, as a headache, as a fever? If your parents were poor, and left their property to others, and if while they live, they do not help you at all, is this shameful to you? Is this what you learned with the philosophers? Did you never hear that the thing which is shameful ought to be blamed, and that which is blamable is worthy of blame? Whom do you blame for an act which is not his own, which he did not do himself? Did you then make your father such as he is, or is it in your power to improve him? Is this power given to you? Well then, ought you to wish the things which are not given to you, or to be ashamed if you do not obtain them? And have you also been accustomed while you were studying philosophy to look to others and to hope for nothing from yourself? Lament then and groan and eat with fear that you may not have food to-morrow. Tremble about your poor slaves lest they steal, lest they run away, lest they die. So live, and continue to live, you who in name only have approached philosophy, and have disgraced its theorems as far as you can by showing them to be useless and unprofitable to those who take them up; you, who have never sought constancy, freedom from perturbation, and from passions; you who have not sought any person for the sake of this object, but many for the sake of syllogisms; you who have never thoroughly examined any of these appearances by yourself, Am I able to bear, or am I not able to bear? What remains for me to do? But as if all your affairs were well and secure, you have been resting on the third topic, that of things being unchanged, in order that you may possess unchanged—what? cowardice, mean spirit, the admiration of the rich, desire without attaining any end, and avoidance (Greek: *echchlisin*) which fails in the attempt? About security in these things you have been anxious.

Ought you not to have gained something in addition from reason, and then to have protected this with security? And whom did you ever see building a battlement all around and encircling it with a wall? And what doorkeeper is placed with no door to watch? But you practise in order to be able to prove—what? You practise that you may not be tossed as on the sea through sophisms, and tossed about from what? Show me first what you hold, what you measure, or what you weigh; and show me the scales or the medimnus (the measure); or how long will you go on measuring the dust? Ought you not to demonstrate those things which make men happy, which make things go on for them in the way as they wish, and why we ought to blame no man, accuse no man, and acquiesce in the administration of the universe?

About Freedom

He is free who lives as he wishes to live; who is neither subject to compulsion nor to hindrance, nor to force; whose movements to action (Greek: *hormai*) are not impeded, whose desires attain their purpose, and who does not fall into that which he would avoid (Greek: *echchliseis aperiptotoi*). Who then chooses to live in error? No man. Who chooses to live deceived, liable to mistake, unjust, unrestrained, discontented, mean? No man. Not one then of the bad lives as he wishes; nor is he then free. And who chooses to live in sorrow, fear, envy, pity, desiring and failing in his desires, attempting to avoid something and falling into it? Not one. Do we then find any of the bad free from sorrow, free from fear, who does not fall into that which he would avoid, and does not obtain that which he wishes? Not one; nor then do we find any bad man free.

Further, then, answer me this question, also: does freedom seem to you to be something great and noble and valuable? How should it not seem so? Is it possible then when a man obtains anything so great and valuable and noble to be mean? It is not possible. When then you see any man subject to another or flattering him contrary to his own opinion, confidently affirm that this man also is not free; and not only if he do this for a bit of supper, but also if he does it for a government (province) or a consulship; and call these men little slaves who for the sake of little matters do these things, and those who do so for the sake of great things call great slaves, as they deserve to be. This is admitted also. Do you think that freedom is a thing independent and self-governing? Certainly. Whomsoever then it is in the power of another to hinder and compel, declare that he is not free. And do not look, I entreat you, after his grandfathers and great-grandfathers, or inquire about his being bought or sold, but if you hear him saying from his heart and with feeling, "Master," even if the twelve fasces precede him (as consul), call him a slave. And if you hear him say, "Wretch that I am, how much I suffer," call him a slave. If, finally, you see him lamenting, complaining, unhappy, call him a slave, though he wears a praetexta. If, then, he is doing nothing of this kind do not yet say that he is free, but learn his opinions, whether they are subject to compulsion, or may produce hindrance, or to bad fortune, and if you find him such, call him a slave who has a holiday in the Saturnalia; say that his master is from home; he will return soon, and you will know what he suffers.

What then is that which makes a man free from hindrance and makes him his own master? For wealth does not do it, nor consulship, nor provincial government, nor royal power; but something else must be discovered. What then is that which when we write makes us free from hindrance and unimpeded? The knowledge of the art of writing. What then is it in playing the lute? The science of playing the lute. Therefore in life also it is the science of life. You have then heard in a general way; but examine the thing also in the several parts. Is it possible that he who desires any of the things which depend on others can be free from hindrance? No. Is it possible for him to be unimpeded? No. Therefore he cannot be free. Consider then, whether we have nothing which is in our own power only, or whether we have all things, or whether some things are in our own power, and others in the power of others. What do you mean? When you wish the body to be entire (sound) is it in your power or not? It is not in my power. When you wish it to be healthy? Neither is this in my power. When you wish it to be handsome? Nor is this. Life or death? Neither is this in my power. Your body then is another's, subject to every man who is stronger than yourself. It is. But your estate is it in your power to have it when you please, and as long as you please, and such as you please? No. And your slaves? No. And your clothes? No. And your house? No. And your horses? Not one of these things. And if you wish by all means your children to live, or your wife, or your brother, or your friends, is it in your power? This also is not in my power.

Whether then have you nothing which is in your own power, which depends on yourself only and cannot be taken from you, or have you anything of the kind? I know not. Look at the thing then thus, and examine it. Is any man able to make you assent to that which is false? No man. In the matter of assent then you are free from hindrance and obstruction. Granted. Well; and can a man force you to desire to move towards that to which you do not choose? He can, for when he threatens me with death or bonds he compels me to desire to move towards it. If then you despise death and bonds, do you still pay any regard to him? No. Is then the despising of death an act of your own or is it not yours? It is my act.

When you have made this preparation, and have practised this discipline, to distinguish that which belongs to another from that which is your own, the things which are subject to hindrance from those which are not, to consider the things free from hindrance to concern yourself, and those which are not free not to concern yourself, to keep your desire steadily fixed to the things which do concern yourself, and turned from the things which do not concern yourself; do you still fear any man? No one. For about what will you be afraid? About the things which are your own, in which consists the nature of good and evil? and who has power over these things? who can take them away? who can impede them? No man can, no more than he can impede God. But will you be afraid about your body and your possessions, about things which are not yours, about things which in no way concern you? and what else have you been studying from the beginning than to distinguish between your own and not your own, the things which are in your power and not in your power, the things subject to hindrance and not subject? and why have you come to the philosophers? was it that you may nevertheless be unfortunate and unhappy? You will then in this way, as I have supposed you to have done, be without fear and disturbance. And what is grief to you? for fear comes from what you expect, but grief from that which is present. But what further will you desire? For of the things which are within the power of the will, as being good and present, you have a proper and regulated desire; but of the things which are not in the power of the will you do not desire any one, and so you do not allow any place to that which is irrational, and impatient, and above measure hasty.

Then after receiving everything from another and even yourself, are you angry and do you blame the giver if he takes anything from you? Who are you, and for what purpose did you come into the world? Did not he (God) introduce you here, did he not show you the light, did he not give you fellow-workers, and perceptions and reason? and as whom did he introduce you here? did he not introduce you as subject to death, and as one to live on the earth with a little flesh, and to observe his administration, and to join with him in the spectacle and the festival for a short time? Will you not then, as long as you have been permitted, after seeing the spectacle and the solemnity, when he leads you out, go with adoration of him and thanks for what you have heard and seen? No; but I would still enjoy the feast. The initiated too would wish to be longer in the initiation; and perhaps also those at Olympia to see other athletes. But the solemnity is ended; go away like a grateful and modest man; make room for others; others also must be born, as you were, and, being born, they must have a place, and houses, and necessary things. And if the first do not retire, what remains? Why are you insatiable? Why are you not content? why do you contract the world? Yes, but I would have my little children with me and my wife. What, are they yours? do they not belong to the giver, and to him who made you? then will you not give up what belongs to others? will you not give way to him who is superior? Why then did he introduce me into the world on these conditions? And if the conditions do not suit you, depart. He has no need of a spectator who is not satisfied. He wants those who join in the festival, those who take part in the chorus, that they may rather applaud, admire, and celebrate with hymns the solemnity. But those who can bear no trouble, and the cowardly, he will not unwillingly see absent from the great assembly (Greek: *panaeguris*) for they did not when they were present behave as they ought to do at a festival nor fill up their place properly, but they lamented, found fault with the deity, fortune, their companions; not seeing both what they had, and their own powers, which they received for contrary purposes, the powers of magnanimity, of a generous mind, manly spirit, and what we are now inquiring about, freedom. For what purpose then have I received these things? To use them. How long? So long as he who has lent them chooses. What if they are necessary to me? Do not attach yourself to them and they will not be necessary; do not say to yourself that they are necessary, and then they are not necessary.

You then, a man may say, are you free? I wish, by the gods, and pray to be free; but I am not yet able to face my masters, I still value my poor body, I value greatly the preservation of it entire, though I do not possess it entire. But I can point out to you a free man, that you may no longer seek an example. Diogenes was free. How was he free? Not because he was born of free parents, but because he was himself free, because he had cast off all the handles of slavery, and it was not possible for any man to approach him, nor had any man the means of laying hold of him to enslave him. He had everything easily loosed, everything only hanging to him. If you laid hold of his property, he would have rather let it go and be yours, than he would have followed you for it; if you had laid hold of his leg, he would have let go his leg; if of all his body, all his poor body; his intimates, friends, country, just the same. For he knew from whence he had them, and from whom, and on what conditions. His true parents indeed, the gods, and his real country he would never have deserted, nor would he have yielded to any man in obedience to them and to their orders, nor would any man have died for his country more readily. For he was not used to inquire when he should be considered to have done anything on behalf of the whole of things (the universe, or all the world), but he remembered that everything which is done comes from thence and is done on behalf of that country and is commanded by him who administers it. Therefore see what Diogenes himself says and writes: "For this reason," he says, "Diogenes, it is in your power to speak both with the King of the Persians and with Archidamus the King of the Lacedaemonians, as you please." Was it because he was born of free parents? I suppose all the Athenians and all the Lacedaemonians, because they were born of slaves, could not talk with them (these kings) as they wished, but feared and paid court to them. Why then does he say that it is in his power? Because I do not consider the poor body to be my own, because I want nothing, because law is everything to me, and nothing else is. These were the things which permitted him to be free.

Think of these things, these opinions, these words; look to these examples, if you would be free, if you desire the thing according to its worth. And what is the wonder if you buy so great a thing at the price of things so many and so great? For the sake of this which is called liberty, some hang themselves, others throw themselves down precipices, and sometimes even whole cities have perished; and will you not for the sake of the true and unassailable and secure liberty give back to God when he demands them the things which he has given? Will you not, as Plato says, study not to die only, but also to endure torture, and exile, and scourging, and, in a word, to give up all which is not your own? If you will not, you will be a slave among slaves, even if you be ten thousand times a consul; and if you make your way up to the palace (Caesar's residence), you will no less be a slave; and you will feel that perhaps philosophers utter words which are contrary to common opinion (paradoxes), as Cleanthes also said, but not words contrary to reason. For you will know by experience that the words are true, and that there is no profit from the things which are valued and eagerly sought to those who have obtained them; and to those who have not yet obtained them there is an imagination (Greek: *phantasia*), that when these things are come, all that is good will come with them; then, when they are come, the feverish feeling is the same, the tossing to and fro is the same, the satiety, the desire of things, which are not present; for freedom is acquired not by the full possession of the things which are desired, but by removing the desire. And that you may know that this is true, as you have labored for those things, so transfer your labor to these: be vigilant for the purpose of acquiring an opinion which will make you free; pay court to a philosopher instead of to a rich old man; be seen about a philosopher's doors; you will not disgrace yourself by being seen; you will not go away empty nor without profit, if you go to the philosopher as you ought, and if not (if you do not succeed), try at least; the trial (attempt) is not disgraceful.

On Familiar Intimacy

To this matter before all you must attend, that you be never so closely connected with any of your former intimates or friends as to come down to the same acts as he does. If you do not observe this rule, you will ruin yourself. But if the thought arises in your mind, "I shall seem disobliging to him and he will not have the same feeling towards me," remember that nothing is done without cost, nor is it possible for a man if he does not do the same things to be the same man that he was. Choose then which of the two you will have, to be equally loved by those by whom you were formerly loved, being the same with your former self; or, being superior, not to obtain from your friends the same that you did before.

What Things We Should Exchange For Other Things

Keep this thought in readiness, when you lose anything external, what you acquire in place of it; and if it be worth more, never say, I have had a loss; neither if you have got a horse in place of an ass, or an ox in place of a sheep, nor a good action in place of a bit of money, nor in place of idle talk such tranquillity as befits a man, nor in place of lewd talk if you have acquired modesty. If you remember this, you will always maintain your character such as it ought to be. But if you do not, consider that the times of opportunity are perishing, and that whatever pains you take about yourself, you are going to waste them all and overturn them. And it needs only a few things for the loss and overturning of all—namely, a small deviation from reason. For the steerer of a ship to upset it, he has no need of the same means as he has need of for saving it; but if he turns it a little to the wind, it is lost; and if he does not do this purposely, but has been neglecting his duty a little, the ship is lost. Something of the kind happens in this case also; if you only fall a nodding a little, all that you have up to this time collected is gone. Attend therefore to the appearances of things, and watch over them; for that which you have to preserve is no small matter, but it is modesty and fidelity and constancy, freedom from the affects, a state of mind undisturbed, freedom from fear, tranquillity, in a word liberty. For what will you sell these things? See what is the value of the things which you will obtain in exchange for these.—But shall I not obtain any such thing for it?—See, and if you do in return get that, see what you receive in place of it. I possess decency, he possesses a tribuneship: he possesses a praetorship, I possess modesty. But I do not make acclamations where it is not becoming: I will not stand up where I ought not; for I am free, and a friend of God. and so I obey him willingly. But I must not claim (seek) anything else, neither body nor possession, nor magistracy, nor good report, nor in fact anything. For he (God) does not allow me to claim (seek) them, for if he had chosen, he would have made them good for me; but he has not done so, and for this reason I cannot transgress his commands. Preserve that which is your own good in everything; and as to every other thing, as it is permitted, and so far as to behave consistently with reason in respect to them, content with this only. If you do not, you will be unfortunate, you will fail in all things, you will be hindered, you will be impeded. These are the laws which have been sent from thence (from God); these are the orders. Of these laws a man ought to be an expositor, to these he ought to submit, not to those of Masurius and Cassius.

To Those Who Are Desirous Of Passing Life In Tranquillity

Remember that not only the desire of power and of riches makes us mean and subject to others, but even the desire of tranquillity, and of leisure, and of travelling abroad, and of learning. For, to speak plainly, whatever the external thing may be, the value which we set upon it places us in subjection to others. What then is the difference between desiring to be a senator or not desiring to be one; what is the difference between desiring power or being content with a private station; what is the difference between saying, I am unhappy, I have nothing to do, but I am bound to my books as a corpse; or saying, I am unhappy, I have no leisure for reading? For as salutations and power are things external and independent of the will, so is a book. For what purpose do you choose to read? Tell me. For if you only direct your purpose to being amused or learning something, you are a silly fellow and incapable of enduring labor. But if you refer reading to the proper end, what else is this than a tranquil and happy life (Greek: *eusoia*)? But if reading does not secure for you a happy and tranquil life, what is the use of it? But it does secure this, the man replies, and for this reason I am vexed that I am deprived of it.—And what is this tranquil and happy life, which any man can impede, I do not say Caesar or Caesar's friend, but a crow, a piper, a fever, and thirty thousand other things? But a tranquil and happy life contains nothing so sure as continuity and freedom from obstacle. Now I am called to do something: I will go then with the purpose of observing the measures (rules) which I must keep, of acting with modesty, steadiness, without desire and aversion to things external; and then that I may attend to men, what they say, how they are moved; and this not with any bad disposition, or that I may have something to blame or to ridicule; but I turn to myself, and ask if I also commit the same faults. How then shall I cease to commit them? Formerly I also acted wrong, but now I do not: thanks to God.

What then is the reason of this? The reason is that we have never read for this purpose, we have never written for this purpose, so that we may in our actions use in a way conformable to nature the appearances presented to us; but we terminate in this, in learning what is said, and in being able to expound it to another, in resolving a syllogism, and in handling the hypothetical syllogism. For this reason where our study (purpose) is, there alone is the impediment. Would you have by all means the things which are not in your power? Be prevented then, be hindered, fail in your purpose. But if we read what is written about action (efforts, Greek: *hormae*), not that we may see what is said about action, but that we may act well; if we read what is said about desire and aversion (avoiding things), in order that we may neither fail in our desires, nor fall into that which we try to avoid; if we read what is said about duty (officium), in order that remembering the relations (of things to one another) we may do nothing irrationally nor contrary to these relations; we should not be vexed, in being hindered as to our readings, but we should be satisfied with doing the acts which are conformable (to the relations), and we should be reckoning not what so far we have been accustomed to reckon: To-day I have read so many verses, I have written so many; but (we should say), To-day I have employed my action as it is taught by the philosophers; I have not employed my desire; I have used avoidance (Greek: *echchlisei*) only with respect to things which are within the power of my will; I have not been afraid of such a person, I have not been prevailed upon by the entreaties of another; I have exercised my patience, my abstinence, my co-operation with others; and so we should thank God for what we ought to thank him.

There is only one way to happiness, and let this rule be ready both in the morning and during the day and by night: the rule is not to look towards things which are out of the power of our will, to think that nothing is our own, to give up all things to the Divinity, to Fortune; to make them the superintendents of these things, whom Zeus also has made so; for a man to observe that only which is his own, that which cannot be hindered; and when we read, to refer our reading to this only, and our writing and our listening. For this reason I cannot call the man industrious, if I hear this only, that he reads and writes; and even if a man adds that he reads all night, I cannot say so, if he knows not to what he should refer his reading. For neither do you say that a man is industrious if he keeps awake for a girl, nor do I. But if he does it (reads and writes) for reputation, I say that he is a lover of reputation. And if he does it for money, I say that he is a lover of money, not a lover of labor; and if he does it through love of learning, I say that he is a lover of learning. But if he refers his labor to his own ruling power that he may keep it in a state conformable to nature and pass his life in that state, then only do I say that he is industrious. For never commend a man on account of these things which are common to all, but on account of his opinions (principles); for these are the things which belong to each man, which make his actions bad or good. Remembering these rules, rejoice in that which is present, and be content with the things which come in season. If you see anything which you have learned and inquired about occurring to you in your course of life (or opportunely applied by you to the acts of life), be delighted at it. If you have laid aside or have lessened bad disposition and a habit of reviling; if you have done so with rash temper, obscene words, hastiness, sluggishness; if you are not moved by what you formerly were, and not in the same way as you once were, you can celebrate a festival daily, to-day because you have behaved well in one act, and to-morrow because you have behaved well in another. How much greater is this a reason for making sacrifices than a consulship or the government of a province? These things come to you from yourself and from the gods. Remember this, who gives these things and to whom, and for what purpose. If you cherish yourself in these thoughts, do you still think that it makes any difference where you shall be happy, where you shall please God? Are not the gods equally distant from all places? Do they not see from all places alike that which is going on?

Against The Quarrelsome And Ferocious

The wise and good man neither himself fights with any person, nor does he allow another, so far as he can prevent it. And an example of this as well as of all other things is proposed to us in the life of Socrates, who not only himself on all occasions avoided fights (quarrels), but would not allow even others to quarrel. See in Xenophon's Symposium how many quarrels he settled, how further he endured Thrasymachus and Polus and Callicles; how he tolerated his wife, and how he tolerated his son who attempted to confute him and to cavil with him. For he remembered well that no man has in his power another man's ruling principle. He wished therefore for nothing else than that which was his own. And what is this? Not that this or that man may act according to nature, for that is a thing which belongs to another; but that while others are doing their own acts, as they choose, he may nevertheless be in a condition conformable to nature and live in it, only doing what is his own to the end that others also may be in a state conformable to nature. For this is the object always set before him by the wise and good man. Is it to be commander (a praetor) of an army? No; but if it is permitted him, his object is in this matter to maintain his own ruling principle. Is it to marry? No; but if marriage is allowed to him, in this matter his object is to maintain himself in a condition conformable to nature. But if he would have his son not to do wrong or his wife, he would have what belongs to another not to belong to another: and to be instructed is this, to learn what things are a man's own and what belongs to another.

How then is there left any place for fighting (quarrelling) to a man who has this opinion (which he ought to have)? Is he surprised at any thing which happens, and does it appear new to him? Does he not expect that which comes from the bad to be worse and more grievous than that what actually befalls him? And does he not reckon as pure gain whatever they (the bad) may do which falls short of extreme wickedness? Such a person has reviled you. Great thanks to him for not having struck you. But he has struck me also. Great thanks that he did not wound you. But he wounded me also. Great thanks that he did not kill you. For when did he learn or in what school that man is a tame animal, that men love one another, that an act of injustice is a great harm to him who does it. Since then he has not learned this and is not convinced of it, why shall he not follow that which seems to be for his own interest? Your neighbor has thrown stones. Have you then done anything wrong? But the things in the house have been broken. Are you then a utensil? No; but a free power of will. What then is given to you (to do) in answer to this? If you are like a wolf, you must bite in return, and throw more stones. But, if you consider what is proper for a man, examine your storehouse, see with what faculties you came into the world. Have you the disposition of a wild beast, have you the disposition of revenge for an injury? When is a horse wretched? When he is deprived of his natural faculties, not when he cannot crow like a cock, but when he cannot run. When is a dog wretched? Not when he cannot fly, but when he cannot track his game. Is then a man also unhappy in this way, not because he cannot strangle lions or embrace statues, for he did not come into the world in the possession of certain powers from nature for this purpose, but because he has lost his probity and his fidelity? People ought to meet and lament such a man for the misfortunes into which he has fallen; not indeed to lament because a man has been born or has died, but because it has happened to him in his lifetime to have lost the things which are his own, not that which he received from his father, not his land and house, and his inn, and his slaves; for not one of these things is a man's own, but all belong to others, are servile, and subject to account (Greek: *hupeithuna*), at different times given to different persons by those who have them in their power: but I mean the things which belong to him as a man, the marks (stamps) in his mind with which he came into the world, such as we seek also on coins, and if we find them we approve of the coins, and if we do not find the marks we reject them. What is the stamp on this sestertius? The stamp of Trajan. Present it. It is the stamp of Nero. Throw it away; it cannot be accepted, it is counterfeit. So also in this case: What is the stamp of his opinions? It is gentleness, a sociable disposition, a tolerant temper, a disposition to mutual affections. Produce these qualities. I accept them: I consider this man a citizen, I accept him as a neighbor, a companion in my voyages. Only see that he has not Nero's stamp. Is he passionate, is he full of resentment, is he fault-finding? If the whim seizes him, does he break the heads of those who come in his way? (If so), why then did you say that he is a man? Is everything judged (determined) by the bare form? If that is so, say that the form in wax is an apple and has the smell and the taste of an apple. But the external figure is not enough: neither then is the nose enough and the eyes to make the man, but he must have the opinions of a man. Here is a man who does not listen to reason, who does not know when he is refuted: he is an ass; in another man the sense of shame is become dead: he is good for nothing, he is anything rather than a man. This man seeks whom he may meet and kick or bite, so that he is not even a sheep or an ass, but a kind of wild beast.

What then? would you have me to be despised?—By whom? by those who know you? and how shall those who know you despise a man who is gentle and modest? Perhaps you mean by those who do not know you? What is that to you? For no other artisan cares for the opinion of those who know not his art. But they will be more hostile to me for this reason. Why do you say "me"? Can any man injure your will, or prevent you from using in a natural way the appearances which are presented to you? In no way can he. Why then are you still disturbed and why do you choose to show yourself afraid? And why do you not come forth and proclaim that you are at peace with all men whatever they may do, and laugh at those chiefly who think that they can harm you? These slaves, you can say, know not either who I am, nor where lies my good or my evil, because they have no access to the things which are mine.

In this way also those who occupy a strong city mock the besiegers (and say): What trouble these men are now taking for nothing; our wall is secure, we have food for a very long time, and all other resources. These are the things which make a city strong and impregnable; but nothing else than his opinions makes a man's soul impregnable. For what wall is so strong, or what body is so hard, or what possession is so safe, or what honor (rank, character) so free from assault (as a man's opinions)? All (other) things everywhere are perishable, easily taken by assault, and if any man in any way is attached to them, he must be disturbed, except what is bad, he must fear, lament, find his desires disappointed, and fall into things which he would avoid. Then do we not choose to make secure the only means of safety which are offered to us, and do we not choose to withdraw ourselves from that which is perishable and servile and to labor at the things which are imperishable and by nature free; and do we not remember that no man either hurts another or does good to another, but that a man's opinions about each thing, is that which hurts him, is that which overturns him; this is fighting, this is civil discord, this is war? That which made Eteocles and Polynices enemies was nothing else than this opinion which they had about royal power, their opinion about exile, that the one is the extreme of evils, the other the greatest good. Now this is the nature of every man to seek the good, to avoid the bad; to consider him who deprives us of the one and involves us in the other an enemy and treacherous, even if he be a brother, or a son, or a father. For nothing is more akin to us than the good; therefore, if these things (externals) are good and evil, neither is a father a friend to sons, nor a brother to a brother, but all the world is everywhere full of enemies, treacherous men, and sycophants. But if the will (Greek: *proairesis*, the purpose, the intention) being what it ought to be, is the only good; and if the will being such as it ought not to be, is the only evil, where is there any strife, where is there reviling? about what? about the things which do not concern us? and strife with whom? with the ignorant, the unhappy, with those who are deceived about the chief things?

Remembering this Socrates managed his own house and endured a very ill-tempered wife and a foolish (ungrateful?) son.

Against Those Who Lament Over Being Pitied

I am grieved, a man says, at being pitied. Whether then is the fact of your being pitied a thing which concerns you or those who pity you? Well, is it in your power to stop this pity? It is in my power, if I show them that I do not require pity. And whether then are you in the condition of not deserving (requiring) pity, or are you not in that condition? I think that I am not; but these persons do not pity me, for the things for which, if they ought to pity me, it would be proper, I mean, for my faults; but they pity me for my poverty, for not possessing honorable offices, for diseases and deaths and other such things. Whether then are you prepared to convince the many, that not one of these things is an evil, but that it is possible for a man who is poor and has no office (Greek: *anarchonti*) and enjoys no honor to be happy; or to show yourself to them as rich and in power? For the second of these things belong to a man who is boastful, silly, and good for nothing. And consider by what means the pretence must be supported. It will be necessary for you to hire slaves and to possess a few silver vessels, and to exhibit them in public, if it is possible, though they are often the same, and to attempt to conceal the fact that they are the same, and to have splendid garments, and all other things for display, and to show that you are a man honored by the great, and to try to sup at their houses, or to be supposed to sup there, and as to your person to employ some mean arts, that you may appear to be more handsome and nobler than you are. These things you must contrive, if you choose to go by the second path in order not to be pitied. But the first way is both impracticable and long, to attempt the very thing which Zeus has not been able to do, to convince all men what things are good and bad. Is this power given to you? This only is given to you, to convince yourself; and you have not convinced yourself. Then I ask you, do you attempt to persuade other men? and who has lived so long with you as you with yourself? and who has so much power of convincing you as you have of convincing yourself; and who is better disposed and nearer to you than you are to yourself? How then have you not yet convinced yourself in order to learn? At present are not things upside down? Is this what you have been earnest about doing, to learn to be free from grief and free from disturbance, and not to be humbled (abject), and to be free? Have you not heard then that there is only one way which leads to this end, to give up (dismiss) the things which do not depend on the will, to withdraw from them, and to admit that they belong to others? For another man then to have an opinion about you, of what kind is it? It is a thing independent of the will—Then is it nothing to you? It is nothing. When then you are still vexed at this and disturbed, do you think that you are convinced about good and evil?

On Freedom From Fear

What makes the tyrant formidable? The guards, you say, and their swords, and the men of the bedchamber, and those who exclude them who would enter. Why then if you bring a boy (child) to the tyrant when he is with his guards, is he not afraid; or is it because the child does not understand these things? If then any man does understand what guards are and that they have swords, and comes to the tyrant for this very purpose because he wishes to die on account of some circumstance and seeks to die easily by the hand of another, is he afraid of the guards? No, for he wishes for the thing which makes the guards formidable. If then any man neither wishing to die nor to live by all means, but only as it may be permitted, approaches the tyrant what hinders him from approaching the tyrant without fear? Nothing. If then a man has the same opinion about his property as the man whom I have instanced has about his body; and also about his children and his wife, and in a word is so affected by some madness or despair that he cares not whether he possesses them or not, but like children who are playing with shells (quarrel) about the play, but do not trouble themselves about the shells, so he too has set no value on the materials (things), but values the pleasure that he has with them and the occupation, what tyrant is then formidable to him, or what guards or what swords?

What hinders a man, who has clearly separated (comprehended) these things, from living with a light heart and bearing easily the reins, quietly expecting everything which can happen, and enduring that which has already happened? Would you have me to bear poverty? Come and you will know what poverty is when it has found one who can act well the part of a poor man. Would you have me to possess power? Let me have power, and also the trouble of it. Well, banishment? Wherever I shall go, there it will be well with me; for here also where I am, it was not because of the place that it was well with me, but because of my opinions which I shall carry off with me, for neither can any man deprive me of them; but my opinions alone are mine and they cannot be taken from me, and I am satisfied while I have them, wherever I may be and whatever I am doing. But now it is time to die. Why do you say to die? Make no tragedy show of the thing, but speak of it as it is. It is now time for the matter (of the body) to be resolved into the things out of which it was composed. And what is the formidable thing here? what is going to perish of the things which are in the universe? what new thing or wondrous is going to happen? Is it for this reason that a tyrant is formidable? Is it for this reason that the guards appear to have swords which are large and sharp? Say this to others; but I have considered about all these things; no man has power over me. I have been made free; I know his commands, no man can now lead me as a slave. I have a proper person to assert my freedom; I have proper judges. (I say) are you not the master of my body? What then is that to me? Are you not the master of my property? What then is that to me? Are you not the master of my exile or of my chains? Well, from all these things and all the poor body itself I depart at your bidding, when you please. Make trial of your power, and you will know how far it reaches.

Whom then can I still fear? Those who are over the bedchamber? Lest they should do, what? Shut me out? If they find that I wish to enter, let them shut me out. Why then do you go to the doors? Because I think it befits me, while the play (sport) lasts, to join in it. How then are you not shut out? Because unless some one allows me to go in, I do not choose to go in, but am always content with that which happens; for I think that what God chooses is better than what I choose. I will attach myself as a minister and follower to him; I have the same movements (pursuits) as he has, I have the same desires; in a word, I have the same will (Greek: *sunthelo*). There is no shutting out for me, but for those who would force their way in. Why then do not I force my way in? Because I know that nothing good is distributed within to those who enter. But when I hear any man called fortunate because he is honored by Caesar, I say what does he happen to get? A province (the government of a province). Does he also obtain an opinion such as he ought? The office of a Prefect. Does he also obtain the power of using his office well? Why do I still strive to enter (Caesar's chamber)? A man scatters dried figs and nuts: the children seize them, and fight with one another; men do not, for they think them to be a small matter. But if a man should throw about shells, even the children do not seize them. Provinces are distributed: let children look to that. Money is distributed; let children look to that. Praetorships, consulships, are distributed; let children scramble for them, let them be shut out, beaten, kiss the hands of the giver, of the slaves: but to me these are only dried figs and nuts. What then? If you fail to get them, while Caesar is scattering them about, do not be troubled; if a dried fig come into your lap, take it and eat it; for so far you may value even a fig. But if I shall stoop down and turn another over, or be turned over by another, and shall flatter those who have got into (Caesar's) chamber, neither is a dried fig worth the trouble, nor anything else of the things which are not good, which the philosophers have persuaded me not to think good.

To A Person Who Had Been Changed To A Character Of Shamelessness

When you see another man in the possession of power (magistracy), set against this the fact that you have not the want (desire) of power; when you see another rich, see what you possess in place of riches: for if you possess nothing in place of them, you are miserable; but if you have not the want of riches, know that you possess more than this man possesses and what is worth much more.

What Things We Ought To Despise And What Things We Ought To Value

The difficulties of all men are about external things, their helplessness is about external. What shall I do? how will it be? how will it turn out? will this happen? will that? All these are the words of those who are turning themselves to things which are not within the power of the will. For who says, How shall I not assent to that which is false? how shall I not turn away from the truth? If a man be of such a good disposition as to be anxious about these things I will remind him of this: Why are you anxious? The thing is in your own power, be assured; do not be precipitate in assenting before you apply the natural rule. On the other side, if a man is anxious (uneasy) about desire, lest it fail in its purpose and miss its end, and with respect to the avoidance of things, lest he should fall into that which he would avoid, I will first kiss (love) him, because he throws away the things about which others are in a flutter (others desire) and their fears, and employs his thoughts about his own affairs and his own condition. Then I shall say to him: If you do not choose to desire that which you will fail to obtain nor to attempt to avoid that into which you will fall, desire nothing which belongs to (which is in the power of) others, nor try to avoid any of the things which are not in your power. If you do not observe this rule, you must of necessity fail in your desires and fall into that which you would avoid. What is the difficulty here? where is there room for the words How will it be? and How will it turn out? and Will this happen or that?

Now is not that which will happen independent of the will? Yes. And the nature of good and of evil, is it not in the things which are within the power of the will? Yes. Is it in your power then to treat according to nature everything which happens? Can any person hinder you? No man. No longer then say to me, How will it be? For, however it may be, you will dispose of it well, and the result to you will be a fortunate one. What would Hercules have been if he said: How shall a great lion not appear to me, or a great boar, or savage men? And what do you care for that? If a great boar appear, you will fight a greater fight; if bad men appear, you will relieve the earth of the bad. Suppose then that I lose my life in this way. You will die a good man, doing a noble act. For since he must certainly die, of necessity a man must be found doing something, either following the employment of a husbandman, or digging, or trading, or serving in a consulship, or suffering from indigestion or from diarrhoea. What then do you wish to be doing when you are found by death? I, for my part, would wish to be found doing something which belongs to a man, beneficent, suitable to the general interest, noble. But if I cannot be found doing things so great, I would be found doing at least that which I cannot be hindered from doing, that which is permitted me to do, correcting myself, cultivating the faculty which makes use of appearances, laboring at freedom from the affects (laboring at tranquillity of mind); rendering to the relations of life their due. If I succeed so far, also (I would be found) touching on (advancing to) the third topic (or head) safety in forming judgments about things. If death surprises me when

I am busy about these things, it is enough for me if I can stretch out my hands to God and say: The means which I have received from thee for seeing thy administration (of the world) and following it I have not neglected; I have not dishonored thee by my acts; see how I have used my perceptions, see how I have used my preconceptions; have I ever blamed thee? have I been discontented with anything that happens, or wished it to be otherwise? have I wished to transgress the (established) relations (of things)? That thou hast given me life, I thank thee for what thou hast given. So long as I have used the things which are thine I am content. Take them back and place them wherever thou mayest choose, for thine were all things, thou gavest them to me. Is it not enough to depart in this state of mind? and what life is better and more becoming than that of a man who is in this state of mind? and what end is more happy?

About Purity (Cleanliness)

Some persons raise a question whether the social feeling is contained in the nature of man; and yet I think that these same persons would have no doubt that love of purity is certainly contained in it, and that if man is distinguished from other animals by anything, he is distinguished by this. When then we see any other animal cleaning itself, we are accustomed to speak of the act with surprise, and to add that the animal is acting like a man; and on the other hand, if a man blames an animal for being dirty, straightway, as if we were making an excuse for it, we say that of course the animal is not a human creature. So we suppose that there is something superior in man, and that we first receive it from the gods. For since the gods by their nature are pure and free from corruption, so far as men approach them by reason, so far do they cling to purity and to a love (habit) of purity. But since it is impossible that man's nature (Greek: *ousia*) can be altogether pure, being mixed (composed) of such materials, reason is applied, as far as it is possible, and reason endeavors to make human nature love purity.

The first then and highest purity is that which is in the soul; and we say the same of impurity. Now you could not discover the impurity of the soul as you could discover that of the body; but as to the soul, what else could you find in it than that which makes it filthy in respect to the acts which are her own? Now the acts of the soul are movement towards an object or movement from it, desire, aversion, preparation, design (purpose), assent. What then is it which in these acts makes the soul filthy and impure? Nothing else than her own bad judgments (Greek: *chrimata*). Consequently the impurity of the soul is the soul's bad opinions; and the purification of the soul is the planting in it of proper opinions; and the soul is pure which has proper opinions, for the soul alone in her own acts is free from perturbation and pollution.

For we ought not even by the appearance of the body to deter the multitude from philosophy; but as in other things, a philosopher should show himself cheerful and tranquil, so also he should in the things that relate to the body. See, ye men, that I have nothing, that I want nothing; see how I am without a house, and without a city, and an exile, if it happens to be so, and without a hearth I live more free from trouble and more happily than all of noble birth and than the rich. But look at my poor body also and observe that it is not injured by my hard way of living. But if a man says this to me, who has the appearance (dress) and face of a condemned man, what god shall persuade me to approach philosophy, if it makes men such persons? Far from it; I would not choose to do so, even if I were going to become a wise man. I indeed would rather that a young man, who is making his first movements towards philosophy, should come to me with his hair carefully trimmed than with it dirty and rough, for there is seen in him a certain notion (appearance) of beauty and a desire of (attempt at) that which is becoming; and where he supposes it to be, there also he strives that it shall be. It is only necessary to show him (what it is), and to say: Young man, you seek beauty, and you do well; you must know then that it (is produced) grows in that part of you where you have the rational faculty; seek it there where you have the movements towards and movements from things, where you have the desires towards and the aversion from things; for this is what you have in yourself of a superior kind; but the poor body is naturally only earth; why do you labor about it to no purpose? if you shall learn nothing else, you will learn from time that the body is nothing. But if a man comes to me daubed with filth, dirty, with a moustache down to his knees, what can I say to him, by what kind of resemblance can I lead him on? For about what has he busied himself which resembles beauty, that I may be able to change him and say, Beauty is not in this, but in that? Would you have me to tell him, that beauty consists not in being daubed with muck, but that it lies in the rational part? Has he any desire of beauty? has he any form of it in his mind? Go and talk to a hog, and tell him not to roll in the mud.

On Attention

When you have remitted your attention for a short time, do not imagine this, that you will recover it when you choose; but let this thought be present to you, that in consequence of the fault committed today your affairs must be in a worse condition for all that follows. For first, and what causes most trouble, a habit of not attending is formed in you; then a habit of deferring your attention. And continually from time to time you drive away by deferring it the happiness of life, proper behavior, the being and living conformably to nature. If then the procrastination of attention is profitable, the complete omission of attention is more profitable; but if it is not profitable, why do you not maintain your attention constant? Today I choose to play. Well then, ought you not to play with attention? I choose to sing. What then hinders you from doing so with attention? Is there any part of life excepted, to which attention does not extend? For will you do it (anything in life) worse by using attention, and better by not attending at all? And what else of the things in life is done better by those who do not use attention? Does he who works in wood work better by not attending to it? Does the captain of a ship manage it better by not attending? and are any of the smaller acts done better by inattention? Do you not see that when you have let your mind loose, it is no longer in your power to recall it, either to propriety, or to modesty, or to moderation; but you do everything that comes into your mind in obedience to your inclinations.

First then we ought to have these (rules) in readiness, and to do nothing without them, and we ought to keep the soul directed to this mark, to pursue nothing external, and nothing which belongs to others (or is in the power of others), but to do as he has appointed who has the power; we ought to pursue altogether the things which are in the power of the will, and all other things as it is permitted. Next to this we ought to remember who we are, and what is our name, and to endeavor to direct our duties towards the character (nature) of our several relations (in life) in this manner: what is the season for singing, what is the season for play, and in whose presence; what will be the consequence of the act; whether our associates will despise us, whether we shall despise them; when to jeer (Greek: *schopsai*), and whom to ridicule; and on what occasion to comply and with whom; and finally, in complying how to maintain our own character. But wherever you have deviated from any of these rules, there is damage immediately, not from anything external, but from the action itself.

What then? is it possible to be free from faults (if you do all this)? It is not possible; but this is possible, to direct your efforts incessantly to being faultless. For we must be content if by never remitting this attention we shall escape at least a few errors. But now when you have said, Tomorrow I will begin to attend, you must be told that you are saying this, Today I will be shameless, disregardful of time and place, mean; it will be in the power of others to give me pain; today I will be passionate and envious. See how many evil things you are permitting yourself to do. If it is good to use attention tomorrow, how much better is it to do so today? if tomorrow it is in your interest to attend, much more is it today, that you may be able to do so tomorrow also, and may not defer it again to the third day.

Against Or To Those Who Readily Tell Their Own Affairs

When a man has seemed to us to have talked with simplicity (candor) about his own affairs, how is it that at last we are ourselves also induced to discover to him our own secrets and we think this to be candid behavior? In the first place, because it seems unfair for a man to have listened to the affairs of his neighbor, and not to communicate to him also in turn our own affairs; next, because we think that we shall not present to them the appearance of candid men when we are silent about our own affairs. Indeed, men are often accustomed to say, I have told you all my affairs, will you tell me nothing of your own? where is this done? Besides, we have also this opinion that we can safely trust him who has already told us his own affairs; for the notion rises in our mind that this man could never divulge our affairs because he would be cautious that we also should not divulge his. In this way also the incautious are caught by the soldiers at Rome. A soldier sits by you in a common dress and begins to speak ill of Caesar; then you, as if you had received a pledge of his fidelity by his having begun the abuse, utter yourself also what you think, and then you are carried off in chains.

Something of this kind happens to us also generally. Now as this man has confidently intrusted his affairs to me, shall I also do so to any man whom I meet? (No), for when I have heard, I keep silence, if I am of such a disposition; but he goes forth and tells all men what he has heard. Then, if I hear what has been done, if I be a man like him, I resolve to be revenged, I divulge what he has told me; I both disturb others, and am disturbed myself. But if I remember that one man does not injure another, and that every man's acts injure and profit him, I secure this, that I do not anything like him, but still I suffer what I do suffer through my own silly talk.

True, but it is unfair when you have heard the secrets of your neighbor for you in your turn to communicate nothing to him. Did I ask you for your secrets, my man? did you communicate your affairs on certain terms, that you should in return hear mine also? If you are a babbler and think that all who meet you are friends, do you wish me also to be like you? But why, if you did well in intrusting your affairs to me, and it is not well for me to intrust mine to you, do you wish me to be so rash? It is just the same as if I had a cask which is water-tight, and you one with a hole in it, and you should come and deposit with me your wine that I might put it into my cask, and then should complain that I also did not intrust my wine to you, for you have a cask with a hole in it. How then is there any equality here? You intrusted your affairs to a man who is faithful and modest, to a man who thinks that his own actions alone are injurious and (or) useful, and that nothing external is. Would you have me intrust mine to you, a man who has dishonored his own faculty of will, and who wishes to gain some small bit of money or some office or promotion in the court (emperor's palace), even if you should be going to murder your own children, like Medea? Where (in what) is this equality (fairness)? But show yourself to me to be faithful, modest, and steady; show me that you have friendly opinions; show that your cask has no hole in it; and you will see how I shall not wait for you to trust me with your own affairs, but I myself shall come to you and ask you to hear mine. For who does not choose to make use of a good vessel? Who does not value a benevolent and faithful adviser? Who will not willingly receive a man who is ready to bear a share, as we may say, of the difficulty of his circumstances, and by this very act to ease the burden, by taking a part of it.

THE ENCHIRIDION

1

Of things some are in our power, and others are not. In our power are opinion (Greek: *hupolaepsis*), movement towards a thing (Greek: *hormae*), desire, aversion (Greek: *echchlisis*), turning from a thing; and in a word, whatever are our acts. Not in our power are the body, property, reputation, offices (magisterial power), and in a word, whatever are not our own acts. And the things in our power are by nature free, not subject to restraint or hindrance; but the things not in our power are weak, slavish, subject to restraint, in the power of others. Remember then, that if you think the things which are by nature slavish to be free, and the things which are in the power of others to be your own, you will be hindered, you will lament, you will be disturbed, you will blame both gods and men; but if you think that only which is your own to be your own, and if you think that what is another's, as it really is, belongs to another, no man will ever compel you, no man will hinder you, you will never blame any man, you will accuse no man, you will do nothing involuntarily (against your will), no man will harm you, you will have no enemy, for you will not suffer any harm.

If then you desire (aim at) such great things remember that you must not (attempt to) lay hold of them with a small effort; but you must leave alone some things entirely, and postpone others for the present. But if you wish for these things also (such great things), and power (office) and wealth, perhaps you will not gain even these very things (power and wealth) because you aim also at those former things (such great things); certainly you will fail in those things through which alone happiness and freedom are secured. Straightway then practise saying to every harsh appearance: You are an appearance, and in no manner what you appear to be. Then examine it by the rules which you possess, and by this first and chiefly, whether it relates to the things which are in our power or to things which are not in our power; and if it relates to anything which is not in our power, be ready to say that it does not concern you.

2

Remember that desire contains in it the profession (hope) of obtaining that which you desire; and the profession (hope) in aversion (turning from a thing) is that you will not fall into that which you attempt to avoid; and he who fails in his desire is unfortunate; and he who falls into that which he would avoid is unhappy. If then you attempt to avoid only the things contrary to nature which are within your power you will not be involved in any of the things which you would avoid. But if you attempt to avoid disease, or death, or poverty, you will be unhappy. Take away then aversion from all things which are not in our power, and transfer it to the things contrary to nature which are in our power. But destroy desire completely for the present. For if you desire anything which is not in our power, you must be unfortunate; but of the things in our power, and which it would be good to desire, nothing yet is before you. But employ only the power of moving towards an object and retiring from it; and these powers indeed only slightly and with exceptions and with remission.

3

In everything which pleases the soul, or supplies a want, or is loved, remember to add this to the (description, notion): What is the nature of each thing, beginning from the smallest? If you love an earthen vessel, say it is an earthen vessel which you love; for when it has been broken you will not be disturbed. If you are kissing your child or wife, say that it is a human being whom you are kissing, for when the wife or child dies you will not be disturbed.

4

When you are going to take in hand any act remind yourself what kind of an act it is. If you are going to bathe, place before yourself what happens in the bath; some splashing the water, others pushing against one another, others abusing one another, and some stealing; and thus with more safety you will undertake the matter, if you say to yourself, I now intend to bathe, and to maintain my will in a manner conformable to nature. And so you will do in every act; for thus if any hindrance to bathing shall happen let this thought be ready. It was not this only that I intended, but I intended also to maintain my will in a way conformable to nature; but I shall not maintain it so if I am vexed at what happens.

5

Men are disturbed not by the things which happen, but by the opinions about the things; for example, death is nothing terrible, for if it were it would have seemed so to Socrates; for the opinion about death that it is terrible, is the terrible thing. When then we are impeded, or disturbed, or grieved, let us never blame others, but ourselves—that is, our opinions. It is the act of an ill-instructed man to blame others for his own bad condition; it is the act of one who has begun to be instructed, to lay the blame on himself; and of one whose instruction is completed, neither to blame another, nor himself.

6

Be not elated at any advantage (excellence) which belongs to another. If a horse when he is elated should say, I am beautiful, one might endure it. But when you are elated, and say, I have a beautiful horse, you must know that you are elated at having a good horse. What then is your own? The use of appearances. Consequently when in the use of appearances you are conformable to nature, then be elated, for then you will be elated at something good which is your own.

7

As on a voyage when the vessel has reached a port, if you go out to get water it is an amusement by the way to pick up a shellfish or some bulb, but your thoughts ought to be directed to the ship, and you ought to be constantly watching if the captain should call, and then you must throw away all those things, that you may not be bound and pitched into the ship like sheep. So in life also, if there be given to you instead of a little bulb and a shell a wife and child, there will be nothing to prevent (you from taking them). But if the captain should call, run to the ship and leave all those things without regard to them. But if you are old, do not even go far from the ship, lest when you are called you make default.

8

Seek not that the things which happen should happen as you wish; but wish the things which happen to be as they are, and you will have a tranquil flow of life.

9

Disease is an impediment to the body, but not to the will, unless the will itself chooses. Lameness is an impediment to the leg, but not to the will. And add this reflection on the occasion of everything that happens; for you will find it an impediment to something else, but not to yourself.

10

On the occasion of every accident (event) that befalls you, remember to turn to yourself and inquire what power you have for turning it to use. If you see a fair man or a fair woman, you will find that the power to resist is temperance (continence). If labor (pain) be presented to you, you will find that it is endurance. If it be abusive words, you will find it to be patience. And if you have been thus formed to the (proper) habit, the appearances will not carry you along with them.

11

Never say about anything, I have lost it, but say I have restored it. Is your child dead? It has been restored. Is your wife dead? She has been restored. Has your estate been taken from you? Has not then this also been restored? But he who has taken it from me is a bad man. But what is it to you, by whose hands the giver demanded it back? So long as he may allow you, take care of it as a thing which belongs to another, as travellers do with their inn.

12

If you intend to improve, throw away such thoughts as these: if I neglect my affairs, I shall not have the means of living: unless I chastise my slave, he will be bad. For it is better to die of hunger and so to be released from grief and fear than to live in abundance with perturbation; and it is better for your slave to be bad than for you to be unhappy. Begin then from little things. Is the oil spilled? Is a little wine stolen? Say on the occasion, at such price is sold freedom from perturbation; at such price is sold tranquillity, but nothing is got for nothing. And when you call your slave, consider that it is possible that he does not hear; and if he does hear, that he will do nothing which you wish. But matters are not so well with him, but altogether well with you, that it should be in his power for you to be not disturbed.

13

If you would improve, submit to be considered without sense and foolish with respect to externals. Wish to be considered to know nothing; and if you shall seem to some to be a person of importance, distrust yourself. For you should know that it is not easy both to keep your will in a condition conformable to nature and (to secure) external things: but if a man is careful about the one, it is an absolute necessity that he will neglect the other.

14

If you would have your children and your wife and your friends to live for ever, you are silly; for you would have the things which are not in your power to be in your power, and the things which belong to others to be yours. So if you would have your slave to be free from faults, you are a fool; for you would have badness not to be badness, but something else. But if you wish not to fail in your desires, you are able to do that. Practise then this which you are able to do. He is the master of every man who has the power over the things which another person wishes or does not wish, the power to confer them on him or to take them away. Whoever then wishes to be free let him neither wish for anything nor avoid anything which depends on others: if he does not observe this rule, he must be a slave.

15

Remember that in life you ought to behave as at a banquet. Suppose that something is carried round and is opposite to you. Stretch out your hand and take a portion with decency. Suppose that it passes by you. Do not detain it. Suppose that it is not yet come to you. Do not send your desire forward to it, but wait till it is opposite to you. Do so with respect to children, so with respect to a wife, so with respect to magisterial offices, so with respect to wealth, and you will be some time a worthy partner of the banquets of the gods.

But if you take none of the things which are set before you, and even despise them, then you will be not only a fellow banqueter with the gods, but also a partner with them in power. For by acting thus Diogenes and Heracleitus and those like them were deservedly divine, and were so called.

16

When you see a person weeping in sorrow either when a child goes abroad or when he is dead, or when the man has lost his property, take care that the appearance do not hurry you away with it, as if he were suffering in external things. But straightway make a distinction in your own mind, and be in readiness to say, it is not that which has happened that afflicts this man, for it does not afflict another, but it is the opinion about this thing which afflicts the man. So far as words then do not be unwilling to show him sympathy, and even if it happens so, to lament with him. But take care that you do not lament internally also.

17

Remember that thou art an actor in a play, of such a kind as the teacher (author) may choose; if short, of a short one; if long, of a long one: if he wishes you to act the part of a poor man, see that you act the part naturally; if the part of a lame man, of a magistrate, of a private person, (do the same). For this is your duty, to act well the part that is given to you; but to select the part, belongs to another.

18

When a raven has croaked inauspiciously, let not the appearance hurry you away with it; but straightway make a distinction in your mind and say, None of these things is signified to me, but either to my poor body, or to my small property, or to my reputation, or to my children, or to my wife: but to me all significations are auspicious if I choose. For whatever of these things results, it is in my power to derive benefit from it.

19

You can be invincible, if you enter into no contest in which it is not in your power to conquer. Take care then when you observe a man honored before others or possessed of great power or highly esteemed for any reason, not to suppose him happy, and be not carried away by the appearance. For if the nature of the good is in our power, neither envy nor jealousy will have a place in us. But you yourself will not wish to be a general or senator (Greek: *prutanis*) or consul, but a free man: and there is only one way to this, to despise (care not for) the things which are not in our power.

20

Remember that it is not he who reviles you or strikes you, who insults you, but it is your opinion about these things as being insulting. When then a man irritates you, you must know that it is your own opinion which has irritated you. Therefore especially try not to be carried away by the appearance. For if you once gain time and delay, you will more easily master yourself.

21

Let death and exile and every other thing which appears dreadful be daily before your eyes; but most of all death: and you will never think of anything mean nor will you desire anything extravagantly.

22

If you desire philosophy, prepare yourself from the beginning to be ridiculed, to expect that many will sneer at you, and say, He has all at once returned to us as a philosopher; and whence does he get this supercilious look for us? Do you not show a supercilious look; but hold on to the things which seem to you best as one appointed by God to this station. And remember that if you abide in the same principles, these men who first ridiculed will afterwards admire you; but if you shall have been overpowered by them, you will bring on yourself double ridicule.

23

If it should ever happen to you to be turned to externals in order to please some person, you must know that you have lost your purpose in life. Be satisfied then in everything with being a philosopher; and if you wish to seem also to any person to be a philosopher, appear so to yourself, and you will be able to do this.

24

Let not these thoughts afflict you, I shall live unhonored and be nobody nowhere. For if want of honor (Greek: *atimia*) is an evil, you cannot be in evil through the means (fault) of another any more than you can be involved in anything base. Is it then your business to obtain the rank of a magistrate, or to be received at a banquet? By no means. How then can this be want of honor (dishonor)? And how will you be nobody nowhere, when you ought to be somebody in those things only which are in your power, in which indeed it is permitted to you to be a man of the greatest worth? But your friends will be without assistance! What do you mean by being without assistance? They will not receive money from you, nor will you make them Roman citizens. Who then told you that these are among the things which are in our power, and not in the power of others? And who can give to another what he has not himself? Acquire money then, your friends say, that we also may have something. If I can acquire money and also keep myself modest and faithful and magnanimous, point out the way, and I will acquire it. But if you ask me to lose the things which are good and my own, in order that you may gain the things which are not good, see how unfair and silly you are. Besides, which would you rather have, money or a faithful and modest friend? For this end then rather help me to be such a man, and do not ask me to do this by which I shall lose that character. But my country, you say, as far as it depends on me, will be without my help. I ask again, what help do you mean? It will not have porticos or baths through you. And what does this mean? For it is not furnished with shoes by means of a smith, nor with arms by means of a shoemaker. But it is enough if every man fully discharges the work that is his own: and if you provided it with another citizen faithful and modest, would you not be useful to it? Yes. Then you also cannot be useless to it. What place then, you say, shall I hold in the city? Whatever you can, if you maintain at the same time your fidelity and modesty. But if when you wish to be useful to the state, you shall lose these qualities, what profit could you be to it, if you were made shameless and faithless?

25

Has any man been preferred before you at a banquet, or in being saluted, or in being invited to a consultation? If these things are good, you ought to rejoice that he has obtained them; but if bad, be not grieved because you have not obtained them. And remember that you cannot, if you do not the same things in order to obtain what is not in our own power, be considered worthy of the same (equal) things. For how can a man obtain an equal share with another when he does not visit a man's doors as that other man does; when he does not attend him when he goes abroad, as the other man does; when he does not praise (flatter) him as another does? You will be unjust then and insatiable, if you do not part with the price, in return for which those things are sold, and if you wish to obtain them for nothing. Well, what is the price of lettuces? An obolus perhaps. If then a man gives up the obolus, and receives the lettuces, and if you do not give up the obolus and do not obtain the lettuces, do not suppose that you receive less than he who has got the lettuces; for as he has the lettuces, so you have the obolus which you did not give. In the same way then in the other matter also you have not been invited to a man's feast, for you did not give to the host the price at which the supper is sold; but he sells it for praise (flattery), he sells it for personal attention. Give then the price, if it is for your interest, for which it is sold. But if you wish both not to give the price and to obtain the things, you are insatiable and silly. Have you nothing then in place of the supper? You have indeed, you have the not flattering of him, whom you did not choose to flatter; you have the not enduring of the man when he enters the room.

26

We may learn the wish (will) of nature from the things in which we do not differ from one another: for instance, when your neighbor's slave has broken his cup, or anything else, we are ready to say forthwith, that it is one of the things which happen. You must know then that when your cup also is broken, you ought to think as you did when your neighbor's cup was broken. Transfer this reflection to greater things also. Is another man's child or wife dead? There is no one who would not say, This is an event incident to man. But when a man's own child or wife is dead, forthwith he calls out, Woe to me, how wretched I am! But we ought to remember how we feel when we hear that it has happened to others.

27

As a mark is not set up for the purpose of missing the aim, so neither does the nature of evil exist in the world.

28

If any person was intending to put your body in the power of any man whom you fell in with on the way, you would be vexed; but that you put your understanding in the power of any man whom you meet, so that if he should revile you, it is disturbed and troubled, are you not ashamed at this?

29

In every act observe the things which come first, and those which follow it; and so proceed to the act. If you do not, at first you will approach it with alacrity, without having thought of the things which will follow; but afterwards, when certain base (ugly) things have shown themselves, you will be ashamed. A man wishes to conquer at the Olympic games. I also wish indeed, for it is a fine thing. But observe both the things which come first, and the things which follow; and then begin the act. You must do everything according to rule, eat according to strict orders, abstain from delicacies, exercise yourself as you are bid at appointed times, in heat, in cold, you must not drink cold water, nor wine as you choose; in a word, you must deliver yourself up to the exercise master as you do to the physician, and then proceed to the contest. And sometimes you will strain the hand, put the ankle out of joint, swallow much dust, sometimes be flogged, and after all this be defeated. When you have considered all this, if you still choose, go to the contest: if you do not you will behave like children, who at one time play at wrestlers, another time as flute players, again as gladiators, then as trumpeters, then as tragic actors. So you also will be at one time an athlete, at another a gladiator, then a rhetorician, then a philosopher, but with your whole soul you will be nothing at all; but like an ape you imitate everything that you see, and one thing after another pleases you. For you have not undertaken anything with consideration, nor have you surveyed it well; but carelessly and with cold desire. Thus some who have seen a philosopher and having heard one speak, as Euphrates speaks—and who can speak as he does?—they wish to be philosophers themselves also. My man, first of all consider what kind of thing it is; and then examine your own nature, if you are able to sustain the character. Do you wish to be a pentathlete or a wrestler? Look at your arms, your thighs, examine your loins. For different men are formed by nature for different things. Do you think that if you do these things, you can eat in the same manner, drink in the same manner, and in the same manner loathe certain things? You must pass sleepless nights, endure toil, go away from your kinsmen, be despised by a slave, in everything have the inferior part, in honor, in office, in the courts of justice, in every little matter. Consider these things, if you would exchange for them, freedom from passions, liberty, tranquillity. If not, take care that, like little children, you be not now a philosopher, then a servant of the publicani, then a rhetorician, then a procurator (manager) for Caesar. These things are not consistent. You must be one man, either good or bad. You must either cultivate your own ruling faculty, or external things. You must either exercise your skill on internal things or on external things; that is you must either maintain the position of a philosopher or that of a common person.

30

Duties are universally measured by relations (Greek: *tais schsesi*). Is a man a father? The precept is to take care of him, to yield to him in all things, to submit when he is reproachful, when he inflicts blows. But suppose that he is a bad father. Were you then by nature made akin to a good father? No; but to a father. Does a brother wrong you? Maintain then your own position towards him, and do not examine what he is doing, but what you must do that your will shall be conformable to nature. For another will not damage you, unless you choose: but you will be damaged then when you shall think that you are damaged. In this way then you will discover your duty from the relation of a neighbor, from that of a citizen, from that of a general, if you are accustomed to contemplate the relations.

31

As to piety towards the gods you must know that this is the chief thing, to have right opinions about them, to think that they exist, and that they administer the All well and justly; and you must fix yourself in this principle (duty), to obey them, and to yield to them in everything which happens, and voluntarily to follow it as being accomplished by the wisest intelligence. For if you do so, you will never either blame the gods, nor will you accuse them of neglecting you. And it is not possible for this to be done in any other way than by withdrawing from the things which are not in our power, and by placing the good and the evil only in those things which are in our power. For if you think that any of the things which are not in our power is good or bad, it is absolutely necessary that, when you do not obtain what you wish, and when you fall into those things which you do not wish, you will find fault and hate those who are the cause of them; for every animal is formed by nature to this, to fly from and to turn from the things which appear harmful and the things which are the cause of the harm, but to follow and admire the things which are useful and the causes of the useful. It is impossible then for a person who thinks that he is harmed to be delighted with that which he thinks to be the cause of the harm, as it is also impossible to be pleased with the harm itself. For this reason also a father is reviled by his son, when he gives no part to his son of the things which are considered to be good; and it was this which made Polynices and Eteocles enemies, the opinion that royal power was a good. It is for this reason that the cultivator of the earth reviles the gods, for this reason the sailor does, and the merchant, and for this reason those who lose their wives and their children. For where the useful (your interest) is, there also piety is. Consequently he who takes care to desire as he ought and to avoid (Greek: *echchlinein*) as he ought, at the same time also cares after piety. But to make libations and to sacrifice and to offer first-fruits according to the custom of our fathers, purely and not meanly nor carelessly nor scantily nor above our ability, is a thing which belongs to all to do.

32

When you have recourse to divination, remember that you do not know how it will turn out, but that you are come to inquire from the diviner. But of what kind it is, you know when you come, if indeed you are a philosopher. For if it is any of the things which are not in our power, it is absolutely necessary that it must be neither good nor bad. Do not then bring to the diviner desire or aversion (Greek: *echchlinein*): if you do, you will approach him with fear. But having determined in your mind that everything which shall turn out (result) is indifferent, and does not concern you, and whatever it may be, for it will be in your power to use it well, and no man will hinder this, come then with confidence to the gods as your advisers. And then when any advice shall have been given, remember whom you have taken as advisers, and whom you will have neglected, if you do not obey them. And go to divination, as Socrates said that you ought, about those matters in which all the inquiry has reference to the result, and in which means are not given either by reason nor by any other art for knowing the thing which is the subject of the inquiry. Wherefore when we ought to share a friend's danger, or that of our country, you must not consult the diviner whether you ought to share it. For even if the diviner shall tell you that the signs of the victims are unlucky, it is plain that this is a token of death, or mutilation of part of the body, or of exile. But reason prevails, that even with these risks, we should share the dangers of our friend, and of our country. Therefore attend to the greater diviner, the Pythian god, who ejected from the temple him who did not assist his friend, when he was being murdered.

33

Immediately prescribe some character and some form to yourself, which you shall observe both when you are alone and when you meet with men.

And let silence be the general rule, or let only what is necessary be said, and in few words. And rarely, and when the occasion calls, we shall say something; but about none of the common subjects, not about gladiators, nor horse-races, nor about athletes, nor about eating or drinking, which are the usual subjects; and especially not about men, as blaming them or praising them, or comparing them. If then you are able, bring over by your conversation, the conversation of your associates, to that which is proper; but if you should happen to be confined to the company of strangers, be silent.

Let not your laughter be much, nor on many occasions, nor excessive.

Refuse altogether to take an oath, if it is possible; if it is not, refuse as far as you are able.

Avoid banquets which are given by strangers and by ignorant persons. But if ever there is occasion to join in them, let your attention be carefully fixed, that you slip not into the manners of the vulgar (the uninstructed). For you must know, that if your companion be impure, he also who keeps company with him must become impure, though he should happen to be pure.

Take (apply) the things which relate to the body as far as the bare use, as food, drink, clothing, house, and slaves; but exclude everything which is for show or luxury.

As to pleasure with women, abstain as far as you can before marriage; but if you do indulge in it, do it in the way which is conformable to custom. Do not however be disagreeable to those who indulge in these pleasures, or reprove them; and do not often boast that you do not indulge in them yourself.

If a man has reported to you, that a certain person speaks ill of you, do not make any defence (answer) to what has been told you; but reply, The man did not know the rest of my faults, for he would not have mentioned these only.

It is not necessary to go to the theatres often: but if there is ever a proper occasion for going, do not show yourself as being a partisan of any man except yourself, that is, desire only that to be done which is done, and for him only to gain the prize who gains the prize; for in this way you will meet with no hindrance. But abstain entirely from shouts and laughter at any (thing or person), or violent emotions. And when you are come away, do not talk much about what has passed on the stage, except about that which may lead to your own improvement. For it is plain, if you do talk much, that you admired the spectacle (more than you ought).

Do not go to the hearing of certain persons' recitations, nor visit them readily. But if you do attend, observe gravity and sedateness, and also avoid making yourself disagreeable.

When you are going to meet with any person, and particularly one of those who are considered to be in a superior condition, place before yourself what Socrates or Zeno would have done in such circumstances, and you will have no difficulty in making a proper use of the occasion.

When you are going to any of those who are in great power, place before yourself that you will not find the man at home, that you will be excluded, that the door will not be opened to you, that the man will not care about you. And if with all this it is your duty to visit him, bear what happens, and never say to yourself that it was not worth the trouble. For this is silly, and marks the character of a man who is offended by externals.

In company take care not to speak much and excessively about your own acts or dangers; for as it is pleasant to you to make mention of your own dangers, it is not so pleasant to others to hear what has happened to you. Take care also not to provoke laughter; for this is a slippery way towards vulgar habits, and is also adapted to diminish the respect of your neighbors. It is a dangerous habit also to approach obscene talk. When then, anything of this kind happens, if there is a good opportunity, rebuke the man who has proceeded to this talk; but if there is not an opportunity, by your silence at least, and blushing and expression of dissatisfaction by your countenance, show plainly that you are displeased at such talk.

34

If you have received the impression (Greek: *phantasion*) of any pleasure, guard yourself against being carried away by it; but let the thing wait for you, and allow yourself a certain delay on your own part. Then think of both times, of the time when you will enjoy the pleasure, and of the time after the enjoyment of the pleasure, when you will repent and will reproach yourself. And set against these things how you will rejoice, if you have abstained from the pleasure, and how you will commend yourself. But if it seem to you seasonable to undertake (do) the thing, take care that the charm of it, and the pleasure, and the attraction of it shall not conquer you; but set on the other side the consideration, how much better it is to be conscious that you have gained this victory.

35

When you have decided that a thing ought to be done, and are doing it, never avoid being seen doing it, though the many shall form an unfavorable opinion about it. For if it is not right to do it, avoid doing the thing; but if it is right, why are you afraid of those who shall find fault wrongly?

36

As the proposition, it is either day, or it is night, is of great importance for the disjunctive argument, but for the conjunctive, is of no value, so in a symposium (entertainment) to select the larger share is of great value for the body, but for the maintenance of the social feeling is worth nothing. When, then, you are eating with another, remember, to look not only to the value for the body of the things set before you, but also to the value of the behavior towards the host which ought to be observed.

37

If you have assumed a character above your strength, you have both acted in this manner in an unbecoming way, and you have neglected that which you might have fulfilled.

38

In walking about, as you take care not to step on a nail, or to sprain your foot, so take care not to damage your own ruling faculty; and if we observe this rule in every act, we shall undertake this act with more security.

39

The measure of possession (property) is to every man the body, as the foot is of the shoe. If then you stand on this rule (the demands of the body), you will maintain the measure; but if you pass beyond it, you must then of necessity be hurried as it were down a precipice. As also in the matter of the shoe, if you go beyond the (necessities of the) foot, the shoe is gilded, then of a purple color, then embroidered; for there is no limit to that which has once passed the true measure.

40

Women forthwith from the age of fourteen are called by the men mistresses (Greek: *churiai, dominae*). Therefore, since they see that there is nothing else that they can obtain, but only the power of lying with men, they begin to decorate themselves, and to place all their hopes in this. It is worth our while then to take care that they may know that they are valued (by men) for nothing else than appearing (being) decent and modest and discreet.

41

It is a mark of a mean capacity to spend much time on the things which concern the body, such as much exercise, much eating, much drinking, much easing of the body, much copulation. But these things should be done as subordinate things; and let all your care be directed to the mind.

42

When any person treats you ill or speaks ill of you, remember that he does this or says this because he thinks that it is his duty. It is not possible then for him to follow that which seems right to you, but that which seems right to himself. Accordingly if he is wrong in his opinion, he is the person who is hurt, for he is the person who has been deceived; for if a man shall suppose the true conjunction to be false, it is not the conjunction which is hindered, but the man who has been deceived about it. If you proceed then from these opinions, you will be mild in temper to him who reviles you; for say on each occasion, It seemed so to him.

43

Everything has two handles, the one by which it may be borne, the other by which it may not. If your brother acts unjustly, do not lay hold of the act by that handle wherein he acts unjustly, for this is the handle which cannot be borne; but lay hold of the other, that he is your brother, that he was nurtured with you, and you will lay hold of the thing by that handle by which it can be borne.

44

These reasonings do not cohere: I am richer than you, therefore I am better than you; I am more eloquent than you, therefore I am better than you. On the contrary, these rather cohere: I am richer than you, therefore my possessions are greater than yours; I am more eloquent than you, therefore my speech is superior to yours. But you are neither possession nor speech.

45

Does a man bathe quickly (early)? do not say that he bathes badly, but that he bathes quickly. Does a man drink much wine? do not say that he does this badly, but say that he drinks much. For before you shall have determined the opinion how do you know whether he is acting wrong? Thus it will not happen to you to comprehend some appearances which are capable of being comprehended, but to assent to others.

46

On no occasion call yourself a philosopher, and do not speak much among the uninstructed about theorems (philosophical rules, precepts); but do that which follows from them. For example, at a banquet do not say how a man ought to eat, but eat as you ought to eat. For remember that in this way Socrates also altogether avoided ostentation. Persons used to come to him and ask to be recommended by him to philosophers, and he used to take them to philosophers, so easily did he submit to being overlooked. Accordingly, if any conversation should arise among uninstructed persons about any theorem, generally be silent; for there is great danger that you will immediately vomit up what you have not digested. And when a man shall say to you that you know nothing, and you are not vexed, then be sure that you have begun the work (of philosophy). For even sheep do not vomit up their grass and show to the shepherds how much they have eaten; but when they have internally digested the pasture, they produce externally wool and milk. Do you also show not your theorems to the uninstructed, but show the acts which come from their digestion.

47

When at a small cost you are supplied with everything for the body, do not be proud of this; nor, if you drink water, say on every occasion, I drink water. But consider first how much more frugal the poor are than we, and how much more enduring of labor. And if you ever wish to exercise yourself in labor and endurance, do it for yourself, and not for others. Do not embrace statues; but if you are ever very thirsty, take a draught of cold water and spit it out, and tell no man.

48

The condition and characteristic of an uninstructed person is this: he never expects from himself profit (advantage) nor harm, but from externals. The condition and characteristic of a philosopher is this: he expects all advantage and all harm from himself. The signs (marks) of one who is making progress are these: he censures no man, he praises no man, he blames no man, he accuses no man, he says nothing about himself as if he were somebody or knew something; when he is impeded at all or hindered, he blames himself; if a man praises him he ridicules the praiser to himself; if a man censures him he makes no defence; he goes about like weak persons, being careful not to move any of the things which are placed, before they are firmly fixed; he removes all desire from himself, and he transfers aversion (Greek: *echchlisin*) to those things only of the things within our power which are contrary to nature; he employs a moderate movement towards everything; whether he is considered foolish or ignorant he cares not; and in a word he watches himself as if he were an enemy and lying in ambush.

49

When a man is proud because he can understand and explain the writings of Chrysippus, say to yourself, If Chrysippus had not written obscurely, this man would have had nothing to be proud of. But what is it that I wish? To understand nature and to follow it. I inquire therefore who is the interpreter? and when I have heard that it is Chrysippus, I come to him (the interpreter). But I do not understand what is written, and therefore I seek the interpreter. And so far there is yet nothing to be proud of. But when I shall have found the interpreter, the thing that remains is to use the precepts (the lessons). This itself is the only thing to be proud of. But if I shall admire the exposition, what else have I been made unless a grammarian instead of a philosopher? except in one thing, that I am explaining Chrysippus instead of Homer. When, then, any man says to me, Read Chrysippus to me, I rather blush, when I cannot show my acts like to and consistent with his words.

50

Whatever things (rules) are proposed to you (for the conduct of life) abide by them, as if they were laws, as if you would be guilty of impiety if you transgressed any of them. And whatever any man shall say about you, do not attend to it; for this is no affair of yours. How long will you then still defer thinking yourself worthy of the best things, and in no matter transgressing the distinctive reason? Have you accepted the theorems (rules), which it was your duty to agree to, and have you agreed to them? what teacher then do you still expect that you defer to him the correction of yourself? You are no longer a youth, but already a full-grown man. If, then, you are negligent and slothful, and are continually making procrastination after procrastination, and proposal (intention) after proposal, and fixing day after day, after which you will attend to yourself, you will not know that you are not making improvement, but you will continue ignorant (uninstructed) both while you live and till you die. Immediately then think it right to live as a full-grown man, and one who is making proficiency, and let everything which appears to you to be the best be to you a law which must not be transgressed. And if anything laborious or pleasant or glorious or inglorious be presented to you, remember that now is the contest, now are the Olympic games, and they cannot be deferred; and that it depends on one defeat and one giving way that progress is either lost or maintained. Socrates in this way became perfect, in all things improving himself, attending to nothing except to reason. But you, though you are not yet a Socrates, ought to live as one who wishes to be a Socrates.

51

The first and most necessary place (part, Greek: *topos*) in philosophy is the use of theorems (precepts, Greek: *theoraemata*), for instance, that we must not lie; the second part is that of demonstrations, for instance, How is it proved that we ought not to lie? The third is that which is confirmatory of these two, and explanatory, for example, How is this a demonstration? For what is demonstration, what is consequence, what is contradiction, what is truth, what is falsehood? The third part (topic) is necessary on account of the second, and the second on account of the first; but the most necessary and that on which we ought to rest is the first. But we do the contrary. For we spend our time on the third topic, and all our earnestness is about it; but we entirely neglect the first. Therefore we lie; but the demonstration that we ought not to lie we have ready to hand.

52

In every thing (circumstance) we should hold these maxims ready to hand:

Lead me, O Zeus, and thou O Destiny,
The way that I am bid by you to go:
To follow I am ready. If I choose not,
I make myself a wretch, and still must follow.

But whoso nobly yields unto necessity,
We hold him wise, and skill'd in things divine.

And the third also: O Crito, if so it pleases the gods, so let it be; Anytus and Melitus are able indeed to kill me, but they cannot harm me.

LETTERS FROM A STOIC

Translated by

GEORGE LONG

Considered to be the greatest Roman philosopher in history, Lucius Annaeus Seneca (known as Seneca the younger) was born in Cordoba (Spain) in C. 4 BC to Seneca the Elder, a Roman knight who was well-known as a teacher of rhetoric, and Helvia, who was from a prominent Baetician family. He was the second of three brothers. When Seneca was about five years old, he was taken to Rome by his aunt, where he was educated at the School of Sextii, which combined Stoicism with Pythagoreanism. There, he studied philosophy and was trained as an orator.

Seneca had a bout of illness when he was in his twenties. He traveled to Egypt to recover and stayed with his aunt and uncle. For a period of about ten years, his aunt took care of him and nursed him back to health. He then returned to Rome with her in 31 AD and began his political career. Seneca's oratorical skills were unparalleled. It is believed that his success infuriated the then emperor Caligula, who gave him a death sentence. Caligula then recanted this order, as he was made to believe that Seneca will anyway have a short life due to his frequent bouts of illness.

Claudius ascended the throne in 41 AD after Caligula's assassination, and accused Seneca of adultery with his niece. By the order of the Senate, Seneca was exiled. He spent the next eight years of his life on the island of Corsica, where he allegedly wrote *Consolation to Helvia* (to comfort his mother who was grieving over the fate of her son) and *Consolation to Polybius*. With the help of Claudius' wife, Agrippina, Seneca was called back to Rome in 49 AD, and a year later was made tutor to Agrippina's son, the future emperor Nero.

Nero became emperor upon Claudius' death. He trusted his new tutor, who had then turned into a royal adviser and perhaps one of the most powerful men in Rome. The initial years of Nero's reign were peaceful. He relied on Seneca and often sought counsel regarding royal matters. He was, however, very young to have the wisdom to manage a kingdom. Slowly and steadily, Seneca's influence on Nero began to diminish and they became estranged. And then there came a day when Nero's volatile nature reared its head. He staged events to kill his own mother. Seneca's pupil had become a monster. Nero's planned strategy to make his mother's murder look like an accident, didn't work. Even so, Seneca came to his pupil's aid at what he considered to be his duty, and helped as required.

Even after all this, Seneca was embroiled in a conspiracy. He was charged with an attempt to assassinate emperor Nero. He had been marked a traitor and was consequently told to commit suicide.

Seneca obeyed and calmly did as he was commanded. The image of Seneca lying in his bathtub with his veins slashed has been an inspiration to many artists. Unfazed in the face of death, Seneca was a man who practiced what he preached. Philosophers, or even people in general, wonder about how to live well and how to prepare for death. Seneca had answers to both of these questions. In his book *Letters from a Stoic*, he wrote that a life lived virtuously is a life well lived. He wrote that death was inevitable, so there was no merit to worrying about it or fearing it.

The writings of Seneca were revived in the Renaissance. His dramas, all of which were tragedies, inspired the writers of that period and helped formulate the genre of the 'revenge tragedy' that was prominent in the Renaissance and continued flourishing in the Jacobean Era. The philosophical writings made Seneca appear to be a very different man than he was pictured through his dramas. Characters in his plays were driven by the very same emotions he wanted his readers to distance themselves from, as is evidenced from his philosophical treatises.

The chronology of Seneca's works has been a matter of debate since very little information on his life is available. His earliest work is believed to be *Consolation to Marcia*. Around 43 or 44 AD, he wrote *Consolation to Helvia* and *Consolation to Polybius,* when he had been exiled and was living in Corsica. Upon his return to Rome, he composed *Letters from a Stoic*, and *Natural Questions* was written in the last few years of his life. The date of composition of Seneca's plays is not clear either. Among the ten plays that he wrote, all of which were widely read during the Renaissance, *Thyestes* is considered his best. *Medea* and *Oedipus* were very popular as well.

Seneca's letters to Lucilius in *Letters from a Stoic* are, in fact, personal essays. These essays advocate Stoicism , a Greek school of thought that held the belief that happiness in life could be attained if one followed reason and a strict moral code. Seneca's writings may be called ancient, but he wrote of things that are still studied and are relevant in modern times. From the importance of friendship to the benefits of living a simple life, Seneca's letters cover everything simply putting across the correct way of life and offering the readers a glimpse into the rich and complicated mind of one of the finest philosophers in history.

VOLUME ONE

LETTER

2

On Discursiveness In Reading

Judging by what you write me, and by what I hear, I am forming a good opinion regarding your future. You do not run hither and thither and distract yourself by changing your abode; for such restlessness is the sign of a disordered spirit. The primary indication, to my thinking, of a well-ordered mind is a man's ability to remain in one place and linger in his own company. Be careful, however, lest this reading of many authors and books of every sort may tend to make you discursive and unsteady. You must linger among a limited number of master-thinkers, and digest their works, if you would derive ideas which shall win firm hold in your mind. Everywhere means nowhere. When a person spends all his time in foreign travel, he ends by having many acquaintances, but no friends. And the same thing must hold true of men who seek intimate acquaintance with no single author, but visit them all in a hasty and hurried manner. Food does no good and is not assimilated into the body if it leaves the stomach as soon as it is eaten; nothing hinders a cure so much as frequent change of medicine; no wound will heal when one salve is tried after another; a plant which is often moved can never grow strong. There is nothing so efficacious that it can be helpful while it is being shifted about. And in reading of many books is distraction.

Accordingly, since you cannot read all the books which you may possess, it is enough to possess only as many books as you can read. "But," you reply, "I wish to dip first into one book and then into another." I tell you that it is the sign of an overnice appetite to toy with many dishes; for when they are manifold and varied, they cloy but do not nourish. So you should always read standard authors; and when you crave a change, fall back upon those whom you read before. Each day acquire something that will fortify you against poverty, against death, indeed against other misfortunes as well; and after you have run over many thoughts, select one to be thoroughly digested that day. This is my own custom; from the many things which I have read, I claim some one part for myself.

The thought for today is one which I discovered in Epicurus;* for I am wont to cross over even into the enemy's camp,—not as a deserter, but as a scout. He says: "Contented poverty is an honourable estate." Indeed, if it be contented, it is not poverty at all. It is not the man who has too little, but the man who craves more, that is poor. What does it matter how much a man has laid up in his safe, or in his warehouse, how large are his flocks and how fat his dividends, if he covets his neighbour's property, and reckons, not his past gains, but his hopes of gains to come? Do you ask what is the proper limit to wealth? It is, first, to have what is necessary, and, second, to have what is enough. Farewell.

---

* Frag. 475 Usener

LETTER

3

On True and False Friendship

You have sent a letter to me through the hand of a "friend" of yours, as you call him. And in your very next sentence you warn me not to discuss with him all the matters that concern you, saying that even you yourself are not accustomed to do this; in other words, you have in the same letter affirmed and denied that he is your friend. Now if you used this word of ours* in the popular sense, and called him "friend" in the same way in which we speak of all candidates for election as "honourable gentlemen," and as we greet all men whom we meet casually, if their names slip us for the moment, with the salutation "my dear sir,"—so be it. But if you consider any man a friend whom you do not trust as you trust yourself, you are mightily mistaken and you do not sufficiently understand what true friendship means. Indeed, I would have you discuss everything with a friend; but first of all discuss the man himself. When friendship is settled, you must trust; before friendship is formed, you must pass judgment. Those persons indeed put last first and confound their duties, who, violating the rules of Theophrastus,** judge a man after they

* i.e., a word which has a special significance to the Stoics; see Ep. xlviii, note.

** Frag. 74 Wimmer.

have made him their friend, instead of making him their friend after they have judged him. Ponder for a long time whether you shall admit a given person to your friendship; but when you have decided to admit him, welcome him with all your heart and soul. Speak as boldly with him as with yourself. As to yourself, although you should live in such a way that you trust your own self with nothing which you could not entrust even to your enemy, yet, since certain matters occur which convention keeps secret, you should share with a friend at least all your worries and reflections. Regard him as loyal, and you will make him loyal. Some, for example, fearing to be deceived, have taught men to deceive; by their suspicions they have given their friend the right to do wrong. Why need I keep back any words in the presence of my friend? Why should I not regard myself as alone when in his company?

There is a class of men who communicate, to anyone whom they meet, matters which should be revealed to friends alone, and unload upon the chance listener whatever irks them. Others, again, fear to confide in their closest intimates; and if it were possible, they would not trust even themselves, burying their secrets deep in their hearts. But we should do neither. It is equally faulty to trust everyone and to trust no one. Yet the former fault is, I should say, the more ingenuous, the latter the more safe. In like manner you should rebuke these two kinds of men,—both those who always lack repose, and those who are always in repose. For love of bustle is not industry,—it is only the restlessness of a hunted mind. And true repose does not consist in condemning all motion as merely vexation; that kind of repose is slackness and inertia. Therefore, you should note the following saying, taken from my reading in Pomponius:* "Some men shrink into dark corners, to such a degree that they see darkly by day." No, men should combine these tendencies, and he who reposes should act and he who acts should take repose. Discuss the problem with Nature; she will tell you that she has created both day and night. Farewell.

---

* See Index.

LETTER

5

On the Philosopher's Mean

I commend you and rejoice in the fact that you are persistent in your studies, and that, putting all else aside, you make it each day your endeavour to become a better man. I do not merely exhort you to keep at it; I actually beg you to do so. I warn you, however, not to act after the fashion of those who desire to be conspicuous rather than to improve, by doing things which will rouse comment as regards your dress or general way of living. Repellent attire, unkempt hair, slovenly beard, open scorn of silver dishes, a couch on the bare earth, and any other perverted forms of self-display, are to be avoided. The mere name of philosophy, however quietly pursued, is an object of sufficient scorn; and what would happen if we should begin to separate ourselves from the customs of our fellow-men? Inwardly, we ought to be different in all respects, but our exterior should conform to society. Do not wear too fine, nor yet too frowzy, a toga. One needs no silver plate, encrusted and embossed in solid gold; but we should not believe the lack of silver and gold to be proof of the simple life. Let us try to maintain a higher standard of life than that of the multitude, but not a contrary standard; otherwise, we shall frighten away and repel the very persons whom we are trying to improve. We also bring it about that they are unwilling to imitate us in anything, because they are afraid lest they might be compelled to imitate us in everything.

The first thing which philosophy undertakes to give is fellow-feeling with all men; in other words, sympathy and sociability. We part company with our promise if we are unlike other men. We must see to it that the means by which we wish to draw admiration be not absurd and odious. Our motto,* as you know, is "Live according to Nature"; but it is quite contrary to nature to torture the body, to hate unlaboured elegance, to be dirty on purpose, to eat food that is not only plain, but disgusting and forbidding. Just as it is a sign of luxury to seek out dainties, so it is madness to avoid that which is customary and can be purchased at no great price. Philosophy calls for plain living, but not for penance; and we may perfectly well be plain and neat at the same time. This is the mean of which I approve; our life should observe a happy medium between the ways of a sage and the ways of the world at large; all men should admire it, but they should understand it also.

"Well then, shall we act like other men? Shall there be no distinction between ourselves and the world?" Yes, a very great one; let men find that we are unlike the common herd, if they look closely. If they visit us at home, they should admire us, rather than our household appointments. He is a great man who uses earthenware dishes as if they were silver; but he is equally great who uses silver as if it were earthenware. It is the sign of an unstable mind not to be able to endure riches.

But I wish to share with you today's profit also. I find in the writings of our** Hecato that the limiting of desires helps also to cure fears: "Cease to hope," he says, "and you will cease to fear." "But how," you will reply, "can things so different go side by side?" In this way, my dear Lucilius: though they do seem at variance, yet they are really united. Just as the same chain fastens the prisoner and the soldier who guards

---

* i.e., of the Stoic school.

** Frag. 25 Fowler.

him, so hope and fear, dissimilar as they are, keep step together; fear follows hope. I am not surprised that they proceed in this way; each alike belongs to a mind that is in suspense, a mind that is fretted by looking forward to the future. But the chief cause of both these ills is that we do not adapt ourselves to the present, but send our thoughts a long way ahead. And so foresight, the noblest blessing of the human race, becomes perverted. Beasts avoid the dangers which they see, and when they have escaped them are free from care; but we men torment ourselves over that which is to come as well as over that which is past. Many of our blessings bring bane to us; for memory recalls the tortures of fear, while foresight anticipates them. The present alone can make no man wretched. Farewell.

LETTER

6

On Sharing Knowledge

I feel, my dear Lucilius, that I am being not only reformed, but transformed. I do not yet, however, assure myself, or indulge the hope, that there are no elements left in me which need to be changed. Of course there are many that should be made more compact, or made thinner, or be brought into greater prominence. And indeed this very fact is proof that my spirit is altered into something better,—that it can see its own faults, of which it was previously ignorant. In certain cases sick men are congratulated because they themselves have perceived that they are sick.

I therefore wish to impart to you this sudden change in myself; I should then begin to place a surer trust in our friendship,—the true friendship which hope and fear and self-interest cannot sever, the friendship in which and for the sake of which men meet death. I can show you many who have lacked, not a friend, but a friendship; this, however, cannot possibly happen when souls are drawn together by identical inclinations into an alliance of honourable desires. And why can it not happen? Because in such cases men know that they have all things in common, especially their troubles.

You cannot conceive what distinct progress I notice that each day brings to me. And when you say: "Give me also a share in these gifts which you have found so helpful," I reply that I am anxious to heap all these privileges upon you, and that I am glad to learn in order that I may teach. Nothing will ever please me, no matter how excellent or beneficial, if I must retain the knowledge of it to myself. And if wisdom were given me under the express condition that it must be kept hidden and not uttered, I should refuse it. No good thing is pleasant to possess, without friends to share it.

I shall therefore send to you the actual books; and in order that you may not waste time in searching here and there for profitable topics, I shall mark certain passages, so that you can turn at once to those which I approve and admire. Of course, however, the living voice and the intimacy of a common life will help you more than the written word. You must go to the scene of action, first, because men put more faith in their eyes than in their ears,[*] and second, because the way is long if one follows precepts, but short and helpful, if one follows patterns. Cleanthes could not have been the express image of Zeno, if he had merely heard his lectures; he shared in his life, saw into his hidden purposes, and watched him to see whether he lived according to his own rules Plato, Aristotle, and the whole throng of sages who were destined to go each his different way, derived more benefit from the character than from the words of Socrates. It was not the class-room of Epicurus, but living together under the same roof, that made great men of Metrodorus, Hermarchus, and Polyaenus. Therefore I summon you, not merely that you may derive benefit, but that you may confer benefit; for we can assist each other greatly.

Meanwhile, I owe you my little daily contribution; you shall be told what pleased me today in the writings of Hecato;[**] it is these words: "What progress, you ask, have I made? I have begun to be a friend to myself." That was indeed a great benefit; such a person can never be alone. You may be sure that such a man is a friend to all mankind. Farewell.

---

* Cf. Herodotus, i. 8 ὦτα τυγχάνει ἀνθρώποισι ἐόντα ἀπιστότερα ὀφθαλμῶν.

** Frag. 26 Fowler.

LETTER

7

On Crowds

Do you ask me what you should regard as especially to be avoided? I say, crowds; for as yet you cannot trust yourself to them with safety. I shall admit my own weakness, at any rate; for I never bring back home the same character that I took abroad with me. Something of that which I have forced to be calm within me is disturbed; some of the foes that I have routed return again. Just as the sick man, who has been weak for a long time, is in such a condition that he cannot be taken out of the house without suffering a relapse, so we ourselves are affected when our souls are recovering from a lingering disease. To consort with the crowd is harmful; there is no person who does not make some vice attractive to us, or stamp it upon us, or taint us unconsciously therewith. Certainly, the greater the mob with which we mingle, the greater the danger.

But nothing is so damaging to good character as the habit of lounging at the games; for then it is that vice steals subtly upon one through the avenue of pleasure. What do you think I mean? I mean that I come home more greedy, more ambitious, more voluptuous, and even more cruel and inhuman,—because I have been among human beings. By chance I attended a mid-day exhibition, expecting some fun, wit, and relaxation,—an exhibition at which men's eyes have respite from the slaughter of their fellow-men. But it was quite the reverse. The previous combats were the essence of compassion; but now all the trifling is put aside and it is pure murder.* The men have no defensive armour. They are exposed to blows at all points, and no one ever strikes in vain. Many persons prefer this programme to the usual pairs and to the bouts "by request." Of course they do; there is no helmet or shield to deflect the weapon. What is the need of defensive armour, or of skill? All these mean delaying death. In the morning they throw men to the lions and the bears; at noon, they throw them to the spectators. The spectators demand that the slayer shall face the man who is to slay him in his turn; and they always reserve the latest conqueror for another butchering. The outcome of every fight is death, and the means are fire and sword. This sort of thing goes on while the arena is empty. You may retort: "But he was a highway robber; he killed a man!" And what of it? Granted that, as a murderer, he deserved this punishment, what crime have you committed, poor fellow, that you should deserve to sit and see this show? In the morning they cried "Kill him! Lash him! Burn him! Why does he meet the sword in so cowardly a way? Why does he strike so feebly? Why doesn't he die game? Whip him to meet his wounds! Let them receive blow for blow, with chests bare and exposed to the stroke!" And when the games stop for the intermission, they announce: "A little throat-cutting in the meantime, so that there may still be something going on!"

Come now; do you** not understand even this truth, that a bad example reacts on the agent? Thank the immortal gods that you are teaching cruelty to a person who cannot learn to be cruel. The young character, which cannot hold fast to righteousness, must be rescued from the mob; it is too easy to side with the majority. Even Socrates, Cato, and Laelius might have been shaken in their moral strength

---

* During the luncheon interval condemned criminals were often driven into the arena and compelled to fight, for the amusement of those spectators who remained throughout the day.

** The remark is addressed to the brutalized spectators.

by a crowd that was unlike them; so true it is that none of us, no matter how much he cultivates his abilities, can withstand the shock of faults that approach, as it were, with so great a retinue. Much harm is done by a single case of indulgence or greed; the familiar friend, if he be luxurious, weakens and softens us imperceptibly; the neighbour, if he be rich, rouses our covetousness; the companion, if he be slanderous, rubs off some of his rust upon us, even though we be spotless and sincere. What then do you think the effect will be on character, when the world at large assaults it! You must either imitate or loathe the world.

But both courses are to be avoided; you should not copy the bad simply because they are many, nor should you hate the many because they are unlike you. Withdraw into yourself, as far as you can. Associate with those who will make a better man of you. Welcome those whom you yourself can improve. The process is mutual; for men learn while they teach. There is no reason why pride in advertising your abilities should lure you into publicity, so that you should desire to recite or harangue before the general public. Of course I should be willing for you to do so if you had a stock-in-trade that suited such a mob; as it is, there is not a man of them who can understand you. One or two individuals will perhaps come in your way, but even these will have to be moulded and trained by you so that they will understand you. You may say: "For what purpose did I learn all these things?" But you need not fear that you have wasted your efforts; it was for yourself that you learned them.

In order, however, that I may not today have learned exclusively for myself, I shall share with you three excellent sayings, of the same general purport, which have come to my attention. This letter will give you one of them as payment of my debt; the other two you may accept as a contribution in advance. Democritus* says: "One man means as much to me as a multitude, and a multitude only as much as one man." The following also was nobly spoken by someone or other, for it is doubtful who the author was; they asked him what

---

* Frag. 302[a] Diels[2].

was the object of all this study applied to an art that would reach but very few. He replied: "I am content with few, content with one, content with none at all." The third saying—and a noteworthy one, too—is by Epicurus,* written to one of the partners of his studies: "I write this not for the many, but for you; each of us is enough of an audience for the other." Lay these words to heart, Lucilius, that you may scorn the pleasure which comes from the applause of the majority. Many men praise you; but have you any reason for being pleased with yourself, if you are a person whom the many can understand? Your good qualities should face inwards. Farewell.

* Frag. 208 Usener.

LETTER

8

On the Philosopher's Seclusion

"Do you bid me," you say, "shun the throng, and withdraw from men, and be content with my own conscience? Where are the counsels of your school, which order a man to die in the midst of active work?" As to the course* which I seem to you to be urging on you now and then, my object in shutting myself up and locking the door is to be able to help a greater number. I never spend a day in idleness; I appropriate even a part of the night for study. I do not allow time for sleep but yield to it when I must, and when my eyes are wearied with waking and ready to fall shut, I keep them at their task. I have withdrawn not only from men, but from affairs, especially from my own affairs; I am working for later generations, writing down some ideas that may be of assistance to them. There are certain wholesome counsels, which may be compared to prescriptions of useful drugs; these I am putting into writing; for I have found them helpful in ministering to my own sores, which, if not wholly cured, have at any rate ceased to spread.

I point other men to the right path, which I have found late in life, when wearied with wandering. I cry out to them:

---

* As contrasted with the general Stoic doctrine of taking part in the world's work.

"Avoid whatever pleases the throng: avoid the gifts of Chance! Halt before every good which Chance brings to you, in a spirit of doubt and fear; for it is the dumb animals and fish that are deceived by tempting hopes. Do you call these things the 'gifts' of Fortune? They are snares. And any man among you who wishes to live a life of safety will avoid, to the utmost of his power, these limed twigs of her favour, by which we mortals, most wretched in this respect also, are deceived; for we think that we hold them in our grasp, but they hold us in theirs. Such a career leads us into precipitous ways, and life on such heights ends in a fall. Moreover, we cannot even stand up against prosperity when she begins to drive us to leeward; nor can we go down, either, 'with the ship at least on her course,' or once for all;[*] Fortune does not capsize us,—she plunges our bows under[**] and dashes us on the rocks.

"Hold fast, then, to this sound and wholesome rule of life; that you indulge the body only so far as is needful for good health. The body should be treated more rigorously, that it may not be disobedient to the mind. Eat merely to relieve your hunger; drink merely to quench your thirst; dress merely to keep out the cold; house yourself merely as a protection against personal discomfort. It matters little whether the house be built of turf, or of variously coloured imported marble; understand that a man is sheltered just as well by a thatch as by a roof of gold. Despise everything that useless toil creates as an ornament and an object of beauty. And reflect that nothing except the soul is worthy of wonder; for to the soul, if it be great, naught is great."[***]

---

* See Ep. lxxxv. 33 for the famous saying of the Rhodian pilot.

** *cernulat*, equivalent to Greek ἀναχαιτίζω, of a horse which throws a rider over its head.

*** Cf. the Stoic precept *nil admirandum.*

When I commune in such terms with myself and with future generations, do you not think that I am doing more good than when I appear as counsel in court, or stamp my seal upon a will, or lend my assistance in the senate, by word or action, to a candidate? Believe me, those who seem to be busied with nothing are busied with the greater tasks; they are dealing at the same time with things mortal and things immortal.

But I must stop, and pay my customary contribution, to balance this letter. The payment shall not be made from my own property; for I am still conning Epicurus.* I read today, in his works, the following sentence: "If you would enjoy real freedom, you must be the slave of Philosophy." The man who submits and surrenders himself to her is not kept waiting; he is emancipated** on the spot. For the very service of Philosophy is freedom.

It is likely that you will ask me why I quote so many of Epicurus's noble words instead of words taken from our own school. But is there any reason why you should regard them as sayings of Epicurus and not common property? How many poets give forth ideas that have been uttered, or may be uttered, by philosophers! I need not touch upon the tragedians and our writers of national drama;*** for these last are also somewhat serious, and stand half-way between comedy and tragedy. What a quantity of sagacious verses lie buried in the mime! How many of Publilius's lines are worthy of being spoken by buskin-clad actors, as well as by wearers of the slipper!**** I shall quote one verse of his, which concerns philosophy, and particularly that phase of it which we were discussing a moment ago, wherein he says that the gifts of Chance are not to be regarded as part of our possessions:

---

* Frag. 199 Usener.

** Literally "spun around" by the master and dismissed to freedom. Cf. Persius, v. 75f.

*** *Fabulae togatae* were plays which dealt with Roman subject matter, as contrasted with adaptations from the Greek, called *palliatae*. The term, in the widest sense includes both comedy and tragedy.

**** i.e., comedians or mimes.

Still alien is whatever you have gained
By coveting.*

I recall that you yourself expressed this idea much more happily and concisely:

What Chance has made yours is not really yours.**

And a third, spoken by you still more happily, shall not be omitted:

The good that could be given, can be removed.***

I shall not charge this up to the expense account, because I have given it to you from your own stock. Farewell.

* *Syri Sententiae*, p. 309 Ribbeck².

** *Com. Rom. Frag.* p. 394 Ribbeck².

*** *ibidem.*

LETTER

9

On Philosophy and Friendship

You desire to know whether Epicurus is right when, in one of his letters,* he rebukes those who hold that the wise man is self-sufficient and for that reason does not stand in need of friendships. This is the objection raised by Epicurus against Stilbo and those who believe** that the Supreme Good is a soul which is insensible to feeling.

We are bound to meet with a double meaning if we try to express the Greek term "lack of feeling" summarily, in a single word, rendering it by the Latin word *impatientia*. For it may be understood in the meaning the opposite to that which we wish it to have. What we mean to express is, a soul which rejects any sensation of evil; but people will interpret the idea as that of a soul which can endure no evil. Consider, therefore, whether it is not better to say "a soul that cannot be harmed," or "a soul entirely beyond the realm of suffering." There is this difference between ourselves and the other school:*** our ideal wise man feels his troubles, but overcomes them; their wise man does not

* Frag. 174 Usener.

** i.e., the Cynics.

*** i.e., the Cynics.

even feel them. But we and they alike hold this idea,—that the wise man is self-sufficient. Nevertheless, he desires friends, neighbours, and associates, no matter how much he is sufficient unto himself. And mark how self-sufficient he is; for on occasion he can be content with a part of himself. If he lose a hand through disease or war, or if some accident puts out one or both of his eyes, he will be satisfied with what is left, taking as much pleasure in his impaired and maimed body as he took when it was sound. But while he does not pine for these parts if they are missing, he prefers not to lose them. In this sense the wise man is self-sufficient, that he can do without friends, not that he desires to do without them. When I say "can," I mean this: he endures the loss of a friend with equanimity.

But he need never lack friends, for it lies in his own control how soon he shall make good a loss. Just as Phidias, if he lose a statue, can straightway carve another, even so our master in the art of making friendships can fill the place of a friend he has lost. If you ask how one can make oneself a friend quickly, I will tell you, provided we are agreed that I may pay my debt* at once and square the account, so far as this letter is concerned. Hecato,** says: "I can show you a philtre, compounded without drugs, herbs, or any witch's incantation: 'If you would be loved, love.'" Now there is great pleasure, not only in maintaining old and established friendships, but also in beginning and acquiring new ones. There is the same difference between winning a new friend and having already won him, as there is between the farmer who sows and the farmer who reaps. The philosopher Attalus used to say: "It is more pleasant to make than to keep a friend, as it is more pleasant to the artist to paint than to have finished painting." When one is busy and absorbed in one's work, the very absorption affords great delight; but when one has withdrawn one's hand from the completed masterpiece, the pleasure is not so keen. Henceforth it is the fruits of his art that he enjoys; it was the art itself that he enjoyed while he was painting. In the case of our children, their

* i.e., the *diurna mercedula*; see Ep. vi, 7.

** Frag. 27 Fowler.

young manhood yields the more abundant fruits, but their infancy was sweeter.

Let us now return to the question. The wise man, I say, self-sufficient though he be, nevertheless desires friends if only for the purpose of practising friendship, in order that his noble qualities may not lie dormant. Not, however, for the purpose mentioned by Epicurus* in the letter quoted above: "That there may be someone to sit by him when he is ill, to help him when he is in prison or in want;" but that he may have someone by whose sick-bed he himself may sit, someone a prisoner in hostile hands whom he himself may set free. He who regards himself only, and enters upon friendships for this reason, reckons wrongly. The end will be like the beginning: he has made friends with one who might assist him out of bondage; at the first rattle of the chain such a friend will desert him. These are the so-called "fair-weather" friendships; one who is chosen for the sake of utility will be satisfactory only so long as he is useful. Hence prosperous men are blockaded by troops of friends; but those who have failed stand amid vast loneliness, their friends fleeing from the very crisis which is to test their worth. Hence, also, we notice those many shameful cases of persons who, through fear, desert or betray. The beginning and the end cannot but harmonize. He who begins to be your friend because it pays will also cease because it pays. A man will be attracted by some reward offered in exchange for his friendship, if he be attracted by aught in friendship other than friendship itself.

For what purpose, then, do I make a man my friend? In order to have someone for whom I may die, whom I may follow into exile, against whose death I may stake my own life, and pay the pledge, too. The friendship which you portray is a bargain and not a friendship; it regards convenience only, and looks to the results. Beyond question the feeling of a lover has in it something akin to friendship; one might call it friendship run mad. But, though this is true, does anyone love

* Frag. 175 Usener.

for the sake of gain, or promotion, or renown? Pure* love, careless of all other things, kindles the soul with desire for the beautiful object, not without the hope of a return of the affection. What then? Can a cause which is more honourable produce a passion that is base? You may retort: "We are not now discussing the question whether friendship is to be cultivated for its own sake." On the contrary, nothing more urgently requires demonstration; for if friendship is to be sought for its own sake, he may seek it who is self-sufficient. "How, then," you ask, "does he seek it?" Precisely as he seeks an object of great beauty, not attracted to it by desire for gain, nor yet frightened by the instability of Fortune. One who seeks friendship for favourable occasions, strips it of all its nobility.

"The wise man is self-sufficient." This phrase, my dear Lucilius, is incorrectly explained by many; for they withdraw the wise man from the world, and force him to dwell within his own skin. But we must mark with care what this sentence signifies and how far it applies; the wise man is sufficient unto himself for a happy existence, but not for mere existence. For he needs many helps towards mere existence; but for a happy existence he needs only a sound and upright soul, one that despises Fortune.

I should like also to state to you one of the distinctions of Chrysippus,** who declares that the wise man is in want of nothing, and yet needs many things.*** "On the other hand," he says, "nothing is needed by the fool, for he does not understand how to use anything, but he is in want of everything." The wise man needs hands, eyes, and many things that are necessary for his daily use; but he is in want of nothing. For want implies a necessity, and nothing is necessary to the wise man. Therefore, although he is self-sufficient, yet he has need of friends. He craves as many friends as possible, not, however, that he may live happily; for he will live happily even without friends.

---

* "Pure love," i.e., love in its essence, unalloyed with other emotions.

** Cf. his *Frag. moral.* 674 von Arnim.

*** The distinction is based upon the meaning of *egere*, "to be in want of" something indispensible, and *opus esse*, "to have need of" something which one can do without.

The Supreme Good calls for no practical aids from outside; it is developed at home, and arises entirely within itself. If the good seeks any portion of itself from without, it begins to be subject to the play of Fortune.

People may say: "But what sort of existence will the wise man have, if he be left friendless when thrown into prison, or when stranded in some foreign nation, or when delayed on a long voyage, or when cast upon a lonely shore?" His life will be like that of Jupiter, who, amid the dissolution of the world, when the gods are confounded together and Nature rests for a space from her work, can retire into himself and give himself over to his own thoughts.* In some such way as this the sage will act; he will retreat into himself, and live with himself. As long as he is allowed to order his affairs according to his judgment, he is self-sufficient—and marries a wife; he is self-sufficient—and brings up children; he is self-sufficient—and yet could not live if he had to live without the society of man. Natural promptings, and not his own selfish needs, draw him into friendships. For just as other things have for us an inherent attractiveness, so has friendship. As we hate solitude and crave society, as nature draws men to each other, so in this matter also there is an attraction which makes us desirous of friendship. Nevertheless, though the sage may love his friends dearly, often comparing them with himself, and putting them ahead of himself, yet all the good will be limited to his own being, and he will speak the words which were spoken by the very Stilbo** whom Epicurus criticizes in his letter. For Stilbo, after his country was captured and his children and his wife lost, as he emerged from the general desolation alone and yet happy, spoke as follows to Demetrius, called Sacker of Cities because of the destruction he brought upon them, in answer to the question whether he had lost anything: "I have all my goods with me!" There is a brave and stout-hearted man for you! The enemy conquered, but Stilbo conquered

* This refers to the Stoic conflagration: after certain cycles their world was destroyed by fire. Cf. E. V. Arnold, *Roman Stoicism*, pp. 192 f.; cf. also Chrysippus, Frag. phys. 1065 von Arnim.

** *Gnomologici Vaticani* 515[a] Sternberg.

his conqueror. "I have lost nothing!" Aye, he forced Demetrius to wonder whether he himself had conquered after all. "My goods are all with me!" In other words, he deemed nothing that might be taken from him to be a good.

We marvel at certain animals because they can pass through fire and suffer no bodily harm; but how much more marvellous is a man who has marched forth unhurt and unscathed through fire and sword and devastation! Do you understand now how much easier it is to conquer a whole tribe than to conquer one *man*? This saying of Stilbo makes common ground with Stoicism; the Stoic also can carry his goods unimpaired through cities that have been burned to ashes; for he is self-sufficient. Such are the bounds which he sets to his own happiness.

But you must not think that our school alone can utter noble words; Epicurus himself, the reviler of Stilbo, spoke similar language;[*] put it down to my credit, though I have already wiped out my debt for the present day.[**] He says: "Whoever does not regard what he has as most ample wealth, is unhappy, though he be master of the whole world." Or, if the following seems to you a more suitable phrase,—for we must try to render the meaning and not the mere words: "A man may rule the world and still be unhappy, if he does not feel that he is supremely happy." In order, however, that you may know that these sentiments are universal,[***] suggested, of course, by Nature, you will find in one of the comic poets this verse:

Unblest is he who thinks himself unblest.[****]

For what does your condition matter, if it is bad in your own eyes? You may say: "What then? If yonder man, rich by base means, and yonder man, lord of many but slave of more, shall call themselves

---

* Frag. 474 Usener.

** Cf. above § 6.

*** i.e., not confined to the Stoics, etc.

**** Author unknown; perhaps, as Buecheler thinks, adapted from the Greek.

happy, will their own opinion make them happy?" It matters not what one says, but what one feels; also, not how one feels on one particular day, but how one feels at all times. There is no reason, however, why you should fear that this great privilege will fall into unworthy hands; only the wise man is pleased with his own. Folly is ever troubled with weariness of itself. Farewell.

LETTER

11

On the Blush of Modesty

Your friend and I have had a conversation. He is a man of ability; his very first words showed what spirit and understanding he possesses, and what progress he has already made. He gave me a foretaste, and he will not fail to answer thereto. For he spoke not from forethought, but was suddenly caught off his guard. When he tried to collect himself, he could scarcely banish that hue of modesty, which is a good sign in a young man; the blush that spread over his face seemed so to rise from the depths. And I feel sure that his habit of blushing will stay with him after he has strengthened his character, stripped off all his faults, and become wise. For by no wisdom can natural weaknesses of the body be removed. That which is implanted and inborn can be toned down by training, but not overcome. The steadiest speaker, when before the public, often breaks into a perspiration, as if he had wearied or over-heated himself; some tremble in the knees when they rise to speak; I know of some whose teeth chatter, whose tongues falter, whose lips quiver. Training and experience can never shake off this habit; nature exerts her own power and through such a weakness makes her presence known even to the strongest. I know that the blush, too, is a habit of this sort, spreading suddenly over the faces of the most dignified men. It is, indeed more prevalent in youth, because of the warmer blood and the sensitive countenance; nevertheless, both seasoned men and aged men are affected by it. Some are most dangerous when they redden, as if they were letting all their sense of shame escape. Sulla, when the blood mantled his cheeks, was in his fiercest mood. Pompey had the most sensitive cast of countenance; he always blushed in the presence of a gathering, and especially at a public assembly. Fabianus also, I remember, reddened when he appeared as a witness before the senate; and his embarrassment became him to a remarkable degree. Such a habit is not due to mental weakness, but to the novelty of a situation; an inexperienced person is not necessarily confused, but is usually affected, because he slips into this habit by natural tendency of the body. Just as certain men are full-blooded, so others are of a quick and mobile blood, that rushes to the face at once.

As I remarked, Wisdom can never remove this habit; for if she could rub out all our faults, she would be mistress of the universe. Whatever is assigned to us by the terms of our birth and the blend in our constitutions, will stick with us, no matter how hard or how long the soul may have tried to master itself. And we cannot forbid these feelings any more than we can summon them. Actors in the theatre, who imitate the emotions, who portray fear and nervousness, who depict sorrow, imitate bashfulness by hanging their heads, lowering their voices, and keeping their eyes fixed and rooted upon the ground. They cannot, however, muster a blush; for the blush cannot be prevented or acquired. Wisdom will not assure us of a remedy, or give us help against it; it comes or goes unbidden, and is a law unto itself.

But my letter calls for its closing sentence. Hear and take to heart this useful and wholesome motto:* "Cherish some man of high character, and keep him ever before your eyes, living as if he were watching you, and ordering all your actions as if he beheld them." Such, my dear Lucilius, is the counsel of Epicurus;** he has quite properly

---

* Epicurus, Frag. 210 Usener.

** Frag. 210 Usener.

given us a guardian and an attendant. We can get rid of most sins, if we have a witness who stands near us when we are likely to go wrong. The soul should have someone whom it can respect,—one by whose authority it may make even its inner shrine more hallowed.* Happy is the man who can make others better, not merely when he is in their company, but even when he is in their thoughts! And happy also is he who can so revere a man as to calm and regulate himself by calling him to mind! One who can so revere another, will soon be himself worthy of reverence. Choose therefore a Cato; or, if Cato seems too severe a model, choose some Laelius, a gentler spirit. Choose a master whose life, conversation, and soul-expressing face have satisfied you; picture him always to yourself as your protector or your pattern. For we must indeed have someone according to whom we may regulate our characters; you can never straighten that which is crooked unless you use a ruler. Farewell.

---

* The figure is taken from the ἄδυτον, the Holy of Holies in a temple. Cf. Vergil, *Aeneid*, vi. 10 *secreta Sibyllas.*

LETTER 12

On Old Age

Wherever I turn, I see evidences of my advancing years. I visited lately my country-place, and protested against the money which was spent on the tumble-down building. My bailiff maintained that the flaws were not due to his own carelessness; "he was doing everything possible, but the house was old." And this was the house which grew under my own hands! What has the future in store for me, if stones of my own age are already crumbling? I was angry, and I embraced the first opportunity to vent my spleen in the bailiff's presence. "It is clear," I cried, "that these plane-trees are neglected; they have no leaves. Their branches are so gnarled and shrivelled; the boles are so rough and unkempt! This would not happen, if someone loosened the earth at their feet, and watered them." The bailiff swore by my protecting deity that "he was doing everything possible, and never relaxed his efforts, but those trees were old." Between you and me, I had planted those trees myself, I had seen them in their first leaf. Then I turned to the door and asked: "Who is that broken-down dotard? You have done well to place him at the entrance; for he is outward bound.* Where did

* A jesting allusion to the Roman funeral; the corpse's feet pointing towards the door.

you get him? What pleasure did it give you to take up for burial some other man's dead?"* But the slave said: "Don't you know me, sir? I am Felicio; you used to bring me little images.** My father was Philositus the steward, and I am your pet slave." "The man is clean crazy," I remarked. "Has my pet slave become a little boy again? But it is quite possible; his teeth are just dropping out."***

I owe it to my country-place that my old age became apparent whithersoever I turned. Let us cherish and love old age; for it is full of pleasure if one knows how to use it. Fruits are most welcome when almost over; youth is most charming at its close; the last drink delights the toper,—the glass which souses him and puts the finishing touch on his drunkenness. Each pleasure reserves to the end the greatest delights which it contains. Life is most delightful when it is on the downward slope, but has not yet reached the abrupt decline. And I myself believe that the period which stands, so to speak, on the edge of the roof, possesses pleasures of its own. Or else the very fact of our not wanting pleasures has taken the place of the pleasures themselves. How comforting it is to have tired out one's appetites, and to have done with them! "But," you say, "it is a nuisance to be looking death in the face!" Death, however, should be looked in the face by young and old alike. We are not summoned according to our rating on the censor's list.**** Moreover, no one is so old that it would be improper for him to hope for another day of existence. And one day, mind you, is a stage on life's journey.

Our span of life is divided into parts; it consists of large circles enclosing smaller. One circle embraces and bounds the rest; it reaches from birth to the last day of existence. The next circle limits the period of our young manhood. The third confines all of childhood in its circumference. Again, there is, in a class by itself, the year; it contains

---

* His former owner should have kept him and buried him.

** Small figures, generally of terra-cotta, were frequently given to children as presents at the Saturnalia. Cf. Macrobius, i. 11. 49 *sigila . . . pro se atque suis piaculum.*

*** i.e., the old slave resembles a child in that he is losing his teeth (but for the second time).

**** i.e., *seniores*, as contrasted with *iuniores.*

within itself all the divisions of time by the multiplication of which we get the total of life. The month is bounded by a narrower ring. The smallest circle of all is the day; but even a day has its beginning and its ending, its sunrise and its sunset. Hence Heraclitus, whose obscure style gave him his surname,* remarked: "One day is equal to every day." Different persons have interpreted the saying in different ways. Some hold that days are equal in number of hours, and this is true; for if by "day" we mean twenty-four hours' time, all days must be equal, inasmuch as the night acquires what the day loses. But others maintain that one day is equal to all days through resemblance, because the very longest space of time possesses no element which cannot be found in a single day,—namely, light and darkness,—and even to eternity day makes these alternations** more numerous, not different when it is shorter and different again when it is longer. Hence, every day ought to be regulated as if it closed the series, as if it rounded out and completed our existence.

Pacuvius, who by long occupancy made Syria his own,*** used to hold a regular burial sacrifice in his own honour, with wine and the usual funeral feasting, and then would have himself carried from the dining room to his chamber, while eunuchs applauded and sang in Greek to a musical accompaniment: "He has lived his life, he has lived his life!" Thus Pacuvius had himself carried out to burial every day. Let us, however, do from a good motive what he used to do from a debased motive; let us go to our sleep with joy and gladness; let us say:

I have lived; the course which Fortune set for me
Is finished.****

---

* ὁ σκοτεινός, "the Obscure," Frag. 106 Diels[2].

** i.e., of light and darkness.

*** *Usus* was the mere enjoyment of a piece of property; *dominium* was the exclusive right to its control. Possession for one, or two, years conferred ownership. See Leage, *Roman Private Law*, pp. 133, 152, and 164. Although Pacuvius was governor so long that the province seemed to belong to him, yet he knew he might die any day.

**** Vergil, *Aeneid*, iv. 653.

And if God is pleased to add another day, we should welcome it with glad hearts. That man is happiest, and is secure in his own possession of himself, who can await the morrow without apprehension. When a man has said: "I have lived!", every morning he arises he receives a bonus.

But now I ought to close my letter. "What?" you say; "shall it come to me without any little offering?" Be not afraid; it brings something,—nay, more than something, a great deal. For what is more noble than the following saying* of which I make this letter the bearer: "It is wrong to live under constraint; but no man is constrained to live under constraint." Of course not. On all sides lie many short and simple paths to freedom; and let us thank God that no man can be kept in life. We may spurn the very constraints that hold us. "Epicurus," you reply, "uttered these words; what are you doing with another's property?" Any truth, I maintain, is my own property. And I shall continue to heap quotations from Epicurus upon you, so that all persons who swear by the words of another, and put a value upon the speaker and not upon the thing spoken, may understand that the best ideas are common property. Farewell.

---

* Epicurus, Sprüche, 9 Wokte.

LETTER

15

On Brawn and Brains

The old Romans had a custom which survived even into my lifetime. They would add to the opening words of a letter: "If you are well, it is well; I also am well." Persons like ourselves would do well to say: "If you are studying philosophy, it is well." For this is just what "being well" means. Without philosophy the mind is sickly, and the body, too, though it may be very powerful, is strong only as that of a madman or a lunatic is strong. This, then, is the sort of health you should primarily cultivate; the other kind of health comes second, and will involve little effort, if you wish to be well physically. It is indeed foolish, my dear Lucilius, and very unsuitable for a cultivated man, to work hard over developing the muscles and broadening the shoulders and strengthening the lungs. For although your heavy feeding produce good results and your sinews grow solid, you can never be a match, either in strength or in weight, for a first-class bull. Besides, by overloading the body with food you strangle the soul and render it less active. Accordingly, limit the flesh as much as possible, and allow free play to the spirit. Many inconveniences beset those who devote themselves to such pursuits. In the first place, they have their exercises, at which they must work and waste their life-force and render it less fit to bear a strain or the severer studies. Second, their keen edge is dulled by heavy eating. Besides, they must take orders from slaves of the vilest stamp,—men who alternate between the oil-flask[*] and the flagon, whose day passes satisfactorily if they have got up a good perspiration and quaffed, to make good what they have lost in sweat, huge draughts of liquor which will sink deeper because of their fasting. Drinking and sweating,—it's the life of a dyspeptic![**]

Now there are short and simple exercises which tire the body rapidly, and so save our time; and time is something of which we ought to keep strict account. These exercises are running, brandishing weights, and jumping,—high-jumping or broad-jumping, or the kind which I may call, "the Priest's dance,"[***] or, in slighting terms, "the clothes-cleaner's jump."[****] Select for practice any one of these, and you will find it plain and easy. But whatever you do, come back soon from body to mind. The mind must be exercised both day and night, for it is nourished by moderate labour; and this form of exercise need not be hampered by cold or hot weather, or even by old age. Cultivate that good which improves with the years. Of course I do not command you to be always bending over your books and your writing materials; the mind must have a change,—but a change of such a kind that it is not unnerved, but merely unbent. Riding in a litter shakes up the body, and does not interfere with study; one may read, dictate, converse, or listen to another; nor does walking prevent any of these things.

You need not scorn voice-culture; but I forbid you to practise raising and lowering your voice by scales and specific intonations. What if you should next propose to take lessons in walking! If you consult the sort of person whom starvation has taught new tricks, you will have someone to regulate your steps, watch every mouthful as you eat,

---

* i.e., the prize-ring; the contestants were rubbed with oil before the fight began.

** *Cardiacus* meant, according to Pliny, *N. H.* xxiii. 1. 24, a sort of dyspepsia accompanied by fever and perspiration. Compare the man in Juvenal v. 32, who will not send a spoonful of wine to a friend ill of this complaint.

*** Named from the Salii, or leaping priests of Mars.

**** The fuller, or washerman, cleansed the clothes by leaping and stamping upon them in the tub.

and go to such lengths as you yourself, by enduring him and believing in him, have encouraged his effrontery to go. "What, then?" you will ask; "is my voice to begin at the outset with shouting and straining the lungs to the utmost?" No; the natural thing is that it be aroused to such a pitch by easy stages, just as persons who are wrangling begin with ordinary conversational tones and then pass to shouting at the top of their lungs. No speaker cries "Help me, citizens!" at the outset of his speech. Therefore, whenever your spirit's impulse prompts you, raise a hubbub, now in louder now in milder tones, according as your voice, as well as your spirit, shall suggest to you, when you are moved to such a performance. Then let your voice, when you rein it in and call it back to earth, come down gently, not collapse; it should trail off in tones half way between high and low, and should not abruptly drop from its raving in the uncouth manner of countrymen. For our purpose is, not to give the voice exercise, but to make it give us exercise.

You see, I have relieved you of no slight bother; and I shall throw in a little complementary present,—it is Greek, too. Here is the proverb; it is an excellent one: "The fool's life is empty of gratitude and full of fears; its course lies wholly toward the future." "Who uttered these words?" you say. The same writer whom I mentioned before.* And what sort of life do you think is meant by the fool's life? That of Baba and Isio?** No; he means our own, for we are plunged by our blind desires into ventures which will harm us, but certainly will never satisfy us; for if we could be satisfied with anything, we should have been satisfied long ago; nor do we reflect how pleasant it is to demand nothing, how noble it is to be contented and not to be dependent upon Fortune. Therefore continually remind yourself, Lucilius, how many ambitions you have attained. When you see many ahead of you, think how many are behind! If you would thank the gods, and be grateful for your past life, you should contemplate how many men you have outstripped. But what have you to do with the others? You have outstripped yourself.

---

* Epicurus, Frag. 491 Usener.

** Court fools of the period.

Fix a limit which you will not even desire to pass, should you have the power. At last, then, away with all these treacherous goods! They look better to those who hope for them than to those who have attained them. If there were anything substantial in them, they would sooner or later satisfy you; as it is, they merely rouse the drinkers' thirst. Away with fripperies which only serve for show! As to what the future's uncertain lot has in store, why should I demand of Fortune that she give, rather than demand of myself that I should not crave? And why should l crave? Shall I heap up my winnings, and forget that man's lot is unsubstantial? For what end should I toil? Lo, today is the last; if not, it is near the last. Farewell.

LETTER

16

On Philosophy, the Guide of Life

It is clear to you, I am sure, Lucilius, that no man can live a happy life, or even a supportable life, without the study of wisdom; you know also that a happy life is reached when our wisdom is brought to completion, but that life is at least endurable even when our wisdom is only begun. This idea, however, clear though it is, must be strengthened and implanted more deeply by daily reflection; it is more important for you to keep the resolutions you have already made than to go on and make noble ones. You must persevere, must develop new strength by continuous study, until that which is only a good inclination becomes a good settled purpose. Hence you no longer need to come to me with much talk and protestations; I know that you have made great progress. I understand the feelings which prompt your words; they are not feigned or specious words. Nevertheless I shall tell you what I think,—that at present I have hopes for you, but not yet perfect trust. And I wish that you would adopt the same attitude towards yourself; there is no reason why you should put confidence in yourself too quickly and readily. Examine yourself; scrutinize and observe yourself in divers ways; but mark, before all else, whether it is in philosophy or merely in life itself* that you have

* i.e., have merely advanced in years.

made progress. Philosophy is no trick to catch the public; it is not devised for show. It is a matter, not of words, but of facts. It is not pursued in order that the day may yield some amusement before it is spent, or that our leisure may be relieved of a tedium that irks us. It moulds and constructs the soul; it orders our life, guides our conduct, shows us what we should do and what we should leave undone; it sits at the helm and directs our course as we waver amid uncertainties. Without it, no one can live fearlessly or in peace of mind. Countless things that happen every hour call for advice; and such advice is to be sought in philosophy.

Perhaps someone will say: "How can philosophy help me, if Fate exists? Of what avail is philosophy, if God rules the universe? Of what avail is it, if Chance governs everything? For not only is it impossible to change things that are determined, but it is also impossible to plan beforehand against what is undetermined; either God has forestalled my plans, and decided what I am to do, or else Fortune gives no free play to my plans." Whether the truth, Lucilius, lies in one or in all of these views, we must be philosophers; whether Fate binds us down by an inexorable law, or whether God as arbiter of the universe has arranged everything, or whether Chance drives and tosses human affairs without method, philosophy ought to be our defence. She will encourage us to obey God cheerfully, but Fortune defiantly; she will teach us to follow God and endure Chance. But it is not my purpose now to be led into a discussion as to what is within our own control,—if foreknowledge is supreme, or if a chain of fated events drags us along in its clutches, or if the sudden and the unexpected play the tyrant over us; I return now to my warning and my exhortation, that you should not allow the impulse of your spirit to weaken and grow cold. Hold fast to it and establish it firmly, in order that what is now impulse may become a habit of the mind.

If I know you well, you have already been trying to find out, from the very beginning of my letter, what little contribution it brings to you. Sift the letter, and you will find it. You need not wonder at any genius of mine; for as yet I am lavish only with other men's property.—But why did I say "other men"? Whatever is well said by anyone is mine.—

This also is a saying of Epicurus:* "If you live according to nature, you will never be poor; if you live according to opinion, you will never be rich." Nature's wants are slight; the demands of opinion are boundless. Suppose that the property of many millionaires is heaped up in your possession. Assume that fortune carries you far beyond the limits of a private income, decks you with gold, clothes you in purple, and brings you to such a degree of luxury and wealth that you can bury the earth under your marble floors; that you may not only possess, but tread upon, riches. Add statues, paintings, and whatever any art has devised for the satisfaction of luxury; you will only learn from such things to crave still greater.

Natural desires are limited; but those which spring from false opinion can have no stopping-point. The false has no limits. When you are travelling on a road, there must be an end; but when astray, your wanderings are limitless. Recall your steps, therefore, from idle things, and when you would know whether that which you seek is based upon a natural or upon a misleading desire, consider whether it can stop at any definite point. If you find, after having travelled far, that there is a more distant goal always in view, you may be sure that this condition is contrary to nature. Farewell.

---

* Frag. 201 Usener.

LETTER

18

On Festivals and Fasting

It is the month of December, and yet the city is at this very moment in a sweat. Licence is given to the general merrymaking. Everything resounds with mighty preparations,—as if the Saturnalia differed at all from the usual business day! So true it is that the difference is nil, that I regard as correct the remark of the man who said: "Once December was a month; now it is a year."*

If I had you with me, I should be glad to consult you and find out what you think should be done,—whether we ought to make no change in our daily routine, or whether, in order not to be out of sympathy with the ways of the public, we should dine in gayer fashion and doff the toga.** As it is now, we Romans have changed our dress for the sake of pleasure and holiday-making, though in former times that was only customary when the State was disturbed and had fallen on evil days. I am sure that, if I know you aright, playing the part of an umpire you would have wished that we should be neither like the liberty-capped***

---

* i.e., the whole year is a Saturnalia.

** For a dinner dress.

*** The *pilleus* was worn by newly freed slaves and by the Roman populace on festal occasions.

throng in all ways, nor in all ways unlike them; unless, perhaps, this is just the season when we ought to lay down the law to the soul, and bid it be alone in refraining from pleasures just when the whole mob has let itself go in pleasures; for this is the surest proof which a man can get of his own constancy, if he neither seeks the things which are seductive and allure him to luxury, nor is led into them. It shows much more courage to remain dry and sober when the mob is drunk and vomiting; but it shows greater self-control to refuse to withdraw oneself and to do what the crowd does, but in a different way,—thus neither making oneself conspicuous nor becoming one of the crowd. For one may keep holiday without extravagance.

I am so firmly determined, however, to test the constancy of your mind that, drawing from the teachings of great men, I shall give you also a lesson: Set aside a certain number of days, during which you shall be content with the scantiest and cheapest fare, with coarse and rough dress, saying to yourself the while: "Is this the condition that I feared?" It is precisely in times of immunity from care that the soul should toughen itself beforehand for occasions of greater stress, and it is while Fortune is kind that it should fortify itself against her violence. In days of peace the soldier performs manœuvres, throws up earthworks with no enemy in sight, and wearies himself by gratuitous toil, in order that he may be equal to unavoidable toil. If you would not have a man flinch when the crisis comes, train him before it comes. Such is the course which those men* have followed who, in their imitation of poverty, have every month come almost to want, that they might never recoil from what they had so often rehearsed.

* The Epicurians. Cf. § 9 and Epicurus, Frag. 158. Usener.

You need not suppose that I mean meals like Timon's, or "paupers' huts,"* or any other device which luxurious millionaires use to beguile the tedium of their lives. Let the pallet be a real one, and the coarse cloak; let the bread be hard and grimy. Endure all this for three or four days at a time, sometimes for more, so that it may be a test of yourself instead of a mere hobby. Then, I assure you, my dear Lucilius, you will leap for joy when filled with a pennyworth of food, and you will understand that a man's peace of mind does not depend upon Fortune; for, even when angry she grants enough for our needs.

There is no reason, however, why you should think that you are doing anything great; for you will merely be doing what many thousands of slaves and many thousands of poor men are doing every day. But you may credit yourself with this item,—that you will not be doing it under compulsion, and that it will be as easy for you to endure it permanently as to make the experiment from time to time. Let us practise our strokes on the "dummy";** let us become intimate with poverty, so that Fortune may not catch us off our guard. We shall be rich with all the more comfort, if we once learn how far poverty is from being a burden.

Even Epicurus, the teacher of pleasure, used to observe stated intervals, during which he satisfied his hunger in niggardly fashion; he wished to see whether he thereby fell short of full and complete happiness, and, if so, by what amount he fell short, and whether this amount was worth purchasing at the price of great effort. At any rate, he makes such a statement in the well known letter written to Polyaenus in the archonship of Charinus.*** Indeed, he boasts that he himself lived on less than a penny, but that Metrodorus, whose progress was not yet so great, needed a whole penny. Do you think

* Cf. Ep. c. 6 and Martial, iii. 48.

** The post which gladiators used when preparing themselves for combats in the arena.

*** Usually identified with Chaerimus, 307-8 B.C. But Wilhelm, *Öster Jahreshefte*, V.136, has shown that there is probably no confusion of names. A Charinus was archon at Athens in 290-89; see Johnson, *Class. Phil.* ix. p. 256.

that there can be fullness on such fare? Yes, and there is pleasure also,—not that shifty and fleeting pleasure which needs a fillip now and then, but a pleasure that is steadfast and sure. For though water, barley-meal, and crusts of barley-bread, are not a cheerful diet, yet it is the highest kind of pleasure to be able to derive pleasure from this sort of food, and to have reduced one's needs to that modicum which no unfairness of Fortune can snatch away. Even prison fare is more generous; and those who have been set apart for capital punishment are not so meanly fed by the man who is to execute them. Therefore, what a noble soul must one have, to descend of one's own free will to a diet which even those who have been sentenced to death have not to fear! This is indeed forestalling the spear-thrusts of Fortune.

So begin, my dear Lucilius, to follow the custom of these men, and set apart certain days on which you shall withdraw from your business and make yourself at home with the scantiest fare. Establish business relations with poverty.

> Dare, O my friend, to scorn the sight of wealth,
> And mould thyself to kinship with thy God.*

For he alone is in kinship with God who has scorned wealth. Of course I do not forbid you to possess it, but I would have you reach the point at which you possess it dauntlessly; this can be accomplished only by persuading yourself that you can live happily without it as well as with it, and by regarding riches always as likely to elude you.

But now I must begin to fold up my letter. "Settle your debts first," you cry. Here is a draft on Epicurus; he will pay down the sum: "Ungoverned anger begets madness."** You cannot help knowing the truth of these words, since you have had not only slaves, but also enemies. But indeed this emotion blazes out against all sorts of persons; it springs from love as much as from hate, and shows itself not less in serious matters than in jest and sport. And it makes no

---

* Vergil, *Aeneid*, viii. 364 f.

** Frag. 484 Usener.

difference how important the provocation may be, but into what kind of soul it penetrates. Similarly with fire; it does not matter how great is the flame, but what it falls upon. For solid timbers have repelled a very great fire; conversely, dry and easily inflammable stuff nourishes the slightest spark into a conflagration. So it is with anger, my dear Lucilius; the outcome of a mighty anger is madness, and hence anger should be avoided, not merely that we may escape excess, but that we may have a healthy mind. Farewell.

LETTER

26

On Old Age and Death

I was just lately telling you that I was within sight of old age.* I am now afraid that I have left old age behind me. For some other word would now apply to my years, or at any rate to my body; since old age means a time of life that is weary rather than crushed. You may rate me in the worn-out class,—of those who are nearing the end.

Nevertheless, I offer thanks to myself, with you as witness; for I feel that age has done no damage to my mind, though I feel its effects on my constitution. Only my vices, and the outward aids to these vices, have reached senility; my mind is strong and rejoices that it has but slight connexion with the body. It has laid aside the greater part of its load. It is alert; it takes issue with me on the subject of old age; it declares that old age is its time of bloom. Let me take it at its word, and let it make the most of the advantages it possesses. The mind bids me do some thinking and consider how much of this peace of spirit and moderation of character I owe to wisdom and how much to my time of life; it bids me distinguish carefully what I cannot do and what I do

* See the twelfth letter. Seneca was by this time at least sixty-five years old, and probably older.

not want to do . . . .* For why should one complain or regard it as a disadvantage, if powers which ought to come to an end have failed? "But," you say, "it is the greatest possible disadvantage to be worn out and to die off, or rather, if I may speak literally, to melt away! For we are not suddenly smitten and laid low; we are worn away, and every day reduces our powers to a certain extent."

But is there any better end to it all than to glide off to one's proper haven, when nature slips the cable? Not that there is anything painful in a shock and a sudden departure from existence; it is merely because this other way of departure is easy,—a gradual withdrawal. I, at any rate, as if the test were at hand and the day were come which is to pronounce its decision concerning all the years of my life, watch over myself and commune thus with myself: "The showing which we have made up to the present time, in word or deed, counts for nothing. All this is but a trifling and deceitful pledge of our spirit, and is wrapped in much charlatanism. I shall leave it to Death to determine what progress I have made. Therefore with no faint heart I am making ready for the day when, putting aside all stage artifice and actor's rouge, I am to pass judgment upon myself,—whether I am merely declaiming brave sentiments, or whether I really feel them; whether all the bold threats I have uttered against fortune are a pretence and a farce. Put aside the opinion of the world; it is always wavering and always takes both sides. Put aside the studies which you have pursued throughout your life; Death will deliver the final judgment in your case. This is what I mean: your debates and learned talks, your maxims gathered from the teachings of the wise, your cultured conversation,—all these afford no proof of the real strength of your soul. Even the most timid man can deliver a bold speech. What you have done in the past will be manifest only at the time when you draw your last breath. I accept the terms; I do not shrink from the decision." This is what I say to myself, but I would have you think that I have said it to you also. You are younger; but what does that matter? There is no fixed count of

* This passage is hopelessly corrupt. The course of the argument requires something like this: For it is just as much to my advantage not to be able to do what I do not want to do, as it is to be able to do whatever gives me pleasure.

our years. You do not know where death awaits you; so be ready for it everywhere.

I was just intending to stop, and my hand was making ready for the closing sentence; but the rites are still to be performed and the travelling money for the letter disbursed. And just assume that I am not telling where I intend to borrow the necessary sum; you know upon whose coffers I depend. Wait for me but a moment, and I will pay you from my own account;* meanwhile, Epicurus will oblige me with these words:** "Think on death," or rather, if you prefer the phrase, on "migration to heaven." The meaning is clear,—that it is a wonderful thing to learn thoroughly how to die. You may deem it superfluous to learn a text that can be used only once; but that is just the reason why we ought to think on a thing. When we can never prove whether we really know a thing, we must always be learning it. "Think on death." In saying this, he bids us think on freedom. He who has learned to die has unlearned slavery; he is above any external power, or, at any rate, he is beyond it. What terrors have prisons and bonds and bars for him? His way out is clear. There is only one chain which binds us to life, and that is the love of life. The chain may not be cast off, but it may be rubbed away, so that, when necessity shall demand, nothing may retard or hinder us from being ready to do at once that which at some time we are bound to do. Farewell.

---

* i.e., the money will be brought from home,—the saying will be one of Seneca's own.

** Epicurus, Frag. 205 Usener.

LETTER

27

On the Good which Abides

"What," say you, "are you giving me advice? Indeed, have you already advised yourself, already corrected your own faults? Is this the reason why you have leisure to reform other men?" No, I am not so shameless as to undertake to cure my fellow-men when I am ill myself. I am, however, discussing with you troubles which concern us both, and sharing the remedy with you, just as if we were lying ill in the same hospital. Listen to me, therefore, as you would if I were talking to myself. I am admitting you to my inmost thoughts, and am having it out with myself, merely making use of you as my pretext. I keep crying out to myself: "Count your years, and you will be ashamed to desire and pursue the same things you desired in your boyhood days. Of this one thing make sure against your dying day,—let your faults die before you die. Away with those disordered pleasures, which must be dearly paid for; it is not only those which are to come that harm me, but also those which have come and gone. Just as crimes, even if they have not been detected when they were committed, do not allow anxiety to end with them; so with guilty pleasures, regret remains even after the pleasures are over. They are not substantial, they are not trustworthy; even if they do not harm us, they are fleeting. Cast about rather for some good which will abide. But there can be no such good except as the soul discovers it for itself within itself. Virtue alone affords everlasting and peace-giving joy; even if some obstacle arise, it is but like an intervening cloud, which floats beneath the sun but never prevails against it."

When will it be your lot to attain this joy? Thus far, you have indeed not been sluggish, but you must quicken your pace. Much toil remains; to confront it, you must yourself lavish all your waking hours, and all your efforts, if you wish the result to be accomplished. This matter cannot be delegated to someone else. The other kind of literary activity* admits of outside assistance. Within our own time there was a certain rich man named Calvisius Sabinus; he had the bank-account and the brains of a freedman.** I never saw a man whose good fortune was a greater offence against propriety. His memory was so faulty that he would sometimes forget the name of Ulysses, or Achilles, or Priam,—names which we know as well as we know those of our own attendants. No major-domo in his dotage, who cannot give men their right names, but is compelled to invent names for them,—no such man, I say, calls off the names*** of his master's tribesmen so atrociously as Sabinus used to call off the Trojan and Achaean heroes. But none the less did he desire to appear learned. So he devised this short cut to learning: he paid fabulous prices for slaves,—one to know Homer by heart and another to know Hesiod; he also delegated a special slave to each of the nine lyric poets. You need not wonder that he paid high prices for these slaves; if he did not find them ready to hand he had them made to order. After collecting this retinue, he began to make life miserable for his guests; he would keep these fellows at the foot of his couch, and ask them from time to time for verses which he might repeat, and then frequently break down in the middle of a word. Satellius Quadratus, a feeder, and consequently

---

* i.e., ordinary studies, or literature, as contrasted with philosophy.

** Compare with the following the vulgarities of Trimalchio in the Satire of Petronius, and the bad taste of Nasidienus in Horace (*Sat.* ii. 8).

*** At the *salutatio*, or morning call. The position of *nomenclator*, "caller-of-names," was originally devoted more strictly to political purposes. Here it is primarily social.

a fawner, upon addle-pated millionaires, and also (for this quality goes with the other two) a flouter of them, suggested to Sabinus that he should have philologists to gather up the bits.* Sabinus remarked that each slave cost him one hundred thousand sesterces; Satellius replied: "You might have bought as many book-cases for a smaller sum." But Sabinus held to the opinion that what any member of his household knew, he himself knew also. This same Satellius began to advise Sabinus to take wrestling lessons,—sickly, pale, and thin as he was, Sabinus answered: "How can I? I can scarcely stay alive now." "Don't say that, I implore you," replied the other, "consider how many perfectly healthy slaves you have!" No man is able to borrow or buy a sound mind; in fact, as it seems to me, even though sound minds were for sale, they would not find buyers. Depraved minds, however, are bought and sold every day.

But let me pay off my debt and say farewell: "Real wealth is poverty adjusted to the law of Nature."** Epicurus has this saying in various ways and contexts; but it can never be repeated too often, since it can never be learned too well. For some persons the remedy should be merely prescribed; in the case of others, it should be forced down their throats. Farewell.

* i.e., all the ideas that dropped out of the head of Sabinus. The slave who picked up the crumbs was called *analecta.*

** Epicurus, Frag. 477 Usener.

LETTER

28

On Travel as a Cure for Discontent

Do you suppose that you alone have had this experience? Are you surprised, as if it were a novelty, that after such long travel and so many changes of scene you have not been able to shake off the gloom and heaviness of your mind? You need a change of soul rather than a change of climate.* Though you may cross vast spaces of sea, and though, as our Vergil** remarks,

Lands and cities are left astern,

your faults will follow you whithersoever you travel. Socrates made the same remark to one who complained; he said: "Why do you wonder that globe-trotting does not help you, seeing that you always take yourself with you? The reason which set you wandering is ever at your heels." What pleasure is there in seeing new lands? Or in surveying cities and spots of interest? All your bustle is useless. Do you ask why such flight does not help you? It is because you flee along with yourself. You must lay aside the

* Cf. Horace, *Ep.* i. 11, 27 *caelum non animum mutant qui trans mare currunt.*

** *Aeneid*, iii. 72.

burdens of the mind; until you do this, no place will satisfy you. Reflect that your present behaviour is like that of the prophetess whom Vergil describes:* she is excited and goaded into fury, and contains within herself much inspiration that is not her own:

> The priestess raves, if haply she may shake
> The great god from her heart.

You wander hither and yon, to rid yourself of the burden that rests upon you, though it becomes more troublesome by reason of your very restlessness, just as in a ship the cargo when stationary makes no trouble, but when it shifts to this side or that, it causes the vessel to heel more quickly in the direction where it has settled. Anything you do tells against you, and you hurt yourself by your very unrest; for you are shaking up a sick man.

That trouble once removed, all change of scene will become pleasant; though you may be driven to the uttermost ends of the earth, in whatever corner of a savage land you may find yourself, that place, however forbidding, will be to you a hospitable abode. The person you are matters more than the place to which you go; for that reason we should not make the mind a bondsman to any one place. Live in this belief: "I am not born for any one corner of the universe; this whole world is my country." If you saw this fact clearly, you would not be surprised at getting no benefit from the fresh scenes to which you roam each time through weariness of the old scenes. For the first would have pleased you in each case, had you believed it wholly yours.** As it is, however, you are not journeying; you are drifting and being driven, only exchanging one place for another, although that which you seek,—to live well,—is found everywhere.*** Can there be any spot so full of confusion as the Forum? Yet you can live quietly

* *Aeneid*, vi. 78 f.

** i.e., had you been able to say *patria mea totus mundus est.*

*** Cf. Horace, *Ep.* i. 11, 28—*navibus atque Quadrigis petimus bene vivere; quod petis, hic est.*

even there, if necessary. Of course, if one were allowed to make one's own arrangements, I should flee far from the very sight and neighbourhood of the Forum. For just as pestilential places assail even the strongest constitution, so there are some places which are also unwholesome for a healthy mind which is not yet quite sound, though recovering from its ailment. I disagree with those who strike out into the midst of the billows and, welcoming a stormy existence, wrestle daily in hardihood of soul with life's problems. The wise man will endure all that, but will not choose it; he will prefer to be at peace rather than at war. It helps little to have cast out your own faults if you must quarrel with those of others. Says one: "There were thirty tyrants surrounding Socrates, and yet they could not break his spirit"; but what does it matter how many masters a man has? "Slavery" has no plural; and he who has scorned it is free,—no matter amid how large a mob of over-lords he stands.

It is time to stop, but not before I have paid duty. "The knowledge of sin is the beginning of salvation." This saying of Epicurus* seems to me to be a noble one. For he who does not know that he has sinned does not desire correction; you must discover yourself in the wrong before you can reform yourself. Some boast of their faults. Do you think that the man has any thought of mending his ways who counts over his vices as if they were virtues? Therefore, as far as possible, prove yourself guilty, hunt up charges against yourself; play the part, first of accuser, then of judge, last of intercessor. At times be harsh with yourself.** Farewell.

---

* Frag. 522 Usener.

** i.e., refuse your own intercession.

LETTER

33

On the Futility of Learning Maxims

You wish me to close these letters also, as I closed my former letters, with certain utterances taken from the chiefs of our school. But they did not interest themselves in choice extracts; the whole texture of their work is full of strength. There is unevenness, you know, when some objects rise conspicuous above others. A single tree is not remarkable if the whole forest rises to the same height. Poetry is crammed with utterances of this sort, and so is history. For this reason I would not have you think that these utterances belong to Epicurus: they are common property and are emphatically our own.* They are, however, more noteworthy in Epicurus, because they appear at infrequent intervals and when you do not expect them, and because it is surprising that brave words should be spoken at any time by a man who made a practice of being effeminate. For that is what most persons maintain. In my own opinion, however, Epicurus is really a brave man, even though he did wear long sleeves.** Fortitude, energy, and

---

* Stoic as well as Epicurean.

** Contrasted with *alte cinctos*. The sleeveless and "girt-up" tunic is the sign of energy; cf. Horace, *Sat.* i. 5. 5, and Suetonius, *Caligula*, 52: the effeminate Caligula would "appear in public with a long-sleeved tunic and bracelets."

readiness for battle are to be found among the Persians,* just as much as among men who have girded themselves up high.

Therefore, you need not call upon me for extracts and quotations; such thoughts as one may extract here and there in the works of other philosophers run through the whole body of our writings. Hence we have no "show-window goods," nor do we deceive the purchaser in such a way that, if he enters our shop, he will find nothing except that which is displayed in the window. We allow the purchasers themselves to get their samples from anywhere they please. Suppose we should desire to sort out each separate motto from the general stock; to whom shall we credit them? To Zeno, Cleanthes, Chrysippus, Panaetius, or Posidonius? We Stoics are not subjects of a despot: each of us lays claim to his own freedom. With them,** on the other hand, whatever Hermarchus says, or Metrodorus, is ascribed to one source. In that brotherhood, everything that any man utters is spoken under the leadership and commanding authority*** of one alone. We cannot, I maintain, no matter how we try, pick out anything from so great a multitude of things equally good.

Only the poor man counts his flock.****

Wherever you direct your gaze, you will meet with something that might stand out from the rest, if the context in which you read it were not equally notable.

For this reason, give over hoping that you can skim, by means of epitomes, the wisdom of distinguished men. Look into their wisdom as a whole; study it as a whole. They are working out a plan and weaving together, line upon line, a masterpiece, from which nothing

---

* Who wore sleeves.

** i.e., the Epicureans.

*** For the phrase *ductu et auspiciis* see Plautus, *Amph.* i. 1. 41 *ut gesserit rem publicam ductu imperio auspicio suo*; and Horace, *Od.* i. 7. 27 *Teucro duce et auspice Teucro.* The original significance of the phrase refers to the right of the commander-in-chief to take the auspices.

**** Ovid, *Metamorphosis*, xiii. 824.

can be taken away without injury to the whole. Examine the separate parts, if you like, provided you examine them as parts of the man himself. She is not a beautiful woman whose ankle or arm is praised, but she whose general appearance makes you forget to admire her single attributes.

If you insist, however, I shall not be niggardly with you, but lavish; for there is a huge multitude of these passages; they are scattered about in profusion,—they do not need to be gathered together, but merely to be picked up. They do not drip forth occasionally; they flow continuously. They are unbroken and are closely connected. Doubtless they would be of much benefit to those who are still novices and worshipping outside the shrine; for single maxims sink in more easily when they are marked off and bounded like a line of verse. That is why we give to children a proverb, or that which the Greeks call *Chria*,* to be learned by heart; that sort of thing can be comprehended by the young mind, which cannot as yet hold more. For a man, however, whose progress is definite, to chase after choice extracts and to prop his weakness by the best known and the briefest sayings and to depend upon his memory, is disgraceful; it is time for him to lean on himself. He should make such maxims and not memorize them. For it is disgraceful even for an old man, or one who has sighted old age, to have a note-book knowledge. "This is what Zeno said." But what have you yourself said? "This is the opinion of Cleanthes." But what is your own opinion? How long shall you march under another man's orders? Take command, and utter some word which posterity will remember. Put forth something from your own stock. For this reason I hold that there is nothing of eminence in all such men as these, who never create anything themselves, but always lurk in the shadow of others, playing the rôle of interpreters, never daring to put once into practice what they have been so long in learning. They have exercised their memories on other men's material. But it is one thing to remember, another to know. Remembering is merely safeguarding something entrusted to

---

* Either "maxims" or "outlines," "themes." For a discussion of them see Quintilian, *Inst. Orat.* i. 9. 3 ff.

the memory; knowing, however, means making everything your own; it means not depending upon the copy and not all the time glancing back at the master. "Thus said Zeno, thus said Cleanthes, indeed!" Let there be a difference between yourself and your book! How long shall you be a learner? From now on be a teacher as well! "But why," one asks,* "should I have to continue hearing lectures on what I can read?" "The living voice," one replies, "is a great help." Perhaps, but not the voice which merely makes itself the mouthpiece of another's words, and only performs the duty of a reporter.

Consider this fact also. Those who have never attained their mental independence begin, in the first place, by following the leader in cases where everyone has deserted the leader; then, in the second place, they follow him in matters where the truth is still being investigated. However, the truth will never be discovered if we rest contented with discoveries already made. Besides, he who follows another not only discovers nothing but is not even investigating. What then? Shall I not follow in the footsteps of my predecessors? I shall indeed use the old road, but if I find one that makes a shorter cut and is smoother to travel, I shall open the new road. Men who have made these discoveries before us are not our masters, but our guides. Truth lies open for all; it has not yet been monopolized. And there is plenty of it left even for posterity to discover. Farewell.

---

* The objector is the assumed auditor. The answer to the objection gives the usual view as to the power of the living voice; to this Seneca assents, provided that the voice has a message of its own.

LETTER

38

On Quiet Conversation

You are right when you urge that we increase our mutual traffic in letters. But the greatest benefit is to be derived from conversation, because it creeps by degrees into the soul. Lectures prepared beforehand and spouted in the presence of a throng have in them more noise but less intimacy. Philosophy is good advice; and no one can give advice at the top of his lungs. Of course we must sometimes also make use of these harangues, if I may so call them, when a doubting member needs to be spurred on; but when the aim is to make a man learn, and not merely to make him wish to learn, we must have recourse to the low-toned words of conversation. They enter more easily, and stick in the memory; for we do not need many words, but, rather, effective words.

Words should be scattered like seed; no matter how small the seed may be, if it has once found favourable ground, it unfolds its strength and from an insignificant thing spreads to its greatest growth. Reason grows in the same way; it is not large to the outward view, but increases as it does its work. Few words are spoken; but if the mind has truly caught them, they come into their strength and spring up. Yes, precepts and seeds have the same quality; they produce much, and yet they are slight things. Only, as I said, let a favourable mind receive and assimilate them. Then of itself the mind also will produce bounteously in its turn, giving back more than it has received. Farewell.

LETTER

40

On the Proper Style for a Philosopher's Discourse

I thank you for writing to me so often; for you are revealing your real self to me in the only way you can. I never receive a letter from you without being in your company forthwith. If the pictures of our absent friends are pleasing to us, though they only refresh the memory and lighten our longing by a solace that is unreal and unsubstantial, how much more pleasant is a letter, which brings us real traces, real evidences, of an absent friend! For that which is sweetest when we meet face to face is afforded by the impress of a friend's hand upon his letter,—recognition.

You write me that you heard a lecture by the philosopher Serapio,* when he landed at your present place of residence. "He is wont," you say, "to wrench up his words with a mighty rush, and he does not let them flow forth one by one, but makes them crowd and dash upon each other.** For the words come in such quantity that a single voice is inadequate to utter them." I do not approve

* This person cannot be identified.

** The explanation of Professor Summers seems sound, that the metaphor is taken from a mountain-torrent. Compare the description of Cratinus' style in Aristophanes, *Ach.* 526, or that of Pindar in Horace, *Od.* iv. 2. 5 ff.

of this in a philosopher; his speech, like his life, should be composed; and nothing that rushes headlong and is hurried is well ordered. That is why, in Homer, the rapid style, which sweeps down without a break like a snow-squall, is assigned to the younger speaker; from the old man eloquence flows gently, sweeter than honey.*

Therefore, mark my words; that forceful manner of speech, rapid and copious, is more suited to a mountebank than to a man who is discussing and teaching an important and serious subject. But I object just as strongly that he should drip out his words as that he should go at top speed; he should neither keep the ear on the stretch, nor deafen it. For that poverty-stricken and thin-spun style also makes the audience less attentive because they are weary of its stammering slowness; nevertheless, the word which has been long awaited sinks in more easily than the word which flits past us on the wing. Finally, people speak of "handing down" precepts to their pupils; but one is not "handing down" that which eludes the grasp. Besides, speech that deals with the truth should be unadorned and plain. This popular style has nothing to do with the truth; its aim is to impress the common herd, to ravish heedless ears by its speed; it does not offer itself for discussion, but snatches itself away from discussion. But how can that speech govern others which cannot itself be governed? May I not also remark that all speech which is employed for the purpose of healing our minds, ought to sink into us? Remedies do not avail unless they remain in the system.

Besides, this sort of speech contains a great deal of sheer emptiness; it has more sound than power. My terrors should be quieted, my irritations soothed, my illusions shaken off, my indulgences checked, my greed rebuked. And which of these cures can be brought about in a hurry? What physician can heal his patient on a flying visit? May I add that such a jargon of confused and ill-chosen words cannot afford pleasure, either? No; but just as you are well satisfied, in the majority of cases, to have seen through tricks which you did not think could

---

* *Iliad*, iii. 222 (Odysseus), and i. 249 (Nestor).

possibly be done*, so in the case of these word-gymnasts,—to have heard them once is amply sufficient. For what can a man desire to learn or to imitate in them? What is he to think of their souls, when their speech is sent into the charge in utter disorder, and cannot be kept in hand? Just as, when you run down hill, you cannot stop at the point where you had decided to stop, but your steps are carried along by the momentum of your body and are borne beyond the place where you wished to halt; so this speed of speech has no control over itself, nor is it seemly for philosophy; since philosophy should carefully place her words, not fling them out, and should proceed step by step.

"What then?" you say; "should not philosophy sometimes take a loftier tone?" Of course she should; but dignity of character should be preserved, and this is stripped away by such violent and excessive force. Let philosophy possess great forces, but kept well under control; let her stream flow unceasingly, but never become a torrent. And I should hardly allow even to an orator a rapidity of speech like this, which cannot be called back, which goes lawlessly ahead; for how could it be followed by jurors, who are often inexperienced and untrained? Even when the orator is carried away by his desire to show off his powers, or by uncontrollable emotion, even then he should not quicken his pace and heap up words to an extent greater than the ear can endure.

You will be acting rightly, therefore, if you do not regard those men who seek how much they may say, rather than how they shall say it, and if for yourself you choose, provided a choice must be made, to speak as Publius Vinicius the stammerer does. When Asellius was asked how Vinicius spoke, he replied: "Gradually"! (It was a remark of Geminus Varius, by the way: "I don't see how you can call that man 'eloquent'; why, he can't get out three words together.") Why, then, should you not choose to speak as Vinicius does? Though of course some wag may cross your path, like the person who said, when Vinicius was dragging out his words one by one, as if he were dictating and not speaking.

---

* Seneca's phrase, *quae fieri posse non crederes*, has been interpreted as a definition of παράδοξα. It is more probable, however, that he is comparing with the juggler's tricks the verbal performances of certain lecturers, whose jargon one marvels at but does not care to hear again.

"Say, haven't you anything to say?" And yet that were the better choice, for the rapidity of Quintus Haterius, the most famous orator of his age, is, in my opinion, to be avoided by a man of sense. Haterius never hesitated, never paused; he made only one start, and only one stop.

However, I suppose that certain styles of speech are more or less suitable to nations also; in a Greek you can put up with the unrestrained style, but we Romans, even when writing, have become accustomed to separate our words.* And our compatriot Cicero, with whom Roman oratory sprang into prominence, was also a slow pacer.** The Roman language is more inclined to take stock of itself, to weigh, and to offer something worth weighing. Fabianus, a man noteworthy because of his life, his knowledge, and, less important than either of these, his eloquence also, used to discuss a subject with dispatch rather than with haste; hence you might call it ease rather than speed. I approve this quality in the wise man; but I do not demand it; only let his speech proceed unhampered, though I prefer that it should be deliberately uttered rather than spouted.

However, I have this further reason for frightening you away from the latter malady, namely, that you could only be successful in practising this style by losing your sense of modesty; you would have to rub all shame from your countenance,*** and refuse to hear yourself speak. For that heedless flow will carry with it many expressions which you would wish to criticize. And, I repeat, you could not attain it and at the same time preserve your sense of shame. Moreover, you would need to practise every day, and transfer your attention from subject matter to words. But words, even if they came to you readily and flowed without any exertion on your part, yet would have to be kept under control. For just as a less ostentatious gait becomes a philosopher, so does a restrained style of speech, far removed from boldness. Therefore, the ultimate kernel of my remarks is this: I bid you be slow of speech. Farewell.

---

* The Greek texts were still written without separation of the words, in contrast with the Roman.

** *Gradarius* may be contrasted with *tolutarius*, "trotter." The word might also mean one who walks with dignified step, as in a religious procession.

*** Cf. Martial, xi. 27. 7 *aut cum perfricuit frontem posuitque pudorem.* After a violent rubbing, the face would not show blushes.

LETTER

41

On the God within Us

You are doing an excellent thing, one which will be wholesome for you, if, as you write me, you are persisting in your effort to attain sound understanding; it is foolish to pray for this when you can acquire it from yourself. We do not need to uplift our hands towards heaven, or to beg the keeper of a temple to let us approach his idol's ear, as if in this way our prayers were more likely to be heard. God is near you, he is with you, he is within you. This is what I mean, Lucilius: a holy spirit indwells within us, one who marks our good and bad deeds, and is our guardian. As we treat this spirit, so are we treated by it. Indeed, no man can be good without the help of God. Can one rise superior to fortune unless God helps him to rise? He it is that gives noble and upright counsel. In each good man

A god doth dwell, but what god know we not.*

If ever you have come upon a grove that is full of ancient trees which have grown to an unusual height, shutting out a view of the sky by a veil of pleached and intertwining branches, then

---

* Vergil, *Aeneid*, viii. 352, *Hoc nemus, hunc, inquit, frondoso vertice collem, Quis deus incertum est, habitat deus*, and cf. Quintillian, i. 10. 88, where he is speaking of Ennius, whom "*sicut sacros vetustate lucos adoremus, in quibus grandia et antiqua robora iam non tantum habent speciem quantem religionem.*"

the loftiness of the forest, the seclusion of the spot, and your marvel at the thick unbroken shade in the midst of the open spaces, will prove to you the presence of deity. Or if a cave, made by the deep crumbling of the rocks, holds up a mountain on its arch, a place not built with hands but hollowed out into such spaciousness by natural causes, your soul will be deeply moved by a certain intimation of the existence of God. We worship the sources of mighty rivers; we erect altars at places where great streams burst suddenly from hidden sources; we adore springs of hot water as divine, and consecrate certain pools because of their dark waters or their immeasurable depth. If you see a man who is unterrified in the midst of dangers, untouched by desires, happy in adversity, peaceful amid the storm, who looks down upon men from a higher plane, and views the gods on a footing of equality, will not a feeling of reverence for him steal over you? Will you not say: "This quality is too great and too lofty to be regarded as resembling this petty body in which it dwells? A divine power has descended upon that man." When a soul rises superior to other souls, when it is under control, when it passes through every experience as if it were of small account, when it smiles at our fears and at our prayers, it is stirred by a force from heaven. A thing like this cannot stand upright unless it be propped by the divine. Therefore, a greater part of it abides in that place from whence it came down to earth. Just as the rays of the sun do indeed touch the earth, but still abide at the source from which they are sent; even so the great and hallowed soul, which has come down in order that we may have a nearer knowledge of divinity, does indeed associate with us, but still cleaves to its origin; on that source it depends, thither it turns its gaze and strives to go, and it concerns itself with our doings only as a being superior to ourselves.

What, then, is such a soul? One which is resplendent with no external good, but only with its own. For what is more foolish than to praise in a man the qualities which come from without? And what is more insane than to marvel at characteristics which may at the next instant be passed on to someone else? A golden bit does not make a better horse. The lion with gilded mane, in process of being trained and forced by weariness to endure the decoration, is sent into the arena in quite a different way from the wild lion whose spirit is unbroken; the latter, indeed, bold in his attack, as nature wished him to be, impressive because of his wild appearance,—and it is his glory that none can look upon him without fear,—is favoured* in preference to the other lion, that languid and gilded brute.

No man ought to glory except in that which is his own. We praise a vine if it makes the shoots teem with increase, if by its weight it bends to the ground the very poles which hold its fruit; would any man prefer to this vine one from which golden grapes and golden leaves hang down? In a vine the virtue peculiarly its own is fertility; in man also we should praise that which is his own. Suppose that he has a retinue of comely slaves and a beautiful house, that his farm is large and large his income; none of these things is in the man himself; they are all on the outside. Praise the quality in him which cannot be given or snatched away, that which is the peculiar property of the man. Do you ask what this is? It is soul, and reason brought to perfection in the soul. For man is a reasoning animal. Therefore, man's highest good is attained, if he has fulfilled the good for which nature designed him at birth. And what is it which this reason demands of him? The easiest thing in the world,—to live in accordance with his own nature. But this is turned into a hard task by the general madness of mankind; we push one another into vice. And how can a man be recalled to salvation, when he has none to restrain him, and all mankind to urge him on? Farewell.

---

* The spectators of the fight, which is to take place between the two lions, applaud the wild lion and bet on him.

LETTER

46

ON A NEW BOOK BY LUCILIUS

I received the book of yours which you promised me. I opened it hastily with the idea of glancing over it at leisure; for I meant only to taste the volume. But by its own charm the book coaxed me into traversing it more at length. You may understand from this fact how eloquent it was; for it seemed to be written in the smooth style,* and yet did not resemble your handiwork or mine, but at first sight might have been ascribed to Titus Livius or to Epicurus. Moreover, I was so impressed and carried along by its charm that I finished it without any postponement. The sunlight called to me, hunger warned, and clouds were lowering; but I absorbed the book from beginning to end.

I was not merely pleased; I rejoiced. So full of wit and spirit it was! I should have added "force," had the book contained moments of repose, or had it risen to energy only at intervals. But I found that there was no burst of force, but an even flow, a style that was vigorous and chaste. Nevertheless I noticed from time to time your sweetness, and here and there that mildness of yours. Your style is lofty and noble; I want you to keep to this manner and this direction. Your subject also contributed

---

* Possibly *levis* in the sense of *light*, referring to size.

something; for this reason you should choose productive topics, which will lay hold of the mind and arouse it.

I shall discuss the book more fully after a second perusal; meantime, my judgment is somewhat unsettled, just as if I had heard it read aloud, and had not read it myself. You must allow me to examine it also. You need not be afraid; you shall hear the truth. Lucky fellow, to offer a man no opportunity to tell you lies at such long range! Unless perhaps, even now, when excuses for lying are taken away, custom serves as an excuse for our telling each other lies! Farewell.

LETTER

47

ON MASTER AND SLAVE

I am glad to learn, through those who come from you, that you live on friendly terms with your slaves. This befits a sensible and well-educated man like yourself. "They are slaves," people declare.* Nay, rather they are men. "Slaves!" No, comrades. "Slaves!" No, they are unpretentious friends. "Slaves!" No, they are our fellow-slaves, if one reflects that Fortune has equal rights over slaves and free men alike.

That is why I smile at those who think it degrading for a man to dine with his slave. But why should they think it degrading? It is only because purse-proud etiquette surrounds a householder at his dinner with a mob of standing slaves. The master eats more than he can hold, and with monstrous greed loads his belly until it is stretched and at length ceases to do the work of a belly; so that he is at greater pains to discharge all the food than he was to stuff it down. All this time the poor slaves may not move their lips, even to speak. The slightest murmur is repressed by the rod; even a chance sound,—a cough, a sneeze, or a hiccup,—is visited with the lash. There is a grievous penalty

* Much of the following is quoted by Macrobius, *Sat.* i. 11. 7 ff., in the passage beginning *vis tu cogitare eos, quos ios tuum vocas, isdem seminibus ortos eodem frui caelo*, etc.

for the slightest breach of silence. All night long they must stand about, hungry and dumb.

The result of it all is that these slaves, who may not talk in their master's presence, talk about their master. But the slaves of former days, who were permitted to converse not only in their master's presence, but actually with him, whose mouths were not stitched up tight, were ready to bare their necks for their master, to bring upon their own heads any danger that threatened him; they spoke at the feast, but kept silence during torture. Finally, the saying, in allusion to this same high-handed treatment, becomes current: "As many enemies as you have slaves." They are not enemies when we acquire them; we make them enemies.

I shall pass over other cruel and inhuman conduct towards them; for we maltreat them, not as if they were men, but as if they were beasts of burden. When we recline at a banquet, one slave mops up the disgorged food, another crouches beneath the table and gathers up the left-overs of the tipsy guests. Another carves the priceless game birds; with unerring strokes and skilled hand he cuts choice morsels along the breast or the rump. Hapless fellow, to live only for the purpose of cutting fat capons correctly,—unless, indeed, the other man is still more unhappy than he, who teaches this art for pleasure's sake, rather than he who learns it because he must. Another, who serves the wine, must dress like a woman and wrestle with his advancing years; he cannot get away from his boyhood; he is dragged back to it; and though he has already acquired a soldier's figure, he is kept beardless by having his hair smoothed away or plucked out by the roots, and he must remain awake throughout the night, dividing his time between his master's drunkenness and his lust; in the chamber he must be a man, at the feast a boy.* Another, whose duty it is to put a valuation on the guests, must stick to his task,

---

* *Glabri*, *delicati*, or *exoleti* were favourite slaves, kept artifically youthful by Romans of the more dissolute class. Cf. Catullus, lxi. 142, and Seneca, *De Brevitate Vitae*, 12. 5 (a passage closely resembling the description given above by Seneca), where the master prides himself upon the elegant appearance and graceful gestures of these favourites.

poor fellow, and watch to see whose flattery and whose immodesty, whether of appetite or of language, is to get them an invitation for tomorrow. Think also of the poor purveyors of food, who note their masters' tastes with delicate skill, who know what special flavours will sharpen their appetite, what will please their eyes, what new combinations will rouse their cloyed stomachs, what food will excite their loathing through sheer satiety, and what will stir them to hunger on that particular day. With slaves like these the master cannot bear to dine; he would think it beneath his dignity to associate with his slave at the same table! Heaven forfend!

But how many masters is he creating in these very men! I have seen standing in the line, before the door of Callistus, the former master,* of Callistus; I have seen the master himself shut out while others were welcomed,—the master who once fastened the "For Sale" ticket on Callistus and put him in the market along with the good-for-nothing slaves. But he has been paid off by that slave who was shuffled into the first lot of those on whom the crier practises his lungs; the slave, too, in his turn has cut *his* name from the list and in his turn has adjudged him unfit to enter his house. The master sold Callistus, but how much has Callistus made his master pay for!

Kindly remember that he whom you call your slave sprang from the same stock, is smiled upon by the same skies, and on equal terms with yourself breathes, lives, and dies. It is just as possible for you to see in him a free-born man as for him to see in you a slave. As a result of the massacres in Marius's** day, many a man of distinguished birth, who was taking the first steps toward senatorial rank by service in the army, was humbled by fortune, one becoming a shepherd, another a caretaker of a country cottage. Despise, then, if you dare, those to whose estate you may at any time descend, even when you are despising them.

---

* The master of Callistus, before he became the favourite of Caligula, is unknown.

** There is some doubt whether we should not read Variana, as Lipsius suggests. This method of qualifying for senator suits the Empire better than the Republic. Variana would refer to the defeat of Varus in Germany, A.D. 9.

I do not wish to involve myself in too large a question, and to discuss the treatment of slaves, towards whom we Romans are excessively haughty, cruel, and insulting. But this is the kernel of my advice: Treat your inferiors as you would be treated by your betters. And as often as you reflect how much power you have over a slave, remember that your master has just as much power over you. "But I have no master," you say. You are still young; perhaps you will have one. Do you not know at what age Hecuba entered captivity, or Croesus, or the mother of Darius, or Plato, or Diogenes?*

Associate with your slave on kindly, even on affable, terms; let him talk with you, plan with you, live with you. I know that at this point all the exquisites will cry out against me in a body; they will say: "There is nothing more debasing, more disgraceful, than this." But these are the very persons whom I sometimes surprise kissing the hands of other men's slaves. Do you not see even this,—how our ancestors removed from masters everything invidious, and from slaves everything insulting? They called the master "father of the household," and the slaves "members of the household," a custom which still holds in the mime. They established a holiday on which masters and slaves should eat together,—not as the only day for this custom, but as obligatory on that day in any case. They allowed the slaves to attain honours in the household and to pronounce judgment;** they held that a household was a miniature commonwealth.

"Do you mean to say," comes the retort, "that I must seat all my slaves at my own table?" No, not any more than that you should invite all free men to it. You are mistaken if you think that I would bar from my table certain slaves whose duties are more humble, as, for example, yonder muleteer or yonder herdsman; I propose to value them according to their character, and not according to their

---

* Plato was about forty years old when he visited Sicily, whence he was afterwards deported by Dionysius the Elder. He was sold into slavery at Aegina and ransomed by a man from Cyrene. Diogenes, while travelling from Athens to Aegina, is said to have been captured by pirates and sold in Crete, where he was purchased by a certain Corinthian and given his freedom.

** i.e., as the praetor himself was normally accustomed to do.

duties. Each man acquires his character for himself, but accident assigns his duties. Invite some to your table because they deserve the honour, and others that they may come to deserve it. For if there is any slavish quality in them as the result of their low associations, it will be shaken off by intercourse with men of gentler breeding. You need not, my dear Lucilius, hunt for friends only in the forum or in the Senate-house; if you are careful and attentive, you will find them at home also. Good material often stands idle for want of an artist; make the experiment, and you will find it so. As he is a fool who, when purchasing a horse, does not consider the animal's points, but merely his saddle and bridle; so he is doubly a fool who values a man from his clothes or from his rank, which indeed is only a robe that clothes us.

"He is a slave." His soul, however, may be that of a freeman. "He is a slave." But shall that stand in his way? Show me a man who is not a slave; one is a slave to lust, another to greed, another to ambition, and all men are slaves to fear. I will name you an ex-consul who is slave to an old hag, a millionaire who is slave to a serving-maid; I will show you youths of the noblest birth in serfdom to pantomime players! No servitude is more disgraceful than that which is self-imposed.

You should therefore not be deterred by these finicky persons from showing yourself to your slaves as an affable person and not proudly superior to them; they ought to respect you rather than fear you. Some may maintain that I am now offering the liberty-cap to slaves in general and toppling down lords from their high estate, because I bid slaves respect their masters instead of fearing them. They say: "This is what he plainly means: slaves are to pay respect as if they were clients or early-morning callers!" Anyone who holds this opinion forgets that what is enough for a god cannot be too little for a master. Respect means love, and love and fear cannot be mingled. So I hold that you are entirely right in not wishing to be feared by your slaves, and in lashing them merely with the tongue; only dumb animals need the thong.

That which annoys us does not necessarily injure us; but we are driven into wild rage by our luxurious lives, so that whatever does not answer our whims arouses our anger. We don the temper of kings. For they, too, forgetful alike of their own strength and of other men's weakness, grow white-hot with rage, as if they had received an injury, when they are entirely protected from danger of such injury by their exalted station. They are not unaware that this is true, but by finding fault they seize upon opportunities to do harm; they insist that they have received injuries, in order that they may inflict them.

I do not wish to delay you longer; for you need no exhortation. This, among other things, is a mark of good character: it forms its own judgments and abides by them; but badness is fickle and frequently changing, not for the better, but for something different. Farewell.

LETTER

48

On Quibbling as Unworthy of the Philosopher

In answer to the letter which you wrote me while travelling,—a letter as long as the journey itself,—I shall reply later. I ought to go into retirement, and consider what sort of advice I should give you. For you yourself, who consult me, also reflected for a long time whether to do so; how much more, then, should I myself reflect, since more deliberation is necessary in settling than in propounding a problem! And this is particularly true when one thing is advantageous to you and another to me. Am I speaking again in the guise of an Epicurean?* But the fact is, the same thing is advantageous to me which is advantageous to you; for I am not your friend unless whatever is at issue concerning you is my concern also. Friendship produces between us a partnership in all our interests. There is no such thing as good

* The Epicureans, who reduced all goods to "utilities," could not regard a friend's advantage as identical to one's own advantage. And yet they laid great stress upon friendship as one of the chief sources of pleasure. For an attempt to reconcile these two positions see Cicero, *De Finibus*, i. 65 ff. Seneca has inadvertantly used a phrase that implies a difference between a friend's interest and one's own. This leads him to reassert the Stoic view of friendship, which adopted as its motto κοινὰ τὰ τῶν φίλων.

or bad fortune for the individual; we live in common. And no one can live happily who has regard to himself alone and transforms everything into a question of his own utility; you must live for your neighbour, if you would live for yourself. This fellowship, maintained with scrupulous care, which makes us mingle as men with our fellow-men and holds that the human race have certain rights in common, is also of great help in cherishing the more intimate fellowship which is based on friendship, concerning which I began to speak above. For he that has much in common with a fellow-man will have all things in common with a friend.

And on this point, my excellent Lucilius, I should like to have those subtle dialecticians of yours advise me how I ought to help a friend, or how a fellow-man, rather than tell me in how many ways the word "friend" is used, and how many meanings the word "man" possesses. Lo, Wisdom and Folly are taking opposite sides. Which shall I join? Which party would you have me follow? On that side, "man" is the equivalent of "friend"; on the other side, "friend" is not the equivalent of "man." The one wants a friend for his own advantage; the other wants to make himself an advantage to his friend.* What *you* have to offer me is nothing but distortion of words and splitting of syllables. It is clear that unless I can devise some very tricky premises and by false deductions tack on to them a fallacy which springs from the truth, I shall not be able to distinguish between what is desirable and what is to be avoided! I am ashamed! Old men as we are, dealing with a problem so serious, we make play of it!

---

* The sides are given in the reverse order in the two clauses: to the Stoic the terms "friend" and "man" are co-extensive; he is the friend of everybody, and his motive in friendship is to be of service; the Epicurean, however, narrows the definition of "friend" and regards him merely as an instrument to his own happiness.

"'Mouse' is a syllable.* Now a mouse eats cheese; therefore, a syllable eats cheese." Suppose now that I cannot solve this problem; see what peril hangs over my head as a result of such ignorance! What a scrape I shall be in! Without doubt I must beware, or some day I shall be catching syllables in a mousetrap, or, if I grow careless, a book may devour my cheese! Unless, perhaps, the following syllogism is shrewder still: "'Mouse' is a syllable. Now a syllable does not eat cheese. Therefore a mouse does not eat cheese." What childish nonsense! Do we knit our brows over this sort of problem? Do we let our beards grow long for this reason? Is this the matter which we teach with sour and pale faces?

Would you really know what philosophy offers to humanity? Philosophy offers counsel. Death calls away one man, and poverty chafes another; a third is worried either by his neighbour's wealth or by his own. So-and-so is afraid of bad luck; another desires to get away from his own good fortune. Some are ill-treated by men, others by the gods. Why, then, do you frame for me such games as these? It is no occasion for jest; you are retained as counsel for unhappy mankind. You have promised to help those in peril by sea, those in captivity, the sick and the needy, and those whose heads are under the poised axe. Whither are you straying? What are you doing?

This friend, in whose company you are jesting, is in fear. Help him, and take the noose from about his neck. Men are stretching out imploring hands to you on all sides; lives ruined and in danger of ruin are begging for some assistance; men's hopes, men's resources, depend upon you. They ask that you deliver them from all their restlessness, that you reveal to them, scattered and wandering as they are, the clear light of truth. Tell them what nature has made necessary, and what superfluous; tell them how simple are the laws that she has laid down, how pleasant and unimpeded life is for those who follow these laws,

---

* In this paragraph Seneca exposes the folly of trying to prove a truth by means of logical tricks, and offers a caricature of those which were current among the philosophers whom he derides.

but how bitter and perplexed it is for those who have put their trust in opinion rather than in nature.

I should deem your games of logic to be of some avail in relieving men's burdens, if you could first show me what part of these burdens they will relieve. What among these games of yours banishes lust? Or controls it? Would that I could say that they were merely of no profit! They are positively harmful. I can make it perfectly clear to you whenever you wish, that a noble spirit when involved in such subtleties is impaired and weakened. I am ashamed to say what weapons they supply to men who are destined to go to war with fortune, and how poorly they equip them! Is this the path to the greatest good? Is philosophy to proceed by such claptrap* and by quibbles which would be a disgrace and a reproach even for expounders** of the law? For what else is it that you men are doing, when you deliberately ensnare the person to whom you are putting questions, than making it appear that the man has lost his case on a technical error?*** But just as the judge can reinstate those who have lost a suit in this way, so philosophy has reinstated these victims of quibbling to their former condition. Why do you men abandon your mighty promises, and, after having assured me in high-sounding language that you will permit the glitter of gold to dazzle my eyesight no more than the gleam of the sword, and that I shall, with mighty

---

* Literally, "or if or if not," words constantly employed by the logicians in legal instruments. For the latter cf. Cicero, *Pro Caecina*, 23. 65 *tum illud, quod dicitur, "sive nive" irrident, tum aucupia verborum et litterarum tendiculas in invidiam vocant.*

** Literally, "to those who sit studying the praetor's edicts." The *album* is the bulletin-board, on which the edicts of the praetor were posted, giving the formulae and stipulations for legal processes of various kinds.

*** In certain actions the praetor appointed a judge and established a formula, indicating the plaintiff's claim and the judge's duty. If the statement was false, or the claim excessive, the plaintiff lost his case; under certain conditions (see last sentence of Seneca § 11) the defendant could claim annulment of the formula and have the case tried again. Such cases were not lost on their merits, and for that reason the lawyer who purposely took such an advantage was doing a contemptible thing.

steadfastness, spurn both that which all men crave and that which all men fear, why do you descend to the ABC's of scholastic pedants? What is your answer?

Is this the path to heaven?*

For that is exactly what philosophy promises to me, that I shall be made equal to God. For this I have been summoned, for this purpose have I come. Philosophy, keep your promise!

Therefore, my dear Lucilius, withdraw yourself as far as possible from these exceptions and objections of so-called philosophers. Frankness, and simplicity beseem true goodness. Even if there were many years left to you, you would have had to spend them frugally in order to have enough for the necessary things; but as it is, when your time is so scant, what madness it is to learn superfluous things! Farewell.

* Vergil, *Aeneid*, ix. 641.

LETTER

53

On the Faults of the Spirit

You can persuade me into almost anything now, for I was recently persuaded to travel by water. We cast off when the sea was lazily smooth; the sky, to be sure, was heavy with nasty clouds, such as usually break into rain or squalls. Still, I thought that the few miles between Puteoli and your dear Parthenope* might be run off in quick time, despite the uncertain and lowering sky. So, in order to get away more quickly, I made straight out to sea for Nesis,** with the purpose of cutting across all the inlets. But when we were so far out that it made little difference to me whether I returned or kept on, the calm weather, which had enticed me, came to naught. The storm had not yet begun, but the ground-swell was on, and the waves kept steadily coming faster. I began to ask the pilot to put me ashore somewhere; he replied that the coast was rough and a bad place

---

* The poetical name for Naples; perhaps it was once a town near by which gave a sort of romantic second title to the larger city. Professor Summers thinks that this poetical name, together with *tua*, indicates a reference to a passage from the verse of Lucilius. Perhaps, however, *tua* means nothing more than "the place which you love so well," being in the neighbourhood of Pompeii, the birthplace of Lucilius.

** An islet near the mouth of the bay wherein Baiae was situated. Puteoli was on the opposite side of the bay from Baiae.

to land, and that in a storm he feared a lee shore more than anything else. But I was suffering too grievously to think of the danger, since a sluggish seasickness which brought no relief was racking me, the sort that upsets the liver without clearing it. Therefore I laid down the law to my pilot, forcing him to make for the shore, willy-nilly. When we drew near, I did not wait for things to be done in accordance with Vergil's orders, until

Prow faced seawards*

or

Anchor plunged from bow;**

I remembered my profession*** as a veteran devotee of cold water, and, clad as I was in my cloak, let myself down into the sea, just as a cold-water bather should. What do you think my feelings were, scrambling over the rocks, searching out the path, or making one for myself? I understood that sailors have good reason to fear the land. It is hard to believe what I endured when I could not endure myself; you may be sure that the reason why Ulysses was shipwrecked on every possible occasion was not so much because the sea-god was angry with him from his birth; he was simply subject to seasickness. And in the future I also, if I must go anywhere by sea, shall only reach my destination in the twentieth year.****

When I finally calmed my stomach (for you know that one does not escape seasickness by escaping from the sea) and refreshed my body with a rubdown, I began to reflect how completely we forget or ignore our failings, even those that affect the body, which are continually

---

* *Aeneid*, vi. 3. This was the usual method of mooring a ship in ancient times.

** *Aeneid*, iii. 277.

*** Compare Ep. lxxxiii. 5.

**** Ulysses took ten years on his journey, because of sea-sickness; Seneca will need twice as many.

reminding us of their existence,—not to mention those which are more serious in proportion as they are more hidden. A slight ague deceives us; but when it has increased and a genuine fever has begun to burn, it forces even a hardy man, who can endure much suffering, to admit that he is ill. There is pain in the foot, and a tingling sensation in the joints; but we still hide the complaint and announce that we have sprained a joint, or else are tired from over-exercise. Then the ailment, uncertain at first, must be given a name; and when it begins to swell the ankles also, and has made both our feet "right" feet,* we are bound to confess that we have the gout. The opposite holds true of diseases of the soul; the worse one is, the less one perceives it. You need not be surprised, my beloved Lucilius. For he whose sleep is light pursues visions during slumber, and sometimes, though asleep, is conscious that he is asleep; but sound slumber annihilates our very dreams and sinks the spirit down so deep that it has no perception of self. Why will no man confess his faults? Because he is still in their grasp; only he who is awake can recount his dream, and similarly a confession of sin is a proof of sound mind.

Let us, therefore, rouse ourselves, that we may be able to correct our mistakes. Philosophy, however, is the only power that can stir us, the only power that can shake off our deep slumber. Devote yourself wholly to philosophy. You are worthy of her; she is worthy of you; greet one another with a loving embrace. Say farewell to all other interests with courage and frankness. Do not study philosophy merely during your spare time.**

If you were ill, you would stop caring for your personal concerns, and forget your business duties; you would not think highly enough of any client to take active charge of his case during a slight abatement of your sufferings. You would try your hardest to be rid of the illness as soon as possible. What, then? Shall you not do the same thing now? Throw aside all hindrances and give up your time to getting a sound

---

* That is, they are so swollen that left and right look alike.

** Literally "on sufferance," whenever other matters permit. Cf. Pliny, *Ep.* vii. 30 *precario studeo,*—"subject to interruption from others."

mind; for no man can attain it if he is engrossed in other matters. Philosophy wields her own authority; she appoints her own time and does not allow it to be appointed for her. She is not a thing to be followed at odd times, but a subject for daily practice; she is mistress, and she commands our attendance. Alexander, when a certain state promised him a part of its territory and half its entire property, replied: "I invaded Asia with the intention, not of accepting what you might give, but of allowing you to keep what I might leave." Philosophy likewise keeps saying to all occupations: "I do not intend to accept the time which you have left over, but I shall allow you to keep what I myself shall leave."

Turn to her, therefore, with all your soul, sit at her feet, cherish her; a great distance will then begin to separate you from other men. You will be far ahead of all mortals, and even the gods will not be far ahead of you. Do you ask what will be the difference between yourself and the gods? They will live longer. But, by my faith, it is the sign of a great artist to have confined a full likeness to the limits of a miniature. The wise man's life spreads out to him over as large a surface as does all eternity to a god. There is one point in which the sage has an advantage over the god; for a god is freed from terrors by the bounty of nature, the wise man by his own bounty. What a wonderful privilege, to have the weaknesses of a man and the serenity of a god! The power of philosophy to blunt the blows of chance is beyond belief. No missile can settle in her body; she is well-protected and impenetrable. She spoils the force of some missiles and wards them off with the loose folds of her gown, as if they had no power to harm; others she dashes aside, and hurls them back with such force that they recoil upon the sender. Farewell.

LETTER

54

On Asthma and Death

My ill-health had allowed me a long furlough, when suddenly it resumed the attack. "What kind of ill-health?" you say. And you surely have a right to ask; for it is true that no kind is unknown to me. But I have been consigned, so to speak, to one special ailment. I do not know why I should call it by its Greek name;* for it is well enough described as "shortness of breath." Its attack is of very brief duration, like that of a squall at sea; it usually ends within an hour. Who indeed could breathe his last for long? I have passed through all the ills and dangers of the flesh; but nothing seems to me more troublesome than this. And naturally so; for anything else may be called illness; but this is a sort of continued "last gasp."** Hence physicians call it "practising how to die." For some day the breath will succeed in doing what it has so often essayed. Do you think I am writing this letter in a merry spirit, just because I have escaped? It would be absurd to take delight in such supposed restoration to health,

---

* i.e., asthma. Seneca thinks that the Latin name is good enough.

** Celcus (iv. 8) gives this disease as the second of those which deal with the respiratory organs; *cum vehementior est, ut spirare aeger sine sono et anhelatione non possit.*

as it would be for a defendant to imagine that he had won his case when he had succeeded in postponing his trial. Yet in the midst of my difficult breathing I never ceased to rest secure in cheerful and brave thoughts.

"What?" I say to myself; "does death so often test me? Let it do so; I myself have for a long time tested death." "When?" you ask. Before I was born. Death is non-existence, and I know already what that means. What was before me will happen again after me. If there is any suffering in this state, there must have been such suffering also in the past, before we entered the light of day. As a matter of fact, however, we felt no discomfort then. And I ask you, would you not say that one was the greatest of fools who believed that a lamp was worse off when it was extinguished than before it was lighted? We mortals also are lighted and extinguished; the period of suffering comes in between, but on either side there is a deep peace. For, unless I am very much mistaken, my dear Lucilius, we go astray in thinking that death only follows, when in reality it has both preceded us and will in turn follow us. Whatever condition existed before our birth, is death. For what does it matter whether you do not begin at all, or whether you leave off, inasmuch as the result of both these states is non-existence?

I have never ceased to encourage myself with cheering counsels of this kind, silently, of course, since I had not the power to speak; then little by little this shortness of breath, already reduced to a sort of panting, came on at greater intervals, and then slowed down and finally stopped. Even by this time, although the gasping has ceased, the breath does not come and go normally; I still feel a sort of hesitation and delay in breathing. Let it be as it pleases, provided there be no sigh from the soul.* Accept this assurance from me: I shall never be frightened when the last hour comes; I am already prepared and do

---

* i.e., that the sigh be physical,—an asthmatic gasp,—and not caused by anguish of the soul.

not plan a whole day ahead. But do you praise* and imitate the man whom it does not irk to die, though he takes pleasure in living. For what virtue is there in going away when you are thrust out? And yet there is virtue even in this: I am indeed thrust out, but it is as if I were going away willingly. For that reason the wise man can never be thrust out, because that would mean removal from a place which he was unwilling to leave; and the wise man does nothing unwillingly. He escapes necessity, because he wills to do what necessity is about to force upon him. Farewell.

* The argument is: I am ready to die, but do not praise me on that account; reserve your praise for him who is not loth to die, though (unlike me) he finds it a pleasure to live (because he is in good health). Yes, for there is no more virtue in accepting death when one hates life, than there is in leaving a place when one is ejected.

LETTER

55

On Vatia's Villa

I have just returned from a ride in my litter; and I am as weary as if I had walked the distance, instead of being seated. Even to be carried for any length of time is hard work, perhaps all the more so because it is an unnatural exercise; for Nature gave us legs with which to do our own walking, and eyes with which to do our own seeing. Our luxuries have condemned us to weakness; we have ceased to be able to do that which we have long declined to do. Nevertheless, I found it necessary to give my body a shaking up, in order that the bile which had gathered in my throat, if that was my trouble, might be shaken out, or, if the very breath within me had become, for some reason, too thick, that the jolting, which I have felt was a good thing for me, might make it thinner. So I insisted on being carried longer than usual, along an attractive beach, which bends between Cumae and Servilius Vatia's country-house,* shut in by the sea on one side and the lake on the other, just like a narrow path. It was packed

* Cumae was on the coast about six miles north of Cape Misenum. Lake Acheron (see § 6) was a salt-water pool between those two points, separated from the sea by a sandbar; it lay near Lake Avernus and probably derived its name from that fact. The Vatia mentioned here is unknown; he must not be confused with Isauricus.

firm under foot, because of a recent storm; since, as you know, the waves, when they beat upon the beach hard and fast, level it out; but a continuous period of fair weather loosens it, when the sand, which is kept firm by the water, loses its moisture.

As my habit is, I began to look about for something there that might be of service to me, when my eyes fell upon the villa which had once belonged to Vatia. So this was the place where that famous praetorian millionaire passed his old age! He was famed for nothing else than his life of leisure, and he was regarded as lucky only for that reason. For whenever men were ruined by their friendship with Asinius Gallus* whenever others were ruined by their hatred of Sejanus, and later** by their intimacy with him,—for it was no more dangerous to have offended him than to have loved him,—people used to cry out: "O Vatia, you alone know how to live!" But what he knew was how to hide, not how to live; and it makes a great deal of difference whether your life be one of leisure or one of idleness. So I never drove past his country-place during Vatia's lifetime without saying to myself: "Here lies Vatia!"

But, my dear Lucilius, philosophy is a thing of holiness, something to be worshipped, so much so that the very counterfeit pleases. For the mass of mankind consider that a person is at leisure who has withdrawn from society, is free from care, self-sufficient, and lives for himself; but these privileges can be the reward only of the wise man. Does he who is a victim of anxiety know how to live for himself? What? Does he even know (and that is of first importance) how to live at all? For the man who has fled from affairs and from men, who has been banished to seclusion by the unhappiness which his own desires have brought upon him, who cannot see his neighbour more happy than himself, who through fear has taken to concealment, like a frightened and sluggish animal,—this person is not living for himself; he is living for his belly,

---

* Son of Asinius Pollio; his frankness got him into trouble and he died of starvation in a dungeon in A.D. 33. Tacitus, *Ann.* i. 32. 2, quotes Augustus, discussing his own successor, as saying of Gallus *avidus et minor*. Sejanus was overthrown and executed in A.D. 31.

** i.e., after his fall.

his sleep, and his lust,—and that is the most shameful thing in the world. He who lives for no one does not necessarily live for himself. Nevertheless, there is so much in steadfastness and adherence to one's purpose that even sluggishness, if stubbornly maintained, assumes an air of authority* with us.

I could not describe the villa accurately; for I am familiar only with the front of the house, and with the parts which are in public view and can be seen by the mere passer-by. There are two grottoes, which cost a great deal of labour, as big as the most spacious hall, made by hand. One of these does not admit the rays of the sun, while the other keeps them until the sun sets. There is also a stream running through a grove of plane-trees, which draws for its supply both on the sea and on Lake Acheron; it intersects the grove just like a race-way,** and is large enough to support fish, although its waters are continually being drawn off. When the sea is calm, however, they do not use the stream, only touching the well-stocked waters when the storms give the fishermen a forced holiday. But the most convenient thing about the villa is the fact that Baiae is next door, it is free from all the inconveniences of that resort, and yet enjoys its pleasures. I myself understand these attractions, and I believe that it is a villa suited to every season of the year. It fronts the west wind, which it intercepts in such a way that Baiae is denied it. So it seems that Vatia was no fool when he selected this place as the best in which to spend his leisure when it was already unfruitful and decrepit.

The place where one lives, however, can contribute little towards tranquillity; it is the mind which must make everything agreeable to itself. I have seen men despondent in a gay and lovely villa, and I have seen them to all appearance full of business in the midst of a solitude. For this reason you should not refuse to believe that your life is well-placed merely because you are not now in Campania. But why are you not there? Just let your thoughts travel, even to this place. You

---

* i.e., imposes on us.

** Literally, "like a Euripus," referring to the narrow strait which divides Euboea from Boeotia at Chalcis. Its current is swift.

may hold converse with your friends when they are absent, and indeed as often as you wish and for as long as you wish. For we enjoy this, the greatest of pleasures, all the more when we are absent from one another. For the presence of friends makes us fastidious; and because we can at any time talk or sit together, when once we have parted we give not a thought to those whom we have just beheld. And we ought to bear the absence of friends cheerfully, just because everyone is bound to be often absent from his friends even when they are present. Include among such cases, in the first place, the nights spent apart, then the different engagements which each of two friends has, then the private studies of each and their excursions into the country, and you will see that foreign travel does not rob us of much. A friend should be retained in the spirit; such a friend can never be absent. He can see every day whomsoever he desires to see.

I would therefore have you share your studies with me, your meals, and your walks. We should be living within too narrow limits if anything were barred to our thoughts. I see you, my dear Lucilius, and at this very moment I hear you; I am with you to such an extent that I hesitate whether I should not begin to write you notes instead of letters. Farewell.

LETTER

56

On Quiet and Study

Beshrew me if I think anything more requisite than silence for a man who secludes himself in order to study! Imagine what a variety of noises reverberates about my ears! I have lodgings right over a bathing establishment. So picture to yourself the assortment of sounds, which are strong enough to make me hate my very powers of hearing! When your strenuous gentleman, for example, is exercising himself by flourishing leaden weights; when he is working hard, or else pretends to be working hard, I can hear him grunt; and whenever he releases his imprisoned breath, I can hear him panting in wheezy and high-pitched tones. Or perhaps I notice some lazy fellow, content with a cheap rubdown, and hear the crack of the pummelling hand on his shoulder, varying in sound according as the hand is laid on flat or hollow. Then, perhaps, a professional* comes along, shouting out the score; that is the finishing touch. Add to this the arresting of an occasional roysterer or pickpocket, the racket of the man who always likes to hear his own voice in the bathroom,** or the enthusiast who

* *Pilicrepus* probably means "ball-counter,"—one who keeps a record of the strokes. Compare our "billiard-marker."

** This was especially true of poets, cf. Horace, *Sat.* i. 4. 76 *suave locus voci resonat conclusus*, and Martial, iii. 44.

plunges into the swimming-tank with unconscionable noise and splashing. Besides all those whose voices, if nothing else, are good, imagine the hair-plucker with his penetrating, shrill voice,—for purposes of advertisement,—continually giving it vent and never holding his tongue except when he is plucking the armpits and making his victim yell instead. Then the cake-seller with his varied cries, the sausageman, the confectioner, and all the vendors of food hawking their wares, each with his own distinctive intonation.

So you say: "What iron nerves or deadened ears, you must have, if your mind can hold out amid so many noises, so various and so discordant, when our friend Chrysippus* is brought to his death by the continual good-morrows that greet him!" But I assure you that this racket means no more to me than the sound of waves or falling water; although you will remind me that a certain tribe once moved their city merely because they could not endure the din of a Nile cataract.** Words seem to distract me more than noises; for words demand attention, but noises merely fill the ears and beat upon them. Among the sounds that din round me without distracting, I include passing carriages, a machinist in the same block, a saw-sharpener near by, or some fellow who is demonstrating with little pipes and flutes at the Trickling Fountain,*** shouting rather than singing.

---

* It is nowhere else related of the famous Stoic philosopher Chrysippus that he objected to the salutations of his friends; and, besides, the morning salutation was a Roman, not a Greek, custom. Lipsius, therefore, was probably right when he proposed to read here, for Chrysippus, Crispus, one of Seneca's friends; cf. *Epigr.* 6.

** The same story is told in *Naturalis Quaestiones*, iv. 2. 5.

*** A cone-shaped fountain, resembling a turning-post (*meta*) in the circus, from which the water spouted through many jets; hence the "sweating" (*sudans*). Its remains may still be seen now not far from the Colosseum on the Velia.

Furthermore, an intermittent noise upsets me more than a steady one. But by this time I have toughened my nerves against all that sort of thing, so that I can endure even a boatswain marking the time in high-pitched tones for his crew. For I force my mind to concentrate, and keep it from straying to things outside itself; all outdoors may be bedlam, provided that there is no disturbance within, provided that fear is not wrangling with desire in my breast, provided that meanness and lavishness are not at odds, one harassing the other. For of what benefit is a quiet neighbourhood, if our emotions are in an uproar?

'Twas night, and all the world was lulled to rest.*

This is not true; for no real rest can be found when reason has not done the lulling. Night brings our troubles to the light, rather than banishes them; it merely changes the form of our worries. For even when we seek slumber, our sleepless moments are as harassing as the daytime. Real tranquillity is the state reached by an unperverted mind when it is relaxed. Think of the unfortunate man who courts sleep by surrendering his spacious mansion to silence, who, that his ear may be disturbed by no sound, bids the whole retinue of his slaves be quiet and that whoever approaches him shall walk on tiptoe; he tosses from this side to that and seeks a fitful slumber amid his frettings! He complains that he has heard sounds, when he has not heard them at all. The reason, you ask? His soul is in an uproar; it must be soothed, and its rebellious murmuring checked. You need not suppose that the soul is at peace when the body is still. Sometimes quiet means disquiet.

We must therefore rouse ourselves to action and busy ourselves with interests that are good, as often as we are in the grasp of an uncontrollable sluggishness. Great generals, when they see that their men are mutinous, check them by some sort of labour or keep them busy with small forays. The much occupied man has no time for wantonness, and it is an obvious commonplace that the evils of leisure can be shaken off by hard work. Although people may often have

---

* A fragment from the Argonautica of Varro Atacinus.

thought that I sought seclusion because I was disgusted with politics and regretted my hapless and thankless position,* yet, in the retreat to which apprehension and weariness have driven me, my ambition sometimes develops afresh. For it is not because my ambition was rooted out that it has abated, but because it was wearied or perhaps even put out of temper by the failure of its plans. And so with luxury, also, which sometimes seems to have departed, and then when we have made a profession of frugality, begins to fret us and, amid our economies, seeks the pleasures which we have merely left but not condemned. Indeed, the more stealthily it comes, the greater is its force. For all unconcealed vices are less serious; a disease also is farther on the road to being cured when it breaks forth from concealment and manifests its power. So with greed, ambition, and the other evils of the mind,—you may be sure that they do most harm when they are hidden behind a pretence of soundness.

Men think that we are in retirement, and yet we are not. For if we have sincerely retired, and have sounded the signal for retreat, and have scorned outward attractions, then, as I remarked above,** no outward thing will distract us; no music of men or of birds*** can interrupt good thoughts, when they have once become steadfast and sure. The mind which starts at words or at chance sounds is unstable and has not yet withdrawn into itself; it contains within itself an element of anxiety and rooted fear, and this makes one a prey to care, as our Vergil says:

> I, whom of yore no dart could cause to flee,
> Nor Greeks, with crowded lines of infantry.
> Now shake at every sound, and fear the air,
> Both for my child and for the load I bear.****

---

* See Introduction, page viii.

** § 4 of this letter.

*** An allusion to the Sirens and Ulysses, cf. § 15 below.

**** Aeneas is escaping from Troy, *Aeneid*, ii. 726 ff.

This man in his first state is wise; he blenches neither at the brandished spear, nor at the clashing armour of the serried foe, nor at the din of the stricken city. This man in his second state lacks knowledge fearing for his own concerns, he pales at every sound; any cry is taken for the battle-shout and overthrows him; the slightest disturbance renders him breathless with fear. It is the load that makes him afraid.* Select anyone you please from among your favourites of Fortune, trailing their many responsibilities, carrying their many burdens, and you will behold a picture of Vergil's hero, "fearing both for his child and for the load he bears."

You may therefore be sure that you are at peace with yourself, when no noise reaches you, when no word shakes you out of yourself, whether it be of flattery or of threat, or merely an empty sound buzzing about you with unmeaning din. "What then?" you say, "is it not sometimes a simpler matter just to avoid the uproar?" I admit this. Accordingly, I shall change from my present quarters. I merely wished to test myself and to give myself practice. Why need I be tormented any longer, when Ulysses found so simple a cure for his comrades** even against the songs of the Sirens? Farewell.

---

* Aeneas carries Anchises; the rich man carries his burden of wealth.

** Not merely by stopping their ears with wax, but also by bidding them row past the Sirens as quickly as possible. *Odyssey*, xii. 182.

LETTER

63

On Grief for Lost Friends

I am grieved to hear that your friend Flaccus is dead, but I would not have you sorrow more than is fitting. That you should not mourn at all I shall hardly dare to insist; and yet I know that it is the better way. But what man will ever be so blessed with that ideal steadfastness of soul, unless he has already risen far above the reach of Fortune? Even such a man will be stung by an event like this, but it will be only a sting. We, however, may be forgiven for bursting into tears, if only our tears have not flowed to excess, and if we have checked them by our own efforts. Let not the eyes be dry when we have lost a friend, nor let them overflow. We may weep, but we must not wail.

Do you think that the law which I lay down for you is harsh, when the greatest of Greek poets has extended the privilege of weeping to one day only, in the lines where he tells us that even Niobe took thought of food?* Do you wish to know the reason for lamentations and excessive weeping? It is because we seek the proofs of our bereavement in our tears, and do not give way to sorrow, but merely parade it. No man goes into mourning for

* Homer, *Iliad*, xix. 229 and xxiv. 602.

his own sake. Shame on our ill-timed folly! There is an element of self-seeking even in our sorrow.

"What," you say, "am I to forget my friend?" It is surely a short-lived memory that you vouchsafe to him, if it is to endure only as long as your grief; presently that brow of yours will be smoothed out in laughter by some circumstance, however casual. It is to a time no more distant than this that I put off the soothing of every regret, the quieting of even the bitterest grief. As soon as you cease to observe yourself, the picture of sorrow which you have contemplated will fade away; at present you are keeping watch over your own suffering. But even while you keep watch it slips away from you, and the sharper it is, the more speedily it comes to an end.

Let us see to it that the recollection of those whom we have lost becomes a pleasant memory to us. No man reverts with pleasure to any subject which he will not be able to reflect upon without pain. So too it cannot but be that the names of those whom we have loved and lost come back to us with a sort of sting; but there is a pleasure even in this sting. For, as my friend Attalus* used to say: "The remembrance of lost friends is pleasant in the same way that certain fruits have an agreeably acid taste, or as in extremely old wines it is their very bitterness that pleases us. Indeed, after a certain lapse of time, every thought that gave pain is quenched, and the pleasure comes to us unalloyed." If we take the word of Attalus for it, "to think of friends who are alive and well is like enjoying a meal of cakes and honey; the recollection of friends who have passed away gives a pleasure that is not without a touch of bitterness. Yet who will deny that even these things, which are bitter and contain an element of sourness, do serve to arouse the stomach?" For my part, I do not agree with him. To me, the thought of my dead friends is sweet and appealing. For I have had them as if I should one day lose them; I have lost them as if I have them still.

---

* The teacher of Seneca, often mentioned by him.

Therefore, Lucilius, act as befits your own serenity of mind, and cease to put a wrong interpretation on the gifts of Fortune. Fortune has taken away, but Fortune has given. Let us greedily enjoy our friends, because we do not know how long this privilege will be ours. Let us think how often we shall leave them when we go upon distant journeys, and how often we shall fail to see them when we tarry together in the same place; we shall thus understand that we have lost too much of their time while they were alive. But will you tolerate men who are most careless of their friends, and then mourn them most abjectly, and do not love anyone unless they have lost him? The reason why they lament too unrestrainedly at such times is that they are afraid lest men doubt whether they really have loved; all too late they seek for proofs of their emotions. If we have other friends, we surely deserve ill at their hands and think ill of them, if they are of so little account that they fail to console us for the loss of one. If, on the other hand, we have no other friends, we have injured ourselves more than Fortune has injured us; since Fortune has robbed us of one friend, but we have robbed ourselves of every friend whom we have failed to make. Again, he who has been unable to love more than one, has had none too much love even for that one.* If a man who has lost his one and only tunic through robbery chooses to bewail his plight rather than look about him for some way to escape the cold, or for something with which to cover his shoulders, would you not think him an utter fool?

You have buried one whom you loved; look about for someone to love. It is better to replace your friend than to weep for him. What I am about to add is, I know, a very hackneyed remark, but I shall not omit it simply because it is a common phrase: A man ends his grief by the mere passing of time, even if he has not ended it of his own accord. But the most shameful cure for sorrow, in the case of a sensible man, is to grow weary of sorrowing. I should prefer

* The reason is, as Lipsius observed, that friendship is essentially a social virtue, and is not confined to one object. The pretended friendship for one and only one is a form of self-love, and is not unselfish love.

you to abandon grief, rather than have grief abandon you; and you should stop grieving as soon as possible, since, even if you wish to do so, it is impossible to keep it up for a long time. Our forefathers* have enacted that, in the case of women, a year should be the limit for mourning; not that they needed to mourn for so long, but that they should mourn no longer. In the case of men, no rules are laid down, because to mourn at all is not regarded as honourable. For all that, what woman can you show me, of all the pathetic females that could scarcely be dragged away from the funeral-pile or torn from the corpse, whose tears have lasted a whole month? Nothing becomes offensive so quickly as grief; when fresh, it finds someone to console it and attracts one or another to itself; but after becoming chronic, it is ridiculed, and rightly. For it is either assumed or foolish.

He who writes these words to you is no other than I, who wept so excessively for my dear friend Annaeus Serenus** that, in spite of my wishes, I must be included among the examples of men who have been overcome by grief. Today, however, I condemn this act of mine, and I understand that the reason why I lamented so greatly was chiefly that I had never imagined it possible for his death to precede mine. The only thought which occurred to my mind was that he was the younger, and much younger, too,—as if the Fates kept to the order of our ages!

Therefore let us continually think as much about our own mortality as about that of all those we love. In former days I ought to have said: "My friend Serenus is younger than I; but what does that matter? He would naturally die after me, but he may precede me." It was just because I did not do this that I was unprepared when Fortune dealt me the sudden blow. Now is the time for you to reflect,

---

* According to tradition, from the time of Numa Pompilius.

** An intimate friend of Seneca, probably a relative, who died in the year 63 from eating poisoned mushrooms (Pliny, *N. H.* xxii. 96). Seneca dedicated to Serenus several of his philosophical essays.

not only that all things are mortal, but also that their mortality is subject to no fixed law. Whatever can happen at any time can happen today. Let us therefore reflect, my beloved Lucilius, that we shall soon come to the goal which this friend, to our own sorrow, has reached. And perhaps, if only the tale told by wise men is true* and there is a bourne to welcome us, then he whom we think we have lost has only been sent on ahead. Farewell.

---

* Cf. the closing chapter of the Agricola of Tacitus: *si, ut sapientibus placet, non cum corpore exstinguuntur magnae animae*, etc.

LETTER

65

On the First Cause

I shared my time yesterday with ill health;* it claimed for itself all the period before noon; in the afternoon, however, it yielded to me. And so I first tested my spirit by reading; then, when reading was found to be possible, I dared to make more demands upon the spirit, or perhaps I should say, to make more concessions to it. I wrote a little, and indeed with more concentration than usual, for I am struggling with a difficult subject and do not wish to be downed. In the midst of this, some friends visited me, with the purpose of employing force and of restraining me, as if I were a sick man indulging in some excess. So conversation was substituted for writing; and from this conversation I shall communicate to you the topic which is still the subject of debate; for we have appointed you referee.** You have more of a task on your hands than you suppose, for the argument is threefold.

---

* For Seneca's troubles in this regard see also Epp. liv. and civ.

** The *arbiter* was a judge appointed to try a case according to *bona fides* (equity), as contrasted with the *iudex* proper, whose duty was defined by the magistrate.

Our Stoic philosophers, as you know, declare that there are two things in the universe which are the source of everything,—namely, cause and matter.* Matter lies sluggish, a substance ready for any use, but sure to remain unemployed if no one sets it in motion. Cause, however, by which we mean reason, moulds matter and turns it in whatever direction it will, producing thereby various concrete results. Accordingly, there must be, in the case of each thing, that from which it is made, and, next, an agent by which it is made. The former is its material, the latter its cause.

All art is but imitation of nature; therefore, let me apply these statements of general principles to the things which have to be made by man. A statue, for example, has afforded matter which was to undergo treatment at the hands of the artist, and has had an artist who was to give form to the matter. Hence, in the case of the statue, the material was bronze, the cause was the workman. And so it goes with all things,—they consist of that which is made, and of the maker. The Stoics believe in one cause only,—the maker; but Aristotle thinks that the word "cause" can be used in three ways: "The first cause," he says, "is the actual matter, without which nothing can be created. The second is the workman. The third is the form, which is impressed upon every work,—a statue, for example." This last is what Aristotle calls the *idos.*** "There is, too," says he, "a fourth,—the purpose of the work as a whole." Now I shall show you what this last means. Bronze is the "first cause" of the statue, for it could never have been made unless there had been something from which it could be cast and moulded. The "second cause" is the artist; for without the skilled hands of a workman that bronze could not have

---

* See Zeller's *Stoics* (translated by Reichel), pp. 139 ff.

** The statue figure is a frequent one in philosophy; cf. Ep. ix. 5. The "form" of Aristotle goes back to the "idea" of Plato. These four causes are the causes of Aristotle, matter (ὕλη), form (εἶδος), force (τὸ κινοῦν), and the end (τὸ τέλος); when they all concur, we pass from possibility to fact. Aristotle gives eight categories in *Phys.* 225 b 5; and ten in *Categ.* 1 b 25,—substance, quantity, quality, relation, place, time, situation, possession, action, passion. For a definition of εἶδος see Aristotle, *Phys* 190 b 20 γίγνεται πᾶν ἔκ τε τοῦ ὑποκειμένου καὶ τῆς μορφῆς (i.e. τοῦ εἴδους).

been shaped to the outlines of the statue. The "third cause" is the form, inasmuch as our statue could never be called The Lance-Bearer or The Boy Binding his Hair,* had not this special shape been stamped upon it. The "fourth cause" is the purpose of the work. For if this purpose had not existed, the statue would not have been made. Now what is this purpose? It is that which attracted the artist, which he followed when he made the statue. It may have been money, if he has made it for sale; or renown, if he has worked for reputation; or religion, if he has wrought it as a gift for a temple. Therefore this also is a cause contributing towards the making of the statue; or do you think that we should avoid including, among the causes of a thing which has been made, that element without which the thing in question would not have been made?

To these four Plato adds a fifth cause,—the pattern which he himself calls the "idea"; for it is this that the artist gazed upon** when he created the work which he had decided to carry out. Now it makes no difference whether he has his pattern outside himself, that he may direct his glance to it, or within himself, conceived and placed there by himself. God has within himself these patterns of all things, and his mind comprehends the harmonies and the measures of the whole totality of things which are to be carried out; he is filled with these shapes which Plato calls the "ideas,"—imperishable, unchangeable, not subject to decay. And therefore, though men die, humanity itself, or the idea of man, according to which man is moulded, lasts on, and though men toil and perish, it suffers no change. Accordingly, there are five causes, as Plato says:*** the material, the agent, the make-up, the model, and the end in view. Last comes

---

* Well-known works of Polyclitus, fifth century B.C.

** Explaining the derivation of the Greek word,—ιδεῖν, "to behold." For a discussion of Plato's "ideas," those "independent, separate, self-existing, perfect, and eternal essences" (*Republic* vi. and vii.) see Adam, *The Republic of Plato*, ii. 168-179. According to Adam, Plato owes his theory of ideas to Socrates, the Eleatics, and the study of geometry; but his debt is not so great as his discovery.

*** i.e., the four categories as established by Aristotle, plus the "idea" of Plato.

the result of all these. Just as in the case of the statue,—to go back to the figure with which we began,—the material is the bronze, the agent is the artist, the make-up is the form which is adapted to the material, the model is the pattern imitated by the agent, the end in view is the purpose in the maker's mind, and, finally, the result of all these is the statue itself. The universe also, in Plato's opinion, possesses all these elements. The agent is God; the source, matter; the form, the shape and the arrangement of the visible world. The pattern is doubtless the model according to which God has made this great and most beautiful creation. The purpose is his object in so doing. Do you ask what God's purpose is? It is goodness. Plato, at any rate, says: "What was God's reason for creating the world? God is good, and no good person is grudging of anything that is good. Therefore, God made it the best world possible." Hand down your opinion, then, O judge; state who seems to you to say what is truest, and not who says what is absolutely true. For to do that is as far beyond our ken as truth itself.

This throng of causes, defined by Aristotle and by Plato, embraces either too much or too little.* For if they regard as "causes" of an object that is to be made everything without which the object cannot be made, they have named too few. Time must be included among the causes; for nothing can be made without time. They must also include place; for if there be no place where a thing can be made, it will not be made. And motion too; nothing is either made or destroyed without motion. There is no art without motion, no change of any kind. Now, however, I am searching for the first, the general cause; this must be simple, inasmuch as matter, too, is simple. Do we ask what cause is? It is surely Creative Reason,**—in other words, God.

---

* The Stoic view (see § 2 of this letter), besides making the four categories of "substance," "form," "variety," and "variety of relation," regarded material things as the only things which possessed being. The Stoics thus differ from Aristotle and Plato in holding that nothing is real except matter; besides, they relate everything to one ultimate cause, the acting force or efficient cause.

** i.e., the λόγος σπερματικός, the creative force in nature, that is, Providence, or the will of Zeus.

For those elements to which you referred are not a great series of independent causes; they all hinge on one alone, and that will be the creative cause. Do you maintain that form is a cause? This is only what the artist stamps upon his work; it is part of a cause, but not the cause. Neither is the pattern a cause, but an indispensable tool of the cause. His pattern is as indispensable to the artist as the chisel or the file; without these, art can make no progress. But for all that, these things are neither parts of the art, nor causes of it. "Then," perhaps you will say, "the purpose of the artist, that which leads him to undertake to create something, is the cause." It may be a cause; it is not, however, the efficient cause, but only an accessory cause. But there are countless accessory causes; what we are discussing is the general cause. Now the statement of Plato and Aristotle is not in accord with their usual penetration, when they maintain that the whole universe, the perfectly wrought work, is a cause. For there is a great difference between a work and the cause of a work.

Either give your opinion, or, as is easier in cases of this kind, declare that the matter is not clear and call for another hearing.* But you will reply: "What pleasure do you get from wasting your time on these problems, which relieve you of none of your emotions, rout none of your desires?" So far as I am concerned, I treat and discuss them as matters which contribute greatly toward calming the spirit, and I search myself first, and then the world about me. And not even now am I, as you think, wasting my time. For all these questions, provided that they be not chopped up and torn apart into such unprofitable refinements, elevate and lighten the soul, which is weighted down by a heavy burden and desires to be freed and to return to the elements of which it was once a part. For this body of ours is a weight upon the soul and its penance; as the load presses down the soul is crushed and is in bondage, unless philosophy has come to its assistance and has bid it take fresh courage by contemplating the universe, and has turned it from things earthly to things divine. There it has its liberty,

* i.e., restate the question and hear the evidence again.

there it can roam abroad;* meantime it escapes the custody in which it is bound, and renews its life in heaven. Just as skilled workmen, who have been engaged upon some delicate piece of work which wearies their eyes with straining, if the light which they have is niggardly or uncertain, go forth into the open air and in some park devoted to the people's recreation delight their eyes in the generous light of day; so the soul, imprisoned as it has been in this gloomy and darkened house, seeks the open sky whenever it can, and in the contemplation of the universe finds rest.

The wise man, the seeker after wisdom, is bound closely, indeed, to his body, but he is an absentee so far as his better self is concerned, and he concentrates his thoughts upon lofty things. Bound, so to speak, to his oath of allegiance, he regards the period of life as his term of service. He is so trained that he neither loves nor hates life; he endures a mortal lot, although he knows that an ampler lot is in store for him. Do you forbid me to contemplate the universe? Do you compel me to withdraw from the whole and restrict me to a part? May I not ask what are the beginnings of all things, who moulded the universe, who took the confused and conglomerate mass of sluggish matter, and separated it into its parts? May I not inquire who is the Master-Builder of this universe, how the mighty bulk was brought under the control of law and order, who gathered together the scattered atoms, who separated the disordered elements and assigned an outward form to elements that lay in one vast shapelessness? Or whence came all the expanse of light? And whether is it fire, or something even brighter than fire?** Am I not

---

* According to the Stoics the soul, which consisted of fire or breath and was a part of the divine essence, rose at death into the ether and became one with the stars. Seneca elsewhere (*Consolatio ad Marciam*) states that the soul went through a sort of purifying process,—a view which may have had some influence on Christian thought. The souls of the good, the Stoics maintained, were destined to last until the end of the world, the souls of the bad to be extinguished before that time.

** The sequence of elements from the earth outwards and upwards was earth, water, air, and fire. The upper fire was ether. Zeno (quoted by Cicero, *Acad.* i. 11. 39) refused to acknowledge a fifth essence: *statuebat enim ignem esse ipsam naturam, quae quaeque gigneret, el mentem et sensus.*

to ask these questions? Must I be ignorant of the heights whence I have descended? Whether I am to see this world but once, or to be born many times? What is my destination afterwards? What abode awaits my soul on its release from the laws of slavery among men? Do you forbid me to have a share in heaven? In other words, do you bid me live with my head bowed down? No, I am above such an existence; I was born to a greater destiny than to be a mere chattel of my body, and I regard this body as nothing but a chain* which manacles my freedom. Therefore, I offer it as a sort of buffer to fortune, and shall allow no wound to penetrate through to my soul. For my body is the only part of me which can suffer injury. In this dwelling, which is exposed to peril, my soul lives free. Never shall this flesh drive me to feel fear, or to assume any pretence that is unworthy of a good man. Never shall I lie in order to honour this petty body. When it seems proper, I shall sever my connexion with it. And at present, while we are bound together, our alliance shall nevertheless not be one of equality; the soul shall bring all quarrels before its own tribunal. To despise our bodies is sure freedom.

To return to our subject; this freedom will be greatly helped by the contemplation of which we were just speaking. All things are made up of matter and of God;** God controls matter, which encompasses him and follows him as its guide and leader. And that which creates, in other words, God, is more powerful and precious than matter, which is acted upon by God. God's place in the universe corresponds to the soul's relation to man. World-matter corresponds to our mortal body; therefore let the lower serve the higher. Let us be brave in the face of hazards. Let us not fear wrongs, or wounds, or bonds, or poverty. And what is death? It is either the end, or a process of change. I have no fear of ceasing to exist; it is the same as not having begun. Nor do I shrink from changing into another state, because I shall, under no conditions, be as cramped as I am now. Farewell.

---

* The "prison of the body" is a frequent figure in Stoic as in all philosophy. See, for example, § 16 of this letter, "the soul in bondage."

** A restatement of the previous remark made in this letter; see note on § 11.

VOLUME TWO

LETTER 77

On Taking One's Own Life

Suddenly there came into our view today the "Alexandrian" ships,—I mean those which are usually sent ahead to announce the coming of the fleet; they are called "mail-boats." The Campanians are glad to see them; all the rabble of Puteoli* stand on the docks, and can recognize the "Alexandrian" boats, no matter how great the crowd of vessels, by the very trim of their sails. For they alone may keep spread their topsails, which all ships use when out at sea, because nothing sends a ship along so well as its upper canvas; that is where most of the speed is obtained. So when the breeze has stiffened and becomes stronger than is comfortable, they set their yards lower; for the wind has less force near the surface of the water. Accordingly, when they have made Capreae and the headland whence

Tall Pallas watches on the stormy peak,**

---

* Puteoli, in the bay of Naples, was the head-quarters in Italy of the important grain-trade with Egypt, on which the Roman magistrates relied to feed the populace.

** Author unknown.

all other vessels are bidden to be content with the mainsail, and the topsail stands out conspicuously on the "Alexandrian" mail-boats.

While everybody was bustling about and hurrying to the waterfront, I felt great pleasure in my laziness, because, although I was soon to receive letters from my friends, I was in no hurry to know how my affairs were progressing abroad, or what news the letters were bringing; for some time now I have had no losses, nor gains either. Even if I were not an old man, I could not have helped feeling pleasure at this; but as it is, my pleasure was far greater. For, however small my possessions might be, I should still have left over more travelling-money than journey to travel, especially since this journey upon which we have set out is one which need not be followed to the end. An expedition will be incomplete if one stops half-way, or anywhere on this side of one's destination; but life is not incomplete if it is honourable. At whatever point you leave off living, provided you leave off nobly, your life is a whole.* Often, however, one must leave off bravely, and our reasons therefore need not be momentous; for neither are the reasons momentous which hold us here.

Tullius Marcellinus,** a man whom you knew very well, who in youth was a quiet soul and became old prematurely, fell ill of a disease which was by no means hopeless; but it was protracted and troublesome, and it demanded much attention; hence he began to think about dying. He called many of his friends together. Each one of them gave Marcellinus advice,—the timid friend urging him to do what he had made up his mind to do; the flattering and wheedling friend giving counsel which he supposed would be more pleasing to Marcellinus when he came to think the matter over; but our Stoic friend, a rare man, and, to praise him in language which he deserves, a man of courage and vigour*** admonished

---

* This thought, found in Ep. xii. 6 and often elsewhere, is a favourite with Seneca.

** It is not likely that this Marcellinus is the same person as the Marcellinus Ep. xxix., because of their different views on philosophy (Summers). But there is no definite evidence for or against.

*** A Roman compliment; the Greeks would have used καλὸς κἀγαθός; cf. Horace, *Ep.* i. 7. 46

Strenuus et fortis causisque Philippus agendis Clarus.

him best of all, as it seems to me. For he began as follows: "Do not torment yourself, my dear Marcellinus, as if the question which you are weighing were a matter of importance. It is not an important matter to live; all your slaves live, and so do all animals; but it is important to die honourably, sensibly, bravely. Reflect how long you have been doing the same thing: food, sleep, lust,—this is one's daily round. The desire to die may be felt, not only by the sensible man or the brave or unhappy man, but even by the man who is merely surfeited."

Marcellinus did not need someone to urge him, but rather someone to help him; his slaves refused to do his bidding. The Stoic therefore removed their fears, showing them that there was no risk involved for the household except when it was uncertain whether the master's death was self-sought or not; besides, it was as bad a practice to kill one's master as it was to prevent him forcibly from killing himself. Then he suggested to Marcellinus himself that it would be a kindly act to distribute gifts to those who had attended him throughout his whole life, when that life was finished, just as, when a banquet is finished,* the remaining portion is divided among the attendants who stand about the table. Marcellinus was of a compliant and generous disposition, even when it was a question of his own property; so he distributed little sums among his sorrowing slaves, and comforted them besides. No need had he of sword or of bloodshed; for three days he fasted and had a tent put up in his very bedroom.** Then a tub was brought in; he lay in it for a long time, and, as the hot water was continually poured over him, he gradually passed away, not without a feeling of pleasure, as he himself remarked,—such a feeling as a slow dissolution is wont to give. Those of us who have ever fainted know from experience what this feeling is.

This little anecdote into which I have digressed will not be displeasing to you. For you will see that your friend departed neither with difficulty nor with suffering. Though he committed suicide, yet he withdrew most gently, gliding out of life. The anecdote may also be

---

* For this frequent "banquet of life" simile see Ep. xcviii. 15 *ipse vitae plenus est*, etc.

** So that the steam might not escape. One thinks of Seneca's last hours: Tac. *Ann.* xv. 64 *stagnum calidae aquae introiit . . . exin balneo inlatus et vapore eius exanimatus.*

of some use; for often a crisis demands just such examples. There are times when we ought to die and are unwilling; sometimes we die and are unwilling. No one is so ignorant as not to know that we must at some time die; nevertheless, when one draws near death, one turns to flight, trembles, and laments. Would you not think him an utter fool who wept because he was not alive a thousand years ago? And is he not just as much of a fool who weeps because he will not be alive a thousand years from now? It is all the same; you will not be, and you were not. Neither of these periods of time belongs to you. You have been cast upon this point of time;* if you would make it longer, how much longer shall you make it? Why weep? Why pray? You are taking pains to no purpose.

> Give over thinking that your prayers can bend
> Divine decrees from their predestined end.**

These decrees are unalterable and fixed; they are governed by a mighty and everlasting compulsion. Your goal will be the goal of all things. What is there strange in this to you? You were born to be subject to this law; this fate befell your father, your mother, your ancestors, all who came before you; and it will befall all who shall come after you. A sequence which cannot be broken or altered by any power binds all things together and draws all things in its course. Think of the multitudes of men doomed to death who will come after you, of the multitudes who will go with you! You would die more bravely, I suppose, in the company of many thousands; and yet there are many thousands, both of men and of animals, who at this very moment, while you are irresolute about death, are breathing their last, in their several ways. But you,—did you believe that you would not some day reach the goal towards which you have always been travelling? No journey but has its end.

You think, I suppose, that it is now in order for me to cite some examples of great men. No, I shall cite rather the case of a boy. The story of the Spartan lad has been preserved: taken captive while still

---

* For the same thought cf. Ep. xlix. 3 *punctum est quod vivimus et adhuc puncto minus.*

** Vergil, *Aeneid*, vi. 376.

a stripling, he kept crying in his Doric dialect, "I will not be a slave!" and he made good his word; for the very first time he was ordered to perform a menial and degrading service,—and the command was to fetch a chamber-pot,—he dashed out his brains against the wall.* So near at hand is freedom, and is anyone still a slave? Would you not rather have your own son die thus than reach old age by weakly yielding? Why therefore are you distressed, when even a boy can die so bravely? Suppose that you refuse to follow him; you will be led. Take into your own control that which is now under the control of another. Will you not borrow that boy's courage, and say: "I am no slave!"? Unhappy fellow, you are a slave to men, you are a slave to your business, you are a slave to life. For life, if courage to die be lacking, is slavery.

Have you anything worth waiting for? Your very pleasures, which cause you to tarry and hold you back, have already been exhausted by you. None of them is a novelty to you, and there is none that has not already become hateful because you are cloyed with it. You know the taste of wine and cordials. It makes no difference whether a hundred or a thousand measures** pass through your bladder; you are nothing but a wine-strainer.*** You are a connoisseur in the flavour of the oyster and of the mullet;**** your luxury has not left you anything untasted for the years that are to come; and yet these are the things from which you are torn away unwillingly. What else is there which you would regret to have taken from you? Friends? But who can be a friend to you? Country? What? Do you think enough of your country to be late to dinner? The light of the sun? You would extinguish it, if you could; for what have you ever done that was fit to be seen in the light? Confess the truth; it is not because you long for the senate

---

* See Plutarch, *Mor.* 234 b, for a similar act of the Spartan boy captured by King Antigonus. Hense (*Rhein. Mus.* xlvii. pp. 220 f.) thinks that this story may be taken from Bion, the third-century satirist and moral philosopher.

** About 5¾ gallons.

*** Cf. Pliny, xiv. 22 *quin immo ut plus capiamus, sacco frangimus vires*. Strained wine could be drunk in greater quantities without intoxication.

**** Cf. Dio Cassius, xl. 54, for the exiled Milo's enjoyment of the mullets of Marseilles.

chamber or the forum, or even for the world of nature, that you would fain put off dying; it is because you are loth to leave the fish-market, though you have exhausted its stores.*

You are afraid of death; but how can you scorn it in the midst of a mushroom supper?** You wish to live; well, do you know how to live? You are afraid to die. But come now: is this life of yours anything but death? Gaius Caesar was passing along the Via Latina, when a man stepped out from the ranks of the prisoners, his grey beard hanging down even to his breast, and begged to be put to death. "What!" said Caesar, "are you alive now?" That is the answer which should be given to men to whom death would come as a relief. "You are afraid to die; what! are you alive now?" "But," says one, "I wish to live, for I am engaged in many honourable pursuits. I am loth to leave life's duties, which I am fulfilling with loyalty and zeal." Surely you are aware that dying is also one of life's duties? You are deserting no duty; for there is no definite number established which you are bound to complete. There is no life that is not short. Compared with the world of nature, even Nestor's life was a short one, or Sattia's,*** the woman who bade carve on her tombstone that she had lived ninety and nine years. Some persons, you see, boast of their long lives; but who could have endured the old lady if she had had the luck to complete her hundredth year? It is with life as it is with a play,—it matters not how long the action is spun out, but how good the acting is. It makes no difference at what point you stop. Stop whenever you choose; only see to it that the closing period is well turned.**** Farewell.

---

* Probably the strong tone of disapproval used in this paragraph is directed against the Roman in general rather than against the industrious Lucilius. It is characteristic of the diatribe.

** Seneca may be recalling the death of the Emperor Claudius.

*** A traditional example of old age, mentioned by Martial and the elder Pliny.

**** Compare the last words of the Emperor Augustus: *amicos percontatus ecquid iis videretur mimum vitae commode transegisse* (Suet. *Aug.* 99).

LETTER

78

On the Healing Power of the Mind

That you are frequently troubled by the snuffling of catarrh and by short attacks of fever which follow after long and chronic catarrhal seizures, I am sorry to hear; particularly because I have experienced this sort of illness myself, and scorned it in its early stages. For when I was still young, I could put up with hardships and show a bold front to illness. But I finally succumbed, and arrived at such a state that I could do nothing but snuffle, reduced as I was to the extremity of thinness.* I often entertained the impulse of ending my life then and there; but the thought of my kind old father kept me back. For I reflected, not how bravely I had the power to die, but how little power he had to bear bravely the loss of me. And so I commanded myself to live. For sometimes it is an act of bravery even to live.

Now I shall tell you what consoled me during those days, stating at the outset that these very aids to my peace of mind were as efficacious as medicine. Honourable consolation results in a cure; and whatever has uplifted the soul helps the body also. My studies were my salvation. I place it to the credit of philosophy

* To such a degree that Seneca's enemy Caligula refrained from executing him, on the ground that he would soon die.

that I recovered and regained my strength. I owe my life to philosophy, and that is the least of my obligations! My friends, too, helped me greatly toward good health; I used to be comforted by their cheering words, by the hours they spent at my bedside, and by their conversation. Nothing, my excellent Lucilius, refreshes and aids a sick man so much as the affection of his friends; nothing so steals away the expectation and the fear of death. In fact, I could not believe that, if they survived me, I should be dying at all. Yes, I repeat, it seemed to me that I should continue to live, not with them, but through them. I imagined myself not to be yielding up my soul, but to be making it over to them.

All these things gave me the inclination to succour myself and to endure any torture; besides, it is a most miserable state to have lost one's zest for dying, and to have no zest in living. These, then, are the remedies to which you should have recourse. The physician will prescribe your walks and your exercise; he will warn you not to become addicted to idleness, as is the tendency of the inactive invalid; he will order you to read in a louder voice and to exercise your lungs* the passages and cavity of which are affected; or to sail and shake up your bowels by a little mild motion; he will recommend the proper food, and the suitable time for aiding your strength with wine or refraining from it in order to keep your cough from being irritated and hacking. But as for me, my counsel to you is this,—and it is a cure, not merely of this disease of yours, but of your whole life,—"Despise death." There is no sorrow in the world, when we have escaped from the fear of death. There are these three serious elements in every disease: fear of death, bodily pain, and interruption of pleasures. Concerning death enough has been said, and I shall add only a word: this fear is not a fear of disease, but a fear of nature. Disease has often postponed death, and a vision of dying has been many a man's salvation.** You will die, not because you are ill, but because you are alive; even when you have been cured, the same end awaits you; when you have recovered, it will be not death, but ill-health, that you have escaped.

---

* Cf. Ep. xv. 7 f.

** i.e., men have become healthier after passing through serious illness.

Let us now return to the consideration of the characteristic disadvantage of disease: it is accompanied by great suffering. The suffering, however, is rendered endurable by interruptions; for the strain of extreme pain must come to an end.* No man can suffer both severely and for a long time; Nature, who loves us most tenderly, has so constituted us as to make pain either endurable or short.** The severest pains have their seat in the most slender parts of our body; nerves, joints, and any other of the narrow passages, hurt most cruelly when they have developed trouble within their contracted spaces. But these parts soon become numb, and by reason of the pain itself lose the sensation of pain, whether because the life-force, when checked in its natural course and changed for the worse, loses the peculiar power through which it thrives and through which it warns us, or because the diseased humours of the body, when they cease to have a place into which they may flow, are thrown back upon themselves, and deprive of sensation the parts where they have caused congestion. So gout, both in the feet and in the hands, and all pain in the vertebrae and in the nerves, have their intervals of rest at the times when they have dulled the parts which they before had tortured; the first twinges,*** in all such cases, are what cause the distress, and their onset is checked by lapse of time, so that there is an end of pain when numbness has set in. Pain in the teeth, eyes, and ears is most acute for the very reason that it begins among the narrow spaces of the body,—no less acute, indeed, than in the head itself. But if it is more violent than usual, it turns to delirium and stupor. This is, accordingly, a consolation for excessive pain,—that you cannot help ceasing to feel it if you feel it to excess. The reason, however, why the inexperienced are impatient when their bodies suffer is, that they have not accustomed themselves to be contented in spirit. They have been closely associated with the body. Therefore a high-minded and sensible man divorces soul from

---

* Cf. Epicurus, Frag. 446 Usener.

** Compare, from among many parallels, Ep. xxiv. 14 *(dolor) levis es, si ferre possum, brevis es, si ferre non possum.*

*** See also Ep. xcv. 17. The word literally means "maggots," "bots," in horses or cattle.

body, and dwells much with the better or divine part, and only as far as he must with this complaining and frail portion.

"But it is a hardship," men say, "to do without our customary pleasures,—to fast, to feel thirst and hunger." These are indeed serious when one first abstains from them. Later the desire dies down, because the appetites themselves which lead to desire are wearied and forsake us; then the stomach becomes petulant, then the food which we craved before becomes hateful. Our very wants die away. But there is no bitterness in doing without that which you have ceased to desire. Moreover, every pain sometimes stops, or at any rate slackens; moreover, one may take precautions against its return, and, when it threatens, may check it by means of remedies. Every variety of pain has its premonitory symptoms; this is true, at any rate, of pain that is habitual and recurrent. One can endure the suffering which disease entails, if one has come to regard its results with scorn. But do not of your own accord make your troubles heavier to bear and burden yourself with complaining. Pain is slight if opinion has added nothing to it; but if, on the other hand, you begin to encourage yourself and say, "It is nothing,—a trifling matter at most; keep a stout heart and it will soon cease"; then in thinking it slight, you will make it slight. Everything depends on opinion; ambition, luxury, greed, hark back to opinion. It is according to opinion that we suffer. A man is as wretched as he has convinced himself that he is. I hold that we should do away with complaint about past sufferings and with all language like this: "None has ever been worse off than I. What sufferings, what evils have I endured! No one has thought that I shall recover. How often have my family bewailed me, and the physicians given me over! Men who are placed on the rack are not torn asunder with such agony!" However, even if all this is true, it is over and gone. What benefit is there in reviewing past sufferings, and in being unhappy, just because once you were unhappy? Besides, every one adds much to his own ills, and tells lies to himself. And that which was bitter to bear is pleasant to have borne; it is natural to rejoice at the ending of one's ills.

Two elements must therefore be rooted out once for all,—the fear of future suffering, and the recollection of past suffering; since the latter no longer concerns me, and the former concerns me not yet. But when set in the very midst of troubles one should say:

> Perchance some day the memory of this sorrow
> Will even bring delight.*

Let such a man fight against them with all his might: if he once gives way, he will be vanquished; but if he strives against his sufferings, he will conquer. As it is, however, what most men do is to drag down upon their own heads a falling ruin which they ought to try to support. If you begin to withdraw your support from that which thrusts toward you and totters and is ready to plunge, it will follow you and lean more heavily upon you; but if you hold your ground and make up your mind to push against it, it will be forced back. What blows do athletes receive on their faces and all over their bodies! Nevertheless, through their desire for fame they endure every torture, and they undergo these things not only because they are fighting but in order to be able to fight. Their very training means torture. So let us also win the way to victory in all our struggles,—for the reward is not a garland or a palm or a trumpeter who calls for silence at the proclamation of our names, but rather virtue, steadfastness of soul, and a peace that is won for all time, if fortune has once been utterly vanquished in any combat. You say, "I feel severe pain." What then; are you relieved from feeling it, if you endure it like a woman? Just as an enemy is more dangerous to a retreating army, so every trouble that fortune brings attacks us all the harder if we yield and turn our backs. "But the trouble is serious." What? Is it for this purpose that we are strong,—that we may have light burdens to bear? Would you have your illness long-drawn-out, or would you have it quick and short? If it is long, it means a respite, allows you a period for resting yourself, bestows upon you the boon of time in plenty; as it arises, so it must also subside. A short and rapid illness will do one of two things: it will quench or be quenched. And what difference does it make whether it is not or I am not? In either case there is an end of pain.

---

* Vergil, *Aeneid*, i. 203.

This, too, will help—to turn the mind aside to thoughts of other things and thus to depart from pain. Call to mind what honourable or brave deeds you have done; consider the good side of your own life.* Run over in your memory those things which you have particularly admired. Then think of all the brave men who have conquered pain: of him who continued to read his book as he allowed the cutting out of varicose veins; of him who did not cease to smile, though that very smile so enraged his torturers that they tried upon him every instrument of their cruelty. If pain can be conquered by a smile, will it not be conquered by reason? You may tell me now of whatever you like—of colds, hard coughing-spells that bring up parts of our entrails, fever that parches our very vitals, thirst, limbs so twisted that the joints protrude in different directions; yet worse than these are the stake, the rack, the red-hot plates, the instrument that reopens wounds while the wounds themselves are still swollen and that drives their imprint still deeper.** Nevertheless there have been men who have not uttered a moan amid these tortures. "More yet!" says the torturer; but the victim has not begged for release. "More yet!" he says again; but no answer has come. "More yet!" the victim has smiled, and heartily, too. Can you not bring yourself, after an example like this, to make a mock at pain?

"But," you object, "my illness does not allow me to be doing anything; it has withdrawn me from all my duties." It is your body that is hampered by ill-health, and not your soul as well. It is for this reason that it clogs the feet of the runner and will hinder the handiwork of the cobbler or the artisan; but if your soul be habitually in practice, you will plead and teach, listen and learn, investigate and meditate. What more is necessary? Do you think that you are doing nothing if you possess self-control in your illness? You will be showing that a disease can be overcome, or at any rate endured. There is, I assure you, a place for virtue even upon a bed of sickness. It is not only the sword and the battle-line that prove the soul alert and unconquered by fear; a man can display

* Literally, perhaps, "the noble rôles which you have played." Summers compares Ep. xiv. 13 *ultimas partes Catonis*—"the closing scenes of Cato's life."

** Cf. Ep. xiv. 4 f. and the *crucibus adfixi, flamma usti*, etc., of Tac. *Ann.* xv. 44.

bravery even when wrapped in his bed-clothes. You have something to do: wrestle bravely with disease. If it shall compel you to nothing, beguile you to nothing, it is a notable example that you display. O what ample matter were there for renown, if we could have spectators of our sickness! Be your own spectator; seek your own applause.

Again, there are two kinds of pleasures. Disease checks the pleasures of the body, but does not do away with them. Nay, if the truth is to be considered, it serves to excite them; for the thirstier a man is, the more he enjoys a drink; the hungrier he is, the more pleasure he takes in food. Whatever falls to one's lot after a period of abstinence is welcomed with greater zest. The other kind, however, the pleasures of the mind, which are higher and less uncertain, no physician can refuse to the sick man. Whoever seeks these and knows well what they are, scorns all the blandishments of the senses. Men say, "Poor sick fellow!" But why? Is it because he does not mix snow with his wine, or because he does not revive the chill of his drink—mixed as it is in a good-sized bowl—by chipping ice into it? Or because he does not have Lucrine* oysters opened fresh at his table? Or because there is no din of cooks about his dining-hall, as they bring in their very cooking apparatus along with their viands? For luxury has already devised this fashion—of having the kitchen accompany the dinner, so that the food may not grow lukewarm, or fail to be hot enough for a palate which has already become hardened. "Poor sick fellow!"—he will eat as much as he can digest. There will be no boar lying before his eyes,** banished from the table as if it were a common meat; and on his sideboard there will be heaped together no breast-meat of birds, because it sickens him to see birds served whole. But what evil has been done to you? You will dine like a sick man, nay, sometimes like a sound man.***

All these things, however, can be easily endured—gruel, warm water, and anything else that seems insupportable to a fastidious man, to one who is wallowing in luxury, sick in soul rather than in body—if

---

* The *lacus Lucrinus* was a salt-water lagoon, near Baiae in Campania.

** i.e., to be looked at; there are better dainties on the table.

*** *Sanus* is used as signifying "sound in body" and as the opposite of *insanus*.

only we cease to shudder at death. And we shall cease, if once we have gained a knowledge of the limits of good and evil; then, and then only, life will not weary us, neither will death make us afraid. For surfeit of self can never seize upon a life that surveys all the things which are manifold, great, divine; only idle leisure is wont to make men hate their lives. To one who roams* through the universe, the truth can never pall; it will be the untruths that will cloy. And, on the other hand, if death comes near with its summons, even though it be untimely in its arrival, though it cut one off in one's prime, a man has had a taste of all that the longest life can give. Such a man has in great measure come to understand the universe. He knows that honourable things do not depend on time for their growth; but any life must seem short to those who measure its length by pleasures which are empty and for that reason unbounded.

Refresh yourself with such thoughts as these, and meanwhile reserve some hours for our letters. There will come a time when we shall be united again and brought together; however short this time may be, we shall make it long by knowing how to employ it. For, as Posidonius says:** "A single day among the learned lasts longer than the longest life of the ignorant." Meanwhile, hold fast to this thought, and grip it close: yield not to adversity; trust not to prosperity; keep before your eyes the full scope of Fortune's power, as if she would surely do whatever is in her power to do. That which has been long expected comes more gently. Farewell.

---

* Perhaps a reminiscence of Lucretius i. 74 *omne immensum peragravit mente animoque.*

** Seneca often quotes Posidonius, as does Cicero also. These words may have been taken from his Προτρεπτικά (or Λόγοι προτρεπτικοί), *Exhortations*, a work in which he maintained that men should make a close study of philosophy, in spite of the varying opinions of its expositors.

LETTER

83

On Drunkenness

You bid me give you an account of each separate day, and of the whole day too; so you must have a good opinion of me if you think that in these days of mine there is nothing to hide. At any rate, it is thus that we should live,—as if we lived in plain sight of all men; and it is thus that we should think,—as if there were someone who could look into our inmost souls; and there is one who can so look. For what avails it that something is hidden from man? Nothing is shut off from the sight of God. He is witness of our souls,* and he comes into the very midst of our thoughts—comes into them, I say, as one who may at any time depart. I shall therefore do as you bid, and shall gladly inform you by letter what I am doing, and in what sequence. I shall keep watching myself continually, and—a most useful habit—shall review each day.** For this is what makes us wicked: that no one of us looks back over his own life. Our thoughts are devoted only to what we are about to do. And yet our plans for the future always depend on the past.

---

* Cf. Ep. xli. 2 *sacer intra nos spiritus, . . . malorum bonorumque nostrorum observator et custos.*

** Cf. Ep. i. 4 *ratio constat inpensae* (referring to his attempt to employ his time profitably).

Today has been unbroken; no one has filched the slightest part of it from me. The whole time has been divided between rest and reading. A brief space has been given over to bodily exercise, and on this ground I can thank old age—my exercise costs very little effort; as soon as I stir, I am tired. And weariness is the aim and end of exercise, no matter how strong one is. Do you ask who are my pacemakers? One is enough for me,—the slave Pharius, a pleasant fellow, as you know; but I shall exchange him for another. At my time of life I need one who is of still more tender years. Pharius, at any rate, says that he and I are at the same period of life; for we are both losing our teeth.* Yet even now I can scarcely follow his pace as he runs, and within a very short time I shall not be able to follow him at all; so you see what profit we get from daily exercise. Very soon does a wide interval open between two persons who travel different ways. My slave is climbing up at the very moment when I am coming down, and you surely know how much quicker the latter is. Nay, I was wrong; for now my life is not coming down; it is falling outright. Do you ask, for all that, how our race resulted today? We raced to a tie,**—something which rarely happens in a running contest. After tiring myself out in this way (for I cannot call it exercise), I took a cold bath; this, at my house, means just short of hot. I, the former cold-water enthusiast, who used to celebrate the new year by taking a plunge into the canal, who, just as naturally as I would set out to do some reading or writing, or to compose a speech, used to inaugurate the first of the year with a plunge into the Virgo aqueduct,*** have changed my allegiance, first to the Tiber, and then to my favourite tank, which is warmed only by the sun, at times when I am most robust and when there is not a flaw in my bodily processes. I have very little energy left for bathing. After the bath, some stale bread and breakfast without a table; no need to wash the hands after such a meal. Then comes a very short nap. You know

---

* See Ep. xii. 3 for a similar witticism.

** *Hieran* (*coronam*), as Lipsius thinks, when the result was doubtful, the garland was offered to the gods. From the Greek ἱερός, sacred.

*** Constructed by Marcus Agrippa; now the fountain of Trevi.

my habit; I avail myself of a scanty bit of sleep,—unharnessing, as it were.* For I am satisfied if I can just stop staying awake. Sometimes I know that I have slept; at other times, I have a mere suspicion.

Lo, now the din of the Races sounds about me! My ears are smitten with sudden and general cheering. But this does not upset my thoughts or even break their continuity. I can endure an uproar with complete resignation. The medley of voices blended in one note sounds to me like the dashing of waves,** or like the wind that lashes the tree-tops, or like any other sound which conveys no meaning.

What is it, then, you ask, to which I have been giving my attention? I will tell you. A thought sticks in my mind, left over from yesterday,—namely, what men of the greatest sagacity have meant when they have offered the most trifling and intricate proofs for problems of the greatest importance,—proofs which may be true, but none the less resemble fallacies. Zeno, that greatest of men, the revered founder of our brave and holy school of philosophy, wishes to discourage us from drunkenness. Listen, then, to his arguments proving that the good man will not get drunk: "No one entrusts a secret to a drunken man; but one will entrust a secret to a good man; therefore, the good man will not get drunk."*** Mark how ridiculous Zeno is made when we set up a similar syllogism in contrast with his. There are many, but one will be enough: "No one entrusts a secret to a man when he is asleep; but one entrusts a secret to a good man; therefore, the good man does not go to sleep."**** Posidonius pleads the cause of our master Zeno in the only possible way; but it cannot, I hold, be pleaded even in this way. For Posidonius maintains that the word "drunken" is used in two ways,—in the one case of a man who is loaded with wine and has no control over himself; in the other, of

---

* The same word is used by Seneca in *De Tranq. An.* xvii. 7 *quidam medio die interiunxerunt et in postmeridianas horas aliquid levioris operae distulerunt.*

** Cf. Ep. lvi. 3 *istum fremitum non magis curo quam fluctum aut deiectum aquae.*

*** Zeno, Frag. 229 von Arnim,—quoting also Philo's εἰ τῷ μεθύοντι οὐκ ἄν τις εὐλόγως λόγον ἀπόρρητον παρακατάθοιτο . . . οὐκ ἄρα μεθύει ὁ ἀστεῖος.

**** Cf. Ep. xlix. 8 *quod non perdidisti, habes; cornua autem non perdidisti; cornua ergo habes,*—and the syllogisms given in Ep. xlviii.

a man who is accustomed to get drunk, and is a slave to the habit. Zeno, he says, meant the latter,—the man who is accustomed to get drunk, not the man who is drunk; and no one would entrust to this person any secret, for it might be blabbed out when the man was in his cups. This is a fallacy. For the first syllogism refers to him who is actually drunk and not to him who is about to get drunk. You will surely admit that there is a great difference between a man who is drunk and a drunkard. He who is actually drunk may be in this state for the first time and may not have the habit, while the drunkard is often free from drunkenness. I therefore interpret the word in its usual meaning, especially since the syllogism is set up by a man who makes a business of the careful use of words, and who weighs his language. Moreover, if this is what Zeno meant, and what he wished it to mean to us, he was trying to avail himself of an equivocal word in order to work in a fallacy; and no man ought to do this when truth is the object of inquiry.

But let us admit, indeed, that he meant what Posidonius says; even so, the conclusion is false,—that secrets are not entrusted to an habitual drunkard. Think how many soldiers who are not always sober have been entrusted by a general or a captain or a centurion with messages which might not be divulged! With regard to the notorious plot to murder Gaius Caesar,—I mean the Caesar who conquered Pompey and got control of the state,—Tillius Cimber was trusted with it no less than Gaius Cassius. Now Cassius throughout his life drank water; while Tillius Cimber was a sot as well as a brawler. Cimber himself alluded to this fact, saying: "*I* carry a master? I cannot carry my liquor!" So let each one call to mind those who, to his knowledge, can be ill trusted with wine, but well trusted with the spoken word; and yet one case occurs to my mind, which I shall relate, lest it fall into oblivion. For life should be provided with conspicuous illustrations. Let us not always be harking back to the dim past.

Lucius Piso, the Director of Public Safety at Rome, was drunk from the very time of his appointment. He used to spend the greater part of the night at banquets, and would sleep until noon. That was the way he spent his morning hours. Nevertheless, he applied himself most diligently to his official duties, which included the guardianship of the city. Even the sainted Augustus trusted him with secret orders when he placed him in command of Thrace.* Piso conquered that country. Tiberius, too, trusted him when he took his holiday in Campania, leaving behind him in the city many a critical matter that aroused both suspicion and hatred. I fancy that it was because Piso's drunkenness turned out well for the Emperor that he appointed to the office of city prefect Cossus, a man of authority and balance, but so soaked and steeped in drink that once, at a meeting of the Senate, whither he had come after banqueting, he was overcome by a slumber from which he could not be roused, and had to be carried home. It was to this man that Tiberius sent many orders, written in his own hand,—orders which he believed he ought not to trust even to the officials of his household. Cossus never let a single secret slip out, whether personal or public.

So let us abolish all such harangues as this: "No man in the bonds of drunkenness has power over his soul. As the very vats are burst by new wine, and as the dregs at the bottom are raised to the surface by the strength of the fermentation; so, when the wine effervesces, whatever lies hidden below is brought up and made visible. As a man overcome by liquor cannot keep down his food when he has over-indulged in wine, so he cannot keep back a secret either. He pours forth impartially both his own secrets and those of other persons." This, of course, is what commonly happens, but so does this,—that we take counsel on serious subjects with those whom we know to be in the habit of drinking freely. Therefore this proposition, which is laid down in the guise of a defence of Zeno's syllogism, is false,—that secrets are not entrusted to the habitual drunkard.

How much better it is to arraign drunkenness frankly and to expose its vices! For even the middling good man avoids them, not to mention the perfect sage, who is satisfied with slaking his thirst; the sage, even if now and then he is led on by good cheer which, for

---

* In 11 B.C., when the Thracians were attacking Macedonia. The campaign lasted for three years, and Piso was rewarded with a triumph at its close.

a friend's sake, is carried somewhat too far, yet always stops short of drunkenness. We shall investigate later the question whether the mind of the sage is upset by too much wine and commits follies like those of the toper; but meanwhile, if you wish to prove that a good man ought not to get drunk, why work it out by logic? Show how base it is to pour down more liquor than one can carry, and not to know the capacity of one's own stomach; show how often the drunkard does things which make him blush when he is sober; state that drunkenness* is nothing but a condition of insanity purposely assumed. Prolong the drunkard's condition to several days; will you have any doubt about his madness? Even as it is, the madness is no less; it merely lasts a shorter time. Think of Alexander of Macedon,** who stabbed Clitus, his dearest and most loyal friend, at a banquet; after Alexander understood what he had done, he wished to die, and assuredly he ought to have died.

Drunkenness kindles and discloses every kind of vice, and removes the sense of shame that veils our evil undertakings.*** For more men abstain from forbidden actions because they are ashamed of sinning than because their inclinations are good. When the strength of wine has become too great and has gained control over the mind, every lurking evil comes forth from its hiding-place. Drunkenness does not create vice, it merely brings it into view; at such times the lustful man does not wait even for the privacy of a bedroom, but without postponement gives free play to the demands of his passions; at such times the unchaste man proclaims and publishes his malady; at such times your cross-grained fellow does not restrain his tongue or his hand. The haughty man increases his arrogance, the ruthless man his cruelty, the slanderer his spitefulness. Every vice is given free play and comes to the front. Besides, we forget who we are, we utter words that are halting and poorly enunciated, the glance is unsteady, the step

---

* Like anger, which was interpreted by the ancients as "short-lived madness."

** For a dramatic account of the murder see Plutarch's *Alexander*, ch. 51.

*** This is the firm conviction of Seneca, himself a most temperate man. §§ 14 and 15 admit that natural genius may triumph over drunkenness; § 17 may allow (with Chrysippus) a certain amount of hilarity; but the general conclusion is obvious.

falters, the head is dizzy, the very ceiling moves about as if a cyclone were whirling the whole house, and the stomach suffers torture when the wine generates gas and causes our very bowels to swell. However, at the time, these troubles can be endured, so long as the man retains his natural strength; but what can he do when sleep impairs his powers, and when that which was drunkenness becomes indigestion?

Think of the calamities caused by drunkenness in a nation! This evil has betrayed to their enemies the most spirited and warlike races; this evil has made breaches in walls defended by the stubborn warfare of many years; this evil has forced under alien sway peoples who were utterly unyielding and defiant of the yoke; this evil has conquered by the wine-cup those who in the field were invincible. Alexander, whom I have just mentioned, passed through his many marches, his many battles, his many winter campaigns (through which he worked his way by overcoming disadvantages of time or place), the many rivers which flowed from unknown sources, and the many seas, all in safety; it was intemperance in drinking that laid him low, and the famous death-dealing bowl of Hercules.*

What glory is there in carrying much liquor? When you have won the prize, and the other banqueters, sprawling asleep or vomiting, have declined your challenge to still other toasts; when you are the last survivor of the revels; when you have vanquished every one by your magnificent show of prowess and there is no man who has proved himself of so great capacity as you,—you are vanquished by the cask. Mark Antony was a great man, a man of distinguished ability; but what ruined him and drove him into foreign habits and un-Roman vices, if it was not drunkenness and—no less potent than wine—love of Cleopatra? This it was that made him an enemy of the state; this it was that rendered him no match for his enemies; this it was that made him cruel, when as he sat at table the heads of the leaders of the state were brought in; when amid the most elaborate feasts and royal

* Lipsius quotes Athenaeus as saying that Boeotian silver cups of large size were so called because the Boeotian Hercules drank from them; Servius, however, on Verg. *Aen.* viii. 278, declared that the name was derived from the large wooden bowl brought by Hercules to Italy and used for sacrificial purposes.

luxury he would identify the faces and hands of men whom he had proscribed;* when, though heavy with wine, he yet thirsted for blood. It was intolerable that he was getting drunk while he did such things; how much more intolerable that he did these things while actually drunk! Cruelty usually follows wine-bibbing; for a man's soundness of mind is corrupted and made savage. Just as a lingering illness makes men querulous and irritable and drives them wild at the least crossing of their desires, so continued bouts of drunkenness bestialize the soul. For when people are often beside themselves, the habit of madness lasts on, and the vices which liquor generated retain their power even when the liquor is gone.

Therefore you should state why the wise man ought not to get drunk. Explain by facts, and not by mere words, the hideousness of the thing, and its haunting evils. Do that which is easiest of all—namely, demonstrate that what men call pleasures are punishments as soon as they have exceeded due bounds. For if you try to prove that the wise man can souse himself with much wine and yet keep his course straight, even though he be in his cups, you may go on to infer by syllogisms that he will not die if he swallows poison, that he will not sleep if he takes a sleeping-potion, that he will not vomit and reject the matter which clogs his stomach when you give him hellebore.** But, when a man's feet totter and his tongue is unsteady, what reason have you for believing that he is half sober and half drunk? Farewell.

---

* "Antony gave orders to those that were to kill Cicero, to cut off his head and right hand . . . ; and, when they were brought before him, he regarded them joyfully, actually bursting out more than once into laughter, and when he had satiated himself with the sight of them, ordered them to be hung up . . . in the forum" (Clough's translation of Plutarch's *Antony*, p. 172).

** A plant which possessed cathartic properties and was widely used by the ancients. It was also applied in cases of mental derangement. The native Latin term is *veratrum*.

LETTER

86

On Scipio's Villa

I am resting at the country-house which once belonged to Scipio Africanus* himself; and I write to you after doing reverence to his spirit and to an altar which I am inclined to think is the tomb** of that great warrior. That his soul has indeed returned to the skies, whence it came, I am convinced, not because he commanded mighty armies—for Cambyses also had mighty armies, and Cambyses was a madman*** who made successful use of his madness—but because he showed moderation and a sense of duty to a marvellous extent. I regard this trait in him as more admirable after his withdrawal from his native land than while he was defending her; for there was the alternative: Scipio should remain in Rome, or Rome should remain free. "It is my wish," said he, "not to infringe in the least upon our laws, or upon our customs; let all Roman citizens have equal rights. O my country, make the most of the good that I have done, but without me. I have been the cause of your freedom, and I shall also be its proof;

* See Ep. li. 11.

** Cf. Livy xxxvii. 53 *morientem rure eo ipso loco sepeliri se iussisse ferunt monumentumque ibi aedificari.*

*** Herodotus iii. 25 ἐμμανής τε ἐὼν καὶ οὐ φρενήρης.

I go into exile, if it is true that I have grown beyond what is to your advantage!"

What can I do but admire this magnanimity, which led him to withdraw into voluntary exile and to relieve the state of its burden? Matters had gone so far that either liberty must work harm to Scipio, or Scipio to liberty. Either of these things was wrong in the sight of heaven. So he gave way to the laws and withdrew to Liternum, thinking to make the state a debtor for his own exile no less than for the exile of Hannibal.*

I have inspected the house, which is constructed of hewn stone; the wall which encloses a forest; the towers also, buttressed out on both sides for the purpose of defending the house; the well, concealed among buildings and shrubbery, large enough to keep a whole army supplied; and the small bath, buried in darkness according to the old style, for our ancestors did not think that one could have a hot bath except in darkness. It was therefore a great pleasure to me to contrast Scipio's ways with our own. Think, in this tiny recess the "terror of Carthage,"** to whom Rome should offer thanks because she was not captured more than once, used to bathe a body wearied with work in the fields! For he was accustomed to keep himself busy and to cultivate the soil with his own hands, as the good old Romans were wont to do. Beneath this dingy roof he stood; and this floor, mean as it is, bore his weight.

But who in these days could bear to bathe in such a fashion? We think ourselves poor and mean if our walls are not resplendent with large and costly mirrors; if our marbles from Alexandria*** are not set off by mosaics of Numidian stone,**** if their borders are not faced over on all sides with difficult patterns, arranged in many colours like paintings; if our vaulted ceilings are not buried in glass; if our

---

* Livy's account (see above) dwells more on the unwillingness of Scipio and his friends to permit the great conqueror to suffer the indignities of a trial.

** A phrase frequent in Roman literature; see Lucretius iii. 1034 *Scipiadas, belli fulmen, Carthaginis horror.*

*** Porphyry, basalt, etc.

**** i.e., the so-called *giallo antico*, with red and yellow tints predominating.

swimming-pools are not lined with Thasian marble,* once a rare and wonderful sight in any temple—pools into which we let down our bodies after they have been drained weak by abundant perspiration; and finally, if the water has not poured from silver spigots. I have so far been speaking of the ordinary bathing-establishments; what shall I say when I come to those of the freedmen? What a vast number of statues, of columns that support nothing, but are built for decoration, merely in order to spend money! And what masses of water that fall crashing from level to level! We have become so luxurious that we will have nothing but precious stones to walk upon.

In this bath of Scipio's there are tiny chinks—you cannot call them windows—cut out of the stone wall in such a way as to admit light without weakening the fortifications; nowadays, however, people regard baths as fit only for moths if they have not been so arranged that they receive the sun all day long through the widest of windows, if men cannot bathe and get a coat of tan at the same time, and if they cannot look out from their bath-tubs over stretches of land and sea.** So it goes; the establishments which had drawn crowds and had won admiration when they were first opened are avoided and put back in the category of venerable antiques as soon as luxury has worked out some new device, to her own ultimate undoing. In the early days, however, there were few baths, and they were not fitted out with any display. For why should men elaborately fit out that which, costs a penny only, and was invented for use, not merely for delight? The bathers of those days did not have water poured over them, nor did it always run fresh as if from a hot spring; and they did not believe that it mattered at all how perfectly pure was the water into which they were to leave their dirt. Ye gods, what a pleasure it is to enter that dark bath, covered with a common sort of roof, knowing that therein your hero Cato, as aedile, or Fabius Maximus, or one of the Cornelia, has warmed the water with his own hands! For this also used to be the duty of the noblest aediles—to enter these places to which the populace resorted, and to demand that

* A white variety, from Thasos, an island off the Thracian coast.

** Cf. Pliny, *Ep.* ii. 17. 12 *piscina, ex qua natantes mare aspiciunt.*

they be cleaned and warmed to a heat required by considerations of use and health, not the heat that men have recently made fashionable, as great as a conflagration—so much so, indeed, that a slave condemned for some criminal offence now ought to be *bathed* alive! It seems to me that nowadays there is no difference between "the bath is on fire," and "the bath is warm."

How some persons nowadays condemn Scipio as a boor because he did not let daylight into his perspiring-room through wide windows, or because he did not roast in the strong sunlight and dawdle about until he could stew in the hot water! "Poor fool," they say, "he did not know how to live! He did not bathe in filtered water; it was often turbid, and after heavy rains almost muddy!" But it did not matter much to Scipio if he had to bathe in that way; he went there to wash off sweat, not ointment. And how do you suppose certain persons will answer me? They will say: "I don't envy Scipio; that was truly an exile's life—to put up with baths like those!" Friend, if you were wiser, you would know that Scipio did not bathe every day. It is stated by those* who have reported to us the old-time ways of Rome that the Romans washed only their arms and legs daily—because those were the members which gathered dirt in their daily toil—and bathed all over only once a week. Here someone will retort: "Yes; pretty dirty fellows they evidently were! How they must have smelled!" But they smelled of the camp, the farm, and heroism. Now that spick-and-span bathing establishments have been devised, men are really fouler than of yore. What says Horatius Flaccus, when he wishes to describe a scoundrel, one who is notorious for his extreme luxury? He says: "Buccillus** smells of perfume." Show me a Buccillus in these days; his smell would be the veritable goat-smell—he would take the place of the Gargonius with whom Horace in the same passage contrasted him. It is nowadays not enough to use ointment, unless you put on a fresh coat two or three times a day, to keep it from evaporating on the body. But why should a man boast of this perfume as if it were his own?

---

* e.g., Varro, in the *Catus*: *balneum non cotidianum.*

** Horace calls him Rufillus (*Sat.* i. 2. 27): *pastillos Rufillus olet, Gargonius hircum.*

If what I am saying shall seem to you too pessimistic, charge it up against Scipio's country-house, where I have learned a lesson from Aegialus, a most careful householder and now the owner of this estate; he taught me that a tree can be transplanted, no matter how far gone in years. We old men must learn this precept; for there is none of us who is not planting an olive-yard for his successor. I have seen them bearing fruit in due season after three or four years of unproductiveness.* And you too shall be shaded by the tree which

> Is slow to grow, but bringeth shade to cheer
> Your grandsons in the far-off years,**

as our poet Vergil says. Vergil sought, however, not what was nearest to the truth, but what was most appropriate, and aimed, not to teach the farmer, but to please the reader. For example, omitting all other errors of his, I will quote the passage in which it was incumbent upon me today to detect a fault:

> In spring sow beans then, too, O clover plant,
> Thou'rt welcomed by the crumbling furrows; and
> The millet calls for yearly care.***

You may judge by the following incident whether those plants should be set out at the same time, or whether both should be sowed in the spring. It is June at the present writing, and we are well on towards July; and I have seen on this very day farmers harvesting beans and sowing millet.

But to return to our olive-yard again. I saw it planted in two ways. If the trees were large, Aegialus took their trunks and cut off the branches to the length of one foot each; he then transplanted along with the ball, after cutting off the roots, leaving only the thick part from which

---

* This seems to be the general meaning of the passage.

** *Georgics*, ii. 58.

*** *Georgics*, i. 215 f.

the roots hang. He smeared this with manure, and inserted it in the hole, not only heaping up the earth about it, but stamping and pressing it down. There is nothing, he says, more effective than this packing process;* in other words, it keeps out the cold and the wind. Besides, the trunk is not shaken so much, and for this reason the packing makes it possible for the young roots to come out and get a hold in the soil. These are of necessity still soft; they have but a slight hold, and a very little shaking uproots them. This ball, moreover, Aegialus lops clean before he covers it up. For he maintains that new roots spring from all the parts which have been shorn. Moreover, the trunk itself should not stand more than three or four feet out of the ground. For there will thus be at once a thick growth from the bottom, nor will there be a large stump, all dry and withered, as is the case with old olive-yards. The second way of setting them out was the following: he set out in similar fashion branches that were strong and of soft bark, as those of young saplings are wont to be. These grow a little more slowly, but, since they spring from what is practically a cutting, there is no roughness or ugliness in them.

This too I have seen recently—an aged vine transplanted from its own plantation. In this case, the fibres also should be gathered together, if possible, and then you should cover up the vine-stem more generously, so that roots may spring up even from the stock. I have seen such plantings made not only in February, but at the very end of March; the plants take hold of and embrace alien elms. But all trees, he declares, which are, so to speak, "thick-stemmed,"** should be assisted with tank-water; if we have this help, we are our own rain-makers.

I do not intend to tell you any more of these precepts, lest, as Aegialus did with me, I may be training you up to be my competitor. Farewell.

---

* In Vitruvius vii. 1 G reads *pinsatione*, referring to the pounding of stones for flooring.

** An agricultural term not elsewhere found.

LETTER

88

On Liberal and Vocational Studies

You have been wishing to know my views with regard to liberal studies.* My answer is this: I respect no study, and deem no study good, which results in money-making. Such studies are profit-bringing occupations, useful only in so far as they give the mind a preparation and do not engage it permanently. One should linger upon them only so long as the mind can occupy itself with nothing greater; they are our apprenticeship, not our real work. Hence you see why "liberal studies" are so called; it is because they are studies worthy of a free-born gentleman. But there is only one really liberal study,—that which gives a man his liberty. It is the study of wisdom, and that is lofty, brave, and great-souled. All other studies are puny and puerile. You surely do not believe that there is good in any of the subjects whose teachers are, as you see, men of the most

* The regular round of education, ἐγκύκλιος παιδεία, including grammar, music, geometry, arithmetic, astrology, and certain phases of rhetoric and dialectic, are in this letter contrasted with liberal studies—those which have for their object the pursuit of virtue. Seneca is thus interpreting *studia liberalia* in a higher sense than his contemporaries would expect. Compare J. R. Lowell's definition of a university, "a place where nothing useful is taught."

ignoble and base stamp? We ought not to be learning such things; we should have done with learning them.

Certain persons have made up their minds that the point at issue with regard to the liberal studies is whether they make men good; but they do not even profess or aim at a knowledge of this particular subject. The scholar* busies himself with investigations into language, and if it be his desire to go farther afield, he works on history, or, if he would extend his range to the farthest limits, on poetry. But which of these paves the way to virtue? Pronouncing syllables, investigating words, memorizing plays, or making rules for the scansion of poetry,—what is there in all this that rids one of fear, roots out desire, or bridles the passions? The question is: do such men teach virtue, or not? If they do not teach it, then neither do they transmit it. If they do teach it, they are philosophers. Would you like to know how it happens that they have not taken the chair for the purpose of teaching virtue? See how unlike their subjects are; and yet their subjects would resemble each other if they taught the same thing.**

It may be, perhaps, that they make you believe that Homer was a philosopher,*** although they disprove this by the very arguments through which they seek to prove it. For sometimes they make of him a Stoic, who approves nothing but virtue, avoids pleasures, and refuses to relinquish honour even at the price of immortality; sometimes they make him an Epicurean, praising the condition of a state in repose, which passes its days in feasting and song; sometimes a Peripatetic,

---

* *Grammaticus* in classical Greek means "one who is familiar with the alphabet"; in the Alexandrian age a "student of literature"; in the Roman age the equivalent of *litteratus*. Seneca means here a "specialist in linguistic science."

** i.e., philosophy (virtue).

*** This theory was approved by Democritus, Hippias of Elis, and the allegorical interpreters; Xenophanes, Heraclitus, and Plato himself condemned Homer for his supposed unphilosophic fabrications.

classifying goodness in three ways;[*] sometimes an Academic, holding that all things are uncertain. It is clear, however, that no one of these doctrines is to be fathered upon Homer, just because they are all there; for they are irreconcilable with one another. We may admit to these men, indeed, that Homer was a philosopher; yet surely he became a wise man before he had any knowledge of poetry. So let us learn the particular things that made Homer wise.

It is no more to the point, of course, for me to investigate whether Homer or Hesiod was the older poet, than to know why Hecuba, although younger than Helen,[**] showed her years so lamentably. What, in your opinion, I say, would be the point in trying to determine the respective ages of Achilles and Patroclus? Do you raise the question, "Through what regions did Ulysses stray?" instead of trying to prevent ourselves from going astray at all times? We have no leisure to hear lectures on the question whether he was sea-tost between Italy and Sicily, or outside our known world (indeed, so long a wandering could not possibly have taken place within its narrow bounds); we ourselves encounter storms of the spirit, which toss us daily, and our depravity drives us into all the ills which troubled Ulysses. For us there is never lacking the beauty to tempt our eyes, or the enemy to assail us; on this side are savage monsters that delight in human blood, on that side the treacherous allurements of the ear, and yonder is shipwreck and all the varied category of misfortunes.[***] Show me rather, by the example of Ulysses, how I am to love my country, my wife, my father, and how, even after suffering shipwreck, I am to sail toward these ends, honourable as

---

* The *tria genera bonorum* of Cicero's *De Fin* v. 84. Cf. *ib.* 18, where the three proper objects of man's search are given as the desire for pleasure, the avoidance of pain, and the attainment of such natural goods as health, strength, and soundness of mind. The Stoics held that the good was absolute.

** Summers compares Lucian, *Gall.* 17. Seneca, however, does not take such gossip seriously.

*** This sentence alludes to Calypso, Circe, the Cyclops, and the Sirens.

they are. Why try to discover whether Penelope was a pattern of purity,* or whether she had the laugh on her contemporaries? Or whether she suspected that the man in her presence was Ulysses, before she knew it was he? Teach me rather what purity is, and how great a good we have in it, and whether it is situated in the body or in the soul.

Now I will transfer my attention to the musician. You, sir, are teaching me how the treble and the bass** are in accord with one another, and how, though the strings produce different notes, the result is a harmony; rather bring my soul into harmony with itself, and let not my purposes be out of tune. You are showing me what the doleful keys*** are; show me rather how, in the midst of adversity, I may keep from uttering a doleful note. The mathematician teaches me how to lay out the dimensions of my estates; but I should rather be taught how to lay out what is enough for a man to own. He teaches me to count, and adapts my fingers to avarice; but I should prefer him to teach me that there is no point in such calculations, and that one is none the happier for tiring out the book-keepers with his possessions—or rather, how useless property is to any man who would find it the greatest misfortune if he should be required to reckon out, by his own wits, the amount of his holdings. What good is there for me in knowing how to parcel out a piece of land, if I know not how to share it with my brother? What good is there in working out to a nicety the dimensions of an acre, and in detecting the error if a piece has so much as escaped my measuring-rod, if I am embittered when an ill-tempered neighbour merely scrapes off a bit of my land? The mathematician teaches me how I may lose none of my boundaries; I, however, seek to learn how to lose them all with a light heart. "But," comes the reply, "I am being driven from the farm which my father and grandfather owned!" Well? Who owned the land before your grandfather? Can you explain what people (I will not say what person) held it originally? You did not enter

* Unfavourable comment by Lycophron, and by Cicero, *De Nat. Deor.* iii. 22 *(Mercurius) ex quo et Penelopa Pana natum ferunt.*

** With *acutae* and *graves* supply *voces*.

*** Perhaps the equivalent of a "minor."

upon it as a master, but merely as a tenant. And whose tenant are you? If your claim is successful, you are tenant of the heir. The lawyers say that public property cannot be acquired privately by possession;* what you hold and call your own is public property—indeed, it belongs to mankind at large. O what marvellous skill! You know how to measure the circle; you find the square of any shape which is set before you; you compute the distances between the stars; there is nothing which does not come within the scope of your calculations. But if you are a real master of your profession, measure me the mind of man! Tell me how great it is, or how puny! You know what a straight line is; but how does it benefit you if you do not know what is straight in this life of ours?

I come next to the person who boasts his knowledge of the heavenly bodies, who knows

> Whither the chilling star of Saturn hides,
> And through what orbit Mercury doth stray.**

Of what benefit will it be to know this? That I shall be disturbed because Saturn and Mars are in opposition, or when Mercury sets at eventide in plain view of Saturn, rather than learn that those stars, wherever they are, are propitious,*** and that they are not subject to change? They are driven along by an unending round of destiny, on a course from which they cannot swerve. They return at stated seasons; they either set in motion, or mark the intervals of the whole world's work. But if they are responsible for whatever happens, how will it

---

* i.e., for a certain term of years; see R. W. Leage, *Roman Private Law*, pp. 133 ff. Compare also Lucretius iii. 971, and Horace, *Ep.* ii. 2. 159.

** Vergil, *Georg.* i. 336 f.

*** Saturn and Mars were regarded as unlucky stars. Astrology, which dates back beyond 3000 B.C. in Babylonia, was developed by the Greeks of the Alexandrian age and got a foothold in Rome by the second century B.C., flourished greatly under Tiberius. Cf. Horace, *Od.* i. 11. 1 f.; Juv. iii. 42 f., and F. Cumont, *Astrology and Religion among the Greeks and Romans* (trans.), esp. pp. 68 ff. and 84 ff.

help you to know the secrets of the immutable? Or if they merely give indications, what good is there in foreseeing what you cannot escape? Whether you know these things or not, they will take place.

Behold the fleeting sun,
The stars that follow in his train, and thou
Shalt never find the morrow play thee false,
Or be misled by nights without a cloud.*

It has, however, been sufficiently and fully ordained that I shall be safe from anything that may mislead me. "What," you say, "does the 'morrow never play me false'? Whatever happens without my knowledge plays me false." I, for my part, do not know what is to be, but I do know what may come to be. I shall have no misgivings in this matter; I await the future in its entirety; and if there is any abatement in its severity, I make the most of it. If the morrow treats me kindly, it is a sort of deception; but it does not deceive me even at that. For just as I know that all things can happen, so I know, too, that they will not happen in every case. I am ready for favourable events in every case, but I am prepared for evil.

In this discussion you must bear with me if I do not follow the regular course. For I do not consent to admit painting into the list of liberal arts, any more than sculpture, marble-working, and other helps toward luxury. I also debar from the liberal studies wrestling and all knowledge that is compounded of oil and mud;** otherwise, I should be compelled to admit perfumers also, and cooks, and all others who lend their wits to the service of our pleasures. For what "liberal" element is there in these ravenous takers of emetics, whose bodies are fed to fatness while their minds are thin and dull?*** Or do we really believe that the training which they give is "liberal" for the young men of Rome, who used to be taught by our ancestors to stand

---

* Vergil, *Georg.* i. 424 ff.

** An allusion to the sand and oil of the wrestling-ring.

*** Cf. Ep. xv. 3 *copia ciborum subtilitas inpeditur.*

straight and hurl a spear, to wield a pike, to guide a horse, and to handle weapons? Our ancestors used to teach their children nothing that could be learned while lying down. But neither the new system nor the old teaches or nourishes virtue. For what good does it do us to guide a horse and control his speed with the curb, and then find that our own passions, utterly uncurbed, bolt with us? Or to beat many opponents in wrestling or boxing, and then to find that we ourselves are beaten by anger?

"What then," you say, "do the liberal studies contribute nothing to our welfare?" Very much in other respects, but nothing at all as regards virtue. For even these arts of which I have spoken, though admittedly of a low grade—depending as they do upon handiwork—contribute greatly toward the equipment of life, but nevertheless have nothing to do with virtue. And if you inquire, "Why, then, do we educate our children in the liberal studies?"* it is not because they can bestow virtue, but because they prepare the soul for the reception of virtue. Just as that "primary course,"** as the ancients called it, in grammar, which gave boys their elementary training, does not teach them the liberal arts, but prepares the ground for their early acquisition of these arts, so the liberal arts do not conduct the soul all the way to virtue, but merely set it going in that direction.

Posidonius*** divides the arts into four classes: first we have those which are common and low, then those which serve for amusement, then those which refer to the education of boys, and, finally, the liberal arts. The common sort belong to workmen and are mere hand-work; they are concerned with equipping life; there is in them no pretence to beauty or honour. The arts of amusement are those which aim to please the eye and the ear. To this class you may assign the stage-machinists, who invent scaffolding that goes aloft of its own accord, or

---

* In a strict sense; not, as in § 2, as Seneca thinks that the term should really be defined—the "liberal" study, i.e. the pursuit of wisdom.

** For the πρώτη ἀγωγή see Quintilian, ii. 1. 4.

*** From what work of Posidonius Seneca is here quoting we do not know; it may be from the Προτρεπτικά, or *Exhortations*, indicating the training preliminary to philosophy.

floors that rise silently into the air, and many other surprising devices, as when objects that fit together then fall apart, or objects which are separate then join together automatically, or objects which stand erect then gradually collapse. The eye of the inexperienced is struck with amazement by these things; for such persons marvel at everything that takes place without warning, because they do not know the causes. The arts which belong to the education of boys, and are somewhat similar to the liberal arts, are those which the Greeks call the "cycle of studies,"* but which we Romans call the "liberal." However, those alone are really liberal—or rather, to give them a truer name, "free"—whose concern is virtue.

"But," one will say, "just as there is a part of philosophy which has to do with nature, and a part which has to do with ethics, and a part which has to do with reasoning, so this group of liberal arts also claims for itself a place in philosophy. When one approaches questions that deal with nature, a decision is reached by means of a word from the mathematician. Therefore mathematics is a department of that branch which it aids."** But many things aid us and yet are not parts of ourselves. Nay, if they were, they would not aid us. Food is an aid to the body, but is not a part of it. We get some help from the service which mathematics renders; and mathematics is as indispensable to philosophy as the carpenter is to the mathematician. But carpentering is not a part of mathematics, nor is mathematics a part of philosophy. Moreover, each has its own limits; for the wise man investigates and learns the causes of natural phenomena, while the mathematician follows up and computes their numbers and their measurements.*** The wise man knows the laws by which the heavenly bodies persist, what powers belong to them, and what attributes; the astronomer merely notes their comings and goings, the rules which govern their settings and their risings, and the occasional periods during which they

* See § 1 note.

** i.e., mathematics is a department of *philosophia naturalis*.

*** This line of argument inversely resembles the criticism by Seneca of Posidonius in Ep. xc.—that the inventions of early science cannot be properly termed a part of philosophy.

seem to stand still, although as a matter of fact no heavenly body can stand still. The wise man will know what causes the reflection in a mirror; but, the mathematician can merely tell you how far the body should be from the reflection, and what shape of mirror will produce a given reflection.* The philosopher will demonstrate that the sun is a large body, while the astronomer will compute just how large, progressing in knowledge by his method of trial and experiment; but in order to progress, he must summon to his aid certain principles. No art, however, is sufficient unto itself, if the foundation upon which it rests depends upon mere favour. Now philosophy asks no favours from any other source; it builds everything on its own soil; but the science of numbers is, so to speak, a structure built on another man's land—it builds on alien soil.** It accepts first principles, and by their favour arrives at further conclusions. If it could march unassisted to the truth, if it were able to understand the nature of the universe, I should say that it would offer much assistance to our minds; for the mind grows by contact with things heavenly, and draws into itself something from on high. There is but one thing that brings the soul to perfection—the unalterable knowledge of good and evil. But there is no other art*** which investigates good and evil.

I should like to pass in review the several virtues. Bravery is a scorner of things which inspire fear; it looks down upon, challenges, and crushes the powers of terror and all that would drive our freedom under the yoke. But do "liberal studies"**** strengthen this virtue? Loyalty is the holiest good in the human heart; it is forced into betrayal by no constraint, and it is bribed by no rewards. Loyalty cries: "Burn me, slay me, kill me! I shall not betray my trust; and the more urgently torture shall seek to find my secret, the deeper in my heart will I bury it!" Can the "liberal arts" produce such a spirit within us? Temperance controls

* See *N. Q.* i. 4 ff.

** According to Roman law, *superficies solo cedit*, "the building goes with the ground."

*** Except philosophy.

**** i.e., in the more commonly accepted sense of the term.

our desires; some it hates and routs, others it regulates and restores to a healthy measure, nor does it ever approach our desires for their own sake. Temperance knows that the best measure of the appetites is not what you want to take, but what you ought to take. Kindliness forbids you to be over-bearing towards your associates, and it forbids you to be grasping. In words and in deeds and in feelings it shows itself gentle and courteous to all men. It counts no evil as another's solely. And the reason why it loves its own good is chiefly because it will some day be the good of another. Do "liberal studies" teach a man such character as this? No; no more than they teach simplicity, moderation and self-restraint, thrift and economy, and that kindliness which spares a neighbour's life as if it were one's own and knows that it is not for man to make wasteful use of his fellow-man.

"But," one says, "since you declare that virtue cannot be attained without the 'liberal studies,' how is it that you deny that they offer any assistance to virtue?"* Because you cannot attain virtue without food, either; and yet food has nothing to do with virtue. Wood does not offer assistance to a ship, although a ship cannot be built except of wood. There is no reason, I say, why you should think that anything is made by the assistance of that without which it cannot be made. We might even make the statement that it is possible to attain wisdom without the "liberal studies"; for although virtue is a thing that must be learned, yet it is not learned by means of these studies.

What reason have I, however, for supposing that one who is ignorant of letters will never be a wise man, since wisdom is not to be found in letters? Wisdom communicates facts** and not words; and it may be true that the memory is more to be depended upon when it has no support outside itself. Wisdom is a large and spacious thing. It needs plenty of free room. One must learn about things divine and human, the past and the future, the ephemeral and the eternal; and one

---

* This usage is a not infrequent one in Latin; cf. Petronius, *Sat.* 42 *neminem nihil boni facere oportet*; *id. ib.* 58; Verg. *Ecl.* v. 25, etc. See Draeger, *Hist. Syn.* ii. 75, and Roby, ii. 2246 ff.

** Cf. Epp. xxxi. 6 and lxxxi. 29 *aestimare res, de quibus . . . cum rerum natura deliberandum est.*

must learn about Time.* See how many questions arise concerning time alone: in the first place, whether it is anything in and by itself; in the second place, whether anything exists prior to time and without time; and again, did time begin along with the universe, or, because there was something even before the universe began, did time also exist then? There are countless questions concerning the soul alone: whence it comes, what is its nature, when it begins to exist, and how long it exists; whether it passes from one place to another and changes its habitation, being transferred successively from one animal shape to another, or whether it is a slave but once, roaming the universe after it is set free; whether it is corporeal or not; what will become of it when it ceases to use us as its medium; how it will employ its freedom when it has escaped from this present prison; whether it will forget all its past, and at that moment begin to know itself when, released from the body, it has withdrawn to the skies.

Thus, whatever phase of things human and divine you have apprehended, you will be wearied by the vast number of things to be answered and things to be learned. And in order that these manifold and mighty subjects may have free entertainment in your soul, you must remove therefrom all superfluous things. Virtue will not surrender herself to these narrow bounds of ours; a great subject needs wide space in which to move. Let all other things be driven out, and let the breast be emptied to receive virtue.

"But it is a pleasure to be acquainted with many arts." Therefore let us keep only as much of them as is essential. Do you regard that man as blameworthy who puts superfluous things on the same footing with useful things, and in his house makes a lavish display of costly objects, but do not deem him blameworthy who has allowed himself to become engrossed with the useless furniture of learning? This desire to know more than is sufficient is a sort of intemperance. Why? Because this unseemly pursuit of the liberal arts makes men

---

* The ancient Stoics defined Time as "extension of the world's motion." The seasons were said to be "alive" because they depended on material conditions. But the Stoics really acknowledged Time to be immaterial. The same problem of corporeality was discussed with regard to the "good."

troublesome, wordy, tactless, self-satisfied bores, who fail to learn the essentials just because they have learned the non-essentials. Didymus the scholar wrote four thousand books. I should feel pity for him if he had only read the same number of superfluous volumes. In these books he investigates Homer's birthplace,* who was really the mother of Aeneas, whether Anacreon was more of a rake or more of a drunkard, whether Sappho was a bad lot,** and other problems the answers to which, if found, were forthwith to be forgotten. Come now, do not tell me that life is long! Nay, when you come to consider our own countrymen also, I can show you many works which ought to be cut down with the axe.

It is at the cost of a vast outlay of time and of vast discomfort to the ears of others that we win such praise as this: "What a learned man you are!" Let us be content with this recommendation, less citified though it be: "What a good man you are!" Do I mean this? Well, would you have me unroll the annals of the world's history and try to find out who first wrote poetry? Or, in the absence of written records, shall I make an estimate of the number of years which lie between Orpheus and Homer? Or shall I make a study of the absurd writings of Aristarchus, wherein he branded the text*** of other men's verses, and wear my life away upon syllables? Shall I then wallow in the geometrician's dust?****

---

* Compare the schoolmaster of Juvenal (vii. 234 ff.), who must know
Nutricem Anchisae, nomen patriamque novercae Anchemoli, dicat quot Acestes vixerit annis, etc.,
and Friedländer's note.

** A tradition, probably begun by the Greek comic-writers, and explained by Professor Smyth (*Greek Melic Poets*, pp. 227 f.) as due to the more independent position of women among the Aeolians. *Transcriber's note: Gummere has euphemistically translated Seneca here. The Latin is "in his an Sappho publica fuerit", and the feminine noun "publica" means "public woman", i.e. a courtesan or prostitute. So Gummere's translation "whether Sappho was a bad lot" is more accurately rendered as "whether Sappho was a prostitute."*

*** Marking supposedly spurious lines by the *obelus*, and using other signs to indicate variations, repetitions, and interpolations. He paid special attention to Homer, Pindar, Hesiod, and the tragedians.

**** The geometricians drew their figures in the dust or sand.

Have I so far forgotten that useful saw "Save your time"? Must I know these things? And what may I choose not to know?

Apion, the scholar, who drew crowds to his lectures all over Greece in the days of Gaius Caesar and was acclaimed a Homerid* by every state, used to maintain that Homer, when he had finished his two poems, the *Iliad* and the *Odyssey*, added a preliminary poem to his work, wherein he embraced the whole Trojan war.** The argument which Apion adduced to prove this statement was that Homer had purposely inserted in the opening line two letters which contained a key to the number of his books. A man who wishes to know many things must know such things as these, and must take no thought of all the time which one loses by ill-health, public duties, private duties, daily duties, and sleep. Apply the measure to the years of your life; they have no room for all these things.

I have been speaking so far of liberal studies; but think how much superfluous and unpractical matter the philosophers contain! Of their own accord they also have descended to establishing nice divisions of syllables, to determining the true meaning of conjunctions and prepositions; they have been envious of the scholars, envious of the mathematicians. They have taken over into their own art all the superfluities of these other arts; the result is that they know more about careful speaking than about careful living. Let me tell you what evils are due to over-nice exactness, and what an enemy it is of truth! Protagoras declares that one can take either side on any question and debate it with equal success—even on this very question, whether every subject can be debated from either point of view. Nausiphanes holds that in things which seem to exist, there is no difference between existence and non-existence. Parmenides maintains that nothing exists of all this which seems to exist, except the universe alone.***

---

* Originally, rhapsodists who recited from Homer; in general, "interpreters and admirers—in short, the whole 'spiritual kindred'—of Homer" (D. B. Monro)

** An ancient explanation of the (now disproved) authorship by Homer of such poems as the *Cypria*, *Little Iliad*, *Sack of Troy*, etc.

*** In other words, the unchangeable, perfect Being of the universe is contrasted with the mutable Non-Being of opinion and unreality.

Zeno of Elea removed all the difficulties by removing one; for he declares that nothing exists. The Pyrrhonean, Megarian, Eretrian, and Academic schools are all engaged in practically the same task; they have introduced a new knowledge, non-knowledge. You may sweep all these theories in with the superfluous troops of "liberal" studies; the one class of men give me a knowledge that will be of no use to me, the other class do away with any hope of attaining knowledge. It is better, of course, to know useless things than to know nothing. One set of philosophers offers no light by which I may direct my gaze toward the truth; the other digs out my very eyes and leaves me blind. If I cleave to Protagoras, there is nothing in the scheme of nature that is not doubtful; if I hold with Nausiphanes, I am sure only of this—that everything is unsure; if with Parmenides, there is nothing except the One;* if with Zeno, there is not even the One.

What are we, then? What becomes of all these things that surround us, support us, sustain us? The whole universe is then a vain or deceptive shadow. I cannot readily say whether I am more vexed at those who would have it that we know nothing, or with those who would not leave us even this privilege. Farewell.

---

* i.e., the universe.

LETTER

90

On the Part Played by Philosophy in the Progress of Man

Who can doubt, my dear Lucilius, that life is the gift of the immortal gods, but that living well* is the gift of philosophy? Hence the idea that our debt to philosophy is greater than our debt to the gods, in proportion as a good life is more of a benefit than mere life, would be regarded as correct, were not philosophy itself a boon which the gods have bestowed upon us. They have given the knowledge thereof to none, but the faculty of acquiring it they have given to all. For if they had made philosophy also a general good, and if we were gifted with understanding at our birth, wisdom would have lost her best attribute—that she is not one of the gifts of fortune. For as it is, the precious and noble characteristic of wisdom is that she does not advance to meet us, that each man is indebted to himself for her, and that we do not seek her at the hands of others.

What would there be in philosophy worthy of your respect, if she were a thing that came by bounty? Her sole function is to discover the truth about things divine and things human. From her side religion never departs, nor duty, nor justice, nor

---

* Cf. Plato, *Crito* 48, "not life itself, but a good life, is chiefly to be desired."

any of the whole company of virtues which cling together in close-united fellowship. Philosophy has taught us to worship that which is divine, to love that which is human;* she has told us that with the gods lies dominion, and among men, fellowship. This fellowship remained unspoiled for a long time, until avarice tore the community asunder and became the cause of poverty, even in the case of those whom she herself had most enriched. For men cease to possess all things the moment they desire all things for their own.

But the first men and those who sprang from them, still unspoiled, followed nature, having one man as both their leader and their law, entrusting themselves to the control of one better than themselves. For nature has the habit of subjecting the weaker to the stronger. Even among the dumb animals those which are either biggest or fiercest hold sway. It is no weakling bull that leads the herd; it is one that has beaten the other males by his might and his muscle. In the case of elephants, the tallest goes first; among men, the best is regarded as the highest. That is why it was to the mind that a ruler was assigned; and for that reason the greatest happiness rested with those peoples among whom a man could not be the more powerful unless he were the better. For that man can safely accomplish what he will who thinks he can do nothing except what he ought to do.

Accordingly, in that age which is maintained to be the golden age,** Posidonius*** holds that the government was under the jurisdiction of the wise. They kept their hands under control, and protected the weaker from the stronger. They gave advice, both to do and not to do;

---

* Compare the "knowledge of things divine and things human" of lxxxix. 5.

** The "Golden Age" motif was a frequent one in Latin literature. Compare, e.g., Tibullus, i. 3. 35 ff., the passage beginning:
Quam bene Saturno vivebant rege, priusquam
Tellus in longas est patefacta vias!
Cf. § 46, summing up the message of Seneca's letter.

*** While modern philosophy would probably side with Seneca rather than Posidonius, it is interesting to know the opinion of Macaulay, who holds (*Essay on Bacon*) that there is much in common between Posidonius and the English inductive philosopher, and thinks but little of Seneca's ideas on the subject. Cf. W. C. Summers, *Select letters of Seneca*, p. 312.

they showed what was useful and what was useless. Their forethought provided that their subjects should lack nothing; their bravery warded off dangers; their kindness enriched and adorned their subjects. For them ruling was a service, not an exercise of royalty. No ruler tried his power against those to whom he owed the beginnings of his power; and no one had the inclination, or the excuse, to do wrong, since the ruler ruled well and the subject obeyed well, and the king could utter no greater threat against disobedient subjects than that they should depart from the kingdom.

But when once vice stole in and kingdoms were transformed into tyrannies, a need arose for laws; and these very laws were in turn framed by the wise. Solon, who established Athens upon a firm basis by just laws, was one of the seven men renowned for their wisdom.* Had Lycurgus lived in the same period, an eighth would have been added to that hallowed number seven. The laws of Zaleucus and Charondas are praised; it was not in the forum or in the offices of skilled counsellors, but in the silent and holy retreat of Pythagoras, that these two men learned the principles of justice which they were to establish in Sicily (which at that time was prosperous) and throughout Grecian Italy.

Up to this point I agree with Posidonius; but that philosophy discovered the arts of which life makes use in its daily round** I refuse to admit, nor will I ascribe to it an artisan's glory. Posidonius says: "When men were scattered over the earth, protected by caves or by the dug-out shelter of a cliff or by the trunk of a hollow tree, it was philosophy that taught them to build houses." But I, for my part, do not hold that philosophy devised these shrewdly-contrived dwellings of ours which rise story upon story, where city crowds against city, any more than that she invented the fish-preserves, which are enclosed for the purpose of saving men's gluttony from having to run the risk of storms, and in order that, no matter how wildly the sea is raging, luxury may have its safe harbours in which to fatten fancy breeds of fish.

* Cleobulus of Rhodes, Periander of Corinth, Pittacus of Mitylene, Bias of Priene, Thales of Miletus, Chilon of Sparta, and Solon of Athens. For some of these substitutions are made in certain lists.

** Cf. Ep. lxxxviii. 20 *ad alia multum, ad virtutem nihil.*

What! Was it philosophy that taught the use of keys and bolts? Nay, what was that except giving a hint to avarice? Was it philosophy that erected all these towering tenements, so dangerous to the persons who dwell in them? Was it not enough for man to provide himself a roof of any chance covering, and to contrive for himself some natural retreat without the help of art and without trouble? Believe me, that was a happy age, before the days of architects, before the days of builders! All this sort of thing was born when luxury was being born,—this matter of cutting timbers square and cleaving a beam with unerring hand as the saw made its way over the marked-out line.

The primal man with wedges split his wood.*

For they were not preparing a roof for a future banquet-ball; for no such use did they carry the pine-trees or the firs along the trembling streets** with a long row of drays—merely to fasten thereon panelled ceilings heavy with gold. Forked poles erected at either end propped up their houses. With close-packed branches and with leaves heaped up and laid sloping they contrived a drainage for even the heaviest rains. Beneath such dwellings, they lived, but they lived in peace. A thatched roof once covered free men; under marble and gold dwells slavery.

On another point also I differ from Posidonius, when he holds that mechanical tools were the invention of wise men. For on that basis one might maintain that those were wise who taught the arts

Of setting traps for game, and liming twigs
For birds, and girdling mighty woods with dogs.***

---

* Vergil, *Georg.* i. 144.

** Cf. Juvenal, iii. 254 ff.:
Longa coruscat
Serraco veniente abies, atque altera pinum Plaustra vehunt, nutant alte populoque minantur.
Compare also the "towering tenements" of § 8.

*** Vergil, *Georg.* i. 139 f.

It was man's ingenuity, not his wisdom, that discovered all these devices. And I also differ from him when he says that wise men discovered our mines of iron and copper, "when the earth, scorched by forest fires, melted the veins of ore which lay near the surface and caused the metal to gush forth."* Nay, the sort of men who discover such things are the sort of men who are busied with them. Nor do I consider this question so subtle as Posidonius thinks, namely, whether the hammer or the tongs came first into use. They were both invented by some man whose mind was nimble and keen, but not great or exalted; and the same holds true of any other discovery which can only be made by means of a bent body and of a mind whose gaze is upon the ground.

The wise man was easy-going in his way of living. And why not? Even in our own times he would prefer to be as little cumbered as possible. How, I ask, can you consistently admire both Diogenes and Daedalus? Which of these two seems to you a wise man—the one who devised the saw, or the one who, on seeing a boy drink water from the hollow of his hand, forthwith took his cup from his wallet and broke it, upbraiding himself with these words:** "Fool that I am, to have been carrying superfluous baggage all this time!" and then curled himself up in his tub and lay down to sleep? In these our own times, which man, pray, do you deem the wiser—the one who invents a process for spraying saffron perfumes to a tremendous height from hidden pipes, who fills or empties canals by a sudden rush of waters, who so cleverly constructs a dining room with a ceiling of movable panels that it presents one pattern after another, the roof changing as often as the courses,***—or the one who proves to others, as well as to himself, that nature has laid upon us no stern and difficult law when she tells us that we can live without the marble-cutter and the engineer,

---

* Cf. T. Rice Holmes, *Ancient Britain*, pp. 121 f., who concludes that the discovery of ore-smelting was accidental.

** Cf. Diog. Laert. vi. 37 θεασάμενός ποτε παιδίον ταῖς χερσὶ ἐξέρριψε τῆς πήρας τὴν κοτύλην, εἰπών, Παιδίον με νενίκηκεν εὐτελεία.

*** Compare the halls of Nero which Seneca may easily have had in mind: (Suet. *Nero* 31) *cenationes laqueatae tabulis eburneis versatilibus . . . praecipua cenationum rotunda, quae perpetuo diebus ac noctibus vice mundi circumageretur.*

that we can clothe ourselves without traffic in silk fabrics, that we can have everything that is indispensable to our use, provided only that we are content with what the earth has placed on its surface? If mankind were willing to listen to this sage, they would know that the cook is as superfluous to them as the soldier. Those were wise men, or at any rate like the wise, who found the care of the body a problem easy to solve. The things that are indispensable require no elaborate pains for their acquisition; it is only the luxuries that call for labour. Follow nature, and you will need no skilled craftsmen.

Nature did not wish us to be harassed. For whatever she forced upon us, she equipped us. "But cold cannot be endured by the naked body." What then? Are there not the skins of wild beasts and other animals, which can protect us well enough, and more than enough, from the cold? Do not many tribes cover their bodies with the bark of trees? Are not the feathers of birds sewn together to serve for clothing? Even at the present day does not a large portion of the Scythian tribe garb itself in the skins of foxes and mice, soft to the touch and impervious to the winds? "For all that, men must have some thicker protection than the skin, in order to keep off the heat of the sun in summer." What then? Has not antiquity produced many retreats which, hollowed out either by the damage wrought by time or by any other occurrence you will, have opened into caverns? What then? Did not the very first-comers take twigs* and weave them by hand into wicker mats, smear them with common mud, and then with stubble and other wild grasses construct a roof, and thus pass their winters secure, the rains carried off by means of the sloping gables? What then? Do not the peoples on the edge of the Syrtes dwell in dug-out houses—and indeed all the tribes who, because of the too fierce blaze of the sun, possess no protection sufficient to keep off the heat except the parched soil itself?

---

* Cf. Ovid, *Met.* i. 121 f.:
Domus antra fuerunt
Et densi frutices et vinctae cortice virgae.
Among many accounts by Roman writers of early man, compare this passage of Ovid, and that in the fifth book of Lucretius.

Nature was not so hostile to man that, when she gave all the other animals an easy rôle in life, she made it impossible for him alone to live without all these artifices. None of these was imposed upon us by her; none of them had to be painfully sought out that our lives might be prolonged. All things were ready for us at our birth; it is we that have made everything difficult for ourselves, through our disdain for what is easy. Houses, shelter, creature comforts, food, and all that has now become the source of vast trouble, were ready at hand, free to all, and obtainable for trifling pains. For the limit everywhere corresponded to the need; it is we that have made all those things valuable, we that have made them admired, we that have caused them to be sought for by extensive and manifold devices. Nature suffices for what she demands. Luxury has turned her back upon nature; each day she expands herself, in all the ages she has been gathering strength, and by her wit promoting the vices. At first, luxury began to lust for what nature regarded as superfluous, then for that which was contrary to nature; and finally she made the soul a bondsman to the body, and bade it be an utter slave to the body's lusts. All these crafts by which the city is patrolled—or shall I say kept in uproar—are but engaged in the body's business; time was when all things were offered to the body as to a slave, but now they are made ready for it as for a master. Accordingly, hence have come the workshops of the weavers and the carpenters; hence the savoury smells of the professional cooks; hence the wantonness of those who teach wanton postures, and wanton and affected singing. For that moderation which nature prescribes, which limits our desires by resources restricted to our needs, has abandoned the field; it has now come to this—that to want only what is enough is a sign both of boorishness and of utter destitution.

It is hard to believe, my dear Lucilius, how easily the charm of eloquence wins even great men away from the truth. Take, for example, Posidonius—who, in my estimation, is of the number of those who have contributed most to philosophy—when he wishes to describe the art of weaving. He tells how, first, some threads are twisted and some drawn out from the soft, loose mass of wool; next, how the upright warp keeps the threads stretched by means of hanging weights; then, how the inserted thread of the woof, which softens the hard texture of the web which holds it fast on either side, is forced by the batten to make a compact union with the warp. He maintains that even the weaver's art was discovered by wise men, forgetting that the more complicated art which he describes was invented in later days—the art wherein

The web is bound to frame; asunder now
The reed doth part the warp. Between the threads
Is shot the woof by pointed shuttles borne;
The broad comb's well-notched teeth then drive it home.*

Suppose he had had the opportunity of seeing the weaving of our own day, which produces the clothing that will conceal nothing, the clothing which affords—I will not say no protection to the body, but none even to modesty!

Posidonius then passes on to the farmer. With no less eloquence he describes the ground which is broken up and crossed again by the plough, so that the earth, thus loosened, may allow freer play to the roots; then the seed is sown, and the weeds plucked out by hand, lest any chance growth or wild plant spring up and spoil the crop. This trade also, he declares, is the creation of the wise,—just as if cultivators of the soil were not even at the present day discovering countless new methods of increasing the soil's fertility! Furthermore, not confining his attention to these arts, he even degrades the wise man by sending him to the mill. For he tells us how the sage, by imitating the processes of nature, began to make bread. "The grain,"** he says, "once taken into the mouth, is crushed by the flinty teeth, which meet in hostile encounter, and whatever grain slips out the tongue turns back to the selfsame teeth. Then it is blended into a mass, that it may the more easily pass down the slippery throat. When this has reached

* Ovid, *Met.* vi. 55 ff.

** Professor Summers calls attention to the similarity of this passage and Cicero, *De Nat. Deor.* ii. 134 ff. *dentibus manditur . . . a lingua adiuvari videtur . . . in alvo . . . calore . . . in reliquum corpus dividantur.*

the stomach, it is digested by the stomach's equable heat; then, and not till then, it is assimilated with the body. Following this pattern," he goes on, "someone placed two rough stones, the one above the other, in imitation of the teeth, one set of which is stationary and awaits the motion of the other set. Then, by the rubbing of the one stone against the other, the grain is crushed and brought back again and again, until by frequent rubbing it is reduced to powder. Then this man sprinkled the meal with water, and by continued manipulation subdued the mass and moulded the loaf. This loaf was, at first, baked by hot ashes or by an earthen vessel glowing hot; later on ovens were gradually discovered and the other devices whose heat will render obedience to the sage's will." Posidonius came very near declaring that even the cobbler's trade was the discovery of the wise man.

Reason did indeed devise all these things, but it was not right reason. It was man, but not the wise man, that discovered them; just as they invented ships, in which we cross rivers and seas—ships fitted with sails for the purpose of catching the force of the winds, ships with rudders added at the stern in order to turn the vessel's course in one direction or another. The model followed was the fish, which steers itself by its tail, and by its slightest motion on this side or on that bends its swift course. "But," says Posidonius, "the wise man did indeed discover all these things; they were, however, too petty for him to deal with himself and so he entrusted them to his meaner assistants." Not so; these early inventions were thought out by no other class of men than those who have them in charge today. We know that certain devices have come to light only within our own memory—such as the use of windows which admit the clear light through transparent tiles,* and such as the vaulted baths, with pipes let into their walls for the purpose of diffusing the heat which maintains an even temperature in their lowest as well as in their highest spaces. Why need I mention the marble with which our temples and our private houses are resplendent? Or the rounded and polished masses

---

* Besides *lapis specularis* (window-glass) the Romans used alabaster, mica, and shells for this purpose.

of stone by means of which we erect colonnades and buildings roomy enough for nations? Or our signs* for whole words, which enable us to take down a speech, however rapidly uttered, matching speed of tongue by speed of hand? All this sort of thing has been devised by the lowest grade of slaves. Wisdom's seat is higher; she trains not the hands, but is mistress of our minds.

Would you know what wisdom has brought forth to light, what she has accomplished? It is not the graceful poses of the body, or the varied notes produced by horn and flute, whereby the breath is received and, as it passes out or through, is transformed into voice. It is not wisdom that contrives arms, or walls, or instruments useful in war; nay, her voice is for peace, and she summons all mankind to concord. It is not she, I maintain, who is the artisan of our indispensable implements of daily use. Why do you assign to her such petty things? You see in her the skilled artisan of life. The other arts, it is true, wisdom has under her control; for he whom life serves is also served by the things which equip life. But wisdom's course is toward the state of happiness; thither she guides us, thither she opens the way for us. She shows us what things are evil and what things are seemingly evil; she strips our minds of vain illusion. She bestows upon us a greatness which is substantial, but she represses the greatness which is inflated, and showy but filled with emptiness; and she does not permit us to be ignorant of the difference between what is great and what is but swollen; nay, she delivers to us the knowledge of the whole of nature and of her own nature. She discloses to us what the gods are and of what sort they are; what are the nether gods, the household deities, and the protecting spirits; what are the souls which have been endowed with lasting life and have been admitted to the second class of divinities,** where is their abode and what their activities, powers, and will.

---

* Suetonius tells us that a certain Ennius, a grammarian of the Augustan age, was the first to develop shorthand on a scientific basis, and that Tiro, Cicero's freedman, had invented the process. He also mentions Seneca as the most scientific and encyclopaedic authority on the subject.

** Possibly either the *manes* or the *indigitamenta* of the early Roman religion.

Such are wisdom's rites of initiation, by means of which is unlocked, not a village shrine, but the vast temple of all the gods—the universe itself, whose true apparitions and true aspects she offers to the gaze of our minds. For the vision of our eyes is too dull for sights so great. Then she goes back to the beginnings of things, to the eternal Reason* which was imparted to the whole, and to the force which inheres in all the seeds of things, giving them the power to fashion each thing according to its kind. Then wisdom begins to inquire about the soul, whence it comes, where it dwells, how long it abides, into how many divisions it falls. Finally, she has turned her attention from the corporeal to the incorporeal, and has closely examined truth and the marks whereby truth is known, inquiring next how that which is equivocal can be distinguished from the truth, whether in life or in language; for in both are elements of the false mingled with the true.

It is my opinion that the wise man has not withdrawn himself, as Posidonius thinks, from those arts which we were discussing, but that he never took them up at all.** For he would have judged that nothing was worth discovering that he would not afterwards judge to be worth using always. He would not take up things which would have to be laid aside.

"But Anacharsis," says Posidonius, "invented the potter's wheel, whose whirling gives shape to vessels."*** Then because the potter's wheel is mentioned in Homer, people prefer to believe that Homer's verses are false rather than the story of Posidonius! But I maintain that Anacharsis

---

* i.e., λόγος.

** Seneca, himself one of the keenest scientific observers in history (witness *Nat. Quaest.*, Epp. lvii., lxxix., etc.), is pushing his argument very far in this letter. His message is clear enough; but the modern combination of natural science, psychology, and philosophy shows that Posidonius had some justification for his theories. Cf. also Lucretius, v. 1105-7 ff.

*** This Scythian prince and friend of Solon, who visited Athens in the sixth century B.C., is also said to have invented the bellows and the anchor. Cf., however, *Iliad* xviii. 600 f. ὡς ὅτε τις τροχὸν ἄρμενον ἐν παλάμῃσιν ἑζόμενος κεραμεὺς πειρήσεται, and Leaf's comment: "The potter's wheel was known in pre-Mycenean times, and was a very ancient invention to the oldest Epic poets." Seneca is right.

was not the creator of this wheel; and even if he was, although he was a wise man when he invented it, yet he did not invent it *qua* "wise man"—just as there are a great many things which wise men do as men, not as wise men. Suppose, for example, that a wise man is exceedingly fleet of foot; he will outstrip all the runners in the race by virtue of being fleet, not by virtue of his wisdom. I should like to show Posidonius some glass-blower who by his breath moulds the glass into manifold shapes which could scarcely be fashioned by the most skilful hand. Nay, these discoveries have been made since we men have ceased to discover wisdom.

But Posidonius again remarks: "Democritus is said to have discovered the arch,* whose effect was that the curving line of stones, which gradually lean toward each other, is bound together by the keystone." I am inclined to pronounce this statement false. For there must have been, before Democritus, bridges and gateways in which the curvature did not begin until about the top. It seems to have quite slipped your memory that this same Democritus discovered how ivory could be softened, how, by boiling, a pebble could be transformed into an emerald,**—the same process used even today for colouring stones which are found to be amenable to this treatment! It may have been a wise man who discovered all such things, but he did not discover them by virtue of being a wise man; for he does many things which we see done just as well, or even more skilfully and dexterously, by men who are utterly lacking in sagacity.

Do you ask what, then, the wise man has found out and what he has brought to light? First of all there is truth, and nature; and nature

---

* Seneca (see next sentence) is right again. The arch was known in Chaldaea and in Egypt before 3000 B.C. Greek bee-hive tombs, Etruscan gateways, and early Roman remains, testify to its immemorial use.

** The ancients judged precious stones merely by their colour; their *smaragdus* included also malachite, jade, and several kinds of quartz. Exposure to heat alters the colour of some stones; and the alchemists believed that the "angelic stone" changed common flints into diamonds, rubies, emeralds, etc. See G. F. Kunz, *The Magic of Jewels and Charms*, p. 16. It was also an ancient superstition that emeralds were produced from jasper.

he has not followed as the other animals do, with eyes too dull to perceive the divine in it. In the second place, there is the law of life, and life he has made to conform to universal principles; and he has taught us, not merely to know the gods, but to follow them, and to welcome the gifts of chance precisely as if they were divine commands. He has forbidden us to give heed to false opinions, and has weighed the value of each thing by a true standard of appraisement. He has condemned those pleasures with which remorse is intermingled, and has praised those goods which will always satisfy; and he has published the truth abroad that he is most happy who has no need of happiness, and that he is most powerful who has power over himself.

I am not speaking of that philosophy which has placed the citizen outside his country and the gods outside the universe, and which has bestowed virtue upon pleasure,* but rather of that philosophy which counts nothing good except what is honourable,—one which cannot be cajoled by the gifts either of man or of fortune, one whose value is that it cannot be bought for any value. That this philosophy existed in such a rude age, when the arts and crafts were still unknown and when useful things could only be learned by use,—this I refuse to believe.

Next there came the fortune-favoured period when the bounties of nature lay open to all, for men's indiscriminate use, before avarice and luxury had broken the bonds which held mortals together, and they, abandoning their communal existence, had separated and turned to plunder. The men of the second age were not wise men, even though they did what wise men should do.** Indeed, there is no other condition of the human race that anyone would regard more highly; and if God should commission a man to fashion earthly creatures and to bestow institutions upon peoples, this man would approve of no other system than that which obtained among the men of that age, when

---

* i.e., the Epicureans, who withdraw from civil life and regarded the gods as taking no part in the affairs of men.

** i.e., live according to nature.

No ploughman tilled the soil, nor was it right
To portion off or bound one's property.
Men shared their gains, and earth more freely gave
Her riches to her sons who sought them not.*

What race of men was ever more blest than that race? They enjoyed all nature in partnership. Nature sufficed for them, now the guardian, as before she was the parent, of all; and this her gift consisted of the assured possession by each man of the common resources. Why should I not even call that race the richest among mortals, since you could not find a poor person among them?

But avarice broke in upon a condition so happily ordained, and, by its eagerness to lay something away and to turn it to its own private use, made all things the property of others, and reduced itself from boundless wealth to straitened need. It was avarice that introduced poverty and, by craving much, lost all. And so, although she now tries to make good her loss, although she adds one estate to another, evicting a neighbour either by buying him out or by wronging him, although she extends her country-seats to the size of provinces and defines ownership as meaning extensive travel through one's own property,—in spite of all these efforts of hers, no enlargement of our boundaries will bring us back to the condition from which we have departed.

When there is no more that we can do, we shall possess much; but we once possessed the whole world! The very soil was more productive when untilled, and yielded more than enough for peoples who refrained from despoiling one another. Whatever gift nature had produced, men found as much pleasure in revealing it to another as in having discovered it. It was possible for no man either to surpass another or to fall short of him; what there was, was divided among unquarrelling friends. Not yet had the stronger begun to lay hands upon the weaker; not yet had the miser, by hiding away what lay before him, begun to shut off his neighbour from even the necessities of life; each cared as much for his neighbour as for himself. Armour lay unused, and the hand, unstained

* Verg. *Georg.* i. 125 ff.

by human blood, had turned all its hatred against wild beasts. The men of that day, who had found in some dense grove protection against the sun, and security against the severity of winter or of rain in their mean hiding-places, spent their lives under the branches of the trees and passed tranquil nights without a sigh. Care vexes us in our purple, and routs us from our beds with the sharpest of goads; but how soft was the sleep the hard earth bestowed upon the men of that day! No fretted and panelled ceilings hung over them, but as they lay beneath the open sky the stars glided quietly above them, and the firmament, night's noble pageant, marched swiftly by, conducting its mighty task in silence. For them by day, as well as by night, the visions of this most glorious abode were free and open. It was their joy to watch the constellations as they sank from mid-heaven, and others, again, as they rose from their hidden abodes. What else but joy could it be to wander among the marvels which dotted the heavens far and wide? But you of the present day shudder at every sound your houses make, and as you sit among your frescoes the slightest creak makes you shrink in terror. *They* had no houses as big as cities. The air, the breezes blowing free through the open spaces, the flitting shade of crag or tree, springs crystal-clear and streams not spoiled by man's work, whether by water-pipe[*] or by any confinement of the channel, but running at will, and meadows beautiful without the use of art,—amid such scenes were their rude homes, adorned with rustic hand. Such a dwelling was in accordance with nature; therein it was a joy to live, fearing neither the dwelling itself nor for its safety. In these days, however, our houses constitute a large portion of our dread.

But no matter how excellent and guileless was the life of the men of that age, they were not wise men; for that title is reserved for the highest achievement. Still, I would not deny that they were men of lofty spirit and—I may use the phrase—fresh from the gods. For there is no doubt that the world produced a better progeny before it was yet worn out. However, not all were endowed with mental faculties of

---

* Cf. Horace, *Ep.* i. 10. 20 f.:
Purior in vicis aqua tendit rumpere plumbum
Quam quae per pronum trepidat cum murmure rivum?

highest perfection, though in all cases their native powers were more sturdy than ours and more fitted for toil. For nature does not bestow virtue; it is an art to become good. They, at least, searched not in the lowest dregs of the earth for gold, nor yet for silver or transparent stones; and they still were merciful even to the dumb animals—so far removed was that epoch from the custom of slaying man by man, not in anger or through fear, but just to make a show! They had as yet no embroidered garments nor did they weave cloth of gold; gold was not yet even mined.

What, then, is the conclusion of the matter? It was by reason of their ignorance of things that the men of those days were innocent; and it makes a great deal of difference whether one wills not to sin or has not the knowledge to sin.* Justice was unknown to them, unknown prudence, unknown also self-control and bravery; but their rude life possessed certain qualities akin to all these virtues. Virtue is not vouchsafed to a soul unless that soul has been trained and taught, and by unremitting practice brought to perfection. For the attainment of this boon, but not in the possession of it, were we born; and even in the best of men, before you refine them by instruction, there is but the stuff of virtue, not virtue itself. Farewell.

---

* Because virtue depends upon reason, and none but voluntary acts should meet with praise or blame.

LETTER

91

On the Lesson to be Drawn from the Burning of Lyons*

Our friend Liberalis** is now downcast; for he has just heard of the fire which has wiped out the colony of Lyons. Such a calamity might upset anyone at all, not to speak of a man who dearly loves his country. But this incident has served to make him inquire about the strength of his own character, which he has trained, I suppose, just to meet situations that he thought might cause him fear. I do not wonder, however, that he was free from apprehension touching an evil so unexpected and practically unheard of as this, since it is without precedent. For fire has damaged many a city, but has annihilated none. Even when fire has been hurled against the walls by the hand of a foe, the flame dies out in many places, and although

---

* In spite of the *centesimus annus* of § 14 (q.v.), the most probable date of this letter, based on Tac. *Ann.* xvi. 13 and other general evidence, is July-September 64 A.D. 58 A.D. would be too early for many reasons—among them that "peace all over the world" would not be a true statement until January of 62. (See the monograph of Jonas, O. Binder, Peiper, and Schultess.)

** Probably Aebutius Liberalis, to whom the treatise De Beneficiis was dedicated.

continually renewed, rarely devours so wholly as to leave nothing for the sword. Even an earthquake has scarcely ever been so violent and destructive as to overthrow whole cities. Finally, no conflagration has ever before blazed forth so savagely in any town that nothing was left for a second. So many beautiful buildings, any single one of which would make a single town famous, were wrecked in one night. In time of such deep peace an event has taken place worse than men can possibly fear even in time of war. Who can believe it? When weapons are everywhere at rest, and when peace prevails throughout the world, Lyons, the pride of Gaul,* is missing!

Fortune has usually allowed all men, when she has assailed them collectively, to have a foreboding of that which they were destined to suffer. Every great creation has had granted to it a period of reprieve before its fall; but in this case, only a single night elapsed between the city at its greatest and the city non-existent. In short, it takes me longer to tell you it has perished than it took for the city to perish.

All this has affected our friend Liberalis, bending his will, which is usually so steadfast and erect in the face of his own trials. And not without reason has he been shaken; for it is the unexpected that puts the heaviest load upon us. Strangeness adds to the weight of calamities, and every mortal feels the greater pain as a result of that which also brings surprise.

Therefore, nothing ought to be unexpected by us. Our minds should be sent forward in advance to meet all problems, and we should consider, not what is wont to happen, but what can happen. For what is there in existence that Fortune, when she has so willed, does not drag down from the very height of its prosperity? And what is there that she does not the more violently assail the more brilliantly it shines? What is laborious or difficult for her? She does not always attack in one way, or even with her full strength; at one time she summons our own hands

---

* That Lyons, situated at the junction of the Arar and the Rhone, was of especial prominence in Gaul, may be also gathered from the fact that it boasted a government mint and the *Ara Augusti*—a shrine established for the annual worship of all the Gallic states. Moreover, the emperor Claudius delivered his famous address in that city (see Tac. *Ann.* xi. 23 f.).

against us; at another time, content with her own powers, she makes use of no agent in devising perils for us. No time is exempt; in the midst of our very pleasures there spring up causes of suffering. War arises in the midst of peace, and that which we depended upon for protection is transformed into a cause of fear; friend becomes enemy, ally becomes foeman. The summer calm is stirred into sudden storms, wilder than the storms of winter.* With no foe in sight we are victims of such fates as foes inflict, and if other causes of disaster fail, excessive good fortune finds them for itself. The most temperate are assailed by illness, the strongest by wasting disease, the most innocent by chastisement, the most secluded by the noisy mob.

Chance chooses some new weapon by which to bring her strength to bear against us, thinking we have forgotten her. Whatever structure has been reared by a long sequence of years, at the cost of great toil and through the great kindness of the gods, is scattered and dispersed by a single day. Nay, he who has said "a day" has granted too long a postponement to swift-coming misfortune; an hour, an instant of time, suffices for the overthrow of empires! It would be some consolation for the feebleness of our selves and our works, if all things should perish as slowly as they come into being; but as it is, increases are of sluggish growth, but the way to ruin is rapid. Nothing, whether public or private, is stable; the destinies of men, no less than those of cities, are in a whirl. Amid the greatest calm terror arises, and though no external agencies stir up commotion, yet evils burst forth from sources whence they were least expected. Thrones which have stood the shock of civil and foreign wars crash to the ground though no one sets them tottering. How few the states which have carried their good fortune through to the end!

We should therefore reflect upon all contingencies, and should fortify our minds against the evils which may possibly come. Exile, the torture of disease, wars, shipwreck,—we must think on these.** Chance

* Cf. Ep. iv. 7, esp. the words *noli huic tranquillitati confidere; momento mare evertitur.*

** The passage bears a striking resemblance to the words of Theseus in an unknown play of Euripides (Nauck. Frag. 964) quoted by Cicero, *Tusc.* iii. 14. 29, and by Plutarch, *Consolation to Apollonius*, 112d.

may tear you from your country or your country from you, or may banish you to the desert; this very place, where throngs are stifling, may become a desert. Let us place before our eyes in its entirety the nature of man's lot, and if we would not be overwhelmed, or even dazed, by those unwonted evils, as if they were novel, let us summon to our minds beforehand, not as great an evil as oftentimes happens, but the very greatest evil that possibly can happen. We must reflect upon fortune fully and completely.

How often have cities in Asia, how often in Achaia, been laid low by a single shock of earthquake! How many towns in Syria, how many in Macedonia, have been swallowed up! How often has this kind of devastation laid Cyprus* in ruins! How often has Paphos collapsed! Not infrequently are tidings brought to us of the utter destruction of entire cities; yet how small a part of the world are we, to whom such tidings often come!

Let us rise, therefore, to confront the operations of Fortune, and whatever happens, let us have the assurance that it is not so great as rumour advertises it to be. A rich city has been laid in ashes, the jewel of the provinces, counted as one of them and yet not included with them;** rich though it was, nevertheless it was set upon a single hill,*** and that not very large in extent. But of all those cities, of whose magnificence and grandeur you hear today, the very traces will be blotted out by time. Do you not see how, in Achaia, the foundations of the most famous cities have already crumbled to nothing, so that no trace is left to show that they ever even existed?**** Not only does that which has been made with hands totter to the ground, not only is that which has been set

---

* Seneca (*N. Q.* vi. 26) speaks of Paphos (on the island of Cyprus) as having been more than once devastated. We know of two such accidents—one under Augustus and another under Vespasian. See the same passage for other earthquake shocks in various places.

** Lyons held an exceptional position in relation to the three Gallic provinces; it was a free town, belonging to none and yet their capital, much like the city of Washington in relation to the United States.

*** A fact mentioned merely to suggest Rome with her seven hills.

**** For example, Mycenae and Tiryns.

in place by man's art and man's efforts overthrown by the passing days; nay, the peaks of mountains dissolve, whole tracts have settled, and places which once stood far from the sight of the sea are now covered by the waves. The mighty power of fires has eaten away the hills through whose sides they used to glow, and has levelled to the ground peaks which were once most lofty—the sailor's solace and his beacon. The works of nature herself are harassed; hence we ought to bear with untroubled minds the destruction of cities. They stand but to fall! This doom awaits them, one and all; it may be that some internal force, and blasts of violence which are tremendous because their way is blocked, will throw off the weight which holds then down; or that a whirlpool of raging currents, mightier because they are hidden in the bosom of the earth, will break through that which resists its power; or that the vehemence of flames will burst asunder the framework of the earth's crust; or that time, from which nothing is safe, will reduce them little by little; or that a pestilential climate will drive their inhabitants away and the mould will corrode their deserted walls. It would be tedious to recount all the ways by which fate may come; but this one thing I know: all the works of mortal man have been doomed to mortality, and in the midst of things which have been destined to die, we live!

Hence it is thoughts like these, and of this kind, which I am offering as consolation to our friend Liberalis, who burns with a love for his country that is beyond belief. Perhaps its destruction has been brought about only that it may be raised up again to a better destiny. Oftentimes a reverse has but made room for more prosperous fortune. Many structures have fallen only to rise to a greater height. Timagenes,* who had a grudge against Rome and her prosperity, used to say that the only reason he was grieved when conflagrations occurred in Rome was his knowledge that better buildings would arise than those which had gone down in the flames. And probably in this city of Lyons, too, all its citizens will earnestly strive that everything shall be rebuilt better

* Probably the writer, and intimate friend of Augustus, who began life in Rome as a captive from Egypt. Falling into disfavour with the Emperor, he took refuge with the malcontent Asinius Pollio at Tusculum, and subsequently died in the East. Cf. Seneca, *De Ira*, iii. 23.

in size and security than what they have lost. May it be built to endure and, under happier auspices, for a longer existence! This is indeed but the hundredth year since this colony was founded—not the limit even of a man's lifetime.* Led forth by Plancus, the natural advantages of its site have caused it to wax strong and reach the numbers which it contains today; and yet how many calamities of the greatest severity has it endured within the space of an old man's life!

Therefore let the mind be disciplined to understand and to endure its own lot, and let it have the knowledge that there is nothing which fortune does not dare—that she has the same jurisdiction over empires as over emperors, the same power over cities as over the citizens who dwell therein. We must not cry out at any of these calamities. Into such a world have we entered, and under such laws do we live. If you like it, obey; if not, depart whithersoever you wish. Cry out in anger if any unfair measures are taken with reference to you individually; but if this inevitable law is binding upon the highest and the lowest alike, be reconciled to fate, by which all things are dissolved. You should not estimate our worth by our funeral mounds or by these monuments of unequal size which line the road; their ashes level all men! We are unequal at birth, but are equal in death. What I say about cities I say also about their inhabitants: Ardea was captured as well as Rome.** The great founder of human law has not made distinctions between us on the basis of high lineage or of illustrious names, except while we live. When, however, we come to the end which awaits mortals, he says: "Depart, ambition! To all creatures that burden the earth let one and the

---

* It was in 43 B.C. that Plancus led out the colonists who were chiefly Roman citizens driven from Vienna. Seneca would have been more accurate had he said "one hundred and eighth (or seventh)." Buecheler and Schultess would (unnecessarily) emend to read *centesimus septimus*. But Seneca was using round numbers.

** Ardea, the earliest capital of Latium, and Rome, the present capital of the empire. Seneca probably refers to Ardea's capture and destruction by the Samnites in the fourth century; Rome was captured by the Celts in 390 B.C. The former greatness of Ardea was celebrated by Vergil, *Aeneid*, vii. 411 ff.:
et nunc magnum manet Ardea nomen,
Sed fortuna fuit.

same* law apply!" For enduring all things, we are equal; no one is more frail than another, no one more certain of his own life on the morrow.

Alexander, king of Macedon, began to study geometry;** unhappy man, because he would thereby learn how puny was that earth of which he had seized but a fraction! Unhappy man, I repeat, because he was bound to understand that he was bearing a false title. For who can be "great" in that which is puny? The lessons which were being taught him were intricate and could be learned only by assiduous application; they were not the kind to be comprehended by a madman, who let his thoughts range beyond the ocean.*** "Teach me something easy!" he cries; but his teacher answers: "These things are the same for all, as hard for one as for another." Imagine that nature is saying to us: "Those things of which you complain are the same for all. I cannot give anything easier to any man, but whoever wishes will make things easier for himself." In what way? By equanimity. You must suffer pain, and thirst, and hunger, and old age too, if a longer stay among men shall be granted you; you must be sick, and you must suffer loss and death. Nevertheless, you should not believe those whose noisy clamour surrounds you; none of these things is an evil, none is beyond your power to bear, or is burdensome. It is only by common opinion that there is anything formidable in them. Your fearing death is therefore like your fear of gossip. But what is more foolish than a man afraid of words? Our friend Demetrius**** is wont to put it cleverly when he says: "For me the talk of ignorant men is like the rumblings which issue from the belly. For," he adds, "what difference does it make to me whether such rumblings come from above or from below?" What madness it is to be afraid of disrepute in the judgment of the disreputable! Just as you have had no cause for shrinking in terror

---

* *Siremps* (or *sirempse*—Plaut. *Amph.* 73), an ancient legal term, is derived by Festus from *similis re ipsa*; but Corssen explains it as from *sic rem pse.*

** i.e., surveying. See Ep. lxxxviii. 10.

*** i.e., Ὠκεανός, the stream which encircles the earth.

**** This plain-living, plain-speaking philosopher appears also in Epp. xx. 9 and lxii. 3. Seneca refers to him as *seminudum, quanto minus quam stramentis incubantem.*

from the talk of men, so you have no cause now to shrink from these things, which you would never fear had not their talk forced fear upon you. Does it do any harm to a good man to be besmirched by unjust gossip? Then let not this sort of thing damage death, either, in our estimation; death also is in bad odour. But no one of those who malign death has made trial of it.

Meanwhile it is foolhardy to condemn that of which you are ignorant. This one thing, however, you do know—that death is helpful to many, that it sets many free from tortures, want, ailments, sufferings, and weariness. We are in the power of nothing when once we have death in our own power! Farewell.

VOLUME THREE

LETTER 104

On Care of Health and Peace of Mind

I have run off to my villa at Nomentum, for what purpose, do you suppose? To escape the city? No; to shake off a fever which was surely working its way into my system. It had already got a grip upon me. My physician kept insisting that when the circulation was upset and irregular, disturbing the natural poise, the disease was under way. I therefore ordered my carriage to be made ready at once, and insisted on departing, in spite of my wife Paulina's* efforts to stop me; for I remembered my master Gallio's** words, when he began to develop a fever in Achaia and took ship at once, insisting that the disease was not of the body but of the place. That is what I remarked to my dear

---

* Pompeia Paulina, the second wife of Seneca; cf. Tac. *Ann.* xv. 60. Though much younger than her husband, she was a model of devotion, and remained loyal to him through all the Neronian persecution.

** Elder brother of Seneca, whose name before his adoption by Lucius Iunius Gallio was Annaeus Novatus. He was governor of Achaia from A.D. July 1, 51 to July 1, 52. See *Acts* xviii. 11 ff., and Duff, *Three Dialogues of Seneca*, p. xliii.

Paulina, who always urges me to take care of my health. I know that her very life-breath comes and goes with my own, and I am beginning, in my solicitude for her, to be solicitous for myself. And although old age has made me braver to bear many things, I am gradually losing this boon that old age bestows. For it comes into my mind that in this old man there is a youth also, and youth needs tenderness. Therefore, since I cannot prevail upon her to love me any more heroically, she prevails upon me to cherish myself more carefully. For one must indulge genuine emotions; sometimes, even in spite of weighty reasons, the breath of life must be called back and kept at our very lips even at the price of great suffering, for the sake of those whom we hold dear; because the good man should not live as long as it pleases him, but as long as he ought. He who does not value his wife, or his friend, highly enough to linger longer in life—he who obstinately persists in dying—is a voluptuary.

The soul should also enforce this command upon itself whenever the needs of one's relatives require; it should pause and humour those near and dear, not only when it desires, but even when it has begun, to die. It gives proof of a great heart to return to life for the sake of others; and noble men have often done this. But this procedure also, I believe, indicates the highest type of kindness: that although the greatest advantage of old age is the opportunity to be more negligent regarding self-preservation and to use life more adventurously, one should watch over one's old age with still greater care if one knows that such action is pleasing, useful, or desirable in the eyes of a person whom one holds dear. This is also a source of no mean joy and profit; for what is sweeter than to be so valued by one's wife that one becomes more valuable to oneself for this reason? Hence my dear Paulina is able to make me responsible, not only for her fears, but also for my own.

So you are curious to know the outcome of this prescription of travel? As soon as I escaped from the oppressive atmosphere of the city, and from that awful odour of reeking kitchens which, when in use, pour forth a ruinous mess of steam and soot, I perceived at once that my health was mending. And how much stronger do you think

I felt when I reached my vineyards! Being, so to speak, let out to pasture, I regularly walked into my meals! So I am my old self again, feeling now no wavering languor in my system, and no sluggishness in my brain. I am beginning to work with all my energy.

But the mere place avails little for this purpose, unless the mind is fully master of itself, and can, at its pleasure, find seclusion even in the midst of business; the man, however, who is always selecting resorts and hunting for leisure, will find something to distract his mind in every place. Socrates is reported to have replied, when a certain person complained of having received no benefit from his travels: "It serves you right! You travelled in your own company!"* O what a blessing it would be for some men to wander away from themselves! As it is, they cause themselves vexation, worry, demoralization, and fear! What profit is there in crossing the sea and in going from one city to another? If you would escape your troubles, you need not another place but another personality. Perhaps you have reached Athens, or perhaps Rhodes; choose any state you fancy, how does it matter what its character may be? You will be bringing to it your own.

Suppose that you hold wealth to be a good: poverty will then distress you, and,—which is most pitiable,—it will be an imaginary poverty. For you may be rich, and nevertheless, because your neighbour is richer, you suppose yourself to be poor exactly by the same amount in which you fall short of your neighbour. You may deem official position a good; you will be vexed at another's appointment or re-appointment to the consulship; you will be jealous whenever you see a name several times in the state records. Your ambition will be so frenzied that you will regard yourself last in the race if there is anyone in front of you. Or you may rate death as the worst of evils, although there is really no evil therein except that which precedes death's coming—fear. You will be frightened out of your wits, not only by real, but by fancied dangers, and will be tossed for ever on the sea of illusion. What benefit will it be to

---

* Cf. Ep. x. 1 "*Mecum loquor.*" "*Cave, rogo, et diligenter adtende; cum homine malo loqueris.*"

Have threaded all the towns of Argolis,
A fugitive through midmost press of foes?*

For peace itself will furnish further apprehension. Even in the midst of safety you will have no confidence if your mind has once been given a shock; once it has acquired the habit of blind panic, it is incapable of providing even for its own safety. For it does not avoid danger, but runs away. Yet we are more exposed to danger when we turn our backs.

You may judge it the most grievous of ills to lose any of those you love; while all the same this would be no less foolish than weeping because the trees which charm your eye and adorn your home lose their foliage. Regard everything that pleases you as if it were a flourishing plant; make the most of it while it is in leaf, for different plants at different seasons must fall and die. But just as the loss of leaves is a light thing, because they are born afresh, so it is with the loss of those whom you love and regard as the delight of your life; for they can be replaced even though they cannot be born afresh. "New friends, however, will not be the same." No, nor will you yourself remain the same; you change with every day and every hour. But in other men you more readily see what time plunders; in your own case the change is hidden, because it will not take place visibly. Others are snatched from sight; we ourselves are being stealthily filched away from ourselves. You will not think about any of these problems, nor will you apply remedies to these wounds. You will of your own volition be sowing a crop of trouble by alternate hoping and despairing. If you are wise, mingle these two elements: do not hope without despair, or despair without hope.

What benefit has travel of itself ever been able to give anyone? No restraint upon pleasure, no bridling of desire, no checking of bad temper, no crushing of the wild assaults of passion, no opportunity to rid the soul of evil. Travelling cannot give us judgment, or shake off our errors; it merely holds our attention for a moment by a certain novelty, as children pause to wonder at something unfamiliar. Besides,

* Vergil, *Aen.* iii. 282 f.

it irritates us, through the wavering of a mind which is suffering from an acute attack of sickness; the very motion makes it more fitful and nervous. Hence the spots we had sought most eagerly we quit still more eagerly, like birds that flit and are off as soon as they have alighted. What travel will give is familiarity with other nations: it will reveal to you mountains of strange shape, or unfamiliar tracts of plain, or valleys that are watered by ever-flowing springs, or the characteristics of some river that comes to our attention. We observe how the Nile rises and swells in summer, or how the Tigris disappears, runs underground through hidden spaces, and then appears with unabated sweep; or how the Maeander,* that oft-rehearsed theme and plaything of the poets, turns in frequent bendings, and often in winding comes close to its own channel before resuming its course. But this sort of information will not make better or sounder men of us.**

We ought rather to spend our time in study, and to cultivate those who are masters of wisdom, learning something which has been investigated, but not settled; by this means the mind can be relieved of a most wretched serfdom, and won over to freedom. Indeed, as long as you are ignorant of what you should avoid or seek, or of what is necessary or superfluous, or of what is right or wrong, you will not be travelling, but merely wandering. There will be no benefit to you in this hurrying to and fro; for you are travelling with your emotions and are followed by your afflictions. Would that they were indeed following you! In that case, they would be farther away; as it is, you are carrying and not leading them. Hence they press about you on all sides, continually chafing and annoying you. It is medicine, not scenery, for which the sick man must go a-searching. Suppose that someone has broken a leg or dislocated a joint: he does not take carriage or ship for other regions, but he calls in the physician to set the fractured limb, or to move it back to its proper place in the socket. What then? When the spirit is broken or wrenched in so many places, do you think that change of place can heal

---

* See Index of Proper Names.

** Although Seneca was deeply interested in such matters, as is proved by Ep. lxxix., the *Naturales Quaestiones*, and an early work on the geography of Egypt.

it? The complaint is too deep-seated to be cured by a journey. Travel does not make a physician or an orator; no art is acquired by merely living in a certain place.

Where lies the truth, then? Can wisdom, the greatest of all the arts, be picked up on a journey? I assure you, travel as far as you like, you can never establish yourself beyond the reach of desire, beyond the reach of bad temper, or beyond the reach of fear; had it been so, the human race would long ago have banded together and made a pilgrimage to the spot. Such ills, as long as you carry with you their causes, will load you down and worry you to skin and bone in your wanderings over land and sea. Do you wonder that it is of no use to run away from them? That from which you are running, is within you. Accordingly, reform your own self, get the burden off your own shoulders, and keep within safe limits the cravings which ought to be removed. Wipe out from your soul all trace of sin. If you would enjoy your travels, make healthy the companion of your travels. As long as this companion is avaricious and mean, greed will stick to you; and while you consort with an overbearing man, your puffed-up ways will also stick close. Live with a hangman, and you will never be rid of your cruelty. If an adulterer be your club-mate, he will kindle the baser passions. If you would be stripped of your faults leave far behind you the patterns of the faults. The miser, the swindler, the bully, the cheat, who will do you much harm merely by being near you, are *within* you.

Change therefore to better associations: live with the Catos, with Laelius, with Tubero. Or, if you enjoy living with Greeks also, spend your time with Socrates and with Zeno: the former will show you how to die if it be necessary; the latter how to die before it is necessary. Live with Chrysippus, with Posidonius:* they will make you acquainted with things earthly and things heavenly; they will bid you work hard over something more than neat turns of language and phrases mouthed forth for the entertainment of listeners; they will bid

* These men are patterns or interpreters of the virtues. The first-named three represent courage, justice, and self-restraint respectively. Socrates is the ideal wise man, Zeno, Chrysippus, and Posidonus are in turn the founder, the classifier, and the modernizer of Stoicism.

you be stout of heart and rise superior to threats. The only harbour safe from the seething storms of this life is scorn of the future, a firm stand, a readiness to receive Fortune's missiles full in the breast, neither skulking nor turning the back. Nature has brought us forth brave of spirit, and, as she has implanted in certain animals a spirit of ferocity, in others craft, in others terror, so she has gifted us with an aspiring and lofty spirit, which prompts us to seek a life of the greatest honour, and not of the greatest security, that most resembles the soul of the universe, which it follows and imitates as far as our mortal steps permit. This spirit thrusts itself forward, confident of commendation and esteem. It is superior to all, monarch of all it surveys; hence it should be subservient to nothing, finding no task too heavy, and nothing strong enough to weigh down the shoulders of a man.

> Shapes dread to look upon, of toil or death*

are not in the least dreadful, if one is able to look upon them with unflinching gaze, and is able to pierce the shadows. Many a sight that is held a terror in the night-time, is turned to ridicule by day. "Shapes dread to look upon, of toil or death": our Vergil has excellently said that these shapes are dread, not in reality, but only "to look upon"—in other words, they seem terrible, but are not. And in these visions what is there, I say, as fear-inspiring as rumour has proclaimed? Why, pray, my dear Lucilius, should a man fear toil, or a mortal death? Countless cases occur to my mind of men who think that what they themselves are unable to do is impossible, who maintain that we utter words which are too big for man's nature to carry out. But how much more highly do I think of these men! They can do these things, but decline to do them. To whom that ever tried have these tasks proved false? To what man did they not seem easier in the doing? Our lack of confidence is not the result of difficulty; the difficulty comes from our lack of confidence.

If, however, you desire a pattern, take Socrates, a long-suffering old man, who was sea-tossed amid every hardship and yet was

---

* *Aeneid*, vi. 277.

unconquered both by poverty (which his troubles at home made more burdensome) and by toil, including the drudgery of military service. He was much tried at home, whether we think of his wife, a woman of rough manners and shrewish tongue, or of the children whose intractability showed them to be more like their mother than their father.* And if you consider the facts, he lived either in time of war, or under tyrants, or under a democracy, which is more cruel than wars and tyrants. The war lasted for twenty-seven years;** then the state became the victim of the Thirty Tyrants, of whom many were his personal enemies. At the last came that climax of condemnation under the gravest of charges: they accused him of disturbing the state religion and corrupting the youth,*** for they declared that he had influenced the youth to defy the gods, to defy the council, and to defy the state in general. Next came the prison, and the cup of poison.**** But all these measures changed the soul of Socrates so little that they did not even change his features. What wonderful and rare distinction! He maintained this attitude up to the very end, and no man ever saw Socrates too much elated or too much depressed. Amid all the disturbance of Fortune, he was undisturbed.

Do you desire another case? Take that of the younger Marcus Cato, with whom Fortune dealt in a more hostile and more persistent fashion. But he withstood her, on all occasions, and in his last moments, at the point of death, showed that a brave man can live in spite of Fortune, can die in spite of her. His whole life was passed either in civil warfare, or under a political regime which was soon to breed civil war. And you may say that he, just as much as Socrates, declared allegiance to liberty in the midst of slavery—unless perchance you

---

* At first a sculptor, then an independent seeker after truth, whose wants were reduced to a minimum. Husband of the shrewish Xanthippe and father of the dull and worthless Lamprocles. Brave soldier at Potidaea, Delium, and Amphipolis.

** 431-404 B.C. (the Peloponnesian War).

*** See Plato's *Apology*, 23 D. They had previously aimed at him a law forbidding the teaching of dialectic.

**** 399 B.C.

think that Pompey, Caesar, and Crassus* were the allies of liberty! No one ever saw Cato change, no matter how often the state changed: he kept himself the same in all circumstances—in the praetorship,** in defeat, under accusation,*** in his province, on the platform, in the army, in death. Furthermore, when the republic was in a crisis of terror, when Caesar was on one side with ten embattled legions at his call, aided by so many foreign nations, and when Pompey was on the other, satisfied to stand alone against all comers, and when the citizens were leaning towards either Caesar or Pompey, Cato alone established a definite party for the Republic. If you would obtain a mental picture of that period, you may imagine on one side the people and the whole proletariat eager for revolution—on the other the senators and knights, the chosen and honoured men of the commonwealth; and there were left between them but these two—the Republic and Cato.

I tell you, you will marvel when you see

> Atreus' son, and Priam, and Achilles, wroth at both.****

Like Achilles, he scorns and disarms each faction. And this is the vote which he casts concerning them both: "If Caesar wins, I slay myself; if Pompey, I go into exile." What was there for a man to fear who, whether in defeat or in victory, had assigned to himself a doom which might have been assigned to him by his enemies in their utmost rage? So he died by his own decision.

You see that man can endure toil: Cato, on foot, led an army through African deserts. You see that thirst can be endured: he marched over sun-baked hills, dragging the remains of a beaten army and with no train of supplies, undergoing lack of water and wearing a heavy suit of armour; always the last to drink of the few springs which

---

* Triumvirs in 60 B.C. and rivals in acquiring unconstitutional power.

** 54 B.C.

*** Perhaps a reference to his mission in Cyprus (58-56 B.C.), and his subsequent arraignment by Clodius.

**** Vergil, *Aen.* i. 458.

they chanced to find. You see that honour, and dishonour too, can be despised: for they report that on the very day when Cato was defeated at the elections, he played a game of ball. You see also that man can be free from fear of those above him in rank: for Cato attacked Caesar and Pompey simultaneously, at a time when none dared fall foul of the one without endeavouring to oblige the other. You see that death can be scorned as well as exile: Cato inflicted exile upon himself and finally death,* and war all the while.

And so, if only we are willing to withdraw our necks from the yoke, we can keep as stout a heart against such terrors as these. But first and foremost, we must reject pleasures; they render us weak and womanish; they make great demands upon us, and, moreover, cause us to make great demands upon Fortune. Second, we must spurn wealth: wealth is the diploma of slavery. Abandon gold and silver, and whatever else is a burden upon our richly-furnished homes; liberty cannot be gained for nothing. If you set a high value on liberty, you must set a low value on everything else. Farewell.

---

* At Utica, in 46 B.C.

LETTER

105

On Facing the World with Confidence

I shall now tell you certain things to which you should pay attention in order to live more safely. Do you however,—such is my judgment,—hearken to my precepts just as if I were counselling you to keep safe your health in your country-place at Ardea.

Reflect on the things which goad man into destroying man: you will find that they are hope, envy, hatred, fear, and contempt. Now, of all these, contempt is the least harmful, so much so that many have skulked behind it as a sort of cure. When a man despises you, he works you injury, to be sure, but he passes on; and no one persistently or of set purpose does hurt to a person whom he despises. Even in battle, prostrate soldiers are neglected: men fight with those who stand their ground. And you can avoid the envious hopes of the wicked so long as you have nothing which can stir the evil desires of others, and so long as you possess nothing remarkable. For people crave even little things, if these catch the attention or are of rare occurrence.

You will escape envy if you do not force yourself upon the public view, if you do not boast your possessions, if you understand how to enjoy things privately. Hatred comes either from running foul of others: and this can be avoided by never provoking anyone; or else it is uncalled for: and common-sense* will keep you safe from it. Yet it has been dangerous to many; some people have been hated without having had an enemy. As to not being feared, a moderate fortune and an easy disposition will guarantee you that; men should know that you are the sort of person who can be offended without danger; and your reconciliation should be easy and sure. Moreover, it is as troublesome to be feared at home as abroad; it is as bad to be feared by a slave as by a gentleman. For every one has strength enough to do you some harm. Besides, he who is feared, fears also; no one has been able to arouse terror and live in peace of mind.

Contempt remains to be discussed. He who has made this quality an adjunct of his own personality, who is despised because he wishes to be despised and not because he *must* be despised, has the measure of contempt under his control. Any inconveniences in this respect can be dispelled by honourable occupations and by friendships with men who have influence with an influential person; with these men it will profit you to engage but not to entangle yourself, lest the cure may cost you more than the risk. Nothing, however, will help you so much as keeping still—talking very little with others, and as much as may be with yourself. For there is a sort of charm about conversation, something very subtle and coaxing, which, like intoxication or love, draws secrets from us. No man will keep to himself what he hears. No one will tell another only as much as he has heard. And he who tells tales will tell names, too. Everyone has someone to whom he entrusts exactly what has been entrusted to him. Though he checks his own garrulity, and is content with one hearer, he will bring about him a nation, if that which was a secret shortly before becomes common talk.

The most important contribution to peace of mind is never to do wrong. Those who lack self-control lead disturbed and tumultuous lives; their crimes are balanced by their fears, and they are never at ease. For they tremble after the deed, and they are embarrassed; their

---

* i.e., tact.

consciences do not allow them to busy themselves with other matters, and continually compel them to give an answer. Whoever expects punishment, receives it, but whoever deserves it, expects it. Where there is an evil conscience something may bring safety, but nothing can bring ease; for a man imagines that, even if he is not under arrest, he may soon be arrested. His sleep is troubled; when he speaks of another man's crime, he reflects upon his own, which seems to him not sufficiently blotted out, not sufficiently hidden from view. A wrongdoer sometimes has the luck to escape notice but never the assurance thereof. Farewell.

LETTER

107

On Obedience To the Universal Will

Where is that common-sense of yours? Where that deftness in examining things? That greatness of soul? Have you come to be tormented by a trifle? Your slaves regarded your absorption in business as an opportunity for them to run away. Well, if your friends deceived you (for by all means let them have the name which we mistakenly bestowed upon them, and so call them, that they may incur more shame by not being such friends)—if your friends, I repeat, deceived you, all your affairs would lack something; as it is, you merely lack men who damaged your own endeavours and considered you burdensome to your neighbours. None of these things is unusual or unexpected. It is as nonsensical to be put out by such events as to complain of being spattered in the street or at getting befouled in the mud. The programme of life is the same as that of a bathing establishment, a crowd, or a journey: sometimes things will be thrown at you, and sometimes they will strike you by accident. Life is not a dainty business. You have started on a long journey; you are bound to slip, collide, fall, become weary, and cry out: "O for Death!"—or in other words, tell lies. At one stage you will leave a comrade behind you, at another you will bury someone, at another you will be apprehensive. It is amid stumblings of this sort that you must travel out this rugged journey.

Does one wish to die? Let the mind be prepared to meet everything; let it know that it has reached the heights round which the thunder plays. Let it know that it has arrived where –

> Grief and avenging Care have set their couch,
> And pallid sickness dwells, and drear Old Age.*

With such messmates must you spend your days. Avoid them you cannot, but despise them you can. And you will despise them, if you often take thought and anticipate the future. Everyone approaches courageously a danger which he has prepared himself to meet long before, and withstands even hardships if he has previously practised how to meet them. But, contrariwise, the unprepared are panic-stricken even at the most trifling things. We must see to it that nothing shall come upon us unforeseen. And since things are all the more serious when they are unfamiliar, continual reflection will give you the power, no matter what the evil may be, not to play the unschooled boy.

"My slaves have run away from me!" Yes, other men have been robbed, blackmailed, slain, betrayed, stamped under foot, attacked by poison or by slander; no matter what trouble you mention, it has happened to many. Again, there are manifold kinds of missiles which are hurled at us. Some are planted in us, some are being brandished and at this very moment are on the way, some which were destined for other men graze us instead. We should not manifest surprise at any sort of condition into which we are born, and which should be lamented by no one, simply because it is equally ordained for all. Yes, I say, equally ordained; for a man might have experienced even that which he has escaped. And an equal law consists, not of that which all have experienced, but of that which is laid down for all. Be sure to prescribe for your mind this sense of equity; we should pay without complaint the tax of our mortality.

---

* Vergil, *Aen.* vi. 274 f.

Winter brings on cold weather; and we must shiver. Summer returns, with its heat; and we must sweat. Unseasonable weather upsets the health; and we must fall ill. In certain places we may meet with wild beasts, or with men who are more destructive than any beasts. Floods, or fires, will cause us loss. And we cannot change this order of things; but what we can do is to acquire stout hearts, worthy of good men, thereby courageously enduring chance and placing ourselves in harmony with Nature. And Nature moderates this world-kingdom which you see, by her changing seasons: clear weather follows cloudy; after a calm, comes the storm; the winds blow by turns; day succeeds night; some of the heavenly bodies rise, and some set. Eternity consists of opposites.

It is to this law that our souls must adjust themselves, this they should follow, this they should obey. Whatever happens, assume that it was bound to happen, and do not be willing to rail at Nature. That which you cannot reform, it is best to endure, and to attend uncomplainingly upon the God under whose guidance everything progresses; for it is a bad soldier who grumbles when following his commander. For this reason we should welcome our orders with energy and vigour, nor should we cease to follow the natural course of this most beautiful universe, into which all our future sufferings are woven.

Let us address Jupiter, the pilot of this world-mass, as did our great Cleanthes in those most eloquent lines—lines which I shall allow myself to render in Latin, after the example of the eloquent Cicero. If you like them, make the most of them; if they displease you, you will understand that I have simply been following the practice of Cicero:

Lead me, O Master of the lofty heavens,
My Father, whithersoever thou shalt wish.
I shall not falter, but obey with speed.
And though I would not, I shall go, and suffer,
In sin and sorrow what I might have done

In noble virtue. Aye, the willing soul
Fate leads, but the unwilling drags along.*

Let us live thus, and speak thus; let Fate find us ready and alert. Here is your great soul—the man who has given himself over to Fate; on the other hand, that man is a weakling and a degenerate who struggles and maligns the order of the universe and would rather reform the gods than reform himself. Farewell.

* Cleanthes, Frag. 527 von Arnim. In Epictetus (*Ench.* 53) these verses are assigned to Cleanthes (omitting the last line); while St. Augustine (*Civ. Dei.* v. 8) quotes them as Seneca's: *Annaei Senecae sunt, nisi fallor, hi versus*. Wilamowitz and others follow the latter view.

LETTER

108

On the Approaches to Philosophy

The topic about which you ask me is one of those where our only concern with knowledge is to have the knowledge. Nevertheless, because it does so far concern us, you are in a hurry; you are not willing to wait for the books which I am at this moment arranging for you, and which embrace the whole department of moral philosophy.* I shall send you the books at once; but I shall, before doing that, write and tell you how this eagerness to learn, with which I see you are aflame, should be regulated, so that it may not get in its own way. Things are not to be gathered at random; nor should they be greedily attacked in the mass; one will arrive at a knowledge of the whole by studying the parts. The burden should be suited to your strength, nor should you tackle more than you can adequately handle. Absorb not all that you wish, but all that you can hold. Only be of a sound mind, and then you will be able to hold all that you wish. For the more the mind receives, the more does it expand.

---

* Cf. Ep. cvi. 2 *scis enim me moralem philosophiam velle conplecti*, etc.

This was the advice, I remember, which Attalus* gave me in the days when I practically laid siege to his class-room, the first to arrive and the last to leave. Even as he paced up and down, I would challenge him to various discussions; for he not only kept himself accessible to his pupils, but met them half-way. His words were: "The same purpose should possess both master and scholar—an ambition in the one case to promote, and in the other to progress." He who studies with a philosopher should take away with him some one good thing every day: he should daily return home a sounder man, or in the way to become sounder. And he will thus return; for it is one of the functions of philosophy to help not only those who study her, but those also who associate with her. He that walks in the sun, though he walk not for that purpose, must needs become sunburned. He who frequents the perfumer's shop and lingers even for a short time, will carry with him the scent of the place. And he who follows a philosopher is bound to derive some benefit therefrom, which will help him even though he be remiss. Mark what I say: "remiss," not "recalcitrant."

"What then?" you say, "do we not know certain men who have sat for many years at the feet of a philosopher and yet have not acquired the slightest tinge of wisdom?" Of course I know such men. There are indeed persevering gentlemen who stick at it; I do not call them pupils of the wise, but merely "squatters."** Certain of them come to hear and not to learn, just as we are attracted to the theatre to satisfy the pleasures of the ear, whether by a speech, or by a song, or by a play. This class, as you will see, constitutes a large part of the listeners, who regard the philosopher's lecture-room merely as a sort of lounging-place for their leisure. They do not set about to lay aside any faults there, or to receive a rule of life, by which they may test their characters; they merely wish to enjoy to the full the delights of the ear. And yet some arrive even with

---

* Seneca's first and most convincing teacher of Stoicism, to whom this letter is a tribute. The ablest of contemporary philosophers, he was banished during the reign of Tiberius. See Index of Proper Names.

** Literally "tenants," "lodgers," of a temporary sort.

notebooks, not to take down the matter, but only the words,* that they may presently repeat them to others with as little profit to these as they themselves received when they heard them. A certain number are stirred by high-sounding phrases, and adapt themselves to the emotions of the speaker with lively change of face and mind—just like the emasculated Phrygian priests** who are wont to be roused by the sound of the flute and go mad to order. But the true hearer is ravished and stirred by the beauty of the subject matter, not by the jingle of empty words. When a bold word has been uttered in defiance of death, or a saucy fling in defiance of Fortune, we take delight in acting straightway upon that which we have heard. Men are impressed by such words, and become what they are bidden to be, should but the impression abide in the mind, and should the populace, who discourage honourable things, not immediately lie in wait to rob them of this noble impulse; only a few can carry home the mental attitude with which they were inspired. It is easy to rouse a listener so that he will crave righteousness; for Nature has laid the foundations and planted the seeds of virtue in us all. And we are all born to these general privileges; hence, when the stimulus is added, the good spirit is stirred as if it were freed from bonds. Have you not noticed how the theatre re-echoes whenever any words are spoken whose truth we appreciate generally and confirm unanimously?

The poor lack much; the greedy man lacks all.***
A greedy man does good to none; he does
Most evil to himself.****

At such verses as these, your meanest miser claps applause and rejoices to hear his own sins reviled. How much more do you think this holds true, when such things are uttered by a philosopher, when

---

* Cf. the dangers of such *lusoria* (Ep. xlviii. 8) and *a rebus studium transferendum est ad verba* (Ep. xl. 14).

** i.e., mendicant Galli, worshippers of Cybele, the Magna Mater.

*** *Syri Sententiae*, Frag. 236 Ribbeck.

**** *Ib.*, Frag. 234 R.

he introduces verses among his wholesome precepts, that he may thus make those verses sink more effectively into the mind of the neophyte! Cleanthes used to say:* "As our breath produces a louder sound when it passes through the long and narrow opening of the trumpet and escapes by a hole which widens at the end, even so the fettering rules of poetry clarify our meaning." The very same words are more carelessly received and make less impression upon us, when they are spoken in prose; but when metre is added and when regular prosody has compressed a noble idea, then the selfsame thought comes, as it were, hurtling with a fuller fling. We talk much about despising money, and we give advice on this subject in the lengthiest of speeches, that mankind may believe true riches to exist in the mind and not in one's bank account, and that the man who adapts himself to his slender means and makes himself wealthy on a little sum, is the truly rich man; but our minds are struck more effectively when a verse like this is repeated:

He needs but little who desires but little.

or,

He hath his wish, whose wish includeth naught
Save that which is enough.**

When we hear such words as these, we are led towards a confession of the truth.

Even men in whose opinion nothing is enough, wonder and applaud when they hear such words, and swear eternal hatred against money. When you see them thus disposed, strike home, keep at them, and charge them with this duty, dropping all double meanings, syllogisms, hair-splitting, and the other side-shows of ineffective smartness. Preach against greed, preach against high living; and when you notice that you have made progress and impressed the minds of your hearers, lay on still harder. You cannot imagine how much progress can be brought about

---

* Frag. 487 von Arnim.

** Pall. Incert. Fab. 65 and 66 Ribbeck.

by an address of that nature, when you are bent on curing your hearers and are absolutely devoted to their best interests. For when the mind is young, it may most easily be won over to desire what is honourable and upright; truth, if she can obtain a suitable pleader, will lay strong hands upon those who can still be taught, those who have been but superficially spoiled.

At any rate, when I used to hear Attalus denouncing sin, error, and the evils of life, I often felt sorry for mankind and regarded Attalus as a noble and majestic being,—above our mortal heights. He called himself a king,* but I thought him more than a king, because he was entitled to pass judgment on kings. And in truth, when he began to uphold poverty, and to show what a useless and dangerous burden was everything that passed the measure of our need, I often desired to leave his lecture-room a poor man. Whenever he castigated our pleasure-seeking lives, and extolled personal purity, moderation in diet, and a mind free from unnecessary, not to speak of unlawful, pleasures, the desire came upon me to limit my food and drink. And that is why some of these habits have stayed with me, Lucilius. For I had planned my whole life with great resolves. And later, when I returned to the duties of a citizen, I did indeed keep a few of these good resolutions. That is why I have forsaken oysters and mushrooms for ever: since they are not really food, but are relishes to bully the sated stomach into further eating, as is the fancy of gourmands and those who stuff themselves beyond their powers of digestion: down with it quickly, and up with it quickly! That is why I have also throughout my life avoided perfumes; because the best scent for the person is no scent at all.** That is why my stomach is unacquainted with wine. That is why throughout my life I have shunned the bath, and have believed that to emaciate the body and sweat it into thinness is at once unprofitable and effeminate. Other resolutions have been broken, but after all in such a way that, in cases where I ceased to practice abstinence, I have observed a limit which is indeed next door to abstinence; perhaps

* A characteristic Stoic paradox.

** An almost proverbial saying; cf. the *recte olet ubi nil olet* of Plautus (*Most.* 273), Cicero, and Martial.

it is even a little more difficult, because it is easier for the will to cut off certain things utterly than to use them with restraint.

Inasmuch as I have begun to explain to you how much greater was my impulse to approach philosophy in my youth than to continue it in my old age, I shall not be ashamed to tell you what ardent zeal Pythagoras inspired in me. Sotion* used to tell me why Pythagoras abstained from animal food, and why, in later times, Sextius did also. In each case, the reason was different, but it was in each case a noble reason. Sextius believed that man had enough sustenance without resorting to blood, and that a habit of cruelty is formed whenever butchery is practised for pleasure. Moreover, he thought we should curtail the sources of our luxury; he argued that a varied diet was contrary to the laws of health, and was unsuited to our constitutions. Pythagoras, on the other hand, held that all beings were inter-related, and that there was a system of exchange between souls which transmigrated from one bodily shape into another. If one may believe him, no soul perishes or ceases from its functions at all, except for a tiny interval—when it is being poured from one body into another. We may question at what time and after what seasons of change the soul returns to man, when it has wandered through many a dwelling-place; but meantime, he made men fearful of guilt and parricide, since they might be, without knowing it, attacking the soul of a parent and injuring it with knife or with teeth—if, as is possible, the related spirit be dwelling temporarily in this bit of flesh! When Sotion had set forth this doctrine, supplementing it with his own proofs, he would say: "You do not believe that souls are assigned, first to one body and then to another, and that our so-called death is merely a change of abode? You do not believe that in cattle, or in wild beasts, or in creatures of the deep, the soul of him who was once a man may linger? You do not believe that nothing on this earth is annihilated, but only changes its haunts? And that animals also have cycles of progress and, so to speak, an orbit for their souls, no less than the heavenly bodies, which revolve in fixed circuits? Great men have put faith in this

* Pythagorean philosopher of the Augustine age, and one of Seneca's early teachers.

idea; therefore, while holding to your own view, keep the whole question in abeyance in your mind. If the theory is true, it is a mark of purity to refrain from eating flesh; if it be false, it is economy. And what harm does it do to you to give such credence? I am merely depriving you of food which sustains lions and vultures."

I was imbued with this teaching, and began to abstain from animal food; at the end of a year the habit was as pleasant as it was easy. I was beginning to feel that my mind was more active; though I would not today positively state whether it really was or not. Do you ask how I came to abandon the practice? It was this way: The days of my youth coincided with the early part of the reign of Tiberius Caesar. Some foreign rites were at that time* being inaugurated, and abstinence from certain kinds of animal food was set down as a proof of interest in the strange cult. So at the request of my father, who did not fear prosecution, but who detested philosophy, I returned to my previous habits; and it was no very hard matter to induce me to dine more comfortably.

Attalus used to recommend a pillow which did not give in to the body; and now, old as I am, I use one so hard that it leaves no trace after pressure. I have mentioned all this in order to show you how zealous neophytes are with regard to their first impulses towards the highest ideals, provided that some one does his part in exhorting them and in kindling their ardour. There are indeed mistakes made, through the fault of our advisers, who teach us how to debate and not how to live; there are also mistakes made by the pupils, who come to their teachers to develop, not their souls, but their wits. Thus the study of wisdom has become the study of words.

Now it makes a great deal of difference what you have in mind when you approach a given subject. If a man is to be a scholar,** and is examining the works of Vergil, he does not interpret the noble passage

* A.D. 19. Cf. Tacitus, *Ann.* ii. 85 *actum de sacris Aegyptiis Iudaicisque pellendis.*

** In this passage Seneca differs (as also in Ep. lxxxviii. § 3) from the earlier Roman idea of *grammaticus* as *poetarum interpres*: he is thinking of one who deals with verbal expressions and the meaning of words. Cf. Sandys, *Hist. Class. Schol.* i. 8 ff.

Time flies away, and cannot be restored*

in the following sense: "We must wake up; unless we hasten, we shall be left behind. Time rolls swiftly ahead, and rolls us with it. We are hurried along ignorant of our destiny; we arrange all our plans for the future, and on the edge of a precipice are at our ease." Instead of this, he brings to our attention how often Vergil, in speaking of the rapidity of time, uses the word "flies" (*fugit*).

The choicest days of hapless human life
Fly first; disease and bitter eld succeed,
And toil, till harsh death rudely snatches all.**

He who considers these lines in the spirit of a philosopher comments on the words in their proper sense: "Vergil never says, 'Time goes,' but 'Time flies,' because the latter is the quickest kind of movement, and in every case our best days are the first to be snatched away; why, then, do we hesitate to bestir ourselves so that we may be able to keep pace with this swiftest of all swift things?" The good flies past and the bad takes its place. Just as the purest wine flows from the top of the jar and the thickest dregs settle at the bottom; so in our human life, that which is best comes first. Shall we allow other men to quaff the best, and keep the dregs for ourselves? Let this phrase cleave to your soul; you should be satisfied thereby as if it were uttered by an oracle:

Each choicest day of hapless human life
Flies first.

Why "choicest day"? Because what's to come is unsure. Why "choicest day"? Because in our youth we are able to learn; we can bend to nobler purposes minds that are ready and still pliable; because this is the time for work, the time for keeping our minds busied in study and in

---

* *Georg.* iii. 284.

** *Georg.* iii. 66 ff.

exercising our bodies with useful effort; for that which remains is more sluggish and lacking in spirit—nearer the end.

Let us therefore strive with all courage, omitting attractions by the way; let us struggle with a single purpose, lest, when we are left behind, we comprehend too late the speed of quick-flying time, whose course we cannot stay. Let every day, as soon as it comes, be welcome as being the choicest, and let it be made our own possession. We must catch that which flees. Now he who scans with a scholar's eye the lines I have just quoted, does not reflect that our first days are the best because disease is approaching and old age weighs upon us and hangs over our heads while we are still thinking about our youth. He thinks rather of Vergil's usual collocation of *disease and eld*; and indeed rightly. For old age is a disease which we cannot cure. "Besides," he says to himself, "think of the epithet that accompanies *eld*; Vergil calls it *bitter*,"—

Disease and bitter eld succeed.

And elsewhere Vergil says:

There dwelleth pale disease and bitter eld.*

There is no reason why you should marvel that each man can collect from the same source suitable matter for his own studies; for in the same meadow the cow grazes, the dog hunts the hare, and the stork the lizard. When Cicero's book *On the State* is opened by a philologist, a scholar, or a follower of philosophy, each man pursues his investigation in his own way. The philosopher wonders that so much could have been said therein against justice. The philologist takes up the same book and comments on the text as follows: There were two Roman kings—one without a father and one without a mother. For we cannot settle who was Servius's mother, and Ancus, the grandson of Numa, has no father on record.** The philologist also notes that the officer whom we call dictator, and about whom we read in our histories under that title, was named in old times

---

* *Aen.* vi. 275.

** Cicero, *De re publica*, ii. 18 *Numae Pompili nepos ex filia rex a populo est Ancus Marcius constitutus . . . siquidem istius regis matrem habemus, ignoramus patrem.*

the *magister populi*; such is the name existing today in the augural records, proved by the fact that he whom the dictator chose as second in command was called *magister equitum*. He will remark, too, that Romulus met his end during an eclipse; that there was an appeal to the people even from the kings (this is so stated in the pontiffs' register and is the opinion of others, including Fenestella*). When the scholar unrolls this same volume, he puts down in his notebook the forms of words, noting that *reapse*, equivalent to *re ipsa*, is used by Cicero, and *sepse*** just as frequently, which means *se ipse*. Then he turns his attention to changes in current usage. Cicero, for example, says: "Inasmuch as we are summoned back from the very calx by his interruption." Now the line in the circus which we call the *creta**** was called the calx by men of old time. Again, he puts together some verses by Ennius, especially those which referred to Africanus:

A man to whom nor friend nor foe could give
Due meed for all his efforts and his deed.****

From this passage the scholar declares that he infers the word *opem* to have meant formerly not merely *assistance*, but *efforts*. For Ennius must mean that neither friend nor foe could pay Scipio a reward worthy of his efforts. Next, he congratulates himself on finding the source of Vergil's words:

Over whose head the mighty gate of Heaven
Thunders,*****

remarking that Ennius stole the idea from Homer, and Vergil from Ennius. For there is a couplet by Ennius, preserved in this same book of Cicero's, *On the State*:******

---

* Fl. in the Augustan Age. *Provocatio* is defined by Greenidge (*Rom. Pub. Life*. p. 64) as "a challenge by an accused to a magistrate to appear before another tribunal."

** A suffix, probably related to the intensive *-pte*

*** Literally, the chalk-marked, or lime-marked, goal-line.

**** Vahlen's *Ennius*, p. 215.

***** *Georg*. iii. 260 f.

****** Vahlen's *Ennius*, p. 216.

If it be right for a mortal to scale the regions of Heaven,
Then the huge gate of the sky opens in glory to *me.*

But that I, too, while engaged upon another task, may not slip into the department of the philologist or the scholar, my advice is this—that all study of philosophy and all reading should be applied to the idea of living the happy life, that we should not hunt out archaic or far-fetched words and eccentric metaphors and figures of speech, but that we should seek precepts which will help us, utterances of courage and spirit which may at once be turned into facts. We should so learn them that words may become deeds. And I hold that no man has treated mankind worse than he who has studied philosophy as if it were some marketable trade, who lives in a different manner from that which he advises. For those who are liable to every fault which they castigate advertise themselves as patterns of useless training. A teacher like that can help me no more than a sea-sick pilot can be efficient in a storm. He must hold the tiller when the waves are tossing him; he must wrestle, as it were, with the sea; he must furl his sails when the storm rages; what good is a frightened and vomiting steersman to *me*? And how much greater, think you, is the storm of life than that which tosses any ship! One must steer, not talk.

All the words that these men utter and juggle before a listening crowd, belong to others. They have been spoken by Plato, spoken by Zeno, spoken by Chrysippus or by Posidonius, and by a whole host of Stoics as numerous as excellent. I shall show you how men can prove their words to be their own: it is by doing what they have been talking about. Since therefore I have given you the message I wished to pass on to you, I shall now satisfy your craving and shall reserve for a new letter a complete answer to your summons; so that you may not approach in a condition of weariness a subject which is thorny and which should be followed with an attentive and painstaking ear. Farewell.

LETTER

114

On Style as a Mirror of Character

You have been asking me why, during certain periods, a degenerate style of speech comes to the fore, and how it is that men's wits have gone downhill into certain vices—in such a way that exposition at one time has taken on a kind of puffed-up strength, and at another has become mincing and modulated like the music of a concert piece. You wonder why sometimes bold ideas—bolder than one could believe—have been held in favour, and why at other times one meets with phrases that are disconnected and full of innuendo, into which one must read more meaning than was intended to meet the ear. Or why there have been epochs which maintained the right to a shameless use of metaphor. For answer, here is a phrase which you are wont to notice in the popular speech—one which the Greeks have made into a proverb: "Man's speech is just like his life."* Exactly as each individual man's actions seem to speak, so people's style of speaking often reproduces the general character of the time, if the morale of the public has relaxed and has

---

* οἷος ὁ βίος, τοιοῦτος καὶ ὁ λόγος. The saying is referred to Socrates by Cicero (*Tusc.* v. 47).

given itself over to effeminacy. Wantonness in speech is proof of public luxury, if it is popular and fashionable, and not confined to one or two individual instances. A man's ability* cannot possibly be of one sort and his soul of another. If his soul be wholesome, well-ordered, serious, and restrained, his ability also is sound and sober. Conversely, when the one degenerates, the other is also contaminated. Do you not see that if a man's soul has become sluggish, his limbs drag and his feet move indolently? If it is womanish, that one can detect the effeminacy by his very gait? That a keen and confident soul quickens the step? That madness in the soul, or anger (which resembles madness), hastens our bodily movements from walking to rushing?

And how much more do you think that this affects one's ability, which is entirely interwoven with the soul,—being moulded thereby, obeying its commands, and deriving therefrom its laws! How Maecenas lived is too well-known for present comment. We know how he walked, how effeminate he was, and how he desired to display himself; also, how unwilling he was that his vices should escape notice. What, then? Does not the looseness of his speech match his ungirt attire?** Are his habits, his attendants, his house, his wife,*** any less clearly marked than his words? He would have been a man of great powers, had he set himself to his task by a straight path, had he not shrunk from making himself understood, had he not been so loose in his style of speech also. You will therefore see that his eloquence was that of an intoxicated man—twisting, turning, unlimited in its slackness.

---

* i.e., that inborn quality which is compounded of character and intelligence.

** Cf. Suetonius, *Aug.* 86, where the Emperor *Maecenatem suum, cuius "myrobrechis," ut ait, "cincinnos"* ("unguent-dripping curls" (Rolfe)) *usque quaque persequitur et imitando per iocum irridet.* Augustus here refers especially to the style of Maecenas as a writer.

*** Terentia. For her charms see Horace, *Od.* ii. 12; for her faults see *De prov.* iii. 10, where Seneca calls her "petulant."

What is more unbecoming than the words:* "A stream and a bank covered with long-tressed woods"? And see how "men plough the channel with boats and, turning up the shallows, leave gardens behind them." Or, "He curls his lady-locks, and bills and coos, and starts a-sighing, like a forest lord who offers prayers with down-bent neck." Or, "An unregenerate crew, they search out people at feasts, and assail households with the wine-cup, and, by hope, exact death." Or, "A Genius could hardly bear witness to his own festival"; or "threads of tiny tapers and crackling meal"; "mothers or wives clothing the hearth."

Can you not at once imagine, on reading through these words, that this was the man who always paraded through the city with a flowing** tunic? For even if he was discharging the absent emperor's duties, he was always in undress when they asked him for the countersign. Or that this was the man who, as judge on the bench, or as an orator, or at any public function, appeared with his cloak wrapped about his head, leaving only the ears exposed,*** like the millionaire's runaway slaves in the farce? Or that this was the man who, at the very time when the state was embroiled in civil strife, when the city was in difficulties and under martial law, was attended in public by two eunuchs—both of them more men than himself? Or that this was the man who had but one wife, and yet was married countless times?**** These words of his, put together so faultily, thrown off so carelessly, and arranged in such marked contrast to the usual practice, declare that the character of their writer was equally unusual, unsound, and eccentric. To be sure, we bestow upon him the highest praise for his humanity; he was sparing with the sword and refrained from bloodshed;***** and he made a show of his power only in the course of his loose living; but he spoiled, by such preposterous finickiness of style, this genuine praise, which was

---

* Maecenas, Frag. 11 Lunderstedt.

** Instead of properly girt up—a mark of slackness.

*** For a similar mark of slovenliness, in Pompey's freedman Demetrius, see Plutarch, *Pompey*, xl. 4.

**** i.e., often repulsed by his wife Terentia, and then restored to grace.

***** i.e., the "ring" of onlookers, the "pit."

his due. For it is evident that he was not really gentle, but effeminate, as is proved by his misleading word-order, his inverted expressions, and the surprising thoughts which frequently contain something great, but in finding expression have become nerveless. One would say that his head was turned by too great success.

This fault is due sometimes to the man, and sometimes to his epoch. When prosperity has spread luxury far and wide, men begin by paying closer attention to their personal appearance. Then they go crazy over furniture. Next, they devote attention to their houses—how to take up more space with them, as if they were country-houses, how to make the walls glitter with marble that has been imported over seas, how to adorn a roof with gold, so that it may match the brightness of the inlaid floors. After that, they transfer their exquisite taste to the dinner-table, attempting to court approval by novelty and by departures from the customary order of dishes, so that the courses which we are accustomed to serve at the end of the meal may be served first, and so that the departing guests may partake of the kind of food which in former days was set before them on their arrival.

When the mind has acquired the habit of scorning the usual things of life, and regarding as mean that which was once customary, it begins to hunt for novelties in speech also; now it summons and displays obsolete and old-fashioned words; now it coins even unknown words or misshapes them; and now a bold and frequent metaphorical usage is made a special feature of style, according to the fashion which has just become prevalent. Some cut the thoughts short, hoping to make a good impression by leaving the meaning in doubt and causing the hearer to suspect his own lack of wit. Some dwell upon them and lengthen them out. Others, too, approach just short of a fault—for a man must really do this if he hopes to attain an imposing effect—but actually love the fault for its own sake. In short, whenever you notice that a degenerate style pleases the critics, you may be sure that character also has deviated from the right standard.

Just as luxurious banquets and elaborate dress are indications of disease in the state, similarly a lax style, if it be popular, shows that the mind (which is the source of the word) has lost its balance. Indeed you ought not to wonder that corrupt speech is welcomed not merely by the more squalid mob* but also by our more cultured throng; for it is only in their dress and not in their judgments that they differ. You may rather wonder that not only the effects of vices, but even vices themselves, meet with approval. For it has ever been thus: no man's ability has ever been approved without something being pardoned. Show me any man, however famous; I can tell you what it was that his age forgave in him, and what it was that his age purposely overlooked. I can show you many men whose vices have caused them no harm, and not a few who have been even helped by these vices. Yes, I will show you persons of the highest reputation, set up as models for our admiration; and yet if you seek to correct their errors, you destroy them; for vices are so intertwined with virtues that they drag the virtues along with them. Moreover, style has no fixed laws; it is changed by the usage of the people, never the same for any length of time. Many orators hark back to earlier epochs for their vocabulary, speaking in the language of the Twelve Tables.** Gracchus, Crassus, and Curio, in their eyes, are too refined and too modern; so back to Appius and Coruncanius!*** Conversely, certain men, in their endeavour to maintain nothing but well-worn and common usages, fall into a humdrum style. These two classes, each in its own way, are degenerate; and it is no less degenerate to use no words except those which are conspicuous, high-sounding, and poetical, avoiding what is familiar and in ordinary usage. One is, I believe, as faulty as the other: the one class are unreasonably elaborate, the other are unreasonably negligent; the former depilate the leg, the latter not even the armpit.****

Let us now turn to the arrangement of words. In this department, what countless varieties of fault I can show you! Some are all for

---

* i.e., the "ring" of onlookers, the "pit."

** Fifth century B.C.

*** i.e., from the second and first centuries B.C., back to the third century.

**** The latter a reasonable mark of good breeding, the former an ostentatious bit of effeminacy. Summers cites Ovid, *A. A.* i. 506 "don't rub your legs smooth with the tight-scraping pumice stone."

abruptness and unevenness of style, purposely disarranging anything which seems to have a smooth flow of language. They would have jolts in all their transitions; they regard as strong and manly whatever makes an uneven impression on the ear. With some others it is not so much an "arrangement" of words as it is a setting to music; so wheedling and soft is their gliding style. And what shall I say of that arrangement in which words are put off and, after being long waited for, just manage to come in at the end of a period? Or again of that softly-concluding style, Cicero-fashion,* with a gradual and gently poised descent always the same and always with the customary arrangement of the rhythm! Nor is the fault only in the style of the sentences, if they are either petty and childish, or debasing, with more daring than modesty should allow, or if they are flowery and cloying, or if they end in emptiness, accomplishing mere sound and nothing more.

Some individual makes these vices fashionable—some person who controls the eloquence of the day; the rest follow his lead and communicate the habit to each other. Thus when Sallust** was in his glory, phrases were lopped off, words came to a close unexpectedly, and obscure conciseness was equivalent to elegance. L. Arruntius, a man of rare simplicity, author of a historical work on the Punic War, was a member and a strong supporter of the Sallust school. There is a phrase in Sallust: *exercitum argento fecit,**** meaning thereby that he *recruited***** an army by means of money. Arruntius began to like this idea; he therefore inserted the verb *facio* all through his book. Hence, in one passage, *fugam nostris fecere;****** in another, *Hiero, rex Syracusanorum, bellum fecit;*(§) and in another, *quae audita Panhormitanos dedere Romanis fecere.*(§) I merely desired

---

* As Cicero (see Ep. xl. 11) was an example of the rhythmical in style, so Pollio is the representative of the "bumpy" (*salebrosa*) manner (Ep. c. 7).

** Flor. 40 B.C.

*** For these Sallust fragments see the edition of Kritz, Nos. 33, *Jug.* 37. 4, and 42; for Arruntius see H. Peter, *Frag. Hist. Rom.* ii. pp. 41 f.

**** Literally, "created," "made."

*****(§) (§) "Brought to pass flight for our men"; "Hiero, king of the Syracusans brought about war"; "The news brought the men of Panormus" (now Palermo, Sicily) "to the point of surrendering to the Romans."

to give you a taste; his whole book is interwoven with such stuff as this. What Sallust reserved for occasional use, Arruntius makes into a frequent and almost continual habit—and there was a reason: for Sallust used the words as they occurred to his mind, while the other writer went afield in search of them. So you see the results of copying another man's vices. Again, Sallust said: *aquis hiemantibus.*[*] Arruntius, in his first book on the Punic War, uses the words: *repente hiemavit tempestas.* (*) And elsewhere, wishing to describe an exceptionally cold year, he says: *totus hiemavit annus.*(*) And in another passage: *inde sexaginta onerarias leves praeter militem et necessarios nautarum hiemante aquilone misit;*(*) and he continues to bolster many passages with this metaphor. In a certain place, Sallust gives the words: *inter arma civilia aequi bonique famas*[**] *petit;* and Arruntius cannot restrain himself from mentioning at once, in the first book, that there were extensive "reminders" concerning Regulus.

These and similar faults, which imitation stamps upon one's style, are not necessarily indications of loose standards or of debased mind; for they are bound to be personal and peculiar to the writer, enabling one to judge thereby of a particular author's temperament; just as an angry man will talk in an angry way, an excitable man in a flurried way, and an effeminate man in a style that is soft and unresisting. You note this tendency in those who pluck out, or thin out, their beards, or who closely shear and shave the upper lip while preserving the rest of the hair and allowing it to grow, or in those who wear cloaks of outlandish colours, who wear transparent togas, and who never deign to do anything which will escape general notice; they endeavour to excite and attract men's attention, and they put up even with censure, provided that they can advertise themselves. That is the style of Maecenas and all the others who stray from the path, not by hazard, but consciously and voluntarily. This is the result of great evil in the soul. As in the case of drink, the tongue does not trip until the mind

---

* (*) (*) (*) "Amid the wintry waters"; "The storm suddenly grew wintry"; "The whole year was like winter"; "Then he dispatched sixty transports of light draught besides the soldiers and the necessary sailors amid a wintry storm."

** The peculiarity here is the use of the plural instead of the singular form. "Amid civil war he seeks reminders of justice and virtue."

is overcome beneath its load and gives way or betrays itself; so that intoxication of style—for what else than this can I call it?—never gives trouble to anyone unless the soul begins to totter. Therefore, I say, take care of the soul; for from the soul issue our thoughts, from the soul our words, from the soul our dispositions, our expressions, and our very gait. When the soul is sound and strong, the style too is vigorous, energetic, manly; but if the soul lose its balance, down comes all the rest in ruins.

> If but the king be safe, your swarm will live
> Harmonious; if he die, the bees revolt.*

The soul is our king. If it be safe, the other functions remain on duty and serve with obedience; but the slightest lack of equilibrium in the soul causes them to waver along with it. And when the soul has yielded to pleasure, its functions and actions grow weak, and any undertaking comes from a nerveless and unsteady source. To persist in my use of this simile—our soul is at one time a king, at another a tyrant. The king, in that he respects things honourable, watches over the welfare of the body which is entrusted to his charge, and gives that body no base, no ignoble commands. But an uncontrolled, passionate, and effeminate soul changes kingship into that most dread and detestable quality—tyranny; then it becomes a prey to the uncontrolled emotions, which dog its steps, elated at first, to be sure, like a populace idly sated with a largess which will ultimately be its undoing, and spoiling what it cannot consume. But when the disease has gradually eaten away the strength, and luxurious habits have penetrated the marrow and the sinews, such a soul exults at the sight of limbs which, through its overindulgence, it has made useless; instead of its own pleasures, it views those of others; it becomes the go-between and witness of the passions which, as the result of self-gratification, it can no longer feel. Abundance of delights is not so pleasing a thing to that soul as it is bitter, because it cannot send

* Vergil, *Georg.* iv. 212 f.

all the dainties of yore down through the over-worked throat and stomach, because it can no longer whirl in the maze of eunuchs and mistresses, and it is melancholy because a great part of its happiness is shut off, through the limitations of the body.

Now is it not madness, Lucilius, for none of us to reflect that he is mortal? Or frail? Or again that he is but one individual? Look at our kitchens, and the cooks, who bustle about over so many fires; is it, think you, for a single belly that all this bustle and preparation of food takes place? Look at the old brands of wine and store-houses filled with the vintages of many ages; is it, think you, a single belly that is to receive the stored wine, sealed with the names of so many consuls, and gathered from so many vineyards? Look, and mark in how many regions men plough the earth, and how many thousands of farmers are tilling and digging; is it, think you, for a single belly that crops are planted in Sicily and Africa? We should be sensible, and our wants more reasonable, if each of us were to take stock of himself, and to measure his bodily needs also, and understand how little he can consume, and for how short a time! But nothing will give you so much help toward moderation as the frequent thought that life is short and uncertain here below; whatever you are doing, have regard to death. Farewell.

LETTER

121

On Instinct in Animals

You will bring suit against me, I feel sure, when I set forth for you today's little problem, with which we have already fumbled long enough. You will cry out again: "What has this to do with character?" Cry out if you like, but let me first of all match you with other opponents,* against whom you may bring suit—such as Posidonius and Archidemus;** these men will stand trial. I shall then go on to say that whatever deals with character does not necessarily produce good character. Man needs one thing for his food, another for his exercise, another for his clothing, another for his instruction, and another for his pleasure. Everything, however, has reference to man's needs, although everything does not make him better. Character is affected by different things in different ways: some things serve to correct and regulate character, and others investigate its nature and origin. And when I seek the reason why Nature brought forth man, and why she set him above other animals, do you suppose that I have left character-study in the rear? No; that is wrong. For how are you to know what character is desirable, unless you have discovered what is best suited to man? Or unless

* i.e., in addition to myself and confirming my statement.

** Frag. 17 von Arnim.

you have studied his nature? You can find out what you should do and what you should avoid, only when you have learned what you owe to your own nature.

"I desire," you say, "to learn how I may crave less, and fear less. Rid me of my unreasoning beliefs. Prove to me that so-called felicity is fickle and empty, and that the word easily admits of a syllable's increase."* I shall fulfil your want, encouraging your virtues and lashing your vices. People may decide that I am too zealous and reckless in this particular; but I shall never cease to hound wickedness, to check the most unbridled emotions, to soften the force of pleasures which will result in pain, and to cry down men's prayers. Of course I shall do this; for it is the greatest evils that we have prayed for, and from that which has made us give thanks comes all that demands consolation.

Meanwhile, allow me to discuss thoroughly some points which may seem now to be rather remote from the present inquiry. We were once debating whether all animals had any feelings about their "constitution."** That this is the case is proved particularly by their making motions of such fitness and nimbleness that they seem to be trained for the purpose. Every being is clever in its own line. The skilled workman handles his tools with an ease born of experience; the pilot knows how to steer his ship skilfully; the artist can quickly lay on the colours which he has prepared in great variety for the purpose of rendering the likeness, and passes with ready eye and hand from palette to canvas. In the same way an animal is agile in all that pertains to the use of its body. We are apt to wonder at skilled dancers because their gestures are perfectly adapted to the meaning of the piece and its accompanying emotions, and their movements match the speed of the dialogue. But that which art gives to the craftsman, is given to the animal by nature. No animal handles its limbs with difficulty, no animal is at a loss how to use its body. This function they exercise immediately at birth. They come into the world with this knowledge; they are born full-trained.

---

* i.e. *felicitas* becomes in*felicitas*.

** i.e., their physical make-up, the elements of their physical being.

But people reply: "The reason why animals are so dexterous in the use of their limbs is that if they move them unnaturally, they will feel pain. They are *compelled* to do thus, according to your school, and it is fear rather than will-power which moves them in the right direction." This idea is wrong. Bodies driven by a compelling force move slowly; but those which move of their own accord possess alertness. The proof that it is not fear of pain which prompts them thus, is, that even when pain checks them they struggle to carry out their natural motions. Thus the child who is trying to stand and is becoming used to carry his own weight, on beginning to test his strength, falls and rises again and again with tears until through painful effort he has trained himself to the demands of nature. And certain animals with hard shells, when turned on their backs, twist and grope with their feet and make motions sideways until they are restored to their proper position. The tortoise on his back feels no suffering; but he is restless because he misses his natural condition, and does not cease to shake himself about until he stands once more upon his feet.

So all these animals have a consciousness of their physical constitution, and for that reason can manage their limbs as readily as they do; nor have we any better proof that they come into being equipped with this knowledge than the fact that no animal is unskilled in the use of its body. But some object as follows: "According to your account, one's constitution consists of a ruling power* in the soul which has a certain relation towards the body. But how can a child comprehend this intricate and subtle principle, which I can scarcely explain even to you? All living creatures should be born logicians, so as to understand a definition which is obscure to the majority of Roman citizens!" Your objection would be true if I spoke of living creatures as understanding "a definition of constitution," and not "their actual constitution." Nature is easier to understand than to explain; hence, the child of whom we were speaking does not understand what

* i.e., the "soul of the world," of which each living soul is a part. The Stoics believed that it was situated in the heart. Zeno called it ἡγεμονικόν, "ruling power"; while the Romans used the term *principale* or *principatus*. The principle described above is ὁρμή (impulse) or τόνος (tension).

"constitution" is, but understands *its own* constitution. He does not know what "a living creature" is, but he feels that he is an animal. Moreover, that very constitution of his own he only understands confusedly, cursorily, and darkly. We also know that we possess souls, but we do not know the essence, the place, the quality, or the source, of the soul. Such as is the consciousness of our souls which we possess, ignorant as we are of their nature and position, even so all animals possess a consciousness of their own constitutions. For they must necessarily feel this, because it is the same agency by which they feel other things also; they must necessarily have a feeling of the principle which they obey and by which they are controlled. Everyone of us understands that there is something which stirs his impulses, but he does not know what it is. He knows that he has a sense of striving, although he does not know what it is or its source. Thus even children and animals have a consciousness of their primary element, but it is not very clearly outlined or portrayed.

"You maintain, do you," says the objector, "that every living thing is at the start adapted to its constitution, but that man's constitution is a reasoning one, and hence man is adapted to himself not merely as a living, but as a reasoning, being? For man is dear to himself in respect of that wherein he is a man. How, then, can a child, being not yet gifted with reason, adapt himself to a reasoning constitution?" But each age has its own constitution, different in the case of the child, the boy, and the old man; they are all adapted to the constitution wherein they find themselves. The child is toothless, and he is fitted to this condition. Then his teeth grow, and he is fitted to that condition also. Vegetation also, which will develop into grain and fruits, has a special constitution when young and scarcely peeping over the tops of the furrows, another when it is strengthened and stands upon a stalk which is soft but strong enough to bear its weight, and still another when the colour changes to yellow, prophesies threshing-time, and hardens in the ear—no matter what may be the constitution into which the plant comes, it keeps it, and conforms thereto. The periods of infancy, boyhood, youth, and old age, are different; but I, who have been infant, boy, and youth, am still the same. Thus, although each has at different times a different constitution, the adaptation of each to its constitution is the same. For nature does not consign boyhood or youth, or old age, to me; it consigns me to them. Therefore, the child is adapted to that constitution which is his at the present moment of childhood, not to that which will be his in youth. For even if there is in store for him any higher phase into which he must be changed, the state in which he is born is also according to nature. First of all, the living being is adapted to itself, for there must be a pattern to which all other things may be referred. I seek pleasure; for whom? For myself. I am therefore looking out for myself. I shrink from pain; on behalf of whom? Myself. Therefore, I am looking out for myself. Since I gauge all my actions with reference to my own welfare, I am looking out for myself before all else. This quality exists in all living beings—not engrafted but inborn.

Nature brings up her own offspring and does not cast them away; and because the most assured security is that which is nearest, every man has been entrusted to his own self. Therefore, as I have remarked in the course of my previous correspondence, even young animals, on issuing from the mother's womb or from the egg, know at once of their own accord what is harmful for them, and avoid death-dealing things.* They even shrink when they notice the shadow of birds of prey which flit overhead.

No animal, when it enters upon life, is free from the fear of death. People may ask: "How can an animal at birth have an understanding of things wholesome or destructive?" The first question, however, is *whether* it can have such understanding, and not *how* it can understand. And it is clear that they have such understanding from the fact that, even if you add understanding, they will act no more adequately than they did in the first place. Why should the hen show no fear of the peacock or the goose, and yet run from the hawk, which is a so much smaller animal not even familiar to the hen? Why should young chickens fear a cat and not a dog? These fowls clearly have a presentiment of harm—

* Seneca is both sound and modern in his account of animal "intelligence." It is instinct, due to sensory-motor reactions, and depending largely upon type heredity.

one not based on actual experiments; for they avoid a thing before they can possibly have experience of it. Furthermore, in order that you may not suppose this to be the result of chance, they do not shrink from certain other things which you would expect them to fear, nor do they ever forget vigilance and care in this regard; they all possess equally the faculty of avoiding what is destructive. Besides, their fear does not grow as their lives lengthen.

Hence indeed it is evident that these animals have not reached such a condition through experience; it is because of an inborn desire for self-preservation. The teachings of experience are slow and irregular; but whatever Nature communicates belongs equally to everyone, and comes immediately. If, however, you require an explanation, shall I tell you how it is that every living thing tries to understand that which is harmful? It feels that it is constructed of flesh; and so it perceives to what an extent flesh may be cut or burned or crushed, and what animals are equipped with the power of doing this damage; it is of animals of this sort that it derives an unfavourable and hostile idea. These tendencies are closely connected; for each animal at the same time consults its own safety, seeking that which helps it, and shrinks from that which will harm it. Impulses towards useful objects, and revulsion from the opposite, are according to nature; without any reflection to prompt the idea, and without any advice, whatever Nature has prescribed, is done.

Do you not see how skillful bees are in building their cells? How completely harmonious in sharing and enduring toil? Do you not see how the spider weaves a web so subtle that man's hand cannot imitate it; and what a task it is to arrange the threads, some directed straight towards the centre, for the sake of making the web solid, and others running in circles and lessening in thickness—for the purpose of tangling and catching in a sort of net the smaller insects for whose ruin the spider spreads the web? This art is born, not taught; and for this reason no animal is more skilled than any other. You will notice that all spider-webs are equally fine, and that the openings in all honeycomb cells are identical in shape. Whatever art communicates is uncertain and uneven; but Nature's assignments are always uniform. Nature has communicated nothing except the duty of taking care of themselves and the skill to do so; that is why living and learning begin at the same time. No wonder that living things are born with a gift whose absence would make birth useless. This is the first equipment that Nature granted them for the maintenance of their existence—the quality of adaptability and self-love. They could not survive except by desiring to do so. Nor would this desire alone have made them prosper, but without it nothing could have prospered. In no animal can you observe any low esteem, or even any carelessness, of self. Dumb beasts, sluggish in other respects, are clever at living. So you will see that creatures which are useless to others are alert for their own preservation.* Farewell.

---

* A theme developed by Cicero (*De fin.* iii. 16): *placet . . . simul atque natum sit animal . . . , ipsum sibi conciliari et commendari ad se conservandum.*

LETTER

122

On Darkness as a Veil for Wickedness

The day has already begun to lessen. It has shrunk considerably, but yet will still allow a goodly space of time if one rises, so to speak, with the day itself. We are more industrious, and we are better men if we anticipate the day and welcome the dawn; but we are base churls if we lie dozing when the sun is high in the heavens, or if we wake up only when noon arrives; and even then to many it seems not yet dawn. Some have reversed the functions of light and darkness; they open eyes sodden with yesterday's debauch only at the approach of night. It is just like the condition of those peoples whom, according to Vergil, Nature has hidden away and placed in an abode directly opposite to our own:

> When in our face the Dawn with panting steeds
> Breathes down, for them the ruddy evening kindles
> Her late-lit fires.*

---

* Vergil, *Georg.* i. 250 ff.

It is not the country of these men, so much as it is their life, that is "directly opposite" to our own. There may be Antipodes dwelling in this same city of ours who, in Cato's words,* "have never seen the sun rise or set." Do you think that these men know *how* to live, if they do not know *when* to live? Do these men fear death, if they have buried themselves alive? They are as weird as the birds of night.** Although they pass their hours of darkness amid wine and perfumes, although they spend the whole extent of their unnatural waking hours in eating dinners—and those too cooked separately to make up many courses—they are not really banqueting; they are conducting their own funeral services. And the dead at least have their banquets by daylight.***

But indeed to one who is active no day is long. So let us lengthen our lives; for the duty and the proof of life consist in action. Cut short the night; use some of it for the day's business. Birds that are being prepared for the banquet, that they may be easily fattened through lack of exercise, are kept in darkness; and similarly, if men vegetate without physical activity, their idle bodies are overwhelmed with flesh, and in their self-satisfied retirement the fat of indolence grows upon them. Moreover, the bodies of those who have sworn allegiance to the hours of darkness have a loathsome appearance. Their complexions are more alarming than those of anaemic invalids; they are lackadaisical and flabby with dropsy; though still alive, they are already carrion. But this, to my thinking, would be among the least of their evils. How much more darkness there is in their souls! Such a man is internally dazed; his vision is darkened; he envies the blind. And what man ever had eyes for the purpose of seeing in the dark?

You ask me how this depravity comes upon the soul—this habit of reversing the daylight and giving over one's whole existence to the night? All vices rebel against Nature; they all abandon the appointed order. It is the motto of luxury to enjoy what is unusual, and not only to

---

* Cato, Frag. p. 110 Jordan.

** i.e., owls, of ill omen.

*** In connexion with the *Parentalia*, Feb. 13-21, and at other anniversary observations, the ceremonies were held in the daytime.

depart from that which is right, but to leave it as far behind as possible, and finally even take a stand in opposition thereto. Do you not believe that men live contrary to Nature who drink fasting,* who take wine into empty veins, and pass to their food in a state of intoxication? And yet this is one of youth's popular vices—to perfect their strength in order to drink on the very threshold of the bath, amid the unclad bathers; nay even to soak in wine and then immediately to rub off the sweat which they have promoted by many a hot glass of liquor! To them, a glass after lunch or one after dinner is *bourgeois*; it is what the country squires do, who are not connoisseurs in pleasure. This unmixed wine delights them just because there is no food to float in it, because it readily makes its way into their muscles; this boozing pleases them just because the stomach is empty.

Do you not believe that men live contrary to Nature who exchange the fashion of their attire with women?** Do not men live contrary to Nature who endeavour to look fresh and boyish at an age unsuitable for such an attempt? What could be more cruel or more wretched? Cannot time and man's estate ever carry such a person beyond an artificial boyhood?*** Do not men live contrary to Nature who crave roses in winter, or seek to raise a spring flower like the lily by means of hot-water heaters and artificial changes of temperature? Do not men live contrary to Nature who grow fruit-trees on the top of a wall? Or raise waving forests upon the roofs and battlements of their houses—the roots starting at a point to which it would be outlandish for the tree-tops to reach? Do not men live contrary to Nature who lay the foundations of bathrooms in the sea and do not imagine that they can enjoy their swim unless the heated pool is lashed as with the waves of a storm?

---

* A vice which Seneca especially abhors; cf. Ep. xv. 3 *multum potionis altius ieiunio iturae.*

** By wearing silk gowns of transparent material.

*** Not literally translated. For the same thought see Ep. xlvii. 7, etc. *Transcriber's note: The Latin which Gummere refused to translate literally is "Numquam vir erit, ut diu virum pati possit? Et cum illum contumeliae sexus eripuisse debuerat, non ne aetas quidem eripiet?" or roughly: "Will he never become a man, so that he can continue to be screwed by men? And though his sex ought to spare him this insult, won't even his age spare him?"*

When men have begun to desire all things in opposition to the ways of Nature, they end by entirely abandoning the ways of Nature. They cry: "It is daytime—let us go to sleep! It is the time when men rest: now for exercise, now for our drive, now for our lunch! Lo, the dawn approaches: it is dinner-time! We should not do as mankind do. It is low and mean to live in the usual and conventional way. Let us abandon the ordinary sort of day. Let us have a morning that is a special feature of ours, peculiar to ourselves!" Such men are, in my opinion, as good as dead. Are they not all but present at a funeral—and before their time too—when they live amid torches and tapers?* I remember that this sort of life was very fashionable at one time: among such men as Acilius Buta, a person of praetorian rank, who ran through a tremendous estate and on confessing his bankruptcy to Tiberius, received the answer: "You have waked up too late!" Julius Montanus was once reading a poem aloud; he was a middling good poet, noted for his friendship with Tiberius, as well as his fall from favour. He always used to fill his poems with a generous sprinkling of sunrises and sunsets. Hence, when a certain person was complaining that Montanus had read all day long, and declared that no man should attend any of his readings, Natta Pinarius** remarked: "I couldn't make a fairer bargain than this: I am ready to listen to him from sunrise to sunset!" Montanus was reading, and had reached the words:***

'Gins the bright morning to spread forth his flames clear-burning; the red dawn
Scatters its light; and the sad-eyed swallow**** returns to her nestlings,
Bringing the chatterers' food, and with sweet bill sharing and serving.

---

* The symbols of a Roman funeral. For the same practice, purposely performed, see Ep. xii. 8 (and the note of W. C. Summers).

** Called by Tacitus, *Ann.* iv. 34, a *Seiani cliens.*

*** Baehrens, *Frag. Poet. Rom.* p. 355.

**** i.e., Procne, in the well-known nightingale myth.

Then Varus, a Roman knight, the hanger-on of Marcus Vinicius,* and a sponger at elegant dinners which he earned by his degenerate wit, shouted: "Bed-time for Buta!" And later, when Montanus declaimed

> Lo, now the shepherds have folded their flocks, and the slow-moving darkness
> 'Gins to spread silence o'er lands that are drowsily lulled into slumber,

this same Varus remarked: "What? Night already? I'll go and pay my morning call on Buta!" You see, nothing was more notorious than Buta's upside-down manner of life. But this life, as I said, was fashionable at one time. And the reason why some men live thus is not because they think that night in itself offers any greater attractions, but because that which is normal gives them no particular pleasure; light being a bitter enemy of the evil conscience, and, when one craves or scorns all things in proportion as they have cost one much or little, illumination for which one does not pay is an object of contempt. Moreover, the luxurious person wishes to be an object of gossip his whole life; if people are silent about him, he thinks that he is wasting his time. Hence he is uncomfortable whenever any of his actions escape notoriety.

Many men eat up their property, and many men keep mistresses. If you would win a reputation among such persons, you must make your programme not only one of luxury but one of notoriety; for in such a busy community wickedness does not discover the ordinary sort of scandal. I heard Pedo Albinovanus, that most attractive story-teller, speaking of his residence above the town-house of Sextus Papinius. Papinius belonged to the tribe of those who shun the light. "About nine o'clock at night I hear the sound of whips. I ask what is going on, and they tell me that Papinius is going over his accounts.** About twelve there is a strenuous shouting; I ask what the matter is, and they say he is

---

* Son of the P. Vinicius ridiculed in Ep. xl. 9. He was husband of Julia, youngest daughter of Germanicus, and was poisoned by Messalina.

** i.e., is punishing his slaves for errors in the day's work.

exercising his voice. About two a.m. I ask the significance of the sound of wheels; they tell me that he is off for a drive. And at dawn there is a tremendous flurry-calling of slaves and butlers, and pandemonium among the cooks. I ask the meaning of this also, and they tell me that he has called for his cordial and his appetizer, after leaving the bath. His dinner," said Pedo, "never went beyond the day,* for he lived very sparingly; he was lavish with nothing but the night. Accordingly, if you believe those who call him tight-fisted and mean, you will call him also a 'slave of the lamp.'"**

You should not be surprised at finding so many special manifestations of the vices; for vices vary, and there are countless phases of them, nor can all their various kinds be classified. The method of maintaining righteousness is simple; the method of maintaining wickedness is complicated, and has infinite opportunity to swerve. And the same holds true of character; if you follow nature, character is easy to manage, free, and with very slight shades of difference; but the sort of person I have mentioned possesses badly warped character, out of harmony with all things, including himself. The chief cause, however, of this disease seems to me to be a squeamish revolt from the normal existence. Just as such persons mark themselves off from others in their dress, or in the elaborate arrangement of their dinners, or in the elegance of their carriages; even so they desire to make themselves peculiar by their way of dividing up the hours of their day. They are unwilling to be wicked in the conventional way, because notoriety is the reward of their sort of wickedness. Notoriety is what all such men seek—men who are, so to speak, *living backwards.*

For this reason, Lucilius, let us keep to the way which Nature has mapped out for us, and let us not swerve therefrom. If we follow Nature, all is easy and unobstructed; but if we combat Nature, our life differs not a whit from that of men who row against the current. Farewell.

---

* i.e., balancing the custom of the ordinary Roman, whose dinner never continued beyond nightfall.

** "'A liver by candle-light,' with a play on the word λίχνος, 'luxurious'" (Summers).

LETTER

123

On the Conflict between Pleasure and Virtue

Wearied with the discomfort rather than with the length of my journey, I have reached my Alban villa late at night, and I find nothing in readiness except myself. So I am getting rid of fatigue at my writing-table: I derive some good from this tardiness on the part of my cook and my baker. For I am communing with myself on this very topic—that nothing is heavy if one accepts it with a light heart, and that nothing need provoke one's anger if one does not add to one's pile of troubles by getting angry. My baker is out of bread; but the overseer, or the house-steward, or one of my tenants can supply me therewith. "Bad bread!" you say. But just wait for it; it will become good. Hunger will make even such bread delicate and of the finest flavour. For that reason I must not eat until hunger bids me; so I shall wait and shall not eat until I can either get good bread or else cease to be squeamish about it. It is necessary that one grow accustomed to slender fare: because there are many problems of time and place which will cross the path even of the rich man and one equipped for pleasure, and bring him up with a round turn. To have whatsoever he wishes is in no man's power; it is in his power not to wish for what he has not, but cheerfully to employ what comes to him. A great step towards independence is a good-humoured stomach, one that is willing to endure rough treatment.

You cannot imagine how much pleasure I derive from the fact that my weariness is becoming reconciled to itself; I am asking for no slaves to rub me down, no bath, and no other restorative except time. For that which toil has accumulated, rest can lighten. This repast, whatever it may be, will give me more pleasure than an inaugural banquet.* For I have made trial of my spirit on a sudden—a simpler and a truer test. Indeed, when a man has made preparations and given himself a formal summons to be patient, it is not equally clear just how much real strength of mind he possesses; the surest proofs are those which one exhibits off-hand, viewing one's own troubles not only fairly but calmly, not flying into fits of temper or wordy wranglings, supplying one's own needs by not craving something which was really due, and reflecting that our habits may be unsatisfied, but never our own real selves. How many things are superfluous we fail to realize until they begin to be wanting; we merely used them not because we needed them but because we had them. And how much do we acquire simply because our neighbours have acquired such things, or because most men possess them! Many of our troubles may be explained from the fact that we live according to a pattern, and, instead of arranging our lives according to reason, are led astray by convention.

There are things which, if done by the few, we should refuse to imitate; yet when the majority have begun to do them, we follow along—just as if anything were more honourable because it is more frequent! Furthermore, wrong views, when they have become prevalent, reach, in our eyes, the standard of righteousness. Everyone now travels with Numidian outriders preceding him, with a troop of slave-runners to clear the way; we deem it disgraceful to have no attendants who will elbow crowds from the road, or will prove, by a great cloud of dust, that a high dignitary is approaching! Everyone now possesses mules that are laden with crystal and myrrhine cups carved by skilled artists of great renown; it is disgraceful for all your baggage to be made

* i.e., a dinner given by an official when he entered upon (*adeo*) his office.

up of that which can be rattled along without danger. Everyone has pages who ride along with ointment-covered faces, so that the heat or the cold will not harm their tender complexions; it is disgraceful that none of your attendant slave-boys should show a healthy cheek, not covered with cosmetics.

You should avoid conversation with all such persons: they are the sort that communicate and engraft their bad habits from one to another. We used to think that the very worst variety of these men were those who vaunted their words; but there are certain men who vaunt their wickedness. Their talk is very harmful; for even though it is not at once convincing, yet they leave the seeds of trouble in the soul, and the evil which is sure to spring into new strength follows us about even when we have parted from them. Just as those who have attended a concert* carry about in their heads the melodies and the charm of the songs they have heard—a proceeding which interferes with their thinking and does not allow them to concentrate upon serious subjects,—even so the speech of flatterers and enthusiasts over that which is depraved sticks in our minds long after we have heard them talk. It is not easy to rid the memory of a catching tune; it stays with us, lasts on, and comes back from time to time. Accordingly, you should close your ears against evil talk, and right at the outset, too; for when such talk has gained an entrance and the words are admitted and are in our minds, they become more shameless. And then we begin to speak as follows: "Virtue, Philosophy, Justice—this is a jargon of empty words. The only way to be happy is to do yourself well. To eat, drink, and spend your money is the only real life, the only way to remind yourself that you are mortal. Our days flow on, and life—which we cannot restore—hastens away from us. Why hesitate to come to our senses? This life of ours will not always admit pleasures; meantime, while it can do so, while it clamours for them, what profit lies in imposing thereupon frugality? Therefore get ahead of death, and let anything that death will filch from you be squandered now upon yourself. You have no mistress,

* For *symphonia* see Ep. li. 4 and note. Compare also the *commissiones*, orchestral exhibitions, composed of many voices, flutes, and brass instruments, Ep. lxxxiv. 10.

no favourite slave to make your mistress envious; you are sober when you make your daily appearance in public; you dine as if you had to show your account-book to 'Papa'; but *that* is not living, it is merely going shares in someone else's existence. And what madness it is to be looking out for the interests of your heir, and to deny yourself everything, with the result that you turn friends into enemies by the vast amount of the fortune you intend to leave! For the more the heir is to get from you, the more he will rejoice in your taking-off! All those sour fellows who criticize other men's lives in a spirit of priggishness and are real enemies to their own lives, playing schoolmaster to the world—you should not consider them as worth a farthing, nor should you hesitate to prefer good living to a good reputation."

These are voices which you ought to shun just as Ulysses did; he would not sail past them until he was lashed to the mast. They are no less potent; they lure men from country, parents, friends, and virtuous ways; and by a hope that, if not base, is ill-starred, they wreck them upon a life of baseness. How much better to follow a straight course and attain a goal where the words "pleasant" and "honourable" have the same meaning!* This end will be possible for us if we understand that there are two classes of objects which either attract us or repel us. We are attracted by such things as riches, pleasures, beauty, ambition, and other such coaxing and pleasing objects; we are repelled by toil, death, pain, disgrace, or lives of greater frugality. We ought therefore to train ourselves so that we may avoid a fear of the one or a desire for the other. Let us fight in the opposite fashion: let us retreat from the objects that allure, and rouse ourselves to meet the objects that attack.

Do you not see how different is the method of descending a mountain from that employed in climbing upwards? Men coming down a slope bend backwards; men ascending a steep place lean forward. For, my dear Lucilius, to allow yourself to put your body's weight ahead when coming down, or, when climbing up, to throw it backward is to comply with vice. The pleasures take one down hill but one must work upwards toward that which is rough and hard to climb; in the one case

---

* i.e., to live by Stoicism rather than by Epicureanism.

let us throw our bodies forward, in the others let us put the check-rein on them.

Do you believe me to be stating now that only those men bring ruin to our ears, who praise pleasure, who inspire us with fear of pain—that element which is in itself provocative of fear? I believe that we are also in injured by those who masquerade under the disguise of the Stoic school and at the same time urge us on into vice. They boast that only the wise man and the learned is a lover.* "He alone has wisdom in this art; the wise man too is best skilled in drinking and feasting. Our study ought to be this alone: up to what age the bloom of love can endure!" All this may be regarded as a concession to the ways of Greece; we ourselves should preferably turn our attention to words like these: "No man is good by chance. Virtue is something which must be learned. Pleasure is low, petty, to be deemed worthless, shared even by dumb animals—the tiniest and meanest of whom fly towards pleasure. Glory is an empty and fleeting thing, lighter than air. Poverty is an evil to no man unless he kick against the goads.** Death is not an evil; why need you ask? Death alone is the equal privilege of mankind. Superstition is the misguided idea of a lunatic; it fears those whom it ought to love; it is an outrage upon those whom it worships. For what difference is there between denying the gods and dishonouring them?"

You should learn such principles as these, nay rather you should learn them by heart; philosophy ought not to try to explain away vice. For a sick man, when his physician bids him live recklessly, is doomed beyond recall. Farewell.

---

* Meaning, in line with the Stoic paradoxes, that only the sage knows how to be rightly in love.

** *Transcriber's note: The Latin is "Paupertas nulli malum est nisi repugnanti," i.e. "Poverty is an evil to noone unless they resist." Gummere's odd phrase "kick against the goads" is actually from the Bible (Acts 26:14)*

LETTER

124

On the True Good as Attained by Reason

Full many an ancient precept could I give,
Didst thou not shrink, and feel it shame to learn
Such lowly duties.*

But you do not shrink, nor are you deterred by any subtleties of study. For your cultivated mind is not wont to investigate such important subjects in a free-and-easy manner. I approve your method in that you make everything count towards a certain degree of progress, and in that you are disgruntled only when nothing can be accomplished by the greatest degree of subtlety. And I shall take pains to show that this is the case now also. Our question is, whether the Good is grasped by the senses or by the understanding; and the corollary thereto is that it does not exist in dumb animals or little children.

Those who rate pleasure as the supreme ideal hold that the Good is a matter of the senses; but we Stoics maintain that it is a matter of the understanding, and we assign it to the mind. If the senses were to pass judgment on what is good, we should never

* Vergil, *Georg.* i. 176 f.

reject any pleasure; for there is no pleasure that does not attract, no pleasure that does not please. Conversely, we should undergo no pain voluntarily; for there is no pain that does not clash with the senses. Besides, those who are too fond of pleasure and those who fear pain to the greatest degree would in that case not deserve reproof. But we condemn men who are slaves to their appetites and their lusts, and we scorn men who, through fear of pain, will dare no manly deed. But what wrong could such men be committing if they looked merely to the senses as arbiters of good and evil? For it is to the senses that you and yours have entrusted the test of things to be sought and things to be avoided!

Reason, however, is surely the governing element in such a matter as this; as reason has made the decision concerning the happy life, and concerning virtue and honour also, so she has made the decision with regard to good and evil. For with them* the vilest part is allowed to give sentence about the better, so that the senses—dense as they are, and dull, and even more sluggish in man than in the other animals,—pass judgment on the Good. Just suppose that one should desire to distinguish tiny objects by the touch rather than by the eyesight! There is no special faculty more subtle and acute than the eye, that would enable us to distinguish between good and evil. You see, therefore, in what ignorance of truth a man spends his days and how abjectly he has overthrown lofty and divine ideals, if he thinks that the sense of touch can pass judgment upon the nature of the Supreme Good and the Supreme Evil! He** says: "Just as every science and every art should possess an element that is palpable and capable of being grasped by the senses (their source of origin and growth), even so the happy life derives its foundation and its beginnings from things that are palpable, and from that which falls within the scope of the senses. Surely you admit that the happy life takes its beginnings from things palpable to the senses." But we define as "happy" those things that are in accord with Nature. And that which is in accord with Nature

* i.e., the Epicureans.

** i.e., the advocate of the "touch" theory.

is obvious and can be seen at once—just as easily as that which is complete. That which is according to Nature, that which is given us as a gift immediately at our birth, is, I maintain, not a Good, but the beginning of a Good. You, however, assign the Supreme Good, pleasure, to mere babies, so that the child at its birth begins at the point whither the perfected man arrives. You are placing the tree-top where the root ought to be. If anyone should say that the child, hidden in its mother's womb, of unknown sex too, delicate, unformed, and shapeless—if one should say that this child is already in a state of goodness, he would clearly seem to be astray in his ideas. And yet how little difference is there between one who has just lately received the gift of life, and one who is still a hidden burden in the bowels of the mother! They are equally developed, as far as their understanding of good or evil is concerned; and a child is as yet no more capable of comprehending the Good than is a tree or any dumb beast.

But why is the Good non-existent in a tree or in a dumb beast? Because there is no reason there, either. For the same cause, then, the Good is non-existent in a child, for the child also has no reason; the child will reach the Good only when he reaches reason.* There are animals without reason, there are animals not yet endowed with reason, and there are animals who possess reason, but only incompletely;** in none of these does the Good exist, for it is reason that brings the Good in its company. What, then, is the distinction between the classes which I have mentioned? In that which does not possess reason, the Good will never exist. In that which is not yet endowed with reason, the Good cannot be existent at the time. And in that which possesses reason but only incompletely, the Good is capable of existing, but does not yet exist. This is what I mean, Lucilius: the Good cannot be discovered in any random person, or at any random age; and it is as far removed from infancy as last is from first, or as that which is complete from that which has just sprung into being. Therefore, it cannot exist in the

* According to the Stoics (and other schools also), the "innate notions," or groundwork of knowledge, begin to be subject to reason after the attainment of a child's seventh year.

** i.e., they are limited to "practical judgment."

delicate body, when the little frame has only just begun to knit together. Of course not—no more than in the seed. Granting the truth of this, we understand that there is a certain kind of Good of a tree or in a plant; but this is not true of its first growth, when the plant has just begun to spring forth out of the ground. There is a certain Good of wheat: it is not yet existent, however, in the swelling stalk, nor when the soft ear is pushing itself out of the husk, but only when summer days and its appointed maturity have ripened the wheat. Just as Nature in general does not produce her Good until she is brought to perfection, even so man's Good does not exist in man until both reason and man are perfected. And what is this Good? I shall tell you: it is a free mind, an upright mind, subjecting other things to itself and itself to nothing. So far is infancy from admitting this Good that boyhood has no hope of it, and even young manhood cherishes the hope without justification; even our old age is very fortunate if it has reached this Good after long and concentrated study. If this, then, is the Good, the good is a matter of the understanding.

"But," comes the retort, "you admitted that there is a certain Good of trees and of grass; then surely there can be a certain Good of a child also." But the true Good is not found in trees or in dumb animals the Good which exists in them is called "good" only by courtesy.* "Then what is it?" you say. Simply that which is in accord with the nature of each. The real Good cannot find a place in dumb animals—not by any means; its nature is more blest and is of a higher class. And where there is no place for reason, the Good does not exist. There are four natures which we should mention here: of the tree, animal, man, and God. The last two, having reasoning power, are of the same nature, distinct only by virtue of the immortality of the one and the mortality of the other. Of one of these, then—to wit God—it is Nature that perfects the Good; of the other—to wit man—pains and study do so. All other things are perfect only in their particular nature, and not truly perfect, since they lack reason.

---

* Just as Academic and Peripatetic philosophers sometimes defined as "goods" what the Stoics called "advantages."

Indeed, to sum up, that alone is perfect which is perfect according to nature as a whole, and nature as a whole is possessed of reason. Other things can be perfect according to their kind. That which cannot contain the happy life cannot contain that which produces the happy life; and the happy life is produced by Goods alone. In dumb animals there is not a trace of the happy life, nor of the means whereby the happy life is produced; in dumb animals the Good does not exist. The dumb animal comprehends the present world about him through his senses alone. He remembers the past only by meeting with something which reminds his senses; a horse, for example, remembers the right road only when he is placed at the starting-point. In his stall, however, he has no memory of the road, no matter how often he may have stepped along it. The third state—the future—does not come within the ken of dumb beasts.

How, then, can we regard as perfect the nature of those who have no experience of time in its perfection? For time is three-fold,—past, present, and future. Animals perceive only the time which is of greatest moment to them within the limits of their coming and going—the present. Rarely do they recollect the past—and that only when they are confronted with present reminders. Therefore the Good of a perfect nature cannot exist in an imperfect nature; for if the latter sort of nature should possess the Good, so also would mere vegetation. I do not indeed deny that dumb animals have strong and swift impulses toward actions which seem according to nature, but such impulses are confused and disordered. The Good however, is never confused or disordered.

"What!" you say, "do dumb animals move in disturbed and ill-ordered fashion?" I should say that they moved in disturbed and ill-ordered fashion, if their nature admitted of order; as it is, they move in accordance with their nature. For that is said to be "disturbed" which can also at some other time be "not disturbed"; so, too, that is said to be in a state of trouble which can be in a state of peace. No man is vicious except one who has the capacity of virtue; in the case of dumb animals their motion is such as results from their nature. But, not to weary you, a certain sort of good will be found in a dumb animal, and a certain sort of virtue, and a certain sort of perfection—but neither the Good, nor virtue, nor perfection in the absolute sense. For this is the privilege of reasoning beings alone, who are permitted to know the cause, the degree, and the means. Therefore, good can exist only in that which possesses reason.

Do you ask now whither our argument is tending, and of what benefit it will be to your mind? I will tell you: it exercises and sharpens the mind, and ensures, by occupying it honourably, that it will accomplish some sort of good. And even that is beneficial which holds men back when they are hurrying into wickedness. However, I will say this also: I can be of no greater benefit to you than by revealing the Good that is rightly yours, by taking you out of the class of dumb animals, and by placing you on a level with God. Why, pray, do you foster and practise your bodily strength? Nature has granted strength in greater degree to cattle and wild beasts. Why cultivate your beauty? After all your efforts, dumb animals surpass you in comeliness. Why dress your hair with such unending attention? Though you let it down in Parthian fashion, or tie it up in the German style, or, as the Scythians do, let it flow wild—yet you will see a mane of greater thickness tossing upon any horse you choose, and a mane of greater beauty bristling upon the neck of any lion. And even after training yourself for speed, you will be no match for the hare. Are you not willing to abandon all these details—wherein you must acknowledge defeat, striving as you are for something that is not your own—and come back to the Good that is really yours?

And what is this Good? It is a clear and flawless mind, which rivals that of God,* raised far above mortal concerns, and counting nothing of its own to be outside itself. You are a reasoning animal. What Good, then, lies within you? Perfect reason. Are you willing to develop this to its farthest limits—to its greatest degree of increase? Only consider yourself happy when all your joys are born of reason, and when—having marked all the objects which men clutch at, or pray

* One of the most conspicuous Stoic paradoxes maintained that "the wise man is a God."

for, or watch over—you find nothing which you will desire; mind, I do not say *prefer*. Here is a short rule by which to measure yourself, and by the test of which you may feel that you have reached perfection: "You will come to your own when you shall understand that those whom the world calls fortunate are really the most unfortunate of all." Farewell.

MEDITATIONS

Translated by

GEORGE LONG

Marcus Aurelius Antoninus was born in Rome, A.D. 121, on the 26th of April. His father, Annius Verus, died while he was praetor. His mother was Domitia Calvilla, also named Lucilla. The Emperor T. Antoninus Pius married Annia Galeria Faustina, the sister of Annius Verus, and was consequently the uncle of M. Antoninus. When Hadrian adopted Antoninus Pius and declared him his successor in the empire, Antoninus Pius adopted both L. Ceionius Commodus, the son of Aelius Caesar, and M. Antoninus, whose original name was M. Annius Verus. Antoninus then took the name of M. Aelius Aurelius Verus, to which was added the title of Caesar in A.D. 139: the name Aelius belonged to Hadrian's family, and Aurelius was the name of Antoninus Pius. When M. Antoninus became Augustus, he dropped the name of Verus and took the name of Antoninus. Accordingly, he is generally known as M. Aurelius Antoninus, or simply M. Antoninus.

The youth was most carefully brought up. He thanks the gods that he had good grandfathers, good parents, a good sister, good teachers, good associates, good kinsmen, and friends—nearly everything good. He had the happy fortune to witness the example of his uncle and adoptive father, Antoninus Pius, and he has recorded in his words the virtues of an excellent man and prudent ruler. Like many young Romans, he tried his hand at poetry and studied rhetoric. Herodes Atticus and M. Cornelius Fronto were his teachers in eloquence. There are extant letters between Fronto and Marcus, which show the great affection of the pupil for the master and the master's great hopes for his industrious pupil. M. Antoninus mentions Fronto among those to whom he was indebted for his education.

When he was eleven years old, he assumed the dress of philosophers, something plain and coarse, became a hard student, and lived a most laborious, abstemious life, even going so far as to injure his health. Finally, he abandoned poetry and rhetoric for philosophy, and he attached himself to the sect of the Stoics. But he did not neglect the study of law, which was a useful preparation for the high place that he was designed to fill. His teacher was L. Volusianus Maecianus, a distinguished jurist. We must suppose that he learned the Roman discipline of arms, which was a necessary part of the education of a man who afterwards led his troops to battle against a warlike race.

Antoninus recorded in his first book the names of his teachers and the obligations that he owed to each of them. The way in which he speaks of what he learned from them might seem to savour vanity or self-praise if we look carelessly at the way in which he has expressed himself, but if anyone draws this conclusion, he will be mistaken. Antoninus means to commemorate the merits of his several teachers, what they taught, and what a pupil might learn from them. Besides, this book, like the eleven other books, was for his own use, and if we may trust the note at the end of the first book, it was written during one of M. Antoninus' campaigns against the Quadi, at a time when the commemoration of the virtues of his illustrious teachers might remind him of their lessons and the practical uses which he might derive from them.

Among his teachers of philosophy was Sextus of Chaeroneia, a grandson of Plutarch. What he learned from this excellent man is told by himself (i. 9). His favourite teacher was Q. Junius Rusticus (i. 7), a philosopher and also a man of practical good sense in public affairs. Rusticus was the adviser to Antoninus after he became emperor. Young men who are destined for high places are not often fortunate in those who are about them, their companions, and teachers and I do not know any example of a young prince having had an education that can be compared with that of M. Antoninus. Such a body of teachers distinguished by their acquirements and their character will hardly be collected again; and as to the pupil, we have not had one like him since.

Hadrian died in July A.D. 138, and was succeeded by Antoninus Pius. M. Antoninus married Faustina, his cousin, the daughter of Pius, probably about A.D. 146, for he had a daughter born in 147. He received from his adoptive father the title of Caesar and was associated with him in the administration of the state. The father and the adopted son lived together in perfect friendship and confidence. Antoninus was a dutiful son, and the emperor Pius loved and esteemed him.

Antoninus Pius died in March, A.D. 161. The Senate, it is said, urged M. Antoninus to take over the sole administration of the empire, but he associated himself with the other adopted son of Pius, L. Ceionius Commodus, who is generally called L. Verus. Thus, Rome had two emperors for the first time. Verus was an indolent man of pleasure, and unworthy of his station. Antoninus, however, bore with him, and it is said Verus had sense enough to pay his colleague the respect due to his character. A virtuous emperor and a loose partner lived together in peace, and their alliance was strengthened by Antoninus giving Verus his daughter Lucilla as a wife.

The reign of Antoninus was first troubled by a Parthian war, in which Verus was sent to command, but he did nothing, and the success that was obtained by the Romans in Armenia and on the Euphrates and Tigris was due to his generals. This Parthian war ended in A.D. 165. Aurelius and Verus had a triumph (A.D. 166) for their victories in the East. A pestilence followed, which carried off great numbers in Rome and Italy and spread to the west of Europe.

The north of Italy was also threatened by the rude people beyond the Alps, from the borders of Gallia to the eastern side of the Hadriatic. These barbarians attempted to break into Italy, as the Germanic nations had attempted nearly three hundred years before, and the rest of the life of Antoninus, with some intervals, was employed in driving back the invaders. In 169, Verus suddenly died, and Antoninus administered the state alone.

During the German wars, Antoninus resided for three years on the Danube at Carnuntum. The Marcomanni were driven out of Pannonia and almost destroyed in their retreat across the Danube; and in A.D. 174, the emperor gained a great victory over the Quadi.

In A.D. 175, Avidius Cassius, a brave and skilled Roman commander who was at the head of the troops in Asia, revolted, and declared himself Augustus. But Cassius was assassinated by some of his officers, and so the rebellion came to an end. Antoninus showed his humanity by his treatment of the family and the partisans of Cassius; and his letter to the Senate, in which he recommends mercy, is extant. (Vulcatius, Avidius Cassius, c. 12.)

Antoninus set out for the East on hearing of Cassius' revolt. Though he appears to have returned to Rome in A.D. 174, he went back to prosecute the war against the Germans, and it is probable that he marched directly to the East from the German war. His wife Faustina, who accompanied him into Asia, died suddenly at the foot of the Taurus, to the great grief of her husband. Capitolinus, who has written the life of Antoninus, and also Dion Cassius, accuses the empress of scandalous infidelity to her husband, and of abominable lewdness. But Capitolinus says that Antoninus either did not know it or pretended not to know it. Nothing is so common as such malicious reports in all ages, and the history of imperial Rome is full of them. Antoninus loved his wife, and he says that she was "obedient, affectionate, and simple." The same scandal had been spread about Faustina's mother, the wife of Antoninus Pius, and yet he too was perfectly satisfied with his wife. Antoninus Pius says after her death, in a letter to Fronto, that he would rather have lived in exile with his wife than in his palace in Rome without her. There are not many men who would give their wives a better character than these two emperors. Capitolinus wrote in the time of Diocletian. He may have intended to tell the truth, but he is a poor, feeble biographer. Dion Cassius, the most malignant of historians, always reports, and perhaps he believed, any scandal against anybody.

Antoninus continued his journey to Syria and Egypt, and on his return to Italy through Athens he was initiated into the Eleusinian mysteries. It was the practice of the emperor to conform to the established rites of the age, and to perform religious ceremonies with due solemnity. We cannot conclude from this that he was a superstitious man, though we might perhaps do so if his book did not show that he was not. But that is only one of many instances where a ruler's public acts do not always prove his real opinions. A prudent governor will not roughly oppose even the superstitions of his people; and though he may wish they were wiser, he will know that he cannot make them so by offending their prejudices.

Antoninus and his son Commodus entered Rome in triumph, perhaps for some German victories, on the 23rd of December, A.D. 176. In the following year Commodus was associated with his father in the empire, and took the name of Augustus. This year A.D. 177 is memorable in ecclesiastical history. Attalus and others were put to death at Lyon for their adherence to the Christian religion. The evidence of this persecution is a letter preserved by Eusebius (Œ.H. V. I; printed in Routh's Reliquiae Sacrae, vol. i, with notes). The letter is from the Christians of Vienna and Lugdunum in Gallia (Vienna and Lyon) to their Christian brethren in Asia and Phrygia; and it is preserved perhaps nearly entirely. It contains a very particular description of the tortures inflicted on the Christians in Gallia, and it states that while the persecution was going on, Attalus, a Christian and a Roman citizen, was loudly demanded by the populace and brought into the amphitheatre; but the governor ordered him to be reserved, with the rest who were in prison, until he had received instructions from the emperor. Many had been tortured before the governor thought of applying to Antoninus. The imperial rescript, says in the letter, that the Christians should be punished, but if they deny their faith, they must be released. On this the work began again. The Christians who were Roman citizens were beheaded; the rest were exposed to the wild beasts in the amphitheatre. Some modern writers on ecclesiastical history, when they use this letter, say nothing of the wonderful stories of the martyrs' sufferings. Sanctus, as the letter says, was burnt with plates of hot iron till his body was sore and had lost all human form; but on being put to the rack he recovered his former appearance under the torture, which was thus a cure instead of a punishment. He was afterwards torn by beasts, placed on an iron chair and roasted. He died at last.

The letter is one piece of evidence. The writer, whoever he was who wrote in the name of the Gallic Christians, is our evidence both for the ordinary and the extraordinary circumstances of the story, and we cannot accept his evidence for one part and reject the other. We often receive small evidence as proof of a thing we believe to be within the limits of probability or possibility, and we reject exactly the same evidence, when the thing to which it refers appears very improbable or impossible. But this is a false method of inquiry, though it is followed by some modern writers, who select what they like from a story and reject the rest of the evidence; or if they do not reject it, they dishonestly suppress it. A man can only act consistently by accepting all this letter or rejecting it all, and we cannot blame him for either. But he who rejects it may still admit that such a letter may be founded on real facts; and he would make this admission as the most probable way of accounting for the existence of the letter; but if, as he would suppose, the writer has stated some things falsely, he cannot tell what part of his story is worthy of credit.

The war on the northern frontier appears to have been uninterrupted during the visit of Antoninus to the East, and on his return the emperor again left Rome to oppose the barbarians. The Germanic people were defeated in a great battle in A.D. 179. During this campaign the emperor was seized with some contagious malady, of which he died in the camp at Sirmium (Mitrovitz), on the Save, in Lower Pannonia, but at Vindebona (Vienna), according to other authorities, on the 17th of March, A.D. 180, in the fifty-ninth year of his age. His son Commodus was with him. The body, or probably the ashes of the emperor, were carried to Rome, and he received the honor of deification. Those who could afford it had his statue or bust; and when Capitolinus wrote, many people still had statues of Antoninus among the Dei Penates or household deities. He was in a manner made a saint. Commodus erected to the memory of his father the Antonine column which is now in the Piazza Colonna in Rome. The bassi rilievi which are placed in a spiral line around the shaft commemorate the victories of Antoninus over the Marcomanni and the Quadi, and the miraculous shower of rain which refreshed the Roman soldiers and discomfited their enemies. The statue of Antoninus was placed on the capital of the column, but it was removed at some time unknown, and a bronze statue of St. Paul was put in the place by Pope Sixtus the Fifth.

The historical evidence for the times of Antoninus is very defective, and some of that which remains is not credible. The most curious is the story about the miracle which happened in A.D. 174, during the war with the Quadi. The Roman army was in danger of perishing by thirst, but a sudden storm drenched them with rain, while it discharged fire and hail on their enemies, and the Romans gained a great victory. All the authorities which speak of the battle also speak of the miracle. The Gentile writers assign it to their gods, and the Christians to the intercession of the Christian legion in the emperor's army. To confirm the Christian statement it is added that the emperor gave the title of Thundering to this legion; but Dacier and others, who maintain the Christian report of the miracle, admit that this title of Thundering or Lightning was not given to this legion because the Quadi were struck with lightning, but because there was a figure of lightning on their shields, and that this title of the legion existed in the time of Augustus. Scaliger also observed that the legion was called Thundering (κεραυνοβόλος or κεραυνοφόρος) before the reign of Antoninus. We learn this from Dion Cassius (Lib. 55, c. 23, and the note of Reimarus), who enumerates all the legions of Augustus' time. The name Thundering of Lightning also appears on an inscription of the reign of Trajan, which was found at Trieste. Eusebius (v. 5), when he relates the miracle, quotes Apolinarius, bishop of Hierapolis, as authority for this name being given to the legion Melitene by the emperor in consequence of the success which he obtained through their prayers; from which we may estimate the value of Apolinarius' testimony. Eusebius does not say in what book of Apolinarius does the statement occur. Dion says that the Thundering Legion was stationed in Cappadocia in the time of Augustus. Valesius also observes that in the Notitia of the Imperium Romanum there is mentioned under the commander of Armenia the Praefectura of the twelfth legion named "Thundering Melitene;" and this position in Armenia will agree with what Dion says of its position in Cappadocia. Accordingly, Valesius concludes that Melitene was not the name of the legion, but of the town in which it was stationed. Melitene was also the name of the district in which this town was situated. The legions did not, he says, take their name from the place where they were on duty, but from the country in which they were raised, and therefore what Eusebius says about the Melitene does not seem probable to him. Yet Valesius, on the authority of Apolinarius and Tertullian, believed that the miracle was worked through the prayers of the Christian soldiers in the emperor's army. Rufinus does not give the name of Melitene to this legion, says Valesius, and probably he purposely omitted it, because he knew that Melitene was the name of a town in Armenia Minor, where the legion was stationed in his time.

The emperor, it is said, made a report of his victory to the Senate, which we may believe, for such was the practice; but we do not know what he said in his letter, for it is not extant. Dacier assumes that the emperor's letter was purposely destroyed by the Senate or the enemies of Christianity, that so honorable a testimony to the Christians and their religion might not be perpetuated. The critic has however not seen that he contradicts himself when he tells us the purport of the letter, for he says that it was destroyed, and even Eusebius could not find it. But there does exist a letter in Greek addressed by Antoninus to the Roman people and the sacred Senate after this memorable victory. It is sometimes printed after Justin's first Apology, but it is totally unconnected with the apologies. This letter is one of the most stupid forgeries of the many which exist, and it cannot possibly be founded even on the genuine report of Antoninus to the Senate. If it were genuine, it would free the emperor from the charge of persecuting men because they were Christians, for he says in this false letter that if a man accuses another only of being a Christian, and the accused confesses, and there is nothing else against him, he must be set free; with this monstrous addition, made by a man inconceivably ignorant, that the informer must be burnt alive.

During the time of Antoninus Pius and Marcus Antoninus there appeared the first Apology of Justinus, and under M. Antoninus the Oration of Tatian against the Greeks, which was a fierce attack on the established religions; the address of Athenagoras to M. Antoninus on behalf of the Christians, and the Apology of Melito, bishop of Sardes, also addressed to the emperor, and that of Apolinarius. The first Apology of Justinus is addressed to T. Antoninus Pius and his two adopted sons, M. Antoninus and L. Verus; but we do not know whether they read it. The second Apology of Justinus is entitled "to the Roman Senate;" but this superscription is from some copyists. In the first chapter Justinus addresses the Romans. In the second chapter he speaks of an affair that had recently happened in the time of M. Antoninus and L,. Verus, as it seems; and he also directly addresses the emperor, saying of a certain woman, "she addressed a petition to thee, the emperor, and thou didst grant the petition." In other passages the writer addresses the two emperors, from which we must conclude that the Apology was directed to them. Eusebius (E.H. iv. 18) states that the second Apology was addressed to the successor of Antoninus Pius, and he names him Antoninus Verus, meaning M. Antoninus. In one passage of this second Apology (c. 8), Justinus, or the writer, whoever he may be, says that even men who followed the Stoic doctrines, when they ordered their lives according to ethical reason, were hated and murdered, such as Heraclitus, Musonius in his own times, and others; for all those who in any way labored to live according to reason and avoided wickedness were always hated; and this was the effect of the work of daemons.

Justinus himself is said to have been put to death at Rome, because he refused to sacrifice to the gods. It cannot have been in the reign of Hadrian, as one authority states; nor in the time of Antoninus Pius, if the second Apology was written in the time of M. Antoninus; and there is evidence that this event took place under M. Antoninus and L. Verus, when Rusticus was praefect of the city.

The persecution in which Polycarp suffered at Smyrna belongs to the time of M. Antoninus. The evidence for it is the letter of the church of Smyrna to the churches of Philomelium and the other Christian churches, and it is preserved by Eusebius (E.H. iv. 15). But the critics do not agree about the time of Polycarp's death, differing in the two extremes to the amount of twelve years. The circumstances of Polycarp's martyrdom were accompanied by miracles, one of which Eusebius (iv. 15) has omitted, but it appears in the oldest Latin version of the letter, which Usher published, and it is supposed that this version was made not long after the time of Eusebius. The notice at the end of the letter states that it was transcribed by Caius from the copy of Irenaeus, the disciple of Polycarp, then transcribed by Socrates at Corinth; "after which I Pionius again wrote it out from the copy above mentioned, having searched it out by the revelation of Polycarp, who directed me to it." The story of Polycarp's martyrdom is embellished with miraculous circumstances which some modern writers on ecclesiastical history take the liberty of omitting.

In order to form a proper notion of the condition of the Christians under M. Antoninus we must go back to Trajan's time. When the younger Pliny was governor of Bithynia, the Christians were numerous in those parts, and the worshipers of the old religion were falling off. The temples were deserted, the festivals neglected, and there were no purchasers of victims for sacrifice. Those who were interested in the maintenance of the old religion thus found that their profits were in danger. Christians of both sexes and all ages were brought before the governor who did not know what to do with them. He could come to no other conclusion than this, that those who confessed to be Christians and persevered in their religion ought to be punished; if for nothing else, for their invincible obstinancy. He found no crimes proved against the Christians, and he could only characterize their religion as a depraved and extravagant superstition, which might be stopped if the people were allowed the opportunity of recanting. Pliny wrote this in a letter to Trajan (Plinius, Ep. x. 97). He asked for the emperor's directions, because he did not know what to do. He remarks that he had never been engaged in judicial inquiries about the Christians, and that accordingly he did not know what to inquire about, or how far to inquire and punish. This proves that it was not a new thing to examine a man's profession of Christianity and to punish him for it.

Trajan's rescript is extant. He approved of the governor's judgment in the matter, but he said that no search must be made after the Christians; if a man was charged with the new religion and convicted, he must not be punished if he affirmed that he was not a Christian, and confirmed his denial by showing his reverence to the heathen gods. He added that no notice must be taken of anonymous information, for such things are a bad example. Trajan was a mild and sensible man; and both motives of mercy and policy probably also induced him to take as little notice of the Christians as he could, to let them live in quiet if it were possible. Trajan's rescript is the first legislative act of the head of the Roman state with reference to Christianity, which is known to us. It does not appear that the Christians were further disturbed under his reign. The martyrdom of Ignatius on the order of Trajan himself is not universally admitted to be an historical fact.

In the time of Hadrian, it was no longer possible for the Roman government to overlook the great increase of the Christians and the hostility of the common sort to them. If the governors in the provinces were willing to let them alone, they could not resist the fanaticism of the heathen community, which looked on the Christians as atheists. The Jews too, who were settled all over the Roman Empire, were as hostile to the Christians as the Gentiles were. With the time of Hadrian began the Christian Apologies, which show plainly what the popular feeling towards the Christians then was. A rescript of Hadrian to Minucius Fundanus, the Proconsul of Asia, which stands at the end of Justin's first Apology, instructs the governor that innocent people must not be troubled, and false accusers must not be allowed to extort money from them; the charges against the Christians must be made in due form, and no attention must be paid to popular clamors; when Christians were regularly prosecuted and convicted of illegal acts, they must be punished according to their deserts; and false accusers also must be punished. Antoninus Pius is said to have published rescripts to the same effect. The terms of Hadrian's rescript seem very favourable to the Christians; but if we understand it in this sense, that they were only to be punished like other people for illegal acts, it would have had no meaning, for that could have been done without asking the emperor's advice. The real purpose of the rescript is that Christians must be punished if they persisted in their belief, and would not prove their renunciation of it by acknowledging the heathen religion. This was Trajan's rule, and we have no reason for supposing that Hadrian granted more to the

Christians than Trajan did. There is also printed at the end of Justin's first Apology a rescript of Antoninus Pius to the Commune of (τὸ κοινὸν τῆς ' Ασίας) and it is also in Eusebius (E.H. iv. 13). The date of the rescript is the third consulship of Antoninus Pius. The rescript declares that the Christians—for they are meant, though the name Christians does not occur in the rescript—were not to be disturbed unless they were attempting something against the Roman rule; and no man was to be punished simply for being a Christian. But this rescript is spurious. Any man moderately acquainted with Roman history will see by the style and tenor that it is a clumsy forgery.

In the time of M. Antoninus the opposition between the old and the new belief was still stronger, and the adherents of the heathen religion urged those in authority to engage in a more regular resistance to the invasions of the Christian faith. Melito in his Apology to M. Antoninus represents the Christians of Asia as persecuted under new imperial orders. Shameless informers, he says, men who were greedy after the property of others, used these orders as a means of robbing those who were doing no harm. He doubts if a just emperor could have ordered anything so unjust; and if the last order was really not from the emperor, the Christians entreat him not to give them up to their enemies. We conclude from this that there were at least imperial rescripts or constitutions of M. Antoninus that laid the foundation of these persecutions. The fact of being a Christian was now a crime and punished, unless the accused denied their religion. Then come the persecutions at Smyrna, which some modern critics place in A.D. 167, ten years before the persecution of Lyon. The governors of the provinces under M. Antoninus might have found enough even in Trajan's rescript to warrant them in punishing Christians, and the fanaticism of the people would drive them to persecution, even if they were unwilling. But besides the fact of the Christians rejecting all the heathen ceremonies, we must not forget that they plainly maintain that all the heathen religions were false. The Christians thus declared war against the heathen rites, and it is hardly necessary to observe that this was a declaration of hostility against the Roman government, which tolerated all the various forms of superstition that existed in the empire, and could not consistently tolerate another religion, which declared that all the rest were false and all the splendid ceremonies of the empire were only a worship of devils.

If we had a true ecclesiastical history, we should know how the Roman emperors attempted to check the new religion; how they enforced their principle of finally punishing Christians, simply as Christians, which Justin in his Apology affirms that they did, and I have no doubt that he tells the truth; how far popular clamor and riots went in this matter, and how far many fanatical and ignorant Christians—for there were many such—contributed to excite the fanaticism on the other side and to embitter the quarrel between the Roman government and the new religion. Our extant ecclesiastical histories are manifestly falsified, and what truth they contain is grossly exaggerated; but the fact is certain that in the time of M. Antoninus the heathen populations were in open hostility to the Christians, and that under Antoninus' rule men were put to death because they were Christians. Eusebius, in the preface to his fifth book, remarks that in the seventeenth year of Antoninus' reign, in some parts of the world, the persecution of the Christians became more violent, and that it proceeded from the populace in the cities; and he adds, in his usual style of exaggeration, that we may infer from what took place in a single nation that myriads of martyrs were made in the habitable earth. The nation which he alludes to is Gallia; and he then proceeds to give the letters of the churches of Vienna and Lugdunum. It is probable that he has assimilated the true cause of the persecutions, the fanaticism of the populace, and that both governors and emperor had a great deal of trouble with these disturbances. How far Marcus was cognizant of these cruel proceedings we do not know, for the historical records of his reign are very defective. He did not make the rule against the Christians, for Trajan did that; and if we admit that he would have been willing to let the Christians alone, we cannot affirm that it was in his power, for it would be a great mistake to suppose that Antoninus had the unlimited authority which some modern sovereigns have had. His power was limited by certain constitutional forms, by the Senate, and by the precedents of his predecessors. We cannot admit that such a man was an active persecutor, for there is no evidence that he was, though it is certain that he had no good opinion of the Christians, as appears from his own words. But he knew nothing of them except their hostility to the Roman religion, and he probably thought that they were dangerous to the state, notwithstanding the professions, false or true, of some of the Apologists. So much I have said, because it would be unfair not to state all that can be urged against a man whom his contemporaries and subsequent ages venerated as a model of virtue and benevolence. If I admitted the genuineness of some documents, he would be altogether clear from the charge of even allowing any persecutions; but as I seek the truth and am sure that they are false, I leave him to bear whatever blame is his due. I add that it is quite certain that Antoninus did not derive any of his ethical principles from a religion of which he knew nothing.

There is no doubt that the Emperor's Reflections—or his Meditations, as they are generally named—is a genuine work. In the first book he speaks of himself, his family, and his teachers; and in other books he mentions himself. Suidas (v. Μάρκος) notices a work of Antoninus in twelve books, which he names the "conduct of his own life;" and he cites the book under several words in his Dictionary, giving the emperor's name, but not the title of the work. There are also passages cited by Suidas from Antoninus without mention of the emperor's name. The true title of the work is unknown. Xylander, who published the first edition of this book (Zürich, 1558, 8vo, with a Latin version), used a manuscript which contained the twelve books, but it is not known where the manuscript is now. The only other complete manuscript which is known to exist is in the Vatican library, but it has no title and no inscriptions of the several books: the eleventh only has the inscription, Μάρκου αὐτοκράτορος marked with an asterisk. The other Vatican manuscripts and the three Florentine contain only excerpts from the emperor's book. All the titles of the excerpts nearly agree with that which Xylander prefixed to his edition, Μάρκου 'Αντωνίνου Αὐτοκράτορος τῶν εἰς ἑαυτὸν βιβλία ιβ. This title has been used by all subsequent editors. We cannot tell whether Antoninus divided his work into books or somebody else did it. If the inscriptions at the end of the first and second books are genuine, he may have made the division himself.

It is plain that the emperor wrote down his thoughts or reflections as the occasions arose; and since they were intended for his own use, it is no improbable conjecture that he left a complete copy behind him written with his own hand; for it is not likely that so diligent a man would use the labor of a transcriber for such a purpose, and expose his most secret thoughts to any other eye. He may have also intended the book for his son Commodus, who however had no taste for his father's philosophy. Some careful hand preserved the precious volume; and a work by Antoninus is mentioned by other late writers besides Suidas.

Many critics have labored on the text of Antoninus. The most complete edition is that by Thomas Gataker, 1652, 4to. The second edition of Gataker was superintended by George Stanhope, 1697, 4to. There is also an edition of 1704. Gataker made and suggested many good corrections, and he also made a new Latin version, which is not a very good specimen of Latin, but it generally expresses the sense of the original, and often better than some of the more recent translations. He added in the margin opposite to each paragraph references to the other parallel passages; and he wrote a commentary, one of the most complete that has been written on any ancient author. This commentary contains the editor's exposition of the more difficult passages, and quotations from all the Greek and Roman writers for the illustration of the text. It is a wonderful monument of learning and labor, and certainly no Englishman has yet done anything like it. At the end of his preface the editor says that he wrote it at Rotherhithe near London, in a severe winter, when he was in the seventy-eighth year of his age, 1651—a time when Milton, Selden, and other great men of the Commonwealth time were living; and the great French scholar Saumaise (Salmasius), with whom Gataker corresponded and received help from him for his edition of Antoninus. The Greek test has also been edited by J. M. Schultz, Leipzig, 1802, 8vo; and by the learned Greek Adamantinus Corais, Paris, 1816, 8vo. The text of Schultz was republished by Tauchnitz, 1821.

There are English, German, French, Italian, and Spanish translations of M. Antoninus, and there may be others. I have not seen all the English translations. There is one by Jeremy Collier, 1702, 8vo, a most coarse and vulgar copy of the original. The latest French translation by Alexis Pierron in the collection of Charpentier is better than Dacier's, which has been honored with an Italian version (Udine, 1772). There is an Italian version (1675), which I have not seen. It is by a cardinal. "A man illustrious in the church, the Cardinal Francis Barberini the elder, nephew of Pope Urban VIII., occupied the last years of his life in translating into his native language the thoughts of the Roman emperor, in order to diffuse among the faithful, the fertilizing and vivifying seeds. He dedicated this translation to his soul, to make it, as he says in his energetic style, redder than his purple at the sight of the virtues of this Gentile" (Pierron, Preface).

I have made this translation at intervals after having used the book for many years. It is made from the Greek, but I have not always followed one text; and I have occasionally compared other versions with my own. I made this translation for my own use, because I found that it was worth the labor; but it may be useful to others also; and therefore, I determined to print it. As the original is sometimes very difficult to understand and still more difficult to translate, it is not possible that I have always avoided error. But I believe that I have not often missed the meaning, and those who will take the trouble to compare the translation with the original should not hastily conclude that I am wrong, if they do not agree with me. Some passages do give the meaning, though at first sight they may not appear to do so; and when I differ from the translators, I think that in some places they are wrong, and in other places I am sure that they are. I have placed in some passages a †, which indicates corruption in the text or great uncertainty in the meaning. I could have made the language more easy and flowing, but I have preferred a ruder style as being better suited to express the character of the original; and sometimes the obscurity which may appear in the version is a fair copy of the obscurity of the Greek. If I should ever revise this version, I would gladly make use of any corrections which may be suggested. I have added an index of some of the Greek terms with the corresponding English. If I have not given the best words for the Greek, I have done the best that I could; and in the text I have always given the same translation of the same word.

The last reflection of the Stoic philosophy that I have observed is in Simplicius' Commentary on the Enchiridion of Epictetus. Simplicius was not a Christian, and such a man was not likely to be converted at a time when Christianity was grossly corrupted. But he was a really religious man, and he concludes his commentary with a prayer to the Deity which no Christian could improve. From the time of Zeno to Simplicius, a period of about nine hundred years, the Stoic philosophy formed the characters of some of the best and greatest men. Finally, it became extinct, and we hear no more of it till the revival of letters in Italy. Angelo Poliziano met with two very inaccurate and incomplete manuscripts of Epictetus' Enchiridion, which he translated into Latin and dedicated to his great patron Lorenzo de' Medici, in whose collection he had found the book. Poliziano's version was printed in the first Bâle edition of the Enchiridion, A. D. 1531 (apud And. Cratandrum). Poliziano recommends the Enchiridion to Lorenzo as a work well suited to his temper, and useful in the difficulties by which he was surrounded.

Epictetus and Antoninus have had readers ever since they were first printed. The little book of Antoninus has been the companion of some great men. Machiavelli's Art of War and Marcus Antoninus were the two books which were used when he was a young man by Captain John Smith, and he could not have found two writers better fitted to form the character of a soldier and a man. Smith is almost unknown and forgotten in England, his native country, but not in America, where he saved the young colony of Virginia. He was great in his heroic mind and his deeds in arms, but greater still in the nobleness of his character. For a man's greatness lies not in wealth and station, as the vulgar believe, nor yet in his intellectual capacity, which is often associated with the meanest moral character, the most abject servility to those in high places, and arrogance to the poor and lowly; but a man's true greatness lies in the consciousness of an honest purpose in life, founded on a just estimate of himself and everything else, on frequent self-examination, and a steady obedience to the rule which he knows to be right, without troubling himself, as the emperor says he should not, about what others may think or say, or whether they do or do not do that which he thinks and says and does.

George Long

BOOK ONE

1

From my grandfather Verus I learned good morals and the government of my temper.

2

From the reputation and remembrance of my father, modesty and a manly character.

3

From my mother, piety and beneficence, and abstinence, not only from evil deeds, but even from evil thoughts; and further, simplicity in my way of living, far removed from the habits of the rich.

4

From my great-grandfather, not to have frequented public schools, and to have had good teachers at home, and to know that on such things a man should spend liberally.

5

From my governor, to be neither of the green nor of the blue party at the games in the Circus, nor a partizan either of the Parmularius or the Scutarius at the gladiators' fights; from him too I learned endurance of labour, and to want little, and to work with my own hands, and not to meddle with other people's affairs, and not to be ready to listen to slander.

6

From Diognetus, not to busy myself about trifling things, and not to give credit to what was said by miracle-workers and jugglers about incantations and the driving away of daemons and such things; and not to breed quails for fighting, nor to give myself up passionately to such things; and to endure freedom of speech; and to have become intimate with philosophy; and to have been a hearer, first of Bacchius, then of Tandasis and Marcianus; and to have written dialogues in my youth; and to have desired a plank bed and skin, and whatever else of the kind belongs to the Grecian discipline.

7

From Rusticus I received the impression that my character required improvement and discipline; and from him I learned not to be led astray to sophistic emulation, nor to writing on speculative matters, nor to delivering little hortatory orations, nor to showing myself off as a man who practises much discipline, or does benevolent acts in order to make a display; and to abstain from rhetoric, and poetry, and fine writing; and not to walk about in the house in my outdoor dress, nor to do other things of the kind; and to write my letters with simplicity, like the letter which Rusticus wrote from Sinuessa to my mother; and with respect to those who have offended me by words, or done me wrong, to be easily disposed to be pacified and reconciled, as soon as they have shown a readiness to be reconciled; and to read carefully, and not to be satisfied with a superficial understanding of a book; nor hastily to give my assent to those who talk overmuch; and I am indebted to him for being acquainted with the *Discourses* of Epictetus, which he communicated to me out of his own collection.

8

From Apollonius I learned freedom of will and undeviating steadiness of purpose; and to look to nothing else, not even for a moment, except to reason; and to be always the same, in sharp pains, on the occasion of the loss of a child, and in long illness; and to see clearly in a living example that the same man can be both most resolute and yielding, and not peevish in giving his instruction; and to have had before my eyes a man who clearly considered his experience and his skill in expounding philosophical principles as the smallest of his merits; and from him I learned how to receive from friends what are esteemed favours, without being either humbled by them or letting them pass unnoticed.

9

From Sextus, a benevolent disposition, and the example of a family governed in a fatherly manner, and the idea of living conformably to nature; and gravity without affectation, and to look carefully after the interests of friends, and to tolerate ignorant persons, and those who form opinions without consideration: he had the power of readily accommodating himself to all, so that intercourse with him was more agreeable than any flattery; and at the same time he was most highly venerated by those who associated with him: and he had the faculty both of discovering and ordering, in an intelligent and methodical way, the principles necessary for life; and he never showed anger or any other passion, but was entirely free from passion, and also most affectionate; and he could express approbation without noisy display, and he possessed much knowledge without ostentation.

10

From Alexander the grammarian, to refrain from fault-finding, and not in a reproachful way to chide those who uttered any barbarous or solecistic or strange-sounding expression; but dexterously to introduce the very expression which ought to have been used, and in the way of answer or giving confirmation, or joining in an inquiry about the thing itself, not about the word, or by some other fit suggestion.

11

From Fronto I learned to observe what envy, and duplicity, and hypocrisy are in a tyrant, and that generally those among us who are called Patricians are rather deficient in paternal affection.

12

From Alexander the Platonic, not frequently nor without necessity to say to any one, or to write in a letter, that I have no leisure; nor continually to excuse the neglect of duties required by our relation to those with whom we live, by alleging urgent occupations.

13

From Catulus, not to be indifferent when a friend finds fault, even if he should find fault without reason, but to try to restore him to his usual disposition; and to be ready to speak well of teachers, as it is reported of Domitius and Athenodotus; and to love my children truly.

14

From my brother Severus, to love my kin, and to love truth, and to love justice; and through him I learned to know Thrasea, Helvidius, Cato, Dion, Brutus; and from him I received the idea of a polity in which there is the same law for all, a polity administered with regard to equal rights and equal freedom of speech, and the idea of a kingly government which respects most of all the freedom of the governed; I learned from him also consistency and undeviating steadiness in my regard for philosophy; and a disposition to do good, and to give to others readily, and to cherish good hopes, and to believe that I am loved by my friends; and in him I observed no concealment of his opinions with respect to those whom he condemned, and that his friends had no need to conjecture what he wished or did not wish, but it was quite plain.

15

From Maximus I learned self-government, and not to be led aside by anything; and cheerfulness in all circumstances, as well as in illness; and a just admixture in the moral character of sweetness and dignity, and to do what was set before me without complaining. I observed that everybody believed that he thought as he spoke, and that in all that he did he never had any bad intention; and he never showed amazement and surprise, and was never in a hurry, and never put off doing a thing, nor was perplexed nor dejected, nor did he ever laugh to disguise his vexation, nor, on the other hand, was he ever passionate or suspicious. He was accustomed to do acts of beneficence, and was ready to forgive, and was free from all falsehood; and he presented the appearance of a man who could not be diverted from right rather than of a man who had been improved. I observed, too, that no man could ever think that he was despised by Maximus, or ever venture to think himself a better man. He had also the art of being humorous in an agreeable way.

16

In my father I observed mildness of temper, and unchangeable resolution in the things which he had determined after due deliberation; and no vainglory in those things which men call honours; and a love of labour and perseverance; and a readiness to listen to those who had anything to propose for the common weal; and undeviating firmness in giving to every man according to his deserts; and a knowledge derived from experience of the occasions for vigorous action and for remission. And I observed that he had overcome all passion for boys; and he considered himself no more than any other citizen; and he released his friends from all obligation to sup with him or to attend him of necessity when he went abroad, and those who had failed to accompany him, by reason of any urgent circumstances, always found him the same. I observed too his habit of careful inquiry in all matters of deliberation, and his persistency, and that he never stopped his investigation through being satisfied with appearances which first present themselves; and that his disposition was to keep his friends, and not to be soon tired of them, nor yet to be extravagant in his affection; and to be satisfied on all occasions, and cheerful; and to foresee things a long way off, and to provide for the smallest without display; and to check immediately popular applause and all flattery; and to be ever watchful over the things which were necessary for the administration of the empire, and to be a good manager of the expenditure, and patiently to endure the blame which he got for such conduct; and he was neither superstitious with respect to the gods, nor did he court men by gifts or by trying to please them, or by flattering the populace; but he showed sobriety in all things and firmness, and never any mean thoughts or action, nor love of novelty. And the things which conduce in any way to the commodity of life, and of which fortune gives an abundant supply, he used without arrogance and without excusing himself; so that when he had them, he enjoyed them without affectation, and when he had them not, he did not want them. No one could ever say of him that he was either a sophist or a home-bred flippant slave or a pedant; but every one acknowledged him to be a man ripe, perfect, above flattery, able to manage his own and other men's affairs. Besides this, he honoured those who were true philosophers, and he did not reproach those who pretended to be philosophers, nor yet was he easily led by them. He was also easy in conversation, and he made himself agreeable without any offensive affectation. He took a reasonable care of his body's health, not as one who was greatly attached to life, nor out of regard to personal appearance, nor yet in a careless way, but so that, through his own attention, he very seldom stood in need of the physician's art or of medicine or external applications. He was most ready to give way without envy to those who possessed any particular faculty, such as that of eloquence or knowledge of the law or of morals, or of anything else; and he gave them his help, that each might enjoy reputation according to his deserts; and he always acted conformably to the institutions of his country, without showing any affectation of doing so. Further, he was not fond of change nor unsteady, but he loved to stay in the same places, and to employ himself about the same things; and after his paroxysms of headache he came immediately fresh and vigorous to his usual occupations. His secrets were not but very few and very rare, and these only about public matters; and he showed prudence and economy in the exhibition of the public spectacles and the construction of public buildings, his donations to the people, and in such things, for he was a man who looked to what ought to be done, not to the reputation which is got by a man's acts. He did not take the bath at unseasonable hours; he was not fond of building houses, nor curious about what he ate, nor about the texture and colour of his clothes, nor about the beauty of his slaves. His dress came from Lorium, his villa on the coast, and from Lanuvium generally. We know how he behaved to the toll-collector at Tusculum who asked his pardon; and such was all his behaviour. There was in him nothing harsh, nor implacable, nor violent, nor, as one may say, anything carried to the sweating point; but he examined all things severally, as if he had abundance of time, and without confusion, in an orderly way, vigorously and consistently. And that might be applied to him which is recorded of Socrates, that he was able both to abstain from, and to enjoy, those things which many are too weak to abstain from, and cannot enjoy without excess. But to be strong enough both to bear the one and to be sober in the other is the mark of a man who has a perfect and invincible soul, such as he showed in the illness of Maximus.

17

To the gods I am indebted for having good grandfathers, good parents, a good sister, good teachers, good associates, good kinsmen and friends, nearly everything good. Further, I owe it to the gods that I was not hurried into any offence against any of them, though I had a disposition which, if opportunity had offered, might have led me to do something of this kind; but, through their favour, there never was such a concurrence of circumstances as put me to the trial. Further, I am thankful to the gods that I was not longer brought up with my grandfather's concubine, and that I preserved the flower of my youth, and that I did not make proof of my virility before the proper season, but even deferred the time; that I was subjected to a ruler and a father who was able to take away all pride from me, and to bring me to the knowledge that it is possible for a man to live in a palace without wanting either guards or embroidered dresses, or torches and statues, and such-like show; but that it is in such a man's power to bring himself very near to the fashion of a private person, without being for this reason either meaner in thought, or more remiss in action, with respect to the things which must be done for the public interest in a manner that befits a ruler. I thank the gods for giving me such a brother, who was able by his moral character to rouse me to vigilance over myself, and who, at the same time, pleased me by his respect and affection; that my children have not been stupid nor deformed in body; that I did not make more proficiency in rhetoric, poetry, and the other studies, in which I should perhaps have been completely engaged, if I had seen that I was making progress in them; that I made haste to place those who brought me up in the station of honour, which they seemed to desire, without putting them off with hope of my doing it some time after, because they were then still young; that I knew Apollonius, Rusticus, Maximus; that I received clear and frequent impressions about living according to nature, and what kind of a life that is, so that, so far as depended on the gods, and their gifts, and help, and inspirations, nothing hindered me from forthwith living according to nature, though I still fall short of it through my own fault, and through not observing the admonitions of the gods, and, I may almost say, their direct instructions; that my body has held out so long in such a kind of life; that I never touched either Benedicta or Theodotus, and that, after having fallen into amatory passions, I was cured; and, though I was often out of humour with Rusticus, I never did anything of which I had occasion to repent; that, though it was my mother's fate to die young, she spent the last years of her life with me; that, whenever I wished to help any man in his need, or on any other occasion, I was never told that I had not the means of doing it; and that to myself the same necessity never happened, to receive anything from another; that I have such a wife, so obedient, and so affectionate, and so simple; that I had abundance of good masters for my children; and that remedies have been shown to me by dreams, both others, and against bloodspitting and giddiness . . .; and that, when I had an inclination to philosophy, I did not fall into the hands of any sophist, and that I did not waste my time on writers of histories, or in the resolution of syllogisms, or occupy myself about the investigation of appearances in the heavens; for all these things require the help of the gods and fortune.

BOOK TWO

Among the Quadi at the Granua

1

Begin the morning by saying to thyself, I shall meet with the busy-body, the ungrateful, arrogant, deceitful, envious, unsocial. All these things happen to them by reason of their ignorance of what is good and evil. But I who have seen the nature of the good that it is beautiful, and of the bad that it is ugly, and the nature of him who does wrong, that it is akin to me, not only of the same blood or seed, but that it participates in the same intelligence and the same portion of the divinity, I can neither be injured by any of them, for no one can fix on me what is ugly, nor can I be angry with my kinsman, nor hate him, For we are made for co-operation, like feet, like hands, like eyelids, like the rows of the upper and lower teeth. To act against one another then is contrary to nature; and it is acting against one another to be vexed and to turn away.

2

Whatever this is that I am, it is a little flesh and breath, and the ruling part. Throw away thy books; no longer distract thyself: it is not allowed; but as if thou wast now dying, despise the flesh; it is blood and bones and a network, a contexture of nerves, veins, and arteries. See the breath also, what kind of a thing it is, air, and not always the same, but every moment sent out and again sucked in. The third then is the ruling part: consider thus: Thou art an old man; no longer let this be a slave, no longer be pulled by the strings like a puppet to unsocial movements, no longer either be dissatisfied with thy present lot, or shrink from the future.

3

All that is from the gods is full of Providence. That which is from fortune is not separated from nature or without an interweaving and involution with the things which are ordered by Providence. From thence all things flow; and there is besides necessity, and that which is for the advantage of the whole universe, of which thou art a part. But that is good for every part of nature which the nature of the whole brings, and what serves to maintain this nature. Now the universe is preserved, as by the changes of the elements so by the changes of things compounded of the elements. Let these principles be enough for thee, let them always be fixed opinions. But cast away the thirst after books, that thou mayest not die murmuring, but cheerfully, truly, and from thy heart thankful to the gods.

4

Remember how long thou hast been putting off these things, and how often thou hast received an opportunity from the gods, and yet dost not use it. Thou must now at last perceive of what universe thou art a part, and of what administrator of the universe thy existence is an efflux, and that a limit of time is fixed for thee, which if thou dost not use for clearing away the clouds from thy mind, it will go and thou wilt go, and it will never return.

5

Every moment think steadily as a Roman and a man to do what thou hast in hand with perfect and simple dignity, and feeling of affection, and freedom, and justice; and to give thyself relief from all other thoughts.

And thou wilt give thyself relief, if thou doest every act of thy life as if it were the last, laying aside all carelessness and passionate aversion from the commands of reason, and all hypocrisy, and self-love, and discontent with the portion which has been given to thee. Thou seest how few the things are, the which if a man lays hold of, he is able to live a life which flows in quiet, and is like the existence of the gods; for the gods on their part will require nothing more from him who observes these things.

6

Do wrong to thyself, do wrong to thyself, my soul; but thou wilt no longer have the opportunity of honouring thyself. Every man's life is sufficient. But thine is nearly finished, though thy soul reverences not itself but places thy felicity in the souls of others.

7

Do the things external which fall upon thee distract thee? Give thyself time to learn something new and good, and cease to be whirled around. But then thou must also avoid being carried about the other way. For those too are triflers who have wearied themselves in life by their activity, and yet have no object to which to direct every movement, and, in a word, all their thoughts.

8

Through not observing what is in the mind of another a man has seldom been seen to be unhappy; but those who do not observe the movements of their own minds must of necessity be unhappy.

9

This thou must always bear in mind, what is the nature of the whole, and what is my nature, and how this is related to that, and what kind of a part it is of what kind of a whole; and that there is no one who hinders thee from always doing and saying the things which are according to the nature of which thou art a part.

10

Theophrastus, in his comparison of bad acts—such a comparison as one would make in accordance with the common notions of mankind—says, like a true philosopher, that the offences which are committed through desire are more blameable than those which are committed through anger. For he who is excited by anger seems to turn away from reason with a certain pain and unconscious contraction; but he who offends through desire, being overpowered by pleasure, seems to be in a manner more intemperate and more womanish in his offences. Rightly then, and in a way worthy of philosophy, he said that the offence which is committed with pleasure is more blameable than that which is committed with pain; and on the whole the one is more like a person who has been first wronged and through pain is compelled to be angry; but the other is moved by his own impulse to do wrong, being carried towards doing something by desire.

11

Since it is possible that thou mayest depart from life this very moment, regulate every act and thought accordingly. But to go away from among men, if there are gods, is not a thing to be afraid of, for the gods will not involve thee in evil; but if indeed they do not exist, or if they have no concern about human affairs, what is it to me to live in a universe devoid of gods or devoid of Providence? But in truth they do exist, and they do care for human things, and they have put all the means in man's power to enable him not to fall into real evils. And as to the rest, if there was anything evil, they would have provided for this also, that it should be altogether in a man's power not to fall into it. Now that which does not make a man worse, how can it make a man's life worse? But neither through ignorance, nor having the knowledge, but not the power to guard against or correct these things, is it possible that the nature of the universe has overlooked them; nor is it possible that it has made so great a mistake, either through want of power or want of skill, that good and evil should happen indiscriminately to the good and the bad. But death certainly, and life, honour and dishonour, pain and pleasure, all these things equally happen to good men and bad, being things which make us neither better nor worse. Therefore they are neither good nor evil.

12

How quickly all things disappear, in the universe the bodies themselves, but in time the remembrance of them; what is the nature of all sensible things, and particularly those which attract with the bait of pleasure or terrify by pain, or are noised abroad by vapoury fame; how worthless, and contemptible, and sordid, and perishable, and dead they are—all this it is the part of the intellectual faculty to observe. To observe too who these are whose opinions and voices give reputation; what death is, and the fact that, if a man looks at it in itself, and by the abstractive power of reflection resolves into their parts all the things which present themselves to the imagination in it, he will then consider it to be nothing else than an operation of nature; and if any one is afraid of an operation of nature, he is a child. This, however, is not only an operation of nature, but it is also a thing which conduces to the purposes of nature. To observe too how man comes near to the deity, and by what part of him, and when this part of man is so disposed.

13

Nothing is more wretched than a man who traverses everything in a round, and pries into the things beneath the earth, as the poet says, and seeks by conjecture what is in the minds of his neighbours, without perceiving that it is sufficient to attend to the daemon within him, and to reverence it sincerely. And reverence of the daemon consists in keeping it pure from passion and thoughtlessness, and dissatisfaction with what comes from gods and men. For the things from the gods merit veneration for their excellence; and the things from men should be dear to us by reason of kinship; and sometimes even, in a manner, they move our pity by reason of men's ignorance of good and bad; this defect being not less than that which deprives us of the power of distinguishing things that are white and black.

14

Though thou shouldst be going to live three thousand years, and as many times ten thousand years, still remember that no man loses any other life than this which he now lives, nor lives any other than this which he now loses. The longest and shortest are thus brought to the same. For the present is the same to all, though that which perishes is not the same; and so that which is lost appears to be a mere moment. For a man cannot lose either the past or the future: for what a man has not, how can any one take this from him? These two things then thou must bear in mind; the one, that all things from eternity are of like forms and come round in a circle, and that it makes no difference whether a man shall see the same things during a hundred years or two hundred, or an infinite time; and the second, that the longest liver and he who will die soonest lose just the same. For the present is the only thing of which a man can be deprived, if it is true that this is the only thing which he has, and that a man cannot lose a thing if he has it not.

15

Remember that all is opinion. For what was said by the Cynic Monimus is manifest: and manifest too is the use of what was said, if a man receives what may be got out of it as far as it is true.

16

The soul of man does violence to itself, first of all, when it becomes an abscess and, as it were, a tumour on the universe, so far as it can. For to be vexed at anything which happens is a separation of ourselves from nature, in some part of which the natures of all other things are contained. In the next place, the soul does violence to itself when it turns away from any man, or even moves towards him with the intention of injuring, such as are the souls of those who are angry. In the third place, the soul does violence to itself when it is overpowered by pleasure or by pain. Fourthly, when it plays a part, and does or says anything insincerely and untruly. Fifthly, when it allows any act of its own and any movement to be without an aim, and does anything thoughtlessly and without considering what it is, it being right that even the smallest things be done with reference to an end; and the end of rational animals is to follow the reason and the law of the most ancient city and polity.

17

Of human life the time is a point, and the substance is in a flux, and the perception dull, and the composition of the whole body subject to putrefaction, and the soul a whirl, and fortune hard to divine, and fame a thing devoid of judgement. And, to say all in a word, everything which belongs to the body is a stream, and what belongs to the soul is a dream and vapour, and life is a warfare and a stranger's sojourn, and after-fame is oblivion. What then is that which is able to conduct a man? One thing and only one, philosophy. But this consists in keeping the daemon within a man free from violence and unharmed, superior to pains and pleasures, doing nothing without purpose, nor yet falsely and with hypocrisy, not feeling the need of another man's doing or not doing anything; and besides, accepting all that happens, and all that is allotted, as coming from thence, wherever it is, from whence he himself came; and, finally, waiting for death with a cheerful mind, as being nothing else than a dissolution of the elements of which every living being is compounded. But if there is no harm to the elements themselves in each continually changing into another, why should a man have any apprehension about the change and dissolution of all the elements? For it is according to nature, and nothing is evil which is according to nature.

BOOK THREE

This in Carnuntum

1

We ought to consider not only that our life is daily wasting away and a smaller part of it is left, but another thing also must be taken into the account, that if a man should live longer, it is quite uncertain whether the understanding will still continue sufficient for the comprehension of things, and retain the power of contemplation which strives to acquire the knowledge of the divine and the human. For if he shall begin to fall into dotage, perspiration and nutrition and imagination and appetite, and whatever else there is of the kind, will not fail; but the power of making use of ourselves, and filling up the measure of our duty, and clearly separating all appearances, and considering whether a man should now depart from life, and whatever else of the kind absolutely requires a disciplined reason, all this is already extinguished. We must make haste then, not only because we are daily nearer to death, but also because the conception of things and the understanding of them cease first.

2

We ought to observe also that even the things which follow after the things which are produced according to nature contain something pleasing and attractive. For instance, when bread is baked some parts are split at the surface, and these parts which thus open, and have a certain fashion contrary to the purpose of the baker's art, are beautiful in a manner, and in a peculiar way excite a desire for eating. And again, figs, when they are quite ripe, gape open; and in the ripe olives the very circumstance of their being near to rottenness adds a peculiar beauty to the fruit. And the ears of corn bending down, and the lion's eyebrows, and the foam which flows from the mouth of wild boars, and many other things—though they are far from being beautiful, if a man should examine them severally—still, because they are consequent upon the things which are formed by nature, help to adorn them, and they please the mind; so that if a man should have a feeling and deeper insight with respect to the things which are produced in the universe, there is hardly one of those which follow by way of consequence which will not seem to him to be in a manner disposed so as to give pleasure. And so he will see even the real gaping jaws of wild beasts with no less pleasure than those which painters and sculptors show by imitation; and in an old woman and an old man he will be able to see a certain maturity and comeliness; and the attractive loveliness of young persons he will be able to look on with chaste eyes; and many such things will present themselves, not pleasing to every man, but to him only who has become truly familiar with nature and her works.

3

Hippocrates after curing many diseases himself fell sick and died. The Chaldaei foretold the deaths of many, and then fate caught them too. Alexander, and Pompeius, and Caius Caesar, after so often completely destroying whole cities, and in battle cutting to pieces many ten thousands of cavalry and infantry, themselves too at last departed from life. Heraclitus, after so many speculations on the conflagration of the universe, was filled with water internally and died smeared all over with mud. And lice destroyed Democritus; and other lice killed Socrates. What means all this? Thou hast embarked, thou hast made the voyage, thou art come to shore; get out. If indeed to another life, there is no want of gods, not even there. But if to a state without sensation, thou wilt cease to be held by pains and pleasures, and to be a slave to the vessel, which is as much inferior as that which serves it is superior: for the one is intelligence and deity; the other is earth and corruption.

4

Do not waste the remainder of thy life in thoughts about others, when thou dost not refer thy thoughts to some object of common utility. For thou losest the opportunity of doing something else when thou hast such thoughts as these, What is such a person doing, and why, and what is he saying, and what is he thinking of, and what is he contriving, and whatever else of the kind makes us wander away from the observation of our own ruling power. We ought then to check in the series of our thoughts everything that is without a purpose and useless, but most of all the over-curious feeling and the malignant; and a man should use himself to think of those things only about which if one should suddenly ask, What hast thou now in thy thoughts? With perfect openness thou mightest, immediately answer, This or That; so that from thy words it should be plain that everything in thee is simple and benevolent, and such as befits a social animal, and one that cares not for thoughts about pleasure or sensual enjoyments at all, nor has any rivalry or envy and suspicion, or anything else for which thou wouldst blush if thou shouldst say that thou hadst it in thy mind. For the man who is such and no longer delays being among the number of the best, is like a priest and minister of the gods, using too the deity which is planted within him, which makes the man uncontaminated by pleasure, unharmed by any pain, untouched by any insult, feeling no wrong, a fighter in the noblest fight, one who cannot be overpowered by any passion, dyed deep with justice, accepting with all his soul everything which happens and is assigned to him as his portion; and not often, nor yet without great necessity and for the general interest, imagining what another says, or does, or thinks. For it is only what belongs to himself that he makes the matter for his activity; and he constantly thinks of that which is allotted to himself out of the sum total of things, and he makes his own acts fair, and he is persuaded that his own portion is good. For the lot which is assigned to each man is carried along with him and carries him along with it. And he remembers also that every rational animal is his kinsman, and that to care for all men is according to man's nature; and a man should hold on to the opinion not of all, but of those only who confessedly live according to nature. But as to those who live not so, he always bears in mind what kind of men they are both at home and from home, both by night and by day, and what they are, and with what men they live an impure life. Accordingly, he does not value at all the praise which comes from such men, since they are not even satisfied with themselves.

5

Labour not unwillingly, nor without regard to the common interest, nor without due consideration, nor with distraction; nor let studied ornament set off thy thoughts, and be not either a man of many words, or busy about too many things. And further, let the deity which is in thee be the guardian of a living being, manly and of ripe age, and engaged in matter political, and a Roman, and a ruler, who has taken his post like a man waiting for the signal which summons him from life, and ready to go, having need neither of oath nor of any man's testimony. Be cheerful also, and seek not external help nor the tranquility which others give. A man then must stand erect, not be kept erect by others.

6

If thou findest in human life anything better than justice, truth, temperance, fortitude, and, in a word, anything better than thy own mind's self-satisfaction in the things which it enables thee to do according to right reason, and in the condition that is assigned to thee without thy own choice; if, I say, thou seest anything better than this, turn to it with all thy soul, and enjoy that which thou hast found to be the best. But if nothing appears to be better than the deity which is planted in thee, which has subjected to itself all thy appetites, and carefully examines all the impressions, and, as Socrates said, has detached itself from the persuasions of sense, and has submitted itself to the gods, and cares for mankind; if thou findest everything else smaller and of less value than this, give place to nothing else, for if thou dost once diverge and incline to it, thou wilt no longer without distraction be able to give the preference to that good thing which is thy proper possession and thy own; for it is not right that anything of any other kind, such as praise from the many, or power, or enjoyment of pleasure, should come into competition with that which is rationally and politically or practically good. All these things, even though they may seem to adapt themselves to the better things in a small degree, obtain the superiority all at once, and carry us away. But do thou, I say, simply and freely choose the better, and hold to it.—But that which is useful is the better.—Well then, if it is useful to thee as a rational being, keep to it; but if it is only useful to thee as an animal, say so, and maintain thy judgement without arrogance: only take care that thou makest the inquiry by a sure method.

7

Never value anything as profitable to thyself which shall compel thee to break thy promise, to lose thy self-respect, to hate any man, to suspect, to curse, to act the hypocrite, to desire anything which needs walls and curtains: for he who has preferred to everything intelligence and daemon and the worship of its excellence, acts no tragic part, does not groan, will not need either solitude or much company; and, what is chief of all, he will live without either pursuing or flying from death; but whether for a longer or a shorter time he shall have the soul inclosed in the body, he cares not at all: for even if he must depart immediately, he will go as readily as if he were going to do anything else which can be done with decency and order; taking care of this only all through life, that his thoughts turn not away from anything which belongs to an intelligent animal and a member of a civil community.

8

In the mind of one who is chastened and purified thou wilt find no corrupt matter, nor impurity, nor any sore skinned over. Nor is his life incomplete when fate overtakes him, as one may say of an actor who leaves the stage before ending and finishing the play. Besides, there is in him nothing servile, nor affected, nor too closely bound to other things, nor yet detached from other things, nothing worthy of blame, nothing which seeks a hiding-place.

9

Reverence the faculty which produces opinion. On this faculty it entirely depends whether there shall exist in thy ruling part any opinion inconsistent with nature and the constitution of the rational animal. And this faculty promises freedom from hasty judgement, and friendship towards men, and obedience to the gods.

10

Throwing away then all things, hold to these only which are few; and besides bear in mind that every man lives only this present time, which is an indivisible point, and that all the rest of his life is either past or it is uncertain. Short then is the time which every man lives, and small the nook of the earth where he lives; and short too the longest posthumous fame, and even this only continued by a succession of poor human beings, who will very soon die, and who know not even themselves, much less him who died long ago.

11

To the aids which have been mentioned let this one still be added:—Make for thyself a definition or description of the thing which is presented to thee, so as to see distinctly what kind of a thing it is in its substance, in its nudity, in its complete entirety, and tell thyself its proper name, and the names of the things of which it has been compounded, and into which it will be resolved. For nothing is so productive of elevation of mind as to be able to examine methodically and truly every object which is presented to thee in life, and always to look at things so as to see at the same time what kind of universe this is, and what kind of use everything performs in it, and what value everything has with reference to the whole, and what with reference to man, who is a citizen of the highest city, of which all other cities are like families; what each thing is, and of what it is composed, and how long it is the nature of this thing to endure which now makes an impression on me, and what virtue I have need of with respect to it, such as gentleness, manliness, truth, fidelity, simplicity, contentment, and the rest. Wherefore, on every occasion a man should say: this comes from God; and this is according to the apportionment and spinning of the thread of destiny, and such-like coincidence and chance; and this is from one of the same stock, and a kinsman and partner, one who knows not however what is according to his nature. But I know; for this reason I behave towards him according to the natural law of fellowship with benevolence and justice. At the same time however in things indifferent I attempt to ascertain the value of each.

12

If thou workest at that which is before thee, following right reason seriously, vigorously, calmly, without allowing anything else to distract thee, but keeping thy divine part pure, as if thou shouldst be bound to give it back immediately; if thou holdest to this, expecting nothing, fearing nothing, but satisfied with thy present activity according to nature, and with heroic truth in every word and sound which thou utterest, thou wilt live happy. And there is no man who is able to prevent this.

13

As physicians have always their instruments and knives ready for cases which suddenly require their skill, so do thou have principles ready for the understanding of things divine and human, and for doing everything, even the smallest, with a recollection of the bond which unites the divine and human to one another. For neither wilt thou do anything well which pertains to man without at the same time having a reference to things divine; nor the contrary.

14

No longer wander at hazard; for neither wilt thou read thy own memoirs, nor the acts of the ancient Romans and Hellenes, and the selections from books which thou wast reserving for thy old age. Hasten then to the end which thou hast before thee, and throwing away idle hopes, come to thy own aid, if thou carest at all for thyself, while it is in thy power.

15

They know not how many things are signified by the words stealing, sowing, buying, keeping quiet, seeing what ought to be done; for this is not effected by the eyes, but by another kind of vision.

16

Body, soul, intelligence: to the body belong sensations, to the soul appetites, to the intelligence principles. To receive the impressions of forms by means of appearances belongs even to animals; to be pulled by the strings of desire belongs both to wild beasts and to men who have made themselves into women, and to a Phalaris and a Nero: and to have the intelligence that guides to the things which appear suitable belongs also to those who do not believe in the gods, and who betray their country, and do their impure deeds when they have shut the doors. If then everything else is common to all that I have mentioned, there remains that which is peculiar to the good man, to be pleased and content with what happens, and with the thread which is spun for him; and not to defile the divinity which is planted in his breast, nor disturb it by a crowd of images, but to preserve it tranquil, following it obediently as a god, neither saying anything contrary to the truth, nor doing anything contrary to justice. And if all men refuse to believe that he lives a simple, modest, and contented life, he is neither angry with any of them, nor does he deviate from the way which leads to the end of life, to which a man ought to come pure, tranquil, ready to depart, and without any compulsion perfectly reconciled to his lot.

BOOK FOUR

1

That which rules within, when it is according to nature, is so affected with respect to the events which happen, that it always easily adapts itself to that which is and is presented to it. For it requires no definite material, but it moves towards its purpose, under certain conditions however; and it makes a material for itself out of that which opposes it, as fire lays hold of what falls into it, by which a small light would have been extinguished: but when the fire is strong, it soon appropriates to itself the matter which is heaped on it, and consumes it, and rises higher by means of this very material.

2

Let no act be done without a purpose, nor otherwise than according to the perfect principles of art.

3

Men seek retreats for themselves, houses in the country, sea-shores, and mountains; and thou too art wont to desire such things very much. But this is altogether a mark of the most common sort of men, for it is in thy power whenever thou shalt choose to retire into thyself. For nowhere either with more quiet or more freedom from trouble does a man retire than into his own soul, particularly when he has within him such thoughts that by looking into them he is immediately in perfect tranquility; and I affirm that tranquility is nothing else than the good ordering of the mind. Constantly then give to thyself this retreat, and renew thyself; and let thy principles be brief and fundamental, which, as soon as thou shalt recur to them, will be sufficient to cleanse the soul completely, and to send thee back free from all discontent with the things to which thou returnest. For with what art thou discontented? With the badness of men? Recall to thy mind this conclusion, that rational animals exist for one another, and that to endure is a part of justice, and that men do wrong involuntarily; and consider how many already, after mutual enmity, suspicion, hatred, and fighting, have been stretched dead, reduced to ashes; and be quiet at last.—But perhaps thou art dissatisfied with that which is assigned to thee out of the universe.—Recall to thy recollection this alternative; either there is providence or atoms, fortuitous concurrence of things; or remember the arguments by which it has been proved that the world is a kind of political community, and be quiet at last.—But perhaps corporeal things will still fasten upon thee.—Consider then further that the mind mingles not with the breath, whether moving gently or violently, when it has once drawn itself apart and discovered its own power, and think also of all that thou hast heard and assented to about pain and pleasure, and be quiet at last.—But perhaps the desire of the thing called fame will torment thee.—See how soon everything is forgotten, and look at the chaos of infinite time on each side of the present, and the emptiness of applause, and the changeableness and want of judgement in those who pretend to give praise, and the narrowness of the space within which it is circumscribed, and be quiet at last. For the whole earth is a point, and how small a nook in it is this thy dwelling, and how few are there in it, and what kind of people are they who will praise thee.

This then remains: Remember to retire into this little territory of thy own, and above all do not distract or strain thyself, but be free, and look at things as a man, as a human being, as a citizen, as a mortal. But among the things readiest to thy hand to which thou shalt turn, let there be these, which are two. One is that things do not touch the soul, for they are external and remain immovable; but our perturbations come only from the opinion which is within. The other is that all these things, which thou seest, change immediately and will no longer be; and constantly bear in mind how many of these changes thou hast already witnessed. The universe is transformation: life is opinion.

4

If our intellectual part is common, the reason also, in respect of which we are rational beings, is common: if this is so, common also is the reason which commands us what to do, and what not to do; if this is so, there is a common law also; if this is so, we are fellow-citizens; if this is so, we are members of some political community; if this is so, the world is in a manner a state. For of what other common political community will any one say that the whole human race are members? And from thence, from this common political community comes also our very intellectual faculty and reasoning faculty and our capacity for law; or whence do they come? For as my earthly part is a portion given to me from certain earth, and that which is watery from another element, and that which is hot and fiery from some peculiar source (for nothing comes out of that which is nothing, as nothing also returns to non-existence), so also the intellectual part comes from some source.

5

Death is such as generation is, a mystery of nature; a composition out of the same elements, and a decomposition into the same; and altogether not a thing of which any man should be ashamed, for it is not contrary to the nature of a reasonable animal, and not contrary to the reason of our constitution.

6

It is natural that these things should be done by such persons, it is a matter of necessity; and if a man will not have it so, he will not allow the fig-tree to have juice. But by all means bear this in mind, that within a very short time both thou and he will be dead; and soon not even your names will be left behind.

7

Take away thy opinion, and then there is taken away the complaint, "I have been harmed." Take away the complaint, "I have been harmed," and the harm is taken away.

8

That which does not make a man worse than he was, also does not make his life worse, nor does it harm him either from without or from within.

9

The nature of that which is universally useful has been compelled to do this.

10

Consider that everything which happens, happens justly, and if thou observest carefully, thou wilt find it to be so. I do not say only with respect to the continuity of the series of things, but with respect to what is just, and as if it were done by one who assigns to each thing its value. Observe then as thou hast begun; and whatever thou doest, do it in conjunction with this, the being good, and in the sense in which a man is properly understood to be good. Keep to this in every action.

11

Do not have such an opinion of things as he has who does thee wrong, or such as he wishes thee to have, but look at them as they are in truth.

12

A man should always have these two rules in readiness; the one, to do only whatever the reason of the ruling and legislating faculty may suggest for the use of men; the other, to change thy opinion, if there is any one at hand who sets thee right and moves thee from any opinion. But this change of opinion must proceed only from a certain persuasion, as of what is just or of common advantage, and the like, not because it appears pleasant or brings reputation.

13

Hast thou reason? I have.—Why then dost not thou use it? For if this does its own work, what else dost thou wish?

14

Thou hast existed as a part. Thou shalt disappear in that which produced thee; but rather thou shalt be received back into its seminal principle by transmutation.

15

Many grains of frankincense on the same altar: one falls before, another falls after; but it makes no difference.

16

Within ten days thou wilt seem a god to those to whom thou art now a beast and an ape, if thou wilt return to thy principles and the worship of reason.

17

Do not act as if thou wert going to live ten thousand years. Death hangs over thee. While thou livest, while it is in thy power, be good.

18

How much trouble he avoids who does not look to see what his neighbour says or does or thinks, but only to what he does himself, that it may be just and pure; or as Agathon says, look not round at the depraved morals of others, but run straight along the line without deviating from it.

19

He who has a vehement desire for posthumous fame does not consider that every one of those who remember him will himself also die very soon; then again also they who have succeeded them, until the whole remembrance shall have been extinguished as it is transmitted through men who foolishly admire and perish. But suppose that those who will remember are even immortal, and that the remembrance will be immortal, what then is this to thee? And I say not what is it to the dead, but what is it to the living? What is praise except indeed so far as it has a certain utility? For thou now rejectest unseasonably the gift of nature, clinging to something else . . .

20

Everything which is in any way beautiful is beautiful in itself, and terminates in itself, not having praise as part of itself. Neither worse then nor better is a thing made by being praised. I affirm this also of the things which are called beautiful by the vulgar, for example, material things and works of art. That which is really beautiful has no need of anything; not more than law, not more than truth, not more than benevolence or modesty. Which of these things is beautiful because it is praised, or spoiled by being blamed? Is such a thing as an emerald made worse than it was, if it is not praised? Or gold, ivory, purple, a lyre, a little knife, a flower, a shrub?

21

If souls continue to exist, how does the air contain them from eternity?—But how does the earth contain the bodies of those who have been buried from time so remote? For as here the mutation of these bodies after a certain continuance, whatever it may be, and their dissolution make room for other dead bodies; so the souls which are removed into the air after subsisting for some time are transmuted and diffused, and assume a fiery nature by being received into the seminal intelligence of the universe, and in this way make room for the fresh souls which come to dwell there. And this is the answer which a man might give on the hypothesis of souls continuing to exist. But we must not only think of the number of bodies which are thus buried, but also of the number of animals which are daily eaten by us and the other animals. For what a number is consumed, and thus in a manner buried in the bodies of those who feed on them! And nevertheless this earth receives them by reason of the changes of these bodies into blood, and the transformations into the aerial or the fiery element.

What is the investigation into the truth in this matter? The division into that which is material and that which is the cause of form, the formal.

22

Do not be whirled about, but in every movement have respect to justice, and on the occasion of every impression maintain the faculty of comprehension or understanding.

23

Everything harmonizes with me, which is harmonious to thee, O Universe. Nothing for me is too early nor too late, which is in due time for thee. Everything is fruit to me which thy seasons bring, O Nature: from thee are all things, in thee are all things, to thee all things return. The poet says, Dear city of Cecrops; and wilt not thou say, Dear city of Zeus?

24

Occupy thyself with few things, says the philosopher, if thou wouldst be tranquil.—But consider if it would not be better to say, Do what is necessary, and whatever the reason of the animal which is naturally social requires, and as it requires. For this brings not only the tranquility which comes from doing well, but also that which comes from doing few things. For the greatest part of what we say and do being unnecessary, if a man takes this away, he will have more leisure and less uneasiness. Accordingly on every occasion a man should ask himself, Is this one of the unnecessary things? Now a man should take away not only unnecessary acts, but also, unnecessary thoughts, for thus superfluous acts will not follow after.

25

Try how the life of the good man suits thee, the life of him who is satisfied with his portion out of the whole, and satisfied with his own just acts and benevolent disposition.

26

Hast thou seen those things? Look also at these. Do not disturb thyself. Make thyself all simplicity. Does any one do wrong? It is to himself that he does the wrong. Has anything happened to thee? Well; out of the universe from the beginning everything which happens has been apportioned and spun out to thee. In a word, thy life is short. Thou must turn to profit the present by the aid of reason and justice. Be sober in thy relaxation.

27

Either it is a well-arranged universe or a chaos huddled together, but still a universe. But can a certain order subsist in thee, and disorder in the All? And this too when all things are so separated and diffused and sympathetic.

28

A black character, a womanish character, a stubborn character, bestial, childish, animal, stupid, counterfeit, scurrilous, fraudulent, tyrannical.

29

If he is a stranger to the universe who does not know what is in it, no less is he a stranger who does not know what is going on in it. He is a runaway, who flies from social reason; he is blind, who shuts the eyes of the understanding; he is poor, who has need of another, and has not from himself all things which are useful for life. He is an abscess on the universe who withdraws and separates himself from the reason of our common nature through being displeased with the things which happen, for the same nature produces this, and has produced thee too: he is a piece rent asunder from the state, who tears his own soul from that of reasonable animals, which is one.

30

The one is a philosopher without a tunic, and the other without a book: here is another half naked: Bread I have not, he says, and I abide by reason.—And I do not get the means of living out of my learning, and I abide by my reason.

31

Love the art, poor as it may be, which thou hast learned, and be content with it; and pass through the rest of life like one who has intrusted to the gods with his whole soul all that he has, making thyself neither the tyrant nor the slave of any man.

32

Consider, for example, the times of Vespasian. Thou wilt see all these things, people marrying, bringing up children, sick, dying, warring, feasting, trafficking, cultivating the ground, flattering, obstinately arrogant, suspecting, plotting, wishing for some to die, grumbling about the present, loving, heaping up treasure, desiring counsulship, kingly power. Well then, that life of these people no longer exists at all. Again, remove to the times of Trajan. Again, all is the same. Their life too is gone. In like manner view also the other epochs of time and of whole nations, and see how many after great efforts soon fell and were resolved into the elements. But chiefly thou shouldst think of those whom thou hast thyself known distracting themselves about idle things, neglecting to do what was in accordance with their proper constitution, and to hold firmly to this and to be content with it. And herein it is necessary to remember that the attention given to everything has its proper value and proportion. For thus thou wilt not be dissatisfied, if thou appliest thyself to smaller matters no further than is fit.

33

The words which were formerly familiar are now antiquated: so also the names of those who were famed of old, are now in a manner antiquated, Camillus, Caeso, Volesus, Leonnatus, and a little after also Scipio and Cato, then Augustus, then also Hadrian and Antoninus. For all things soon pass away and become a mere tale, and complete oblivion soon buries them. And I say this of those who have shone in a wondrous way. For the rest, as soon as they have breathed out their breath, they are gone, and no man speaks of them. And, to conclude the matter, what is even an eternal remembrance? A mere nothing. What then is that about which we ought to employ our serious pains? This one thing, thoughts just, and acts social, and words which never lie, and a disposition which gladly accepts all that happens, as necessary, as usual, as flowing from a principle and source of the same kind.

34

Willingly give thyself up to Clotho, one of the Fates, allowing her to spin thy thread into whatever things she pleases.

35

Everything is only for a day, both that which remembers and that which is remembered.

36

Observe constantly that all things take place by change, and accustom thyself to consider that the nature of the Universe loves nothing so much as to change the things which are and to make new things like them. For everything that exists is in a manner the seed of that which will be. But thou art thinking only of seeds which are cast into the earth or into a womb: but this is a very vulgar notion.

37

Thou wilt soon die, and thou art not yet simple, not free from perturbations, nor without suspicion of being hurt by external things, nor kindly disposed towards all; nor dost thou yet place wisdom only in acting justly.

38

Examine men's ruling principles, even those of the wise, what kind of things they avoid, and what kind they pursue.

39

What is evil to thee does not subsist in the ruling principle of another; nor yet in any turning and mutation of thy corporeal covering. Where is it then? It is in that part of thee in which subsists the power of forming opinions about evils. Let this power then not form such opinions, and all is well. And if that which is nearest to it, the poor body, is burnt, filled with matter and rottenness, nevertheless let the part which forms opinions about these things be quiet, that is, let it judge that nothing is either bad or good which can happen equally to the bad man and the good. For that which happens equally to him who lives contrary to nature and to him who lives according to nature, is neither according to nature nor contrary to nature.

40

Constantly regard the universe as one living being, having one substance and one soul; and observe how all things have reference to one perception, the perception of this one living being; and how all things act with one movement; and how all things are the cooperating causes of all things which exist; observe too the continuous spinning of the thread and the contexture of the web.

41

Thou art a little soul bearing about a corpse, as Epictetus used to say.

42

It is no evil for things to undergo change, and no good for things to subsist in consequence of change.

43

Time is like a river made up of the events which happen, and a violent stream; for as soon as a thing has been seen, it is carried away, and another comes in its place, and this will be carried away too.

44

Everything which happens is as familiar and well known as the rose in spring and the fruit in summer; for such is disease, and death, and calumny, and treachery, and whatever else delights fools or vexes them.

45

In the series of things those which follow are always aptly fitted to those which have gone before; for this series is not like a mere enumeration of disjointed things, which has only a necessary sequence, but it is a rational connection: and as all existing things are arranged together harmoniously, so the things which come into existence exhibit no mere succession, but a certain wonderful relationship.

46

Always remember the saying of Heraclitus, that the death of earth is to become water, and the death of water is to become air, and the death of air is to become fire, and reversely. And think too of him who forgets whither the way leads, and that men quarrel with that with which they are most constantly in communion, the reason which governs the universe; and the things which daily meet with seem to them strange: and consider that we ought not to act and speak as if we were asleep, for even in sleep we seem to act and speak; and that we ought not, like children who learn from their parents, simply to act and speak as we have been taught.

47

If any god told thee that thou shalt die tomorrow, or certainly on the day after tomorrow, thou wouldst not care much whether it was on the third day or on the morrow, unless thou wast in the highest degree mean-spirited—for how small is the difference?—So think it no great thing to die after as many years as thou canst name rather than tomorrow.

48

Think continually how many physicians are dead after often contracting their eyebrows over the sick; and how many astrologers after predicting with great pretensions the deaths of others; and how many philosophers after endless discourses on death or immortality; how many heroes after killing thousands; and how many tyrants who have used their power over men's lives with terrible insolence as if they were immortal; and how many cities are entirely dead, so to speak, Helice and Pompeii and Herculaneum, and others innumerable. Add to the reckoning all whom thou hast known, one after another. One man after burying another has been laid out dead, and another buries him: and all this in a short time. To conclude, always observe how ephemeral and worthless human things are, and what was yesterday a little mucus tomorrow will be a mummy or ashes. Pass then through this little space of time conformably to nature, and end thy journey in content, just as an olive falls off when it is ripe, blessing nature who produced it, and thanking the tree on which it grew.

49

Be like the promontory against which the waves continually break, but it stands firm and tames the fury of the water around it.

Unhappy am I because this has happened to me.—Not so, but happy am I, though this has happened to me, because I continue free from pain, neither crushed by the present nor fearing the future. For such a thing as this might have happened to every man; but every man would not have continued free from pain on such an occasion. Why then is that rather a misfortune than this a good fortune? And dost thou in all cases call that a man's misfortune, which is not a deviation from man's nature? And does a thing seem to thee to be a deviation from man's nature, when it is not contrary to the will of man's nature? Well, thou knowest the will of nature. Will then this which has happened prevent thee from being just, magnanimous, temperate, prudent, secure against inconsiderate opinions and falsehood; will it prevent thee from having modesty, freedom, and everything else, by the presence of which man's nature obtains all that is its own? Remember too on every occasion which leads thee to vexation to apply this principle: not that this is a misfortune, but that to bear it nobly is good fortune.

50

It is a vulgar, but still a useful help towards contempt of death, to pass in review those who have tenaciously stuck to life. What more then have they gained than those who have died early? Certainly they lie in their tombs somewhere at last, Cadicianus, Fabius, Julianus, Lepidus, or any one else like them, who have carried out many to be buried, and then were carried out themselves. Altogether the interval is small between birth and death; and consider with how much trouble, and in company with what sort of people and in what a feeble body this interval is laboriously passed. Do not then consider life a thing of any value. For look to the immensity of time behind thee, and to the time which is before thee, another boundless space. In this infinity then what is the difference between him who lives three days and him who lives three generations?

51

Always run to the short way; and the short way is the natural: accordingly say and do everything in conformity with the soundest reason. For such a purpose frees a man from trouble, and warfare, and all artifice and ostentatious display.

BOOK FIVE

1

In the morning when thou risest unwillingly, let this thought be present—I am rising to the work of a human being. Why then am I dissatisfied if I am going to do the things for which I exist and for which I was brought into the world? Or have I been made for this, to lie in the bed-clothes and keep myself warm?—But this is more pleasant.—Dost thou exist then to take thy pleasure, and not at all for action or exertion? Dost thou not see the little plants, the little birds, the ants, the spiders, the bees working together to put in order their several parts of the universe? And art thou unwilling to do the work of a human being, and dost thou not make haste to do that which is according to thy nature?—But it is necessary to take rest also.—It is necessary: however nature has fixed bounds to this too: she has fixed bounds both to eating and drinking, and yet thou goest beyond these bounds, beyond what is sufficient; yet in thy acts it is not so, but thou stoppest short of what thou canst do. So thou lovest not thyself, for if thou didst, thou wouldst love thy nature and her will. But those who love their several arts exhaust themselves in working at them unwashed and without food; but thou valuest thy own own nature less than the turner values the turning art, or the dancer the dancing art, or the lover of money values his money, or the vainglorious man his little glory. And such men, when they have a violent affection to a thing, choose neither to eat nor to sleep rather than to perfect the things which they care for. But are the acts which concern society more vile in thy eyes and less worthy of thy labour?

2

How easy it is to repel and to wipe away every impression which is troublesome or unsuitable, and immediately to be in all tranquility.

3

Judge every word and deed which are according to nature to be fit for thee; and be not diverted by the blame which follows from any people nor by their words, but if a thing is good to be done or said, do not consider it unworthy of thee. For those persons have their peculiar leading principle and follow their peculiar movement; which things do not thou regard, but go straight on, following thy own nature and the common nature; and the way of both is one.

4

I go through the things which happen according to nature until I shall fall and rest, breathing out my breath into that element out of which I daily draw it in, and falling upon that earth out of which my father collected the seed, and my mother the blood, and my nurse the milk; out of which during so many years I have been supplied with food and drink; which bears me when I tread on it and abuse it for so many purposes.

5

Thou sayest, Men cannot admire the sharpness of thy wits.—Be it so: but there are many other things of which thou canst not say, I am not formed for them by nature. Show those qualities then which are altogether in thy power, sincerity, gravity, endurance of labour, aversion to pleasure, contentment with thy portion and with few things, benevolence, frankness, no love of superfluity, freedom from trifling magnanimity. Dost thou not see how many qualities thou art immediately able to exhibit, in which there is no excuse of natural incapacity and unfitness, and yet thou still remainest voluntarily below the mark? Or art thou compelled through being defectively furnished by nature to murmur, and to be stingy, and to flatter, and to find fault with thy poor body, and to try to please men, and to make great display, and to be so restless in thy mind? No, by the gods: but thou mightest have been delivered from these things long ago. Only if in truth thou canst be charged with being rather slow and dull of comprehension, thou must exert thyself about this also, not neglecting it nor yet taking pleasure in thy dulness.

6

One man, when he has done a service to another, is ready to set it down to his account as a favour conferred. Another is not ready to do this, but still in his own mind he thinks of the man as his debtor, and he knows what he has done. A third in a manner does not even know what he has done, but he is like a vine which has produced grapes, and seeks for nothing more after it has once produced its proper fruit. As a horse when he has run, a dog when he has tracked the game, a bee when it has made the honey, so a man when he has done a good act, does not call out for others to come and see, but he goes on to another act, as a vine goes on to produce again the grapes in season.—Must a man then be one of these, who in a manner act thus without observing it?—Yes.—But this very thing is necessary, the observation of what a man is doing: for, it may be said, it is characteristic of the social animal to perceive that he is working in a social manner, and indeed to wish that his social partner also should perceive it.—It is true what thou sayest, but thou dost not rightly understand what is now said: and for this reason thou wilt become one of those of whom I spoke before, for even they are misled by a certain show of reason. But if thou wilt choose to understand the meaning of what is said, do not fear that for this reason thou wilt omit any social act.

7

A prayer of the Athenians: Rain, rain, O dear Zeus, down on the ploughed fields of the Athenians and on the plains.

In truth we ought not to pray at all, or we ought to pray in this simple and noble fashion.

8

Just as we must understand when it is said, That Aesculapius prescribed to this man horse-exercise, or bathing in cold water or going without shoes; so we must understand it when it is said, That the nature of the universe prescribed to this man disease or mutilation or loss or anything else of the kind. For in the first case Prescribed means something like this: he prescribed this for this man as a thing adapted to procure health; and in the second case it means: That which happens to (or, suits) every man is fixed in a manner for him suitably to his destiny. For this is what we mean when we say that things are suitable to us, as the workmen say of squared stones in walls or the pyramids, that they are suitable, when they fit them to one another in some kind of connexion. For there is altogether one fitness, harmony. And as the universe is made up out of all bodies to be such a body as it is, so out of all existing causes necessity (destiny) is made up to be such a cause as it is. And even those who are completely ignorant understand what I mean, for they say, It (necessity, destiny) brought this to such a person.—This then was brought and this was precribed to him. Let us then receive these things, as well as those which Aesculapius prescribes. Many as a matter of course even among his prescriptions are disagreeable, but we accept them in the hope of health. Let the perfecting and accomplishment of the things, which the common nature judges to be good, be judged by thee to be of the same kind as thy health. And so accept everything which happens, even if it seem disagreeable, because it leads to this, to the health of the universe and to the prosperity and felicity of Zeus (the universe). For he would not have brought on any man what he has brought, if it were not useful for the whole. Neither does the nature of anything, whatever it may be, cause anything which is not suitable to that which is directed by it. For two reasons then it is right to be content with that which happens to thee; the one, because it was done for thee and prescribed for thee, and in a manner had reference to thee, originally from the most ancient causes spun with thy destiny; and the other, because even that which comes severally to every man is to the power which administers the universe a cause of felicity and perfection, nay even of its very continuance. For the integrity of the whole is mutilated, if thou cuttest off anything whatever from the conjunction and the continuity either of the parts or of the causes. And thou dost cut off, as far as it is in thy power, when thou art dissatisfied, and in a manner triest to put anything out of the way.

9

Be not disgusted, nor discouraged, nor dissatisfied, if thou dost not succeed in doing everything according to right principles; but when thou bast failed, return back again, and be content if the greater part of what thou doest is consistent with man's nature, and love this to which thou returnest; and do not return to philosophy as if she were a master, but act like those who have sore eyes and apply a bit of sponge and egg, or as another applies a plaster, or drenching with water. For thus thou wilt not fail to obey reason, and thou wilt repose in it. And remember that philosophy requires only the things which thy nature requires; but thou wouldst have something else which is not according to nature.—It may be objected, Why what is more agreeable than this which I am doing?—But is not this the very reason why pleasure deceives us? And consider if magnanimity, freedom, simplicity, equanimity, piety, are not more agreeable. For what is more agreeable than wisdom itself, when thou thinkest of the security and the happy course of all things which depend on the faculty of understanding and knowledge?

10

Things are in such a kind of envelopment that they have seemed to philosophers, not a few nor those common philosophers, altogether unintelligible; nay even to the Stoics themselves they seem difficult to understand. And all our assent is changeable; for where is the man who never changes? Carry thy thoughts then to the objects themselves, and consider how short-lived they are and worthless, and that they may be in the possession of a filthy wretch or a whore or a robber. Then turn to the morals of those who live with thee, and it is hardly possible to endure even the most agreeable of them, to say nothing of a man being hardly able to endure himself. In such darkness then and dirt and in so constant a flux both of substance and of time, and of motion and of things moved, what there is worth being highly prized or even an object of serious pursuit, I cannot imagine. But on the contrary it is a man's duty to comfort himself, and to wait for the natural dissolution and not to be vexed at the delay, but to rest in these principles only: the one, that nothing will happen to me which is not conformable to the nature of the universe; and the other, that it is in my power never to act contrary to my god and daemon: for there is no man who will compel me to this.

11

About what am I now employing my own soul? On every occasion I must ask myself this question, and inquire, what have I now in this part of me which they call the ruling principle? And whose soul have I now? That of a child, or of a young man, or of a feeble woman, or of a tyrant, or of a domestic animal, or of a wild beast?

12

What kind of things those are which appear good to the many, we may learn even from this. For if any man should conceive certain things as being really good, such as prudence, temperance, justice, fortitude, he would not after having first conceived these endure to listen to anything which should not be in harmony with what is really good. But if a man has first conceived as good the things which appear to the many to be good, he will listen and readily receive as very applicable that which was said by the comic writer. Thus even the many perceive the difference. For were it not so, this saying would not offend and would not be rejected in the first case, while we receive it when it is said of wealth, and of the means which further luxury and fame, as said fitly and wittily. Go on then and ask if we should value and think those things to be good, to which after their first conception in the mind the words of the comic writer might be aptly applied—that he who has them, through pure abundance has not a place to ease himself in.

13

I am composed of the formal and the material; and neither of them will perish into non-existence, as neither of them came into existence out of non-existence. Every part of me then will be reduced by change into some part of the universe, and that again will change into another part of the universe, and so on for ever. And by consequence of such a change I too exist, and those who begot me, and so on for ever in the other direction. For nothing hinders us from saying so, even if the universe is administered according to definite periods of revolution.

14

Reason and the reasoning art (philosophy) are powers which are sufficient for themselves and for their own works. They move then from a first principle which is their own, and they make their way to the end which is proposed to them; and this is the reason why such acts are named catorthoseis or right acts, which word signifies that they proceed by the right road.

15

None of these things ought to be called a man's, which do not belong to a man, as man. They are not required of a man, nor does man's nature promise them, nor are they the means of man's nature attaining its end. Neither then does the end of man lie in these things, nor yet that which aids to the accomplishment of this end, and that which aids towards this end is that which is good. Besides, if any of these things did belong to man, it would not be right for a man to despise them and to set himself against them; nor would a man be worthy of praise who showed that he did not want these things, nor would he who stinted himself in any of them be good, if indeed these things were good. But now the more of these things a man deprives himself of, or of other things like them, or even when he is deprived of any of them, the more patiently he endures the loss, just in the same degree he is a better man.

16

Such as are thy habitual thoughts, such also will be the character of thy mind; for the soul is dyed by the thoughts. Dye it then with a continuous series of such thoughts as these: for instance, that where a man can live, there he can also live well. But he must live in a palace;—well then, he can also live well in a palace. And again, consider that for whatever purpose each thing has been constituted, for this it has been constituted, and towards this it is carried; and its end is in that towards which it is carried; and where the end is, there also is the advantage and the good of each thing. Now the good for the reasonable animal is society; for that we are made for society has been shown above. Is it not plain that the inferior exist for the sake of the superior? But the things which have life are superior to those which have not life, and of those which have life the superior are those which have reason.

17

To seek what is impossible is madness: and it is impossible that the bad should not do something of this kind.

18

Nothing happens to any man which he is not formed by nature to bear. The same things happen to another, and either because he does not see that they have happened or because he would show a great spirit he is firm and remains unharmed. It is a shame then that ignorance and conceit should be stronger than wisdom.

19

Things themselves touch not the soul, not in the least degree; nor have they admission to the soul, nor can they turn or move the soul: but the soul turns and moves itself alone, and whatever judgements it may think proper to make, such it makes for itself the things which present themselves to it.

20

In one respect man is the nearest thing to me, so far as I must do good to men and endure them. But so far as some men make themselves obstacles to my proper acts, man becomes to me one of the things which are indifferent, no less than the sun or wind or a wild beast. Now it is true that these may impede my action, but they are no impediments to my affects and disposition, which have the power of acting conditionally and changing: for the mind converts and changes every hindrance to its activity into an aid; and so that which is a hindrance is made a furtherance to an act; and that which is an obstacle on the road helps us on this road.

21

Reverence that which is best in the universe; and this is that which makes use of all things and directs all things. And in like manner also reverence that which is best in thyself; and this is of the same kind as that. For in thyself also, that which makes use of everything else, is this, and thy life is directed by this.

22

That which does no harm to the state, does no harm to the citizen. In the case of every appearance of harm apply this rule: if the state is not harmed by this, neither am I harmed. But if the state is harmed, thou must not be angry with him who does harm to the state. Show him where his error is.

23

Often think of the rapidity with which things pass by and disappear, both the things which are and the things which are produced. For substance is like a river in a continual flow, and the activities of things are in constant change, and the causes work in infinite varieties; and there is hardly anything which stands still. And consider this which is near to thee, this boundless abyss of the past and of the future in which all things disappear. How then is he not a fool who is puffed up with such things or plagued about them and makes himself miserable? for they vex him only for a time, and a short time.

24

Think of the universal substance, of which thou hast a very small portion; and of universal time, of which a short and indivisible interval has been assigned to thee; and of that which is fixed by destiny, and how small a part of it thou art.

25

Does another do me wrong? Let him look to it. He has his own disposition, his own activity. I now have what the universal nature wills me to have; and I do what my nature now wills me to do.

26

Let the part of thy soul which leads and governs be undisturbed by the movements in the flesh, whether of pleasure or of pain; and let it not unite with them, but let it circumscribe itself and limit those affects to their parts. But when these affects rise up to the mind by virtue of that other sympathy that naturally exists in a body which is all one, then thou must not strive to resist the sensation, for it is natural: but let not the ruling part of itself add to the sensation the opinion that it is either good or bad.

27

Live with the gods. And he does live with the gods who constantly shows to them, his own soul is satisfied with that which is assigned to him, and that it does all that the daemon wishes, which Zeus hath given to every man for his guardian and guide, a portion of himself. And this is every man's understanding and reason.

28

Art thou angry with him whose armpits stink? Art thou angry with him whose mouth smells foul? What good will this danger do thee? He has such a mouth, he has such arm-pits: it is necessary that such an emanation must come from such things—but the man has reason, it will be said, and he is able, if he takes pain, to discover wherein he offends—I wish thee well of thy discovery. Well then, and thou hast reason: by thy rational faculty stir up his rational faculty; show him his error, admonish him. For if he listens, thou wilt cure him, and there is no need of anger. Neither tragic actor nor whore . . .

29

As thou intendest to live when thou art gone out, . . . so it is in thy power to live here. But if men do not permit thee, then get away out of life, yet so as if thou wert suffering no harm. The house is smoky, and I quit it. Why dost thou think that this is any trouble? But so long as nothing of the kind drives me out, I remain, am free, and no man shall hinder me from doing what I choose; and I choose to do what is according to the nature of the rational and social animal.

30

The intelligence of the universe is social. Accordingly it has made the inferior things for the sake of the superior, and it has fitted the superior to one another. Thou seest how it has subordinated, co-ordinated and assigned to everything its proper portion, and has brought together into concord with one another the things which are the best.

31

How hast thou behaved hitherto to the gods, thy parents, brethren, children, teachers, to those who looked after thy infancy, to thy friends, kinsfolk, to thy slaves? Consider if thou hast hitherto behaved to all in such a way that this may be said of thee:

> Never has wronged a man in deed or word.

And call to recollection both how many things thou hast passed through, and how many things thou hast been able to endure: and that the history of thy life is now complete and thy service is ended: and how many beautiful things thou hast seen: and how many pleasures and pains thou hast despised; and how many things called honourable thou hast spurned; and to how many ill-minded folks thou hast shown a kind disposition.

32

Why do unskilled and ignorant souls disturb him who has skill and knowledge? What soul then has skill and knowledge? That which knows beginning and end, and knows the reason which pervades all substance and through all time by fixed periods (revolutions) administers the universe.

33

Soon, very soon, thou wilt be ashes, or a skeleton, and either a name or not even a name; but name is sound and echo. And the things which are much valued in life are empty and rotten and trifling, and like little dogs biting one another, and little children quarrelling, laughing, and then straightway weeping. But fidelity and modesty and justice and truth are fled

Up to Olympus from the wide-spread earth.

What then is there which still detains thee here? If the objects of sense are easily changed and never stand still, and the organs of perception are dull and easily receive false impressions; and the poor soul itself is an exhalation from blood. But to have good repute amidst such a world as this is an empty thing. Why then dost thou not wait in tranquility for thy end, whether it is extinction or removal to another state? And until that time comes, what is sufficient? Why, what else than to venerate the gods and bless them, and to do good to men, and to practise tolerance and self-restraint; but as to everything which is beyond the limits of the poor flesh and breath, to remember that this is neither thine nor in thy power.

34

Thou canst pass thy life in an equable flow of happiness, if thou canst go by the right way, and think and act in the right way. These two things are common both to the soul of God and to the soul of man, and to the soul of every rational being, not to be hindered by another; and to hold good to consist in the disposition to justice and the practice of it, and in this to let thy desire find its termination.

35

If this is neither my own badness, nor an effect of my own badness, and the common weal is not injured, why am I troubled about it? And what is the harm to the common weal?

36

Do not be carried along inconsiderately by the appearance of things, but give help to all according to thy ability and their fitness; and if they should have sustained loss in matters which are indifferent, do not imagine this to be a damage. For it is a bad habit. But as the old man, when he went away, asked back his foster-child's top, remembering that it was a top, so do thou in this case also.

When thou art calling out on the Rostra, hast thou forgotten, man, what these things are?—Yes; but they are objects of great concern to these people—wilt thou too then be made a fool for these things?

37

I was once a fortunate man, but I lost it, I know not how.—But fortunate means that a man has assigned to himself a good fortune: and a good fortune is good disposition of the soul, good emotions, good actions.

BOOK SIX

1

The substance of the universe is obedient and compliant; and the reason which governs it has in itself no cause for doing evil, for it has no malice, nor does it do evil to anything, nor is anything harmed by it. But all things are made and perfected according to this reason.

2

Let it make no difference to thee whether thou art cold or warm, if thou art doing thy duty; and whether thou art drowsy or satisfied with sleep; and whether ill-spoken of or praised; and whether dying or doing something else. For it is one of the acts of life, this act by which we die: it is sufficient then in this act also to do well what we have in hand.

3

Look within. Let neither the peculiar quality of anything nor its value escape thee.

4

All existing things soon change, and they will either be reduced to vapour, if indeed all substance is one, or they will be dispersed.

5

The reason which governs knows what its own disposition is, and what it does, and on what material it works.

6

The best way of avenging thyself is not to become like the wrong doer.

7

Take pleasure in one thing and rest in it, in passing from one social act to another social act, thinking of God.

8

The ruling principle is that which rouses and turns itself, and while it makes itself such as it is and such as it wills to be, it also makes everything which happens appear to itself to be such as it wills.

9

In conformity to the nature of the universe every single thing is accomplished, for certainly it is not in conformity to any other nature that each thing is accomplished, either a nature which externally comprehends this, or a nature which is comprehended within this nature, or a nature external and independent of this.

10

The universe is either a confusion, and a mutual involution of things, and a dispersion; or it is unity and order and providence. If then it is the former, why do I desire to tarry in a fortuitous combination of things and such a disorder? And why do I care about anything else than how I shall at last become earth? And why am I disturbed, for the dispersion of my elements will happen whatever I do. But if the other supposition is true, I venerate, and I am firm, and I trust in him who governs.

11

When thou hast been compelled by circumstances to be disturbed in a manner, quickly return to thyself and do not continue out of tune longer than the compulsion lasts; for thou wilt have more mastery over the harmony by continually recurring to it.

12

If thou hadst a step-mother and a mother at the same time, thou wouldst be dutiful to thy step-mother, but still thou wouldst constantly return to thy mother. Let the court and philosophy now be to thee step-mother and mother: return to philosophy frequently and repose in her, through whom what thou meetest with in the court appears to thee tolerable, and thou appearest tolerable in the court.

13

When we have meat before us and such eatables we receive the impression, that this is the dead body of a fish, and this is the dead body of a bird or of a pig; and again, that this Falernian is only a little grape juice, and this purple robe some sheep's wool dyed with the blood of a shell-fish: such then are these impressions, and they reach the things themselves and penetrate them, and so we see what kind of things they are. Just in the same way ought we to act all through life, and where there are things which appear most worthy of our approbation, we ought to lay them bare and look at their worthlessness and strip them of all the words by which they are exalted. For outward show is a wonderful perverter of thc reason, and when thou art most sure that thou art employed about things worth thy pains, it is then that it cheats thee most. Consider then what Crates says of Xenocrates himself.

14

Most of the things which the multitude admire are referred to objects of the most general kind, those which are held together by cohesion or natural organization, such as stones, wood, fig-trees, vines, olives. But those which are admired by men who are a little more reasonable are referred to the things which are held together by a living principle, as flocks, herds. Those which are admired by men who are still more instructed are the things which are held together by a rational soul, not however a universal soul, but rational so far as it is a soul skilled in some art, or expert in some other way, or simply rational so far as it possesses a number of slaves. But he who values rational soul, a soul universal and fitted for political life, regards nothing else except this; and above all things he keeps his soul in a condition and in an activity conformable to reason and social life, and he co-operates to this end with those who are of the same kind as himself.

15

Some things are hurrying into existence, and others are hurrying out of it; and of that which is coming into existence part is already extinguished. Motions and changes are continually renewing the world, just as the uninterrupted course of time is always renewing the infinite duration of ages. In this flowing stream then, on which there is no abiding, what is there of the things which hurry by on which a man would set a high price? It would be just as if a man should fall in love with one of the sparrows which fly by, but it has already passed out of sight. Something of this kind is the very life of every man, like the exhalation of the blood and the respiration of the air. For such as it is to have once drawn in the air and to have given it back, which we do every moment, just the same is it with the whole respiratory power, which thou didst receive at thy birth yesterday and the day before, to give it back to the element from which thou didst first draw it.

16

Neither is transpiration, as in plants, a thing to be valued, nor respiration, as in domesticated animals and wild beasts, nor the receiving of impressions by the appearances of things, nor being moved by desires as puppets by strings, nor assembling in herds, nor being nourished by food; for this is just like the act of separating and parting with the useless part of our food. What then is worth being valued? To be received with clapping of hands? No. Neither must we value the clapping of tongues, for the praise which comes from the many is a clapping of tongues. Suppose then that thou hast given up this worthless thing called fame, what remains that is worth valuing? This in my opinion, to move thyself and to restrain thyself in conformity to thy proper constitution, to which end both all employments and arts lead. For every art aims at this, that the thing which has been made should be adapted to the work for which it has been made; and both the vine-planter who looks after the vine, and the horse-breaker, and he who trains the dog, seek this end. But the education and the teaching of youth aim at something. In this then is the value of the education and the teaching. And if this is well, thou wilt not seek anything else. Wilt thou not cease to value many other things too? Then thou wilt be neither free, nor sufficient for thy own happiness, nor without passion. For of necessity thou must be envious, jealous, and suspicious of those who can take away those things, and plot against those who have that which is valued by thee. Of necessity a man must be altogether in a state of perturbation who wants any of these things; and besides, he must often find fault with the gods. But to reverence and honour thy own mind will make thee content with thyself, and in harmony with society, and in agreement with the gods, that is, praising all that they give and have ordered.

17

Above, below, all around are the movements of the elements. But the motion of virtue is in none of these: it is something more divine, and advancing by a way hardly observed it goes happily on its road.

18

How strangely men act. They will not praise those who are living at the same time and living with themselves; but to be themselves praised by posterity, by those whom they have never seen or ever will see, this they set much value on. But this is very much the same as if thou shouldst be grieved because those who have lived before thee did not praise thee.

19

If a thing is difficult to be accomplished by thyself, do not think that it is impossible for man: but if anything is possible for man and conformable to his nature, think that this can be attained by thyself too.

20

In the gymnastic exercises suppose that a man has torn thee with his nails, and by dashing against thy head has inflicted a wound. Well, we neither show any signs of vexation, nor are we offended, nor do we suspect him afterwards as a treacherous fellow; and yet we are on our guard against him, not however as an enemy, nor yet with suspicion, but we quietly get out of his way. Something like this let thy behaviour be in all the other parts of life; let us overlook many things in those who are like antagonists in the gymnasium. For it is in our power, as I said, to get out of the way, and to have no suspicion nor hatred.

21

If any man is able to convince me and show me that I do not think or act right, I will gladly change; for I seek the truth by which no man was ever injured. But he is injured who abides in his error and ignorance.

22

I do my duty: other things trouble me not; for they are either things without life, or things without reason, or things that have rambled and know not the way.

23

As to the animals which have no reason and generally all things and objects, do thou, since thou hast reason and they have none, make use of them with a generous and liberal spirit. But towards human beings, as they have reason, behave in a social spirit. And on all occasions call on the gods, and do not perplex thyself about the length of time in which thou shalt do this; for even three hours so spent are sufficient.

24

Alexander the Macedonian and his groom by death were brought to the same state; for either they were received among the same seminal principles of the universe, or they were alike dispersed among the atoms.

25

Consider how many things in the same indivisible time take place in each of us, things which concern the body and things which concern the soul: and so thou wilt not wonder if many more things, or rather all things which come into existence in that which is the one and all, which we call Cosmos, exist in it at the same time.

26

If any man should propose to thee the question, how the name Antoninus is written, wouldst thou with a straining of the voice utter each letter? What then if they grow angry, wilt thou be angry too? Wilt thou not go on with composure and number every letter? just so then in this life also remember that every duty is made up of certain parts. These it is thy duty to observe and without being disturbed or showing anger towards those who are angry with thee to go on thy way and finish that which is set before thee.

27

How cruel it is not to allow men to strive after the things which appear to them to be suitable to their nature and profitable! And yet in a manner thou dost not allow them to do this, when thou art vexed because they do wrong. For they are certainly moved towards things because they suppose them to be suitable to their nature and profitable to them.—But it is not so.—Teach them then, and show them without being angry.

28

Death is a cessation of the impressions through the senses, and of the pulling of the strings which move the appetites, and of the discursive movements of the thoughts, and of the service to the flesh.

29

It is a shame for the soul to be first to give way in this life, when thy body does not give way.

30

Take care that thou art not made into a Caesar, that thou art not dyed with this dye; for such things happen. Keep thyself then simple, good, pure, serious, free from affectation, a friend of justice, a worshipper of the gods, kind, affectionate, strenuous in all proper acts. Strive to continue to be such as philosophy wished to make thee. Reverence the gods, and help men. Short is life. There is only one fruit of this terrene life, a pious disposition and social acts. Do everything as a disciple of Antoninus. Remember his constancy in every act which was conformable to reason, and his evenness in all things, and his piety, and the serenity of his countenance, and his sweetness, and his disregard of empty fame, and his efforts to understand things; and how he would never let anything pass without having first most carefully examined it and clearly understood it; and how he bore with those who blamed him unjustly without blaming them in return; how he did nothing in a hurry; and how he listened not to calumnies, and how exact an examiner of manners and actions he was; and not given to reproach people, nor timid, nor suspicious, nor a sophist; and with how little he was satisfied, such as lodging, bed, dress, food, servants; and how laborious and patient; and how he was able on account of his sparing diet to hold out to the evening, not even requiring to relieve himself by any evacuations except at the usual hour; and his firmness and uniformity in his friendships; and how he tolerated freedom of speech in those who opposed his opinions; and the pleasure that he had when any man showed him anything better; and how religious he was without superstition. Imitate all this that thou mayest have as good a conscience, when thy last hour comes, as he had.

31

Return to thy sober senses and call thyself back; and when thou hast roused thyself from sleep and hast perceived that they were only dreams which troubled thee, now in thy waking hours look at these (the things about thee) as thou didst look at those (the dreams).

32

I consist of a little body and a soul. Now to this little body all things are indifferent, for it is not able to perceive differences. But to the understanding those things only are indifferent, which are not the works of its own activity. But whatever things are the works of its own activity, all these are in its power. And of these however only those which are done with reference to the present; for as to the future and the past activities of the mind, even these are for the present indifferent.

33

Neither the labour which the hand does nor that of the foot is contrary to nature, so long as the foot does the foot's work and the hand the hand's. So then neither to a man as a man is his labour contrary to nature, so long as it does the things of a man. But if the labour is not contrary to his nature, neither is it an evil to him.

34

How many pleasures have been enjoyed by robbers, patricides, tyrants.

35

Dost thou not see how the handicraftsmen accommodate themselves up to a certain point to those who are not skilled in their craft—nevertheless they cling to the reason (the principles) of their art and do not endure to depart from it? Is it not strange if the architect and the physician shall have more respect to the reason (the principles) of their own arts than man to his own reason, which is common to him and the gods?

36

Asia, Europe are corners of the universe: all the sea a drop in the universe; Athos a little clod of the universe: all the present time is a point in eternity. All things are little, changeable, perishable. All things come from thence, from that universal ruling power either directly proceeding or by way of sequence. And accordingly the lion's gaping jaws, and that which is poisonous, and every harmful thing, as a thorn, as mud, are after-products of the grand and beautiful. Do not then imagine that they are of another kind from that which thou dost venerate, but form a just opinion of the source of all.

37

He who has seen present things has seen all, both everything which has taken place from all eternity and everything which will be for time without end; for all things are of one kin and of one form.

38

Frequently consider the connexion of all things in the universe and their relation to one another. For in a manner all things are implicated with one another, and all in this way are friendly to one another; for one thing comes in order after another, and this is by virtue of the active movement and mutual conspiration and the unity of the substance.

39

Adapt thyself to the things with which thy lot has been cast: and the men among whom thou hast received thy portion, love them, but do it truly, sincerely.

40

Every instrument, tool, vessel, if it does that for which it has been made, is well, and yet he who made it is not there. But in the things which are held together by nature there is within and there abides in them the power which made them; wherefore the more is it fit to reverence this power, and to think, that, if thou dost live and act according to its will, everything in thee is in conformity to intelligence. And thus also in the universe the things which belong to it are in conformity to intelligence.

41

Whatever of the things which are not within thy power thou shalt suppose to be good for thee or evil, it must of necessity be that, if such a bad thing befall thee or the loss of such a good thing, thou wilt blame the gods, and hate men too, those who are the cause of the misfortune or the loss, or those who are suspected of being likely to be the cause; and indeed we do much injustice, because we make a difference between these things. But if we judge only those things which are in our power to be good or bad, there remains no reason either for finding fault with God or standing in a hostile attitude to man.

42

We are all working together to one end, some with knowledge and design, and others without knowing what they do; as men also when they are asleep, of whom it is Heraclitus, I think, who says that they are labourers and co-operators in the things which take place in the universe. But men co-operate after different fashions: and even those co-operate abundantly, who find fault with what happens and those who try to oppose it and to hinder it; for the universe had need even of such men as these. It remains then for thee to understand among what kind of workmen thou placest thyself; for he who rules all things will certainly make a right use of thee, and he will receive thee among some part of the co-operators and of those whose labours conduce to one end. But be not thou such a part as the mean and ridiculous verse in the play, which Chrysippus speaks of.

43

Does the sun undertake to do the work of the rain, or Aesculapius the work of the Fruit-bearer (the earth)? And how is it with respect to each of the stars, are they not different and yet they work together to the same end?

44

If the gods have determined about me and about the things which must happen to me, they have determined well, for it is not easy even to imagine a deity without forethought; and as to doing me harm, why should they have any desire towards that? For what advantage would result to them from this or to the whole, which is the special object of their providence? But if they have not determined about me individually, they have certainly determined about the whole at least, and the things which happen by way of sequence in this general arrangement I ought to accept with pleasure and to be content with them. But if they determine about nothing—which it is wicked to believe, or if we do believe it, let us neither sacrifice nor pray nor swear by them nor do anything else which we do as if the gods were present and lived with us—but if however the gods determine about none of the things which concern us, I am able to determine about myself, and I can inquire about that which is useful; and that is useful to every man which is conformable to his own constitution and nature. But my nature is rational and social; and my city and country, so far as I am Antoninus, is Rome, but so far as I am a man, it is the world. The things then which are useful to these cities are alone useful to me.

45

Whatever happens to every man, this is for the interest of the universal: this might be sufficient. But further thou wilt observe this also as a general truth, if thou dost observe, that whatever is profitable to any man is profitable also to other men. But let the word profitable be taken here in the common sense as said of things of the middle kind, neither good nor bad.

46

As it happens to thee in the amphitheatre and such places, that the continual sight of the same things and the uniformity make the spectacle wearisome, so it is in the whole of life; for all things above, below, are the same and from the same. How long then?

47

Think continually that all kinds of men and of all kinds of pursuits and of all nations are dead, so that thy thoughts come down even to Philistion and Phoebus and Origanion. Now turn thy thoughts to the other kinds of men. To that place then we must remove, where there are so many great orators, and so many noble philosophers, Heraclitus, Pythagoras, Socrates; so many heroes of former days, and so many generals after them, and tyrants; besides these, Eudoxus, Hipparchus, Archimedes, and other men of acute natural talents, great minds, lovers of labour, versatile, confident, mockers even of the perishable and ephemeral life of man, as Menippus and such as are like him. As to all these consider that they have long been in the dust. What harm then is this to them; and what to those whose names are altogether unknown? One thing here is worth a great deal, to pass thy life in truth and justice, with a benevolent disposition even to liars and unjust men.

48

When thou wishest to delight thyself, think of the virtues of those who live with thee; for instance, the activity of one, and the modesty of another, and the liberality of a third, and some other good quality of a fourth. For nothing delights so much as the examples of the virtues, when they are exhibited in the morals of those who live with us and present themselves in abundance, as far as is possible. Wherefore we must keep them before us.

49

Thou art not dissatisfied, I suppose, because thou weighest only so many litrae and not three hundred. Be not dissatisfied then that thou must live only so many years and not more; for as thou art satisfied with the amount of substance which has been assigned to thee, so be content with the time.

50

Let us try to persuade them (men). But act even against their will, when the principles of justice lead that way. If however any man by using force stands in thy way, betake thyself to contentment and tranquility, and at the same time employ the hindrance towards the exercise of some other virtue; and remember that thy attempt was with a reservation, that thou didst not desire to do impossibilities. What then didst thou desire?—Some such effort as this.—But thou attainest thy object, if the things to which thou wast moved are accomplished.

51

He who loves fame considers another man's activity to be his own good; and he who loves pleasure, his own sensations; but he who has understanding, considers his own acts to be his own good.

52

It is in our power to have no opinion about a thing, and not to be disturbed in our soul; for things themselves have no natural power to form our judgements.

53

Accustom thyself to attend carefully to what is said by another, and as much as it is possible, be in the speaker's mind.

54

That which is not good for the swarm, neither is it good for the bee.

55

If sailors abused the helmsman or the sick the doctor, would they listen to anybody else; or how could the helmsman secure the safety of those in the ship or the doctor the health of those whom he attends?

56

How many together with whom I came into the world are already gone out of it.

57

To the jaundiced honey tastes bitter, and to those bitten by mad dogs water causes fear; and to little children the ball is a fine thing. Why then am I angry? Dost thou think that a false opinion has less power than the bile in the jaundiced or the poison in him who is bitten by a mad dog?

58

No man will hinder thee from living according to the reason of thy own nature: nothing will happen to thee contrary to the reason of the universal nature.

59

What kind of people are those whom men wish to please, and for what objects, and by what kind of acts? How soon will time cover all things, and how many it has covered already.

BOOK SEVEN

1

What is badness? It is that which thou hast often seen. And on the occasion of everything which happens keep this in mind, that it is that which thou hast often seen. Everywhere up and down thou wilt find the same things, with which the old histories are filled, those of the middle ages and those of our own day; with which cities and houses are filled now. There is nothing new: all things are both familiar and short-lived.

2

How can our principles become dead, unless the impressions (thoughts) which correspond to them are extinguished? But it is in thy power continuously to fan these thoughts into a flame. I can have that opinion about anything, which I ought to have. If I can, why am I disturbed? The things which are external to my mind have no relation at all to my mind.—Let this be the state of thy affects, and thou standest erect. To recover thy life is in thy power. Look at things again as thou didst use to look at them; for in this consists the recovery of thy life.

3

The idle business of show, plays on the stage, flocks of sheep, herds, exercises with spears, a bone cast to little dogs, a bit of bread into fish-ponds, labourings of ants and burden-carrying, runnings about of frightened little mice, puppets pulled by stringsall alike. It is thy duty then in the midst of such things to show good humour and not a proud air; to understand however that every man is worth just so much as the things are worth about which he busies himself.

4

In discourse thou must attend to what is said, and in every movement thou must observe what is doing. And in the one thou shouldst see immediately to what end it refers, but in the other watch carefully what is the thing signified.

5

Is my understanding sufficient for this or not? If it is sufficient, I use it for the work as an instrument given by the universal nature. But if it is not sufficient, then either I retire from the work and give way to him who is able to do it better, unless there be some reason why I ought not to do so; or I do it as well as I can, taking to help me the man who with the aid of my ruling principle can do what is now fit and useful for the general good. For whatsoever either by myself or with another I can do, ought to be directed to this only, to that which is useful and well suited to society.

6

How many after being celebrated by fame have been given up to oblivion; and how many who have celebrated the fame of others have long been dead.

7

Be not ashamed to be helped; for it is thy business to do thy duty like a soldier in the assault on a town. How then, if being lame thou canst not mount up on the battlements alone, but with the help of another it is possible?

8

Let not future things disturb thee, for thou wilt come to them, if it shall be necessary, having with thee the same reason which now thou usest for present things.

9

All things are implicated with one another, and the bond is holy; and there is hardly anything unconnected with any other thing. For things have been co-ordinated, and they combine to form the same universe (order). For there is one universe made up of all things, and one God who pervades all things, and one substance, and one law, one common reason in all intelligent animals, and one truth; if indeed there is also one perfection for all animals which are of the same stock and participate in the same reason.

10

Everything material soon disappears in the substance of the whole; and everything formal (causal) is very soon taken back into the universal reason; and the memory of everything is very soon overwhelmed in time.

11

To the rational animal the same act is according to nature and according to reason.

12

Be thou erect, or be made erect.

13

Just as it is with the members in those bodies which are united in one, so it is with rational beings which exist separate, for they have been constituted for one co-operation. And the perception of this will be more apparent to thee, if thou often sayest to thyself that I am a member (*melos*) of the system of rational beings. But if (using the letter r) thou sayest that thou art a part (*meros*) thou dost not yet love men from thy heart; beneficence does not yet delight thee for its own sake; thou still doest it barely as a thing of propriety, and not yet as doing good to thyself.

14

Let there fall externally what will on the parts which can feel the effects of this fall. For those parts which have felt will complain, if they choose. But I, unless I think that what has happened is an evil, am not injured. And it is in my power not to think so.

15

Whatever any one does or says, I must be good, just as if the gold, or the emerald, or the purple were always saying this, Whatever any one does or says, I must be emerald and keep my colour.

16

The ruling faculty does not disturb itself; I mean, does not frighten itself or cause itself pain. But if any one else can frighten or pain it, let him do so. For the faculty itself will not by its own opinion turn itself into such ways. Let the body itself take care, if it can, that is suffer nothing, and let it speak, if it suffers. But the soul itself, that which is subject to fear, to pain, which has completely the power of forming an opinion about these things, will suffer nothing, for it will never deviate into such a judgement. The leading principle in itself wants nothing, unless it makes a want for itself; and therefore it is both free from perturbation and unimpeded, if it does not disturb and impede itself.

17

Eudaemonia (happiness) is a good daemon, or a good thing. What then art thou doing here, O imagination? Go away, I entreat thee by the gods, as thou didst come, for I want thee not. But thou art come according to thy old fashion. I am not angry with thee: only go away.

18

Is any man afraid of change? Why what can take place without change? What then is more pleasing or more suitable to the universal nature? And canst thou take a bath unless the wood undergoes a change? And canst thou be nourished, unless the food undergoes a change? And can anything else that is useful be accomplished without change? Dost thou not see then that for thyself also to change is just the same, and equally necessary for the universal nature?

19

Through the universal substance as through a furious torrent all bodies are carried, being by their nature united with and cooperating with the whole, as the parts of our body with one another. How many a Chrysippus, how many a Socrates, how many an Epictetus has time already swallowed up? And let the same thought occur to thee with reference to every man and thing.

20

One thing only troubles me, lest I should do something which the constitution of man does not allow, or in the way which it does not allow, or what it does not allow now.

21

Near is thy forgetfulness of all things; and near the forgetfulness of thee by all.

22

It is peculiar to man to love even those who do wrong. And this happens, if when they do wrong it occurs to thee that they are kinsmen, and that they do wrong through ignorance and unintentionally, and that soon both of you will die; and above all, that the wrong-doer has done thee no harm, for he has not made thy ruling faculty worse than it was before.

23

The universal nature out of the universal substance, as if it were wax, now moulds a horse, and when it has broken this up, it uses the material for a tree, then for a man, then for something else; and each of these things subsists for a very short time. But it is no hardship for the vessel to be broken up, just as there was none in its being fastened together.

24

A scowling look is altogether unnatural; when it is often assumed, the result is that all comeliness dies away, and at last is so completely extinguished that it cannot be again lighted up at all. Try to conclude from this very fact that it is contrary to reason. For if even the perception of doing wrong shall depart, what reason is there for living any longer?

25

Nature which governs the whole will soon change all things which thou seest, and out of their substance will make other things, and again other things from the substance of them, in order that the world may be ever new.

26

When a man has done thee any wrong, immediately consider with what opinion about good or evil he has done wrong. For when thou hast seen this, thou wilt pity him, and wilt neither wonder nor be angry. For either thou thyself thinkest the same thing to be good that he does or another thing of the same kind. It is thy duty then to pardon him. But if thou dost not think such things to be good or evil, thou wilt more readily be well disposed to him who is in error.

27

Think not so much of what thou hast not as of what thou hast: but of the things which thou hast select the best, and then reflect how eagerly they would have been sought, if thou hadst them not. At the same time however take care that thou dost not through being so pleased with them accustom thyself to overvalue them, so as to be disturbed if ever thou shouldst not have them.

28

Retire into thyself. The rational principle which rules has this nature, that it is content with itself when it does what is just, and so secures tranquility.

29

Wipe out the imagination. Stop the pulling of the strings. Confine thyself to the present. Understand well what happens either to thee or to another. Divide and distribute every object into the causal (formal) and the material. Think of thy last hour. Let the wrong which is done by a man stay there where the wrong was done.

30

Direct thy attention to what is said. Let thy understanding enter into the things that are doing and the things which do them.

31

Adorn thyself with simplicity and modesty and with indifference towards the things which lie between virtue and vice. Love mankind. Follow God. The poet says that Law rules all.—And it is enough to remember that Law rules all.

32

About death: Whether it is a dispersion, or a resolution into atoms, or annihilation, it is either extinction or change.

33

About pain: The pain which is intolerable carries us off; but that which lasts a long time is tolerable; and the mind maintains its own tranquility by retiring into itself, and the ruling faculty is not made worse. But the parts which are harmed by pain, let them, if they can, give their opinion about it.

34

About fame: Look at the minds of those who seek fame, observe what they are, and what kind of things they avoid, and what kind of things they pursue. And consider that as the heaps of sand piled on one another hide the former sands, so in life the events which go before are soon covered by those which come after.

35

From Plato: The man who has an elevated mind and takes a view of all time and of all substance, dost thou suppose it possible for him to think that human life is anything great? it is not possible, he said.—Such a man then will think that death also is no evil.—Certainly not.

36

From Antisthenes: It is royal to do good and to be abused.

37

It is a base thing for the countenance to be obedient and to regulate and compose itself as the mind commands, and for the mind not to be regulated and composed by itself.

38

It is not right to vex ourselves at things,
For they care nought about it.

39

To the immortal gods and us give joy.

40

Life must be reaped like the ripe ears of corn:
One man is born; another dies.

41

If gods care not for me and for my children,
There is a reason for it.

42

For the good is with me, and the just.

43

No joining others in their wailing, no violent emotion.

44

From Plato: But I would make this man a sufficient answer, which is this: Thou sayest not well, if thou thinkest that a man who is good for anything at all ought to compute the hazard of life or death, and should not rather look to this only in all that he does, whether he is doing what is just or unjust, and the works of a good or a bad man.

45

For thus it is, men of Athens, in truth: wherever a man has placed himself thinking it the best place for him, or has been placed by a commander, there in my opinion he ought to stay and to abide the hazard, taking nothing into the reckoning, either death or anything else, before the baseness of deserting his post.

46

But, my good friend, reflect whether that which is noble and good is not something different from saving and being saved; for as to a man living such or such a time, at least one who is really a man, consider if this is not a thing to be dismissed from the thoughts: and there must be no love of life: but as to these matters a man must intrust them to the deity and believe what the women say, that no man can escape his destiny, the next inquiry being how he may best live the time that he has to live.

47

Look round at the courses of the stars, as if thou wert going along with them; and constantly consider the changes of the elements into one another; for such thoughts purge away the filth of the terrene life.

48

This is a fine saying of Plato: That he who is discoursing about men should look also at earthly things as if he viewed them from some higher place; should look at them in their assemblies, armies, agricultural labours, marriages, treaties, births, deaths, noise of the courts of justice, desert places, various nations of barbarians, feasts, lamentations, markets, a mixture of all things and an orderly combination of contraries.

49

Consider the past; such great changes of political supremacies. Thou mayest foresee also the things which will be. For they will certainly be of like form, and it is not possible that they should deviate from the order of the things which take place now: accordingly to have contemplated human life for forty years is the same as to have contemplated it for ten thousand years. For what more wilt thou see?

50

That which has grown from the earth to the earth,
But that which has sprung from heavenly seed,
Back to the heavenly realms returns.

This is either a dissolution of the mutual involution of the atoms, or a similar dispersion of the unsentient elements.

51

With food and drinks and cunning magic arts
Turning the channel's course to 'scape from death.
The breeze which heaven has sent
We must endure, and toil without complaining.

52

Another may be more expert in casting his opponent; but he is not more social, nor more modest, nor better disciplined to meet all that happens, nor more considerate with respect to the faults of his neighbours.

53

Where any work can be done conformably to the reason which is common to gods and men, there we have nothing to fear: for where we are able to get profit by means of the activity which is successful and proceeds according to our constitution, there no harm is to be suspected.

54

Everywhere and at all times it is in thy power piously to acquiesce in thy present condition, and to behave justly to those who are about thee, and to exert thy skill upon thy present thoughts, that nothing shall steal into them without being well examined.

55

Do not look around thee to discover other men's ruling principles, but look straight to this, to what nature leads thee, both the universal nature through the things which happen to thee, and thy own nature through the acts which must be done by thee. But every being ought to do that which is according to its constitution; and all other things have been constituted for the sake of rational beings, just as among irrational things the inferior for the sake of the superior, but the rational for the sake of one another.

The prime principle then in man's constitution is the social. And the second is not to yield to the persuasions of the body, for it is the peculiar office of the rational and intelligent motion to circumscribe itself, and never to be overpowered either by the motion of the senses or of the appetites, for both are animal; but the intelligent motion claims superiority and does not permit itself to be overpowered by the others. And with good reason, for it is formed by nature to use all of them. The third thing in the rational constitution is freedom from error and from deception. Let then the ruling principle holding fast to these things go straight on, and it has what is its own.

56

Consider thyself to be dead, and to have completed thy life up to the present time; and live according to nature the remainder which is allowed thee.

57

Love that only which happens to thee and is spun with the thread of thy destiny. For what is more suitable?

58

In everything which happens keep before thy eyes those to whom the same things happened, and how they were vexed, and treated them as strange things, and found fault with them: and now where are they? Nowhere. Why then dost thou too choose to act in the same way? And why dost thou not leave these agitations which are foreign to nature, to those who cause them and those who are moved by them? And why art thou not altogether intent upon the right way of making use of the things which happen to thee? For then thou wilt use them well, and they will be a material for thee to work on. Only attend to thyself, and resolve to be a good man in every act which thou doest: and remember . . .

59

Look within. Within is the fountain of good, and it will ever bubble up, if thou wilt ever dig.

60

The body ought to be compact, and to show no irregularity either in motion or attitude. For what the mind shows in the face by maintaining in it the expression of intelligence and propriety, that ought to be required also in the whole body. But all of these things should be observed without affectation.

61

The art of life is more like the wrestler's art than the dancer's, in respect of this, that it should stand ready and firm to meet onsets which are sudden and unexpected.

62

Constantly observe who those are whose approbation thou wishest to have, and what ruling principles they possess. For then thou wilt neither blame those who offend involuntarily, nor wilt thou want their approbation, if thou lookest to the sources of their opinions and appetites.

63

Every soul, the philosopher says, is involuntarily deprived of truth; consequently in the same way it is deprived of justice and temperance and benevolence and everything of the kind. It is most necessary to bear this constantly in mind, for thus thou wilt be more gentle towards all.

64

In every pain let this thought be present, that there is no dishonour in it, nor does it make the governing intelligence worse, for it does not damage the intelligence either so far as the intelligence is rational or so far as it is social. Indeed in the case of most pains let this remark of Epicurus aid thee, that pain is neither intolerable nor everlasting, if thou bearest in mind that it has its limits, and if thou addest nothing to it in imagination: and remember this too, that we do not perceive that many things which are disagreeable to us are the same as pain, such as excessive drowsiness, and the being scorched by heat, and the having no appetite. When then thou art discontented about any of these things, say to thyself, that thou art yielding to pain.

65

Take care not to feel towards the inhuman, as they feel towards men.

66

How do we know if Telauges was not superior in character to Socrates? For it is not enough that Socrates died a more noble death, and disputed more skilfully with the sophists, and passed the night in the cold with more endurance, and that when he was bid to arrest Leon of Salamis, he considered it more noble to refuse, and that he walked in a swaggering way in the streets—though as to this fact one may have great doubts if it was true. But we ought to inquire, what kind of a soul it was that Socrates possessed, and if he was able to be content with being just towards men and pious towards the gods, neither idly vexed on account of men's villainy, nor yet making himself a slave to any man's ignorance, nor receiving as strange anything that fell to his share out of the universal, nor enduring it as intolerable, nor allowing his understanding to sympathize with the affects of the miserable flesh.

67

Nature has not so mingled the intelligence with the composition of the body, as not to have allowed thee the power of circumscribing thyself and of bringing under subjection to thyself all that is thy own; for it is very possible to be a divine man and to be recognised as such by no one. Always bear this in mind; and another thing too, that very little indeed is necessary for living a happy life. And because thou hast despaired of becoming a dialectician and skilled in the knowledge of nature, do not for this reason renounce the hope of being both free and modest and social and obedient to God.

68

It is in thy power to live free from all compulsion in the greatest tranquility of mind, even if all the world cry out against thee as much as they choose, and even if wild beasts tear in pieces the members of this kneaded matter which has grown around thee. For what hinders the mind in the midst of all this from maintaining itself in tranquility and in a just judgement of all surrounding things and in a ready use of the objects which are presented to it, so that the judgement may say to the thing which falls under its observation: This thou art in substance (reality), though in men's opinion thou mayest appear to be of a different kind; and the use shall say to that which falls under the hand: Thou art the thing that I was seeking; for to me that which presents itself is always a material for virtue both rational and political, and in a word, for the exercise of art, which belongs to man or God. For everything which happens has a relationship either to God or man, and is neither new nor difficult to handle, but usual and apt matter to work on.

69

The perfection of moral character consists in this, in passing every day as the last, and in being neither violently excited nor torpid nor playing the hypocrite.

70

The gods who are immortal are not vexed because during so long a time they must tolerate continually men such as they are and so many of them bad; and besides this, they also take care of them in all ways. But thou, who art destined to end so soon, art thou wearied of enduring the bad, and this too when thou art one of them?

71

It is a ridiculous thing for a man not to fly from his own badness, which is indeed possible, but to fly from other men's badness, which is impossible.

72

Whatever the rational and political (social) faculty finds to be neither intelligent nor social, it properly judges to be inferior to itself.

73

When thou hast done a good act and another has received it, why dost thou look for a third thing besides these, as fools do, either to have the reputation of having done a good act or to obtain a return?

74

No man is tired of receiving what is useful. But it is useful to act according to nature. Do not then be tired of receiving what is useful by doing it to others.

75

The nature of the All moved to make the universe. But now either everything that takes place comes by way of consequence or continuity; or even the chief things towards which the ruling power of the universe directs its own movement are governed by no rational principle. If this is remembered it will make thee more tranquil in many things.

BOOK EIGHT

1

This reflection also tends to the removal of the desire of empty fame, that it is no longer in thy power to have lived the whole of thy life, or at least thy life from thy youth upwards, like a philosopher; but both to many others and to thyself it is plain that thou art far from philosophy. Thou hast fallen into disorder then, so that it is no longer easy for thee to get the reputation of a philosopher; and thy plan of life also opposes it. If then thou hast truly seen where the matter lies, throw away the thought, How thou shalt seem to others, and be content if thou shalt live the rest of thy life in such wise as thy nature wills. Observe then what it wills, and let nothing else distract thee; for thou hast had experience of many wanderings without having found happiness anywhere, not in syllogisms, nor in wealth, nor in reputation, nor in enjoyment, nor anywhere. Where is it then? In doing what man's nature requires. How then shall a man do this? If he has principles from which come his affects and his acts. What principles? Those which relate to good and bad: the belief that there is nothing good for man, which does not make him just, temperate, manly, free; and that there is nothing bad, which does not do the contrary to what has been mentioned.

2

On the occasion of every act ask thyself, How is this with respect to me? Shall I repent of it? A little time and I am dead, and all is gone. What more do I seek, if what I am now doing is work of an intelligent living being, and a social being, and one who is under the same law with God?

3

Alexander and Gaius and Pompeius, what are they in comparison with Diogenes and Heraclitus and Socrates? For they were acquainted with things, and their causes (forms), and their matter, and the ruling principles of these men were the same. But as to the others, how many things had they to care for, and to how many things were they slaves?

4

Consider that men will do the same things nevertheless, even though thou shouldst burst.

5

This is the chief thing: Be not perturbed, for all things are according to the nature of the universal; and in a little time thou wilt be nobody and nowhere, like Hadrian and Augustus. In the next place having fixed thy eyes steadily on thy business look at it, and at the same time remembering that it is thy duty to be a good man, and what man's nature demands, do that without turning aside; and speak as it seems to thee most just, only let it be with a good disposition and with modesty and without hypocrisy.

6

The nature of the universal has this work to do, to remove to that place the things which are in this, to change them, to take them away hence, and to carry them there. All things are change, yet we need not fear anything new. All things are familiar to us; but the distribution of them still remains the same.

7

Every nature is contented with itself when it goes on its way well; and a rational nature goes on its way well, when in its thoughts it assents to nothing false or uncertain, and when it directs its movements to social acts only, and when it confines its desires and aversions to the things which are in its power, and when it is satisfied with everything that is assigned to it by the common nature. For of this common nature every particular nature is a part, as the nature of the leaf is a part of the nature of the plant; except that in the plant the nature of the leaf is part of a nature which has not perception or reason, and is subject to be impeded; but the nature of man is part of a nature which is not subject to impediments, and is intelligent and just, since it gives to everything in equal portions and according to its worth, times, substance, cause (form), activity, and incident. But examine, not to discover that any one thing compared with any other single thing is equal in all respects, but by taking all the parts together of one thing and comparing them with all the parts together of another.

8

Thou hast not leisure or ability to read. But thou hast leisure or ability to check arrogance: thou hast leisure to be superior to pleasure and pain: thou hast leisure to be superior to love of fame, and not to be vexed at stupid and ungrateful people, nay even to care for them.

9

Let no man any longer hear thee finding fault with the court life or with thy own.

10

Repentance is a kind of self-reproof for having neglected something useful; but that which is good must be something useful, and the perfect good man should look after it. But no such man would ever repent of having refused any sensual pleasure. Pleasure then is neither good nor useful.

11

This thing, what is it in itself, in its own constitution? What is its substance and material? And what its causal nature (or form)? And what is it doing in the world? And how long does it subsist?

12

When thou risest from sleep with reluctance, remember that it is according to thy constitution and according to human nature to perform social acts, but sleeping is common also to irrational animals. But that which is according to each individual's nature is also more peculiarly its own, and more suitable to its nature, and indeed also more agreeable.

13

Constantly and, if it be possible, on the occasion of every impression on the soul, apply to it the principles of Physic, of Ethic, and of Dialectic.

14

Whatever man thou meetest with, immediately say to thyself: What opinions has this man about good and bad? For if with respect to pleasure and pain and the causes of each, and with respect to fame and ignominy, death and life, he has such and such opinions, it will seem nothing wonderful or strange to me, if he does such and such things; and I shall bear in mind that he is compelled to do so.

15

Remember that as it is a shame to be surprised if the fig-tree produces figs, so it is to be surprised if the world produces such and such things of which it is productive; and for the physician and the helmsman it is a shame to be surprised, if a man has a fever, or if the wind is unfavourable.

16

Remember that to change thy opinion and to follow him who corrects thy error is as consistent with freedom as it is to persist in thy error. For it is thy own, the activity which is exerted according to thy own movement and judgement, and indeed according to thy own understanding too.

17

If a thing is in thy own power, why dost thou do it? But if it is in the power of another, whom dost thou blame? The atoms (chance) or the gods? Both are foolish. Thou must blame nobody. For if thou canst, correct that which is the cause; but if thou canst not do this, correct at least the thing itself; but if thou canst not do even this, of what use is it to thee to find fault? For nothing should be done without a purpose.

18

That which has died falls not out of the universe. If it stays here, it also changes here, and is dissolved into its proper parts, which are elements of the universe and of thyself. And these too change, and they murmur not.

19

Everything exists for some end, a horse, a vine. Why dost thou wonder? Even the sun will say, I am for some purpose, and the rest of the gods will say the same. For what purpose then art thou? to enjoy pleasure? See if common sense allows this.

20

Nature has had regard in everything no less to the end than to the beginning and the continuance, just like the man who throws up a ball.

What good is it then for the ball to be thrown up, or harm for it to come down, or even to have fallen? And what good is it to the bubble while it holds together, or what harm when it is burst? The same may be said of a light also.

21

Turn it (the body) inside out, and see what kind of thing it is; and when it has grown old, what kind of thing it becomes, and when it is diseased.

Short-lived are both the praiser and the praised, and the rememberer and the remembered: and all this in a nook of this part of the world; and not even here do all agree, no, not any one with himself: and the whole earth too is a point.

22

Attend to the matter which is before thee, whether it is an opinion or an act or a word.

Thou sufferest this justly: for thou choosest rather to become good tomorrow than to be good today.

23

Am I doing anything? I do it with reference to the good of mankind. Does anything happen to me? I receive it and refer it to the gods, and the source of all things, from which all that happens is derived.

24

Such as bathing appears to thee—oil, sweat, dirt, filthy water, all things disgusting—so is every part of life and everything.

25

Lucilla saw Verus die, and then Lucilla died. Secunda saw Maximus die, and then Secunda died. Epitynchanus saw Diotimus die, and Epitynchanus died. Antoninus saw Faustina die, and then Antoninus died. Such is everything. Celer saw Hadrian die, and then Celer died. And those sharp-witted men, either seers or men inflated with pride, where are they? For instance the sharp-witted men, Charax and Demetrius the Platonist and Eudaemon, and any one else like them. All ephemeral, dead long ago. Some indeed have not been remembered even for a short time, and others have become the heroes of fables, and again others have disappeared even from fables. Remember this then, that this little compound, thyself, must either be dissolved, or thy poor breath must be extinguished, or be removed and placed elsewhere.

26

It is satisfaction to a man to do the proper works of a man. Now it is a proper work of a man to be benevolent to his own kind, to despise the movements of the senses, to form a just judgement of plausible appearances, and to take a survey of the nature of the universe and of the things which happen in it.

27

There are three relations between thee and other things: the one to the body which surrounds thee; the second to the divine cause from which all things come to all; and the third to those who live with thee.

28

Pain is either an evil to the body—then let the body say what it thinks of it—or to the soul; but it is in the power of the soul to maintain its own serenity and tranquility, and not to think that pain is an evil. For every judgement and movement and desire and aversion is within, and no evil ascends so high.

29

Wipe out thy imaginations by often saying to thyself: now it is in my power to let no badness be in this soul, nor desire nor any perturbation at all; but looking at all things I see what is their nature, and I use each according to its value.—Remember this power which thou hast from nature.

30

Speak both in the senate and to every man, whoever he may be, appropriately, not with any affectation: use plain discourse.

31

Augustus' court, wife, daughter, descendants, ancestors, sister, Agrippa, kinsmen, intimates, friends, Areius, Maecenas, physicians and sacrificing priests—the whole court is dead. Then turn to the rest, not considering the death of a single man, but of a whole race, as of the Pompeii; and that which is inscribed on the tombs—The last of his race. Then consider what trouble those before them have had that they might leave a successor; and then, that of necessity some one must be the last. Again here consider the death of a whole race.

32

It is thy duty to order thy life well in every single act; and if every act does its duty, as far as is possible, be content; and no one is able to hinder thee so that each act shall not do its duty.—But something external will stand in the way.—Nothing will stand in the way of thy acting justly and soberly and considerately.—But perhaps some other active power will be hindered.—Well, but by acquiescing in the hindrance and by being content to transfer thy efforts to that which is allowed, another opportunity of action is immediately put before thee in place of that which was hindered, and one which will adapt itself to this ordering of which we are speaking.

33

Receive wealth or prosperity without arrogance; and be ready to let it go.

34

If thou didst ever see a hand cut off, or a foot, or a head, lying anywhere apart from the rest of the body, such does a man make himself, as far as he can, who is not content with what happens, and separates himself from others, or does anything unsocial. Suppose that thou hast detached thyself from the natural unity—for thou wast made by nature a part, but now thou hast cut thyself off—yet here there is this beautiful provision, that it is in thy power again to unite thyself. God has allowed this to no other part, after it has been separated and cut asunder, to come together again. But consider the kindness by which he has distinguished man, for he has put it in his power not to be separated at all from the universal; and when he has been separated, he has allowed him to return and to be united and to resume his place as a part.

35

As the nature of the universal has given to every rational being all the other powers that it has, so we have received from it this power also. For as the universal nature converts and fixes in its predestined place everything which stands in the way and opposes it, and makes such things a part of itself, so also the rational animal is able to make every hindrance its own material, and to use it for such purposes as it may have designed.

36

Do not disturb thyself by thinking of the whole of thy life. Let not thy thoughts at once embrace all the various troubles which thou mayest expect to befall thee: but on every occasion ask thyself, What is there in this which is intolerable and past bearing? For thou wilt be ashamed to confess. In the next place remember that neither the future nor the past pains thee, but only the present. But this is reduced to a very little, if thou only circumscribest it, and chidest thy mind, if it is unable to hold out against even this.

37

Does Panthea or Pergamus now sit by the tomb of Verus? Does Chaurias or Diotimus sit by the tomb of Hadrian? That would be ridiculous. Well, suppose they did sit there, would the dead be conscious of it? And if the dead were conscious, would they be pleased? And if they were pleased, would that make them immortal? Was it not in the order of destiny that these persons too should first become old women and old men and then die? What then would those do after these were dead? All this is foul smell and blood in a bag.

38

If thou canst see sharp, look and judge wisely, says the philosopher.

39

In the constitution of the rational animal I see no virtue which is opposed to justice; but I see a virtue which is opposed to love of pleasure, and that is temperance.

40

If thou takest away thy opinion about that which appears to give thee pain, thou thyself standest in perfect security.—Who is this self?—The reason.—But I am not reason.—Be it so. Let then the reason itself not trouble itself. But if any other part of thee suffers, let it have its own opinion about itself.

41

Hindrance to the perceptions of sense is an evil to the animal nature. Hindrance to the movements (desires) is equally an evil to the animal nature. And something else also is equally an impediment and an evil to the constitution of plants. So then that which is a hindrance to the intelligence is an evil to the intelligent nature. Apply all these things then to thyself. Does pain or sensuous pleasure affect thee? The senses will look to that.—Has any obstacle opposed thee in thy efforts towards an object? if indeed thou wast making this effort absolutely (unconditionally, or without any reservation), certainly this obstacle is an evil to thee considered as a rational animal. But if thou takest into consideration the usual course of things, thou hast not yet been injured nor even impeded. The things however which are proper to the understanding no other man is used to impede, for neither fire, nor iron, nor tyrant, nor abuse, touches it in any way. When it has been made a sphere, it continues a sphere.

42

It is not fit that I should give myself pain, for I have never intentionally given pain even to another.

43

Different things delight different people. But it is my delight to keep the ruling faculty sound without turning away either from any man or from any of the things which happen to men, but looking at and receiving all with welcome eyes and using everything according to its value.

44

See that thou secure this present time to thyself: for those who rather pursue posthumous fame do consider that the men of after time will be exactly such as these whom they cannot bear now; and both are mortal.

And what is it in any way to thee if these men of after time utter this or that sound, or have this or that opinion about thee?

45

Take me and cast me where thou wilt; for there I shall keep my divine part tranquil, that is, content, if it can feel and act conformably to its proper constitution. Is this change of place sufficient reason why my soul should be unhappy and worse than it was, depressed, expanded, shrinking, affrighted? And what wilt thou find which is sufficient reason for this?

46

Nothing can happen to any man which is not a human accident, nor to an ox which is not according to the nature of an ox, nor to a vine which is not according to the nature of a vine, nor to a stone which is not proper to a stone. If then there happens to each thing both what is usual and natural, why shouldst thou complain? For the common nature brings nothing which may not be borne by thee.

47

If thou art pained by any external thing, it is not this thing that disturbs thee, but thy own judgement about it. And it is in thy power to wipe out this judgement now. But if anything in thy own disposition gives thee pain, who hinders thee from correcting thy opinion? And even if thou art pained because thou art not doing some particular thing which seems to thee to be right, why dost thou not rather act than complain?—But some insuperable obstacle is in the way?—Do not be grieved then, for the cause of its not being done depends not on thee.—But it is not worth while to live if this cannot be done.—Take thy departure then from life contentedly, just as he dies who is in full activity, and well pleased too with the things which are obstacles.

48

Remember that the ruling faculty is invincible, when self-collected it is satisfied with itself, if it does nothing which it does not choose to do, even if it resist from mere obstinacy. What then will it be when it forms a judgement about anything aided by reason and deliberately? Therefore the mind which is free from passions is a citadel, for man has nothing more secure to which he can fly for, refuge and for the future be inexpugnable. He then who has not seen this is an ignorant man; but he who has seen it and does not fly to this refuge is unhappy.

49

Say nothing more to thyself than what the first appearances report. Suppose that it has been reported to thee that a certain person speaks ill of thee. This has been reported; but that thou hast been injured, that has not been reported. I see that my child is sick. I do see; but that he is in danger, I do not see. Thus then always abide by the first appearances, and add nothing thyself from within, and then nothing happens to thee. Or rather add something, like a man who knows everything that happens in the world.

50

A cucumber is bitter.—Throw it away.—There are briars in the road.—Turn aside from them.—This is enough. Do not add, And why were such things made in the world? For thou wilt be ridiculed by a man who is acquainted with nature, as thou wouldst be ridiculed by a carpenter and shoemaker if thou didst find fault because thou seest in their workshop shavings and cuttings from the things which they make. And yet they have places into which they can throw these shavings and cuttings, and the universal nature has no external space; but the wondrous part of her art is that though she has circumscribed herself, everything within her which appears to decay and to grow old and to be useless she changes into herself, and again makes other new things from these very same, so that she requires neither substance from without nor wants a place into which she may cast that which decays. She is content then with her own space, and her own matter and her own art.

51

Neither in thy actions be sluggish nor in thy conversation without method, nor wandering in thy thoughts, nor let there be in thy soul inward contention nor external effusion, nor in life be so busy as to have no leisure.

Suppose that men kill thee, cut thee in pieces, curse thee. What then can these things do to prevent thy mind from remaining pure, wise, sober, just? For instance, if a man should stand by a limpid pure spring, and curse it, the spring never ceases sending up potable water; and if he should cast clay into it or filth, it will speedily disperse them and wash them out, and will not be at all polluted. How then shalt thou possess a perpetual fountain and not a mere well? By forming thyself hourly to freedom conjoined with contentment, simplicity and modesty.

52

He who does not know what the world is, does not know where he is. And he who does not know for what purpose the world exists, does not know who he is, nor what the world is. But he who has failed in any one of these things could not even say for what purpose he exists himself. What then dost thou think of him who avoids or seeks the praise of those who applaud, of men who know not either where they are or who they are?

53

Dost thou wish to be praised by a man who curses himself thrice every hour? Wouldst thou wish to please a man who does not please himself? Does a man please himself who repents of nearly everything that he does?

54

No longer let thy breathing only act in concert with the air which surrounds thee, but let thy intelligence also now be in harmony with the intelligence which embraces all things. For the intelligent power is no less diffused in all parts and pervades all things for him who is willing to draw it to him than the aerial power for him who is able to respire it.

55

Generally, wickedness does no harm at all to the universe; and particularly, the wickedness of one man does no harm to another. It is only harmful to him who has it in his power to be released from it, as soon as he shall choose.

56

To my own free will the free will of my neighbour is just as indifferent as his poor breath and flesh. For though we are made especially for the sake of one another, still the ruling power of each of us has its own office, for otherwise my neighbour's wickedness would be my harm, which God has not willed in order that my unhappiness may not depend on another.

57

The sun appears to be poured down, and in all directions indeed it is diffused, yet it is not effused. For this diffusion is extension: Accordingly its rays are called Extensions [aktines] because they are extended [apo tou ekteinesthai]. But one may judge what kind of a thing a ray is, if he looks at the sun's light passing through a narrow opening into a darkened room, for it is extended in a right line, and as it were is divided when it meets with any solid body which stands in the way and intercepts the air beyond; but there the light remains fixed and does not glide or fall off. Such then ought to be the outpouring and diffusion of the understanding, and it should in no way be an effusion, but an extension, and it should make no violent or impetuous collision with the obstacles which are in its way; nor yet fall down, but be fixed and enlighten that which receives it. For a body will deprive itself of the illumination, if it does not admit it.

58

He who fears death either fears the loss of sensation or a different kind of sensation. But if thou shalt have no sensation, neither wilt thou feel any harm; and if thou shalt acquire another kind of sensation, thou wilt be a different kind of living being and thou wilt not cease to live.

59

Men exist for the sake of one another. Teach them then or bear with them.

60

In one way an arrow moves, in another way the mind. The mind indeed, both when it exercises caution and when it is employed about inquiry, moves straight onward not the less, and to its object.

61

Enter into every man's ruling faculty; and also let every other man enter into thine.

BOOK NINE

1

He who acts unjustly acts impiously. For since the universal nature has made rational animals for the sake of one another to help one another according to their deserts, but in no way to injure one another, he who transgresses her will, is clearly guilty of impiety towards the highest divinity. And he too who lies is guilty of impiety to the same divinity; for the universal nature is the nature of things that are; and things that are have a relation to all things that come into existence. And further, this universal nature is named truth, and is the prime cause of all things that are true. He then who lies intentionally is guilty of impiety inasmuch as he acts unjustly by deceiving; and he also who lies unintentionally, inasmuch as he is at variance with the universal nature, and inasmuch as he disturbs the order by fighting against the nature of the world; for he fights against it, who is moved of himself to that which is contrary to truth, for he had received powers from nature through the neglect of which he is not able now to distinguish falsehood from truth. And indeed he who pursues pleasure as good, and avoids pain as evil, is guilty of impiety. For of necessity such a man must often find fault with the universal nature, alleging that it assigns things to the bad and the good contrary to their deserts, because frequently the bad are in the enjoyment of pleasure and possess the things which procure pleasure, but the good have pain for their share and the things which cause pain. And further, he who is afraid of pain will sometimes also be afraid of some of the things which will happen in the world, and even this is impiety. And he who pursues pleasure will not abstain from injustice, and this is plainly impiety. Now with respect to the things towards which the universal nature is equally affected—for it would not have made both, unless it was equally affected towards both—towards these they who wish to follow nature should be of the same mind with it, and equally affected. With respect to pain, then, and pleasure, or death and life, or honour and dishonour, which the universal nature employs equally, whoever is not equally affected is manifestly acting impiously. And I say that the universal nature employs them equally, instead of saying that they happen alike to those who are produced in continuous series and to those who come after them by virtue of a certain original movement of Providence, according to which it moved from a certain beginning to this ordering of things, having conceived certain principles of the things which were to be, and having determined powers productive of beings and of changes and of such like successions.

2

It would be a man's happiest lot to depart from mankind without having had any taste of lying and hypocrisy and luxury and pride. However to breathe out one's life when a man has had enough of these things is the next best voyage, as the saying is. Hast thou determined to abide with vice, and has not experience yet induced thee to fly from this pestilence? For the destruction of the understanding is a pestilence, much more indeed than any such corruption and change of this atmosphere which surrounds us. For this corruption is a pestilence of animals so far as they are animals; but the other is a pestilence of men so far as they are men.

3

Do not despise death, but be well content with it, since this too is one of those things which nature wills. For such as it is to be young and to grow old, and to increase and to reach maturity, and to have teeth and beard and grey hairs, and to beget, and to be pregnant and to bring forth, and all the other natural operations which the seasons of thy life bring, such also is dissolution. This, then, is consistent with the character of a reflecting man, to be neither careless nor impatient nor contemptuous with respect to death, but to wait for it as one of the operations of nature. As thou now waitest for the time when the child shall come out of thy wife's womb, so be ready for the time when thy soul shall fall out of this envelope. But if thou requirest also a vulgar kind of comfort which shall reach thy heart, thou wilt be made best reconciled to death by observing the objects from which thou art going to be removed, and the morals of those with whom thy soul will no longer be mingled. For it is no way right to be offended with men, but it is thy duty to care for them and to bear with them gently; and yet to remember that thy departure will be not from men who have the same principles as thyself. For this is the only thing, if there be any, which could draw us the contrary way and attach us to life, to be permitted to live with those who have the same principles as ourselves. But now thou seest how great is the trouble arising from the discordance of those who live together, so that thou mayest say, Come quick, O death, lest perchance I, too, should forget myself.

4

He who does wrong does wrong against himself. He who acts unjustly acts unjustly to himself, because he makes himself bad.

5

He often acts unjustly who does not do a certain thing; not only he who does a certain thing.

6

Thy present opinion founded on understanding, and thy present conduct directed to social good, and thy present disposition of contentment with everything which happens—that is enough.

7

Wipe out imagination: check desire: extinguish appetite: keep the ruling faculty in its own power.

8

Among the animals which have not reason one life is distributed; but among reasonable animals one intelligent soul is distributed: just as there is one earth of all things which are of an earthy nature, and we see by one light, and breathe one air, all of us that have the faculty of vision and all that have life.

9

All things which participate in anything which is common to them all move towards that which is of the same kind with themselves. Everything which is earthy turns towards the earth, everything which is liquid flows together, and everything which is of an aerial kind does the same, so that they require something to keep them asunder, and the application of force. Fire indeed moves upwards on account of the elemental fire, but it is so ready to be kindled together with all the fire which is here, that even every substance which is somewhat dry, is easily ignited, because there is less mingled with it of that which is a hindrance to ignition. Accordingly then everything also which participates in the common intelligent nature moves in like manner towards that which is of the same kind with itself, or moves even more. For so much as it is superior in comparison with all other things, in the same degree also is it more ready to mingle with and to be fused with that which is akin to it. Accordingly among animals devoid of reason we find swarms of bees, and herds of cattle, and the nurture of young birds, and in a manner, loves; for even in animals there are souls, and that power which brings them together is seen to exert itself in the superior degree, and in such a way as never has been observed in plants nor in stones nor in trees. But in rational animals there are political communities and friendships, and families and meetings of people; and in wars, treaties and armistices. But in the things which are still superior, even though they are separated from one another, unity in a manner exists, as in the stars. Thus the ascent to the higher degree is able to produce a sympathy even in things which are separated. See, then, what now takes place. For only intelligent animals have now forgotten this mutual desire and inclination, and in them alone the property of flowing together is not seen. But still though men strive to avoid this union, they are caught and held by it, for their nature is too strong for them; and thou wilt see what I say, if thou only observest. Sooner, then, will one find anything earthy which comes in contact with no earthy thing than a man altogether separated from other men.

10

Both man and God and the universe produce fruit; at the proper seasons each produces it. But if usage has especially fixed these terms to the vine and like things, this is nothing. Reason produces fruit both for all and for itself, and there are produced from it other things of the same kind as reason itself.

11

If thou art able, correct by teaching those who do wrong; but if thou canst not, remember that indulgence is given to thee for this purpose. And the gods, too, are indulgent to such persons; and for some purposes they even help them to get health, wealth, reputation; so kind they are. And it is in thy power also; or say, who hinders thee?

12

Labour not as one who is wretched, nor yet as one who would be pitied or admired: but direct thy will to one thing only, to put thyself in motion and to check thyself, as the social reason requires.

13

Today I have got out of all trouble, or rather I have cast out all trouble, for it was not outside, but within and in my opinions.

14

All things are the same, familiar in experience, and ephemeral in time, and worthless in the matter. Everything now is just as it was in the time of those whom we have buried.

15

Things stand outside of us, themselves by themselves, neither knowing aught of themselves, nor expressing any judgement. What is it, then, which does judge about them? The ruling faculty.

16

Not in passivity, but in activity lie the evil and the good of the rational social animal, just as his virtue and his vice lie not in passivity, but in activity.

17

For the stone which has been thrown up it is no evil to come down, nor indeed any good to have been carried up.

18

Penetrate inwards into men's leading principles, and thou wilt see what judges thou art afraid of, and what kind of judges they are of themselves.

19

All things are changing: and thou thyself art in continuous mutation and in a manner in continuous destruction, and the whole universe too.

20

It is thy duty to leave another man's wrongful act there where it is.

21

Termination of activity, cessation from movement and opinion, and in a sense their death, is no evil. Turn thy thoughts now to the consideration of thy life, thy life as a child, as a youth, thy manhood, thy old age, for in these also every change was a death. Is this anything to fear? Turn thy thoughts now to thy life under thy grandfather, then to thy life under thy mother, then to thy life under thy father; and as thou findest many other differences and changes and terminations, ask thyself, Is this anything to fear? In like manner, then, neither are the termination and cessation and change of thy whole life a thing to be afraid of.

22

Hasten to examine thy own ruling faculty and that of the universe and that of thy neighbour: thy own that thou mayest make it just: and that of the universe, that thou mayest remember of what thou art a part; and that of thy neighbour, that thou mayest know whether he has acted ignorantly or with knowledge, and that thou mayest also consider that his ruling faculty is akin to thine.

23

As thou thyself art a component part of a social system, so let every act of thine be a component part of social life. Whatever act of thine then has no reference either immediately or remotely to a social end, this tears asunder thy life, and does not allow it to be one, and it is of the nature of a mutiny, just as when in a popular assembly a man acting by himself stands apart from the general agreement.

24

Quarrels of little children and their sports, and poor spirits carrying about dead bodies, such is everything; and so what is exhibited in the representation of the mansions of the dead strikes our eyes more clearly.

25

Examine into the quality of the form of an object, and detach it altogether from its material part, and then contemplate it; then determine the time, the longest which a thing of this peculiar form is naturally made to endure.

26

Thou hast endured infinite troubles through not being contented with thy ruling faculty, when it does the things which it is constituted by nature to do. But enough of this.

27

When another blames thee or hates thee, or when men say about thee anything injurious, approach their poor souls, penetrate within, and see what kind of men they are. Thou wilt discover that there is no reason to take any trouble that these men may have this or that opinion about thee. However thou must be well disposed towards them, for by nature they are friends. And the gods too aid them in all ways, by dreams, by signs, towards the attainment of those things on which they set a value.

28

The periodic movements of the universe are the same, up and down from age to age. And either the universal intelligence puts itself in motion for every separate effect, and if this is so, be thou content with that which is the result of its activity; or it puts itself in motion once, and everything else comes by way of sequence in a manner; or indivisible elements are the origin of all things.—In a word, if there is a god, all is well; and if chance rules, do not thou also be governed by it.

29

Soon will the earth cover us all: then the earth, too, will change, and the things also which result from change will continue to change for ever, and these again for ever. For if a man reflects on the changes and transformations which follow one another like wave after wave and their rapidity, he will despise everything which is perishable.

30

The universal cause is like a winter torrent: it carries everything along with it. But how worthless are all these poor people who are engaged in matters political, and, as they suppose, are playing the philosopher! All drivellers. Well then, man: do what nature now requires. Set thyself in motion, if it is in thy power, and do not look about thee to see if any one will observe it; nor yet expect Plato's Republic: but be content if the smallest thing goes on well, and consider such an event to be no small matter. For who can change men's opinions? And without a change of opinions what else is there than the slavery of men who groan while they pretend to obey? Come now and tell me of Alexander and Philip and Demetrius of Phalerum. They themselves shall judge whether they discovered what the common nature required, and trained themselves accordingly. But if they acted like tragedy heroes, no one has condemned me to imitate them. Simple and modest is the work of philosophy. Draw me not aside to indolence and pride.

31

Look down from above on the countless herds of men and their countless solemnities, and the infinitely varied voyagings in storms and calms, and the differences among those who are born, who live together, and die. And consider, too, the life lived by others in olden time, and the life of those who will live after thee, and the life now lived among barbarous nations, and how many know not even thy name, and how many will soon forget it, and how they who perhaps now are praising thee will very soon blame thee, and that neither a posthumous name is of any value, nor reputation, nor anything else.

32

Let there be freedom from perturbations with respect to the things which come from the external cause; and let there be justice in the things done by virtue of the internal cause, that is, let there be movement and action terminating in this, in social acts, for this is according to thy nature.

33

Thou canst remove out of the way many useless things among those which disturb thee, for they lie entirely in thy opinion; and thou wilt then gain for thyself ample space by comprehending the whole universe in thy mind, and by contemplating the eternity of time, and observing the rapid change of every several thing, how short is the time from birth to dissolution, and the illimitable time before birth as well as the equally boundless time after dissolution.

34

All that thou seest will quickly perish, and those who have been spectators of its dissolution will very soon perish too. And he who dies at the extremest old age will be brought into the same condition with him who died prematurely.

35

What are these men's leading principles, and about what kind of things are they busy, and for what kind of reasons do they love and honour? Imagine that thou seest their poor souls laid bare. When they think that they do harm by their blame or good by their praise, what an idea!

36

Loss is nothing else than change. But the universal nature delights in change, and in obedience to her all things are now done well, and from eternity have been done in like form, and will be such to time without end. What, then, dost thou say? That all things have been and all things always will be bad, and that no power has ever been found in so many gods to rectify these things, but the world has been condemned to be found in never ceasing evil?

37

The rottenness of the matter which is the foundation of everything! Water, dust, bones, filth: or again, marble rocks, the callosities of the earth; and gold and silver, the sediments; and garments, only bits of hair; and purple dye, blood; and everything else is of the same kind. And that which is of the nature of breath is also another thing of the same kind, changing from this to that.

38

Enough of this wretched life and murmuring and apish tricks. Why art thou disturbed? What is there new in this? What unsettles thee? Is it the form of the thing? Look at it. Or is it the matter? Look at it. But besides these there is nothing. Towards the gods, then, now become at last more simple and better. It is the same whether we examine these things for a hundred years or three.

39

If any man has done wrong, the harm is his own. But perhaps he has not done wrong.

40

Either all things proceed from one intelligent source and come together as in one body, and the part ought not to find fault with what is done for the benefit of the whole; or there are only atoms, and nothing else than mixture and dispersion. Why, then, art thou disturbed? Say to the ruling faculty, Art thou dead, art thou corrupted, art thou playing the hypocrite, art thou become a beast, dost thou herd and feed with the rest?

41

Either the gods have no power or they have power. If, then, they have no power, why dost thou pray to them? But if they have power, why dost thou not pray for them to give thee the faculty of not fearing any of the things which thou fearest, or of not desiring any of the things which thou desirest, or not being pained at anything, rather than pray that any of these things should not happen or happen? for certainly if they can co-operate with men, they can co-operate for these purposes. But perhaps thou wilt say, the gods have placed them in thy power. Well, then, is it not better to use what is in thy power like a free man than to desire in a slavish and abject way what is not in thy power? And who has told thee that the gods do not aid us even in the things which are in our power? Begin, then, to pray for such things, and thou wilt see. One man prays thus: How shall I be able to lie with that woman? Do thou pray thus: How shall I not desire to lie with her? Another prays thus: How shall I be released from this? Another prays: How shall I not desire to be released? Another thus: How shall I not lose my little son? Thou thus: How shall I not be afraid to lose him? In fine, turn thy prayers this way, and see what comes.

42

Epicurus says, In my sickness my conversation was not about my bodily sufferings, nor, says he, did I talk on such subjects to those who visited me; but I continued to discourse on the nature of things as before, keeping to this main point, how the mind, while participating in such movements as go on in the poor flesh, shall be free from perturbations and maintain its proper good. Nor did I, he says, give the physicians an opportunity of putting on solemn looks, as if they were doing something great, but my life went on well and happily. Do, then, the same that he did both in sickness, if thou art sick, and in any other circumstances; for never to desert philosophy in any events that may befall us, nor to hold trifling talk either with an ignorant man or with one unacquainted with nature, is a principle of all schools of philosophy; but to be intent only on that which thou art now doing and on the instrument by which thou doest it.

43

When thou art offended with any man's shameless conduct, immediately ask thyself, Is it possible, then, that shameless men should not be in the world? It is not possible. Do not, then, require what is impossible. For this man also is one of those shameless men who must of necessity be in the world. Let the same considerations be present to thy mind in the case of the knave, and the faithless man, and of every man who does wrong in any way. For at the same time that thou dost remind thyself that it is impossible that such kind of men should not exist, thou wilt become more kindly disposed towards every one individually. It is useful to perceive this, too, immediately when the occasion arises, what virtue nature has given to man to oppose to every wrongful act. For she has given to man, as an antidote against the stupid man, mildness, and against another kind of man some other power. And in all cases it is possible for thee to correct by teaching the man who is gone astray; for every man who errs misses his object and is gone astray. Besides wherein hast thou been injured? For thou wilt find that no one among those against whom thou art irritated has done anything by which thy mind could be made worse; but that which is evil to thee and harmful has its foundation only in the mind. And what harm is done or what is there strange, if the man who has not been instructed does the acts of an uninstructed man? Consider whether thou shouldst not rather blame thyself, because thou didst not expect such a man to err in such a way. For thou hadst means given thee by thy reason to suppose that it was likely that he would commit this error, and yet thou hast forgotten and art amazed that he has erred. But most of all when thou blamest a man as faithless or ungrateful, turn to thyself. For the fault is manifestly thy own, whether thou didst trust that a man who had such a disposition would keep his promise, or when conferring thy kindness thou didst not confer it absolutely, nor yet in such way as to have received from thy very act all the profit. For what more dost thou want when thou hast done a man a service? Art thou not content that thou hast done something conformable to thy nature, and dost thou seek to be paid for it? Just as if the eye demanded a recompense for seeing, or the feet for walking. For as these members are formed for a particular purpose, and by working according to their several constitutions obtain what is their own; so also as man is formed by nature to acts of benevolence, when he has done anything benevolent or in any other way conducive to the common interest, he has acted conformably to his constitution, and he gets what is his own.

BOOK TEN

1

Wilt thou, then, my soul, never be good and simple and one and naked, more manifest than the body which surrounds thee? Wilt thou never enjoy an affectionate and contented disposition? Wilt thou never be full and without a want of any kind, longing for nothing more, nor desiring anything, either animate or inanimate, for the enjoyment of pleasures? Nor yet desiring time wherein thou shalt have longer enjoyment, or place, or pleasant climate, or society of men with whom thou mayest live in harmony? But wilt thou be satisfied with thy present condition, and pleased with all that is about thee, and wilt thou convince thyself that thou hast everything and that it comes from the gods, that everything is well for thee, and will be well whatever shall please them, and whatever they shall give for the conservation of the perfect living being, the good and just and beautiful, which generates and holds together all things, and contains and embraces all things which are dissolved for the production of other like things? Wilt thou never be such that thou shalt so dwell in community with gods and men as neither to find fault with them at all, nor to be condemned by them?

2

Observe what thy nature requires, so far as thou art governed by nature only: then do it and accept it, if thy nature, so far as thou art a living being, shall not be made worse by it.

And next thou must observe what thy nature requires so far as thou art a living being. And all this thou mayest allow thyself, if thy nature, so far as thou art a rational animal, shall not be made worse by it. But the rational animal is consequently also a political (social) animal. Use these rules, then, and trouble thyself about nothing else.

3

Everything which happens either happens in such wise as thou art formed by nature to bear it, or as thou art not formed by nature to bear it. If, then, it happens to thee in such way as thou art formed by nature to bear it, do not complain, but bear it as thou art formed by nature to bear it. But if it happens in such wise as thou art not formed by nature to bear it, do not complain, for it will perish after it has consumed thee. Remember, however, that thou art formed by nature to bear everything, with respect to which it depends on thy own opinion to make it endurable and tolerable, by thinking that it is either thy interest or thy duty to do this.

4

If a man is mistaken, instruct him kindly and show him his error. But if thou art not able, blame thyself, or blame not even thyself.

5

Whatever may happen to thee, it was prepared for thee from all eternity; and the implication of causes was from eternity spinning the thread of thy being, and of that which is incident to it.

6

Whether the universe is a concourse of atoms, or nature is a system, let this first be established, that I am a part of the whole which is governed by nature; next, I am in a manner intimately related to the parts which are of the same kind with myself. For remembering this, inasmuch as I am a part, I shall be discontented with none of the things which are assigned to me out of the whole; for nothing is injurious to the part, if it is for the advantage of the whole. For the whole contains nothing which is not for its advantage; and all natures indeed have this common principle, but the nature of the universe has this principle besides, that it cannot be compelled even by any external cause to generate anything harmful to itself. By remembering, then, that I am a part of such a whole, I shall be content with everything that happens. And inasmuch as I am in a manner intimately related to the parts which are of the same kind with myself, I shall do nothing unsocial, but I shall rather direct myself to the things which are of the same kind with myself, and I shall turn an my efforts to the common interest, and divert them from the contrary. Now, if these things are done so, life must flow on happily, just as thou mayest observe that the life of a citizen is happy, who continues a course of action which is advantageous to his fellow-citizens, and is content with whatever the state may assign to him.

7

The parts of the whole, everything, I mean, which is naturally comprehended in the universe, must of necessity perish; but let this be understood in this sense, that they must undergo change. But if this is naturally both an evil and a necessity for the parts, the whole would not continue to exist in a good condition, the parts being subject to change and constituted so as to perish in various ways. For whether did nature herself design to do evil to the things which are parts of herself, and to make them subject to evil and of necessity fall into evil, or have such results happened without her knowing it? Both these suppositions, indeed, are incredible. But if a man should even drop the term Nature (as an efficient power), and should speak of these things as natural, even then it would be ridiculous to affirm at the same time that the parts of the whole are in their nature subject to change, and at the same time to be surprised or vexed as if something were happening contrary to nature, particularly as the dissolution of things is into those things of which each thing is composed. For there is either a dispersion of the elements out of which everything has been compounded, or a change from the solid to the earthy and from the airy to the aerial, so that these parts are taken back into the universal reason, whether this at certain periods is consumed by fire or renewed by eternal changes. And do not imagine that the solid and the airy part belong to thee from the time of generation. For all this received its accretion only yesterday and the day before, as one may say, from the food and the air which is inspired. This, then, which has received the accretion, changes, not that which thy mother brought forth. But suppose that this which thy mother brought forth implicates thee very much with that other part, which has the peculiar quality of change, this is nothing in fact in the way of objection to what is said.

8

When thou hast assumed these names, good, modest, true, rational, a man of equanimity, and magnanimous, take care that thou dost not change these names; and if thou shouldst lose them, quickly return to them. And remember that the term Rational was intended to signify a discriminating attention to every several thing and freedom from negligence; and that Equanimity is the voluntary acceptance of the things which are assigned to thee by the common nature; and that Magnanimity is the elevation of the intelligent part above the pleasurable or painful sensations of the flesh, and above that poor thing called fame, and death, and all such things. If, then, thou maintainest thyself in the possession of these names, without desiring to be called by these names by others, thou wilt be another person and wilt enter on another life. For to continue to be such as thou hast hitherto been, and to be tom in pieces and defiled in such a life, is the character of a very stupid man and one overfond of his life, and like those half-devoured fighters with wild beasts, who though covered with wounds and gore, still intreat to be kept to the following day, though they will be exposed in the same state to the same claws and bites. Therefore fix thyself in the possession of these few names: and if thou art able to abide in them, abide as if thou wast removed to certain islands of the Happy. But if thou shalt perceive that thou fallest out of them and dost not maintain thy hold, go courageously into some nook where thou shalt maintain them, or even depart at once from life, not in passion, but with simplicity and freedom and modesty, after doing this one laudable thing at least in thy life, to have gone out of it thus. In order, however, to the remembrance of these names, it will greatly help thee, if thou rememberest the gods, and that they wish not to be flattered, but wish all reasonable beings to be made like themselves; and if thou rememberest that what does the work of a fig-tree is a fig-tree, and that what does the work of a dog is a dog, and that what does the work of a bee is a bee, and that what does the work of a man is a man.

9

Mimi, war, astonishment, torpor, slavery, will daily wipe out those holy principles of thine. How many things without studying nature dost thou imagine, and how many dost thou neglect? But it is thy duty so to look on and so to do everything, that at the same time the power of dealing with circumstances is perfected, and the contemplative faculty is exercised, and the confidence which comes from the knowledge of each several thing is maintained without showing it, but yet not concealed. For when wilt thou enjoy simplicity, when gravity, and when the knowledge of every several thing, both what it is in substance, and what place it has in the universe, and how long it is formed to exist and of what things it is compounded, and to whom it can belong, and who are able both to give it and take it away?

10

A spider is proud when it has caught a fly, and another when he has caught a poor hare, and another when he has taken a little fish in a net, and another when he has taken wild boars, and another when he has taken bears, and another when he has taken Sarmatians. Are not these robbers, if thou examinest their opinions?

11

Acquire the contemplative way of seeing how all things change into one another, and constantly attend to it, and exercise thyself about this part of philosophy. For nothing is so much adapted to produce magnanimity. Such a man has put off the body, and as he sees that he must, no one knows how soon, go away from among men and leave everything here, he gives himself up entirely to just doing in all his actions, and in everything else that happens he resigns himself to the universal nature. But as to what any man shall say or think about him or do against him, he never even thinks of it, being himself contented with these two things, with acting justly in what he now does, and being satisfied with what is now assigned to him; and he lays aside all distracting and busy pursuits, and desires nothing else than to accomplish the straight course through the law, and by accomplishing the straight course to follow God.

12

What need is there of suspicious fear, since it is in thy power to inquire what ought to be done? And if thou seest clear, go by this way content, without turning back: but if thou dost not see clear, stop and take the best advisers. But if any other things oppose thee, go on according to thy powers with due consideration, keeping to that which appears to be just. For it is best to reach this object, and if thou dost fail, let thy failure be in attempting this. He who follows reason in all things is both tranquil and active at the same time, and also cheerful and collected.

13

Inquire of thyself as soon as thou wakest from sleep, whether it will make any difference to thee, if another does what is just and right. It will make no difference.

Thou hast not forgotten, I suppose, that those who assume arrogant airs in bestowing their praise or blame on others, are such as they are at bed and at board, and thou hast not forgotten what they do, and what they avoid and what they pursue, and how they steal and how they rob, not with hands and feet, but with their most valuable part, by means of which there is produced, when a man chooses, fidelity, modesty, truth, law, a good daemon (happiness)?

14

To her who gives and takes back all, to nature, the man who is instructed and modest says, Give what thou wilt; take back what thou wilt. And he says this not proudly, but obediently and well pleased with her.

15

Short is the little which remains to thee of life. Live as on a mountain. For it makes no difference whether a man lives there or here, if he lives everywhere in the world as in a state (political community). Let men see, let them know a real man who lives according to nature. If they cannot endure him, let them kill him. For that is better than to live thus as men do.

16

No longer talk at all about the kind of man that a good man ought to be, but be such.

17

Constantly contemplate the whole of time and the whole of substance, and consider that all individual things as to substance are a grain of a fig, and as to time, the turning of a gimlet.

18

Look at everything that exists, and observe that it is already in dissolution and in change, and as it were putrefaction or dispersion, or that everything is so constituted by nature as to die.

19

Consider what men are when they are eating, sleeping, generating, easing themselves and so forth. Then what kind of men they are when they are imperious and arrogant, or angry and scolding from their elevated place. But a short time ago to how many they were slaves and for what things; and after a little time consider in what a condition they will be.

20

That is for the good of each thing, which the universal nature brings to each. And it is for its good at the time when nature brings it.

21

"The earth loves the shower"; and "the solemn aether loves": and the universe loves to make whatever is about to be. I say then to the universe, that I love as thou lovest. And is not this too said, that "this or that loves (is wont) to be produced"?

22

Either thou livest here and hast already accustomed thyself to it, or thou art going away, and this was thy own will; or thou art dying and hast discharged thy duty. But besides these things there is nothing. Be of good cheer, then.

23

Let this always be plain to thee, that this piece of land is like any other; and that all things here are the same with things on top of a mountain, or on the sea-shore, or wherever thou choosest to be. For thou wilt find just what Plato says, Dwelling within the walls of a city as in a shepherd's fold on a mountain.

24

What is my ruling faculty now to me? And of what nature am I now making it? And for what purpose am I now using it? Is it void of understanding? Is it loosed and rent asunder from social life? Is it melted into and mixed with the poor flesh so as to move together with it?

25

He who flies from his master is a runaway; but the law is master, and he who breaks the law is a runaway. And he also who is grieved or angry or afraid, is dissatisfied because something has been or is or shall be of the things which are appointed by him who rules all things, and he is Law, and assigns to every man what is fit. He then who fears or is grieved or is angry is a runaway.

26

A man deposits seed in a womb and goes away, and then another cause takes it, and labours on it and makes a child. What a thing from such a material! Again, the child passes food down through the throat, and then another cause takes it and makes perception and motion, and in fine life and strength and other things; how many and how strange I Observe then the things which are produced in such a hidden way, and see the power just as we see the power which carries things downwards and upwards, not with the eyes, but still no less plainly.

27

Constantly consider how all things such as they now are, in time past also were; and consider that they will be the same again. And place before thy eyes entire dramas and stages of the same form, whatever thou hast learned from thy experience or from older history; for example, the whole court of Hadrian, and the whole court of Antoninus, and the whole court of Philip, Alexander, Croesus; for all those were such dramas as we see now, only with different actors.

28

Imagine every man who is grieved at anything or discontented to be like a pig which is sacrificed and kicks and screams.

Like this pig also is he who on his bed in silence laments the bonds in which we are held. And consider that only to the rational animal is it given to follow voluntarily what happens; but simply to follow is a necessity imposed on all.

29

Severally on the occasion of everything that thou doest, pause and ask thyself, if death is a dreadful thing because it deprives thee of this.

30

When thou art offended at any man's fault, forthwith turn to thyself and reflect in what like manner thou dost err thyself; for example, in thinking that money is a good thing, or pleasure, or a bit of reputation, and the like. For by attending to this thou wilt quickly forget thy anger, if this consideration also is added, that the man is compelled: for what else could he do? or, if thou art able, take away from him the compulsion.

31

When thou hast seen Satyron the Socratic, think of either Eutyches or Hymen, and when thou hast seen Euphrates, think of Eutychion or Silvanus, and when thou hast seen Alciphron think of Tropaeophorus, and when thou hast seen Xenophon think of Crito or Severus, and when thou hast looked on thyself, think of any other Caesar, and in the case of every one do in like manner. Then let this thought be in thy mind, Where then are those men? Nowhere, or nobody knows where. For thus continuously thou wilt look at human things as smoke and nothing at all; especially if thou reflectest at the same time that what has once changed will never exist again in the infinite duration of time. But thou, in what a brief space of time is thy existence? And why art thou not content to pass through this short time in an orderly way? What matter and opportunity for thy activity art thou avoiding? For what else are all these things, except exercises for the reason, when it has viewed carefully and by examination into their nature the things which happen in life? Persevere then until thou shalt have made these things thy own, as the stomach which is strengthened makes all things its own, as the blazing fire makes flame and brightness out of everything that is thrown into it.

32

Let it not be in any man's power to say truly of thee that thou art not simple or that thou are not good; but let him be a liar whoever shall think anything of this kind about thee; and this is altogether in thy power. For who is he that shall hinder thee from being good and simple? Do thou only determine to live no longer, unless thou shalt be such. For neither does reason allow thee to live, if thou art not such.

33

What is that which as to this material (our life) can be done or said in the way most conformable to reason. For whatever this may be, it is in thy power to do it or to say it, and do not make excuses that thou art hindered. Thou wilt not cease to lament till thy mind is in such a condition that, what luxury is to those who enjoy pleasure, such shall be to thee, in the matter which is subjected and presented to thee, the doing of the things which are conformable to man's constitution; for a man ought to consider as an enjoyment everything which it is in his power to do according to his own nature. And it is in his power everywhere. Now, it is not given to a cylinder to move everywhere by its own motion, nor yet to water nor to fire, nor to anything else which is governed by nature or an irrational soul, for the things which check them and stand in the way are many. But intelligence and reason are able to go through everything that opposes them, and in such manner as they are formed by nature and as they choose. Place before thy eyes this facility with which the reason will be carried through all things, as fire upwards, as a stone downwards, as a cylinder down an inclined surface, and seek for nothing further. For all other obstacles either affect the body only which is a dead thing; or, except through opinion and the yielding of the reason itself, they do not crush nor do any harm of any kind; for if they did, he who felt it would immediately become bad. Now, in the case of all things which have a certain constitution, whatever harm may happen to any of them, that which is so affected becomes consequently worse; but in the like case, a man becomes both better, if one may say so, and more worthy of praise by making a right use of these accidents. And finally remember that nothing harms him who is really a citizen, which does not harm the state; nor yet does anything harm the state, which does not harm law (order); and of these things which are called misfortunes not one harms law. What then does not harm law does not harm either state or citizen.

34

To him who is penetrated by true principles even the briefest precept is sufficient, and any common precept, to remind him that he should be free from grief and fear. For example

Leaves, some the wind scatters on the ground . . . so is the race of men.

Leaves, also, are thy children; and leaves, too, are they who cry out as if they were worthy of credit and bestow their praise, or on the contrary curse, or secretly blame and sneer; and leaves, in like manner, are those who shall receive and transmit a man's fame to aftertimes. For all such things as these "are produced in the season of spring," as the poet says; then the wind casts them down; then the forest produces other leaves in their places. But a brief existence is common to all things, and yet thou avoidest and pursuest all things as if they would be eternal. A little time, and thou shalt close thy eyes; and him who has attended thee to thy grave another soon will lament.

35

The healthy eye ought to see all visible things and not to say, I wish for green things; for this is the condition of a diseased eye. And the healthy hearing and smelling ought to be ready to perceive all that can be heard and smelled. And the healthy stomach ought to be with respect to all food just as the mill with respect to all things which it is formed to grind. And accordingly the healthy understanding ought to be prepared for everything which happens; but that which says, Let my dear children live, and let all men praise whatever I may do, is an eye which seeks for green things, or teeth which seek for soft things.

36

There is no man so fortunate that there shall not be by him when he is dying some who are pleased with what is going to happen. Suppose that he was a good and wise man, will there not be at last some one to say to himself, Let us at last breathe freely being relieved from this schoolmaster? It is true that he was harsh to none of us, but I perceived that he tacitly condemns us.—This is what is said of a good man. But in our own case how many other things are there for which there are many who wish to get rid of us. Thou wilt consider this then when thou art dying, and thou wilt depart more contentedly by reflecting thus: I am going away from such a life, in which even my associates in behalf of whom I have striven so much, prayed, and cared, themselves wish me to depart, hoping perchance to get some little advantage by it. Why then should a man cling to a longer stay here? Do not however for this reason go away less kindly disposed to them, but preserving thy own character, and friendly and benevolent and mild, and on the other hand not as if thou wast torn away; but as when a man dies a quiet death, the poor soul is easily separated from the body, such also ought thy departure from men to be, for nature united thee to them and associated thee. But does she now dissolve the union? Well, I am separated as from kinsmen, not however dragged resisting, but without compulsion; for this too is one of the things according to nature.

37

Accustom thyself as much as possible on the occasion of anything being done by any person to inquire with thyself, For what object is this man doing this? But begin with thyself, and examine thyself first.

38

Remember that this which pulls the strings is the thing which is hidden within: this is the power of persuasion, this is life, this, if one may so say, is man. In contemplating thyself never include the vessel which surrounds thee and these instruments which are attached about it. For they are like to an axe, differing only in this that they grow to the body. For indeed there is no more use in these parts without the cause which moves and checks them than in the weaver's shuttle, and the writer's pen and the driver's whip.

BOOK ELEVEN

1

These are the properties of the rational soul: it sees itself, analyses itself, and makes itself such as it chooses; the fruit which it bears itself enjoys—for the fruits of plants and that in animals which corresponds to fruits others enjoy—it obtains its own end, wherever the limit of life may be fixed. Not as in a dance and in a play and in such like things, where the whole action is incomplete, if anything cuts it short; but in every part and wherever it may be stopped, it makes what has been set before it full and complete, so that it can say, I have what is my own. And further it traverses the whole universe, and the surrounding vacuum, and surveys its form, and it extends itself into the infinity of time, and embraces and comprehends the periodical renovation of all things, and it comprehends that those who come after us will see nothing new, nor have those before us seen anything more, but in a manner he who is forty years old, if he has any understanding at all, has seen by virtue of the uniformity that prevails all things which have been and all that will be. This too is a property of the rational soul, love of one's neighbour, and truth and modesty, and to value nothing more more than itself, which is also the property of Law. Thus then right reason differs not at all from the reason of justice.

2

Thou wilt set little value on pleasing song and dancing and the pancratium, if thou wilt distribute the melody of the voice into its several sounds, and ask thyself as to each, if thou art mastered by this; for thou wilt be prevented by shame from confessing it: and in the matter of dancing, if at each movement and attitude thou wilt do the same; and the like also in the matter of the pancratium. In all things, then, except virtue and the acts of virtue, remember to apply thyself to their several parts, and by this division to come to value them little: and apply this rule also to thy whole life.

3

What a soul that is which is ready, if at any moment it must be separated from the body, and ready either to be extinguished or dispersed or continue to exist; but so that this readiness comes from a man's own judgement, not from mere obstinacy, as with the Christians, but considerately and with dignity and in a way to persuade another, without tragic show.

4

Have I done something for the general interest? Well then I have had my reward. Let this always be present to thy mind, and never stop doing such good.

5

What is thy art? To be good. And how is this accomplished well except by general principles, some about the nature of the universe, and others about the proper constitution of man?

6

At first tragedies were brought on the stage as means of reminding men of the things which happen to them, and that it is according to nature for things to happen so, and that, if you are delighted with what is shown on the stage, you should not be troubled with that which takes place on the larger stage. For you see that these things must be accomplished thus, and that even they bear them who cry out "O Cithaeron." And, indeed, some things are said well by the dramatic writers, of which kind is the following especially:—

Me and my children if the gods neglect,
This has its reason too.
And again
We must not chale and fret at that which happens.
And
Life's harvest reap like the wheat's fruitful ear.
And other things of the same kind.

After tragedy the old comedy was introduced, which had a magisterial freedom of speech, and by its very plainness of speaking was useful in reminding men to beware of insolence; and for this purpose too Diogenes used to take from these writers.

But as to the middle comedy which came next, observe what it was, and again, for what object the new comedy was introduced, which gradually sunk down into a mere mimic artifice. That some good things are said even by these writers, everybody knows: but the whole plan of such poetry and dramaturgy, to what end does it look!

7

How plain does it appear that there is not another condition of life so well suited for philosophising as this in which thou now happenest to be.

8

A branch cut off from the adjacent branch must of necessity be cut off from the whole tree also. So too a man when he is separated from another man has fallen off from the whole social community. Now as to a branch, another cuts it off, but a man by his own act separates himself from his neighbour when he hates him and turns away from him, and he does not know that he has at the same time cut himself off from the whole social system. Yet he has this privilege certainly from Zeus who framed society, for it is in our power to grow again to that which is near to us, and be to come a part which helps to make up the whole. However, if it often happens, this kind of separation, it makes it difficult for that which detaches itself to be brought to unity and to be restored to its former condition. Finally, the branch, which from the first grew together with the tree, and has continued to have one life with it, is not like that which after being cut off is then ingrafted, for this is something like what the gardeners mean when they say that it grows with the rest of the tree, but that it has not the same mind with it.

9

As those who try to stand in thy way when thou art proceeding according to right reason, will not be able to turn thee aside from thy proper action, so neither let them drive thee from thy benevolent feelings towards them, but be on thy guard equally in both matters, not only in the matter of steady judgement and action, but also in the matter of gentleness towards those who try to hinder or otherwise trouble thee. For this also is a weakness, to be vexed at them, as well as to be diverted from thy course of action and to give way through fear; for both are equally deserters from their post, the man who does it through fear, and the man who is alienated from him who is by nature a kinsman and a friend.

10

There is no nature which is inferior to art, for the arts imitate the nature of things. But if this is so, that nature which is the most perfect and the most comprehensive of all natures, cannot fall short of the skill of art. Now all arts do the inferior things for the sake of the superior; therefore the universal nature does so too. And, indeed, hence is the origin of justice, and in justice the other virtues have their foundation: for justice will not be observed, if we either care for middle things (things indifferent), or are easily deceived and careless and changeable.

11

If the things do not come to thee, the pursuits and avoidances of which disturb thee, still in a manner thou goest to them. Let then thy judgement about them be at rest, and they will remain quiet, and thou wilt not be seen either pursuing or avoiding.

12

The spherical form of the soul maintains its figure, when it is neither extended towards any object, nor contracted inwards, nor dispersed nor sinks down, but is illuminated by light, by which it sees the truth, the truth of all things and the truth that is in itself.

13

Suppose any man shall despise me. Let him look to that himself. But I will look to this, that I be not discovered doing or saying anything deserving of contempt. Shall any man hate me? Let him look to it. But I will be mild and benevolent towards every man, and ready to show even him his mistake, not reproachfully, nor yet as making a display of my endurance, but nobly and honestly, like the great Phocion, unless indeed he only assumed it. For the interior parts ought to be such, and a man ought to be seen by the gods neither dissatisfied with anything nor complaining. For what evil is it to thee, if thou art now doing what is agreeable to thy own nature, and art satisfied with that which at this moment is suitable to the nature of the universe, since thou art a human being placed at thy post in order that what is for the common advantage may be done in some way?

14

Men despise one another and flatter one another; and men wish to raise themselves above one another, and crouch before one another.

15

How unsound and insincere is he who says, I have determined to deal with thee in a fair way.—What art thou doing, man? There is no occasion to give this notice. It will soon show itself by acts. The voice ought to be plainly written on the forehead. Such as a man's character is, he immediately shows it in his eyes, just as he who is beloved forthwith reads everything in the eyes of lovers. The man who is honest and good ought to be exactly like a man who smells strong, so that the bystander as soon as he comes near him must smell whether he choose or not. But the affectation of simplicity is like a crooked stick. Nothing is more disgraceful than a wolfish friendship (false friendship). Avoid this most of all. The good and simple and benevolent show all these things in the eyes, and there is no mistaking.

16

As to living in the best way, this power is in the soul, if it be indifferent to things which are indifferent. And it will be indifferent, if it looks on each of these things separately and all together, and if it remembers that not one of them produces in us an opinion about itself, nor comes to us; but these things remain immovable, and it is we ourselves who produce the judgements about them, and, as we may say, write them in ourselves, it being in our power not to write them, and it being in our power, if perchance these judgements have imperceptibly got admission to our minds, to wipe them out; and if we remember also that such attention will only be for a short time, and then life will be at an end. Besides, what trouble is there at all in doing this? For if these things are according to nature, rejoice in them, and they will be easy to thee: but if contrary to nature, seek what is conformable to thy own nature, and strive towards this, even if it bring no reputation; for every man is allowed to seek his own good.

17

Consider whence each thing is come, and of what it consists, and into what it changes, and what kind of a thing it will be when it has changed, and that it will sustain no harm.

18

If any have offended against thee, consider *first*: What is my relation to men, and that we are made for one another; and in another respect, I was made to be set over them, as a ram over the flock or a bull over the herd. But examine the matter from first principles, from this: If all things are not mere atoms, it is nature which orders all things: if this is so, the inferior things exist for the sake of the superior, and these for the sake of one another.

Second, consider what kind of men they are at table, in bed, and so forth: and particularly, under what compulsions in respect of opinions they are; and as to their acts, consider with what pride they do what they do.

Third, that if men do rightly what they do, we ought not to be displeased; but if they do not right, it is plain that they do so involuntarily and in ignorance. For as every soul is unwillingly deprived of the truth, so also is it unwillingly deprived of the power of behaving to each man according to his deserts. Accordingly men are pained when they are called unjust, ungrateful, and greedy, and in a word wrong-doers to their neighbours.

Fourth, consider that thou also doest many things wrong, and that thou art a man like others; and even if thou dost abstain from certain faults, still thou hast the disposition to commit them, though either through cowardice, or concern about reputation, or some such mean motive, thou dost abstain from such faults.

Fifth, consider that thou dost not even understand whether men are doing wrong or not, for many things are done with a certain reference to circumstances. And in short, a man must learn a great deal to enable him to pass a correct judgement on another man's acts.

Sixth, consider when thou art much vexed or grieved, that man's life is only a moment, and after a short time we are all laid out dead.

Seventh, that it is not men's acts which disturb us, for those acts have their foundation in men's ruling principles, but it is our own opinions which disturb us. Take away these opinions then, and resolve to dismiss thy judgement about an act as if it were something grievous, and thy anger is gone. How then shall I take away these opinions? By reflecting that no wrongful act of another brings shame on thee: for unless that which is shameful is alone bad, thou also must of necessity do many things wrong, and become a robber and everything else.

Eighth, consider how much more pain is brought on us by the anger and vexation caused by such acts than by the acts themselves, at which we are angry and vexed.

Ninth, consider that a good disposition is invincible, if it be genuine, and not an affected smile and acting a part. For what will the most violent man do to thee, if thou continuest to be of a kind disposition towards him, and if, as opportunity offers, thou gently admonishest him and calmly correctest his errors at the very time when he is trying to do thee harm, saying, Not so, my child: we are constituted by nature for something else: I shall certainly not be injured, but thou art injuring thyself, my child.—And show him with gentle tact and by general principles that this is so, and that even bees do not do as he does, nor any animals which are formed by nature to be gregarious. And thou must do this neither with any double meaning nor in the way of reproach, but affectionately and without any rancour in thy soul; and not as if thou wert lecturing him, nor yet that any bystander may admire, but either when he is alone, and if others are present . . .

Remember these nine rules, as if thou hadst received them as a gift from the Muses, and begin at last to be a man while thou livest. But thou must equally avoid flattering men and being veied at them, for both are unsocial and lead to harm. And let this truth be present to thee in the excitement of anger, that to be moved by passion is not manly, but that mildness and gentleness, as they are more agreeable to human nature, so also are they more manly; and he who possesses these qualities possesses strength, nerves and courage, and not the man who is subject to fits of passion and discontent. For in the same degree in which a man's mind is nearer to freedom from all passion, in the same degree also is it nearer to strength: and as the sense of pain is a characteristic of weakness, so also is anger. For he who yields to pain and he who yields to anger, both are wounded and both submit.

But if thou wilt, receive also a *tenth* present from the leader of the Muses (Apollo), and it is this—that to expect bad men not to do wrong is madness, for he who expects this desires an impossibility. But to allow men to behave so to others, and to expect them not to do thee any wrong, is irrational and tyrannical.

19

There are four principal aberrations of the superior faculty against which thou shouldst be constantly on thy guard, and when thou hast detected them, thou shouldst wipe them out and say on each occasion thus: this thought is not necessary: this tends to destroy social union: this which thou art going to say comes not from the real thoughts; for thou shouldst consider it among the most absurd of things for a man not to speak from his real thoughts. But the fourth is when thou shalt reproach thyself for anything, for this is an evidence of the diviner part within thee being overpowered and yielding to the less honourable and to the perishable part, the body, and to its gross pleasures.

20

Thy aerial part and all the fiery parts which are mingled in thee, though by nature they have an upward tendency, still in obedience to the disposition of the universe they are overpowered here in the compound mass (the body). And also the whole of the earthy part in thee and the watery, though their tendency is downward, still are raised up and occupy a position which is not their natural one. In this manner then the elemental parts obey the universal, for when they have been fixed in any place perforce they remain there until again the universal shall sound the signal for dissolution. Is it not then strange that thy intelligent part only should be disobedient and discontented with its own place? And yet no force is imposed on it, but only those things which are conformable to its nature: still it does not submit, but is carried in the opposite direction. For the movement towards injustice and intemperance and to anger and grief and fear is nothing else than the act of one who deviates from nature. And also when the ruling faculty is discontented with anything that happens, then too it deserts its post: for it is constituted for piety and reverence towards the gods no less than for justice. For these qualities also are comprehended under the generic term of contentment with the constitution of things, and indeed they are prior to acts of justice.

21

He who has not one and always the same object in life, cannot be one and the same all through his life. But what I have said is not enough, unless this also is added, what this object ought to be. For as there is not the same opinion about all the things which in some way or other are considered by the majority to be good, but only about some certain things, that is, things which concern the common interest; so also ought we to propose to ourselves an object which shall be of a common kind (social) and political. For he who directs all his own efforts to this object, will make all his acts alike, and thus will always be the same.

22

Think of the country mouse and of the town mouse, and of the alarm and trepidation of the town mouse.

23

Socrates used to call the opinions of the many by the name of Lamiae, bugbears to frighten children.

24

The Lacedaemonians at their public spectacles used to set seats in the shade for strangers, but themselves sat down anywhere.

25

Socrates excused himself to Perdiccas for not going to him, saying, It is because I would not perish by the worst of all ends, that is, I would not receive a favour and then be unable to return it.

26

In the writings of the Ephesians there was this precept, constantly to think of some one of the men of former times who practised virtue.

27

The Pythagoreans bid us in the morning look to the heavens that we may be reminded of those bodies which continually do the same things and in the same manner perform their work, and also be reminded of their purity and nudity. For there is no veil over a star.

28

Consider what a man Socrates was when he dressed himself in a skin, after Xanthippe had taken his cloak and gone out, and what Socrates said to his friends who were ashamed of him and drew back from him when they saw him dressed thus.

29

Neither in writing nor in reading wilt thou be able to lay down rules for others before thou shalt have first learned to obey rules thyself. Much more is this so in life.

30

A slave thou art: free speech is not for thee.

31

And my heart laughed within.

32

And virtue they will curse, speaking harsh words.

33

To look for the fig in winter is a madman's act: such is he who looks for his child when it is no longer allowed.

34

When a man kisses his child, said Epictetus, he should whisper to himself, "Tomorrow perchance thou wilt die."—But those are words of bad omen.—"No word is a word of bad omen," said Epictetus, "which expresses any work of nature; or if it is so, it is also a word of bad omen to speak of the ears of corn being reaped."

35

The unripe grape, the ripe bunch, the dried grape, all are changes, not into nothing, but into something which exists not yet.

36

No man can rob us of our free will.

37

Epictetus also said, A man must discover an art (or rules) with respect to giving his assent; and in respect to his movements he must be careful that they be made with regard to circumstances, that they be consistent with social interests, that they have regard to the value of the object; and as to sensual desire, he should altogether keep away from it; and as to avoidance (aversion) he should not show it with respect to any of the things which are not in our power.

38

The dispute then, he said, is not about any common matter, but about being mad or not.

39

Socrates used to say, What do you want? Souls of rational men or irrational?—Souls of rational men.—Of what rational men? Sound or unsound?—Sound.—Why then do you not seek for them?—Because we have them.—Why then do you fight and quarrel?

BOOK TWELVE

1

All those things at which thou wishest to arrive by a circuitous road, thou canst have now, if thou dost not refuse them to thyself. And this means, if thou wilt take no notice of all the past, and trust the future to providence, and direct the present only conformably to piety and justice. Conformably to piety, that thou mayest be content with the lot which is assigned to thee, for nature designed it for thee and thee for it. Conformably to justice, that thou mayest always speak the truth freely and without disguise, and do the things which are agreeable to law and according to the worth of each. And let neither another man's wickedness hinder thee, nor opinion nor voice, nor yet the sensations of the poor flesh which has grown about thee; for the passive part will look to this. If then, whatever the time may be when thou shalt be near to thy departure, neglecting everything else thou shalt respect only thy ruling faculty and the divinity within thee, and if thou shalt be afraid not because thou must some time cease to live, but if thou shalt fear never to have begun to live according to nature—then thou wilt be a man worthy of the universe which has produced thee, and thou wilt cease to be a stranger in thy native land, and to wonder at things which happen daily as if they were something unexpected, and to be dependent on this or that.

2

God sees the minds (ruling principles) of all men bared of the material vesture and rind and impurities. For with his intellectual part alone he touches the intelligence only which has flowed and been derived from himself into these bodies. And if thou also usest thyself to do this, thou wilt rid thyself of thy much trouble. For he who regards not the poor flesh which envelops him, surely will not trouble himself by looking after raiment and dwelling and fame and such like externals and show.

3

The things are three of which thou art composed, a little body, a little breath (life), intelligence. Of these the first two are thine, so far as it is thy duty to take care of them; but the third alone is properly thine. Therefore if thou shalt separate from thyself, that is, from thy understanding, whatever others do or say, and whatever thou hast done or said thyself, and whatever future things trouble thee because they may happen, and whatever in the body which envelops thee or in the breath (life), which is by nature associated with the body, is attached to thee independent of thy will, and whatever the external circumfluent vortex whirls round, so that the intellectual power exempt from the things of fate can live pure and free by itself, doing what is just and accepting what happens and saying the truth: if thou wilt separate, I say, from this ruling faculty the things which are attached to it by the impressions of sense, and the things of time to come and of time that is past, and wilt make thyself like Empedocles' sphere, All round, and in its joyous rest reposing;

and if thou shalt strive to live only what is really thy life, that is, the present—then thou wilt be able to pass that portion of life which remains for thee up to the time of thy death, free from perturbations, nobly, and obedient to thy own daemon (to the god that is within thee).

4

I have often wondered how it is that every man loves himself more than all the rest of men, but yet sets less value on his own opinion of himself than on the opinion of others. If then a god or a wise teacher should present himself to a man and bid him to think of nothing and to design nothing which he would not express as soon as he conceived it, he could not endure it even for a single day. So much more respect have we to what our neighbours shall think of us than to what we shall think of ourselves.

5

How can it be that the gods after having arranged all things well and benevolently for mankind, have overlooked this alone, that some men and very good men, and men who, as we may say, have had most communion with the divinity, and through pious acts and religious observances have been most intimate with the divinity, when they have once died should never exist again, but should be completely extinguished?

But if this is so, be assured that if it ought to have been otherwise, the gods would have done it. For if it were just, it would also be possible; and if it were according to nature, nature would have had it so. But because it is not so, if in fact it is not so, be thou convinced that it ought not to have been so:— for thou seest even of thyself that in this inquiry thou art disputing with the diety; and we should not thus dispute with the gods, unless they were most excellent and most just;—but if this is so, they would not have allowed anything in the ordering of the universe to be neglected unjustly and irrationally.

6

Practise thyself even in the things which thou despairest of accomplishing. For even the left hand, which is ineffectual for all other things for want of practice, holds the bridle more vigorously than the right hand; for it has been practised in this.

7

Consider in what condition both in body and soul a man should be when he is overtaken by death; and consider the shortness of life, the boundless abyss of time past and future, the feebleness of all matter.

8

Contemplate the formative principles (forms) of things bare of their coverings; the purposes of actions; consider what pain is, what pleasure is, and death, and fame; who is to himself the cause of his uneasiness; how no man is hindered by another; that everything is opinion.

9

In the application of thy principles thou must be like the pancratiast, not like the gladiator; for the gladiator lets fall the sword which he uses and is killed; but the other always has his hand, and needs to do nothing else than use it.

10

See what things are in themselves, dividing them into matter, form and purpose.

11

What a power man has to do nothing except what God will approve, and to accept all that God may give him.

12

With respect to that which happens conformably to nature, we ought to blame neither gods, for they do nothing wrong either voluntarily or involuntarily, nor men, for they do nothing wrong except involuntarily. Consequently we should blame nobody.

13

How ridiculous and what a stranger he is who is surprised at anything which happens in life.

14–15

Either there is a fatal necessity and invincible order, or a kind Providence, or a confusion without a purpose and without a director (Book IV). If then there is an invincible necessity, why dost thou resist? But if there is a Providence which allows itself to be propitiated, make thyself worthy of the help of the divinity. But if there is a confusion without governor, be content that in such a tempest thou hast in thyself a certain ruling intelligence. And even if the tempest carry thee away, let it carry away the poor flesh, the poor breath, everything else; for the intelligence at least it will not carry away.

Does the light of the lamp shine without losing its splendour until it is extinguished; and shall the truth which is in thee and justice and temperance be extinguished before thy death?

16

When a man has presented the appearance of having done wrong, say, How then do I know if this is a wrongful act? And even if he has done wrong, how do I know that he has not condemned himself? and so this is like tearing his own face. Consider that he, who would not have the bad man do wrong, is like the man who would not have the fig-tree to bear juice in the figs and infants to cry and the horse to neigh, and whatever else must of necessity be. For what must a man do who has such a character? If then thou art irritable, cure this man's disposition.

17–18

If it is not right, do not do it: if it is not true, do not say it. For let thy efforts be. In everything always observe what the thing is which produces for thee an appearance, and resolve it by dividing it into the formal, the material, the purpose, and the time within which it must end.

19

Perceive at last that thou hast in thee something better and more divine than the things which cause the various affects, and as it were pull thee by the strings. What is there now in my mind? Is it fear, or suspicion, or desire, or anything of the kind?

20

First, do nothing inconsiderately, nor without a purpose. Second, make thy acts refer to nothing else than to a social end.

21

Consider that before long thou wilt be nobody and nowhere, nor will any of the things exist which thou now seest, nor any of those who are now living. For all things are formed by nature to change and be turned and to perish in order that other things in continuous succession may exist.

22

Consider that everything is opinion, and opinion is in thy power. Take away then, when thou choosest, thy opinion, and like a mariner, who has doubled the promontory, thou wilt find calm, everything stable, and a waveless bay.

23

Any one activity whatever it may be, when it has ceased at its proper time, suffers no evil because it has ceased; nor he who has done this act, does he suffer any evil for this reason that the act has ceased. In like manner then the whole which consists of all the acts, which is our life, if it cease at its proper time, suffers no evil for this reason that it has ceased; nor he who has terminated this series at the proper time, has he been ill dealt with. But the proper time and the limit nature fixes, sometimes as in old age the peculiar nature of man, but always the universal nature, by the change of whose parts the whole universe continues ever young and perfect. And everything which is useful to the universal is always good and in season. Therefore the termination of life for every man is no evil, because neither is it shameful, since it is both independent of the will and not opposed to the general interest, but it is good, since it is seasonable and profitable to and congruent with the universal. For thus too he is moved by the deity who is moved in the same manner with the deity and moved towards the same things in his mind.

24

These three principles thou must have in readiness. *First*, in the things which thou doest do nothing either inconsiderately or otherwise than as justice herself would act; but with respect to what may happen to thee from without, consider that it happens either by chance or according to Providence, and thou must neither blame chance nor accuse Providence. *Second*, consider what every being is from the seed to the time of its receiving a soul, and from the reception of a soul to the giving back of the same, and of what things every being is compounded and into what things it is resolved. *Third*, if thou shouldst suddenly be raised up above the earth, and shouldst look down on human things, and observe the variety of them how great it is, and at the same time also shouldst see at a glance how great is the number of beings who dwell around in the air and the aether, consider that as often as thou shouldst be raised up, thou wouldst see the same things, sameness of form and shortness of duration. Are these things to be proud of?

25

Cast away opinion: thou art saved. Who then hinders thee from casting it away?

26

When thou art troubled about anything, thou hast forgotten this, that all things happen according to the universal nature; and forgotten this, that a man's wrongful act is nothing to thee; and further thou hast forgotten this, that everything which happens, always happened so and will happen so, and now happens so everywhere; forgotten this too, how close is the kinship between a man and the whole human race, for it is a community, not of a little blood or seed, but of intelligence. And thou hast forgotten this too, that every man's intelligence is a god, and is an efflux of the deity; and forgotten this, that nothing is a man's own, but that his child and his body and his very soul came from the deity; forgotten this, that everything is opinion; and lastly thou hast forgotten that every man lives the present time only, and loses only this.

27

Constantly bring to thy recollection those who have complained greatly about anything, those who have been most conspicuous by the greatest fame or misfortunes or enmities or fortunes of any kind: then think where are they all now? Smoke and ash and a tale, or not even a tale. And let there be present to thy mind also everything of this sort, how Fabius Catullinus lived in the country, and Lucius Lupus in his gardens, and Stertinius at Baiae, and Tiberius at Capreae and Velius

Rufus (or Rufus at Velia); and in fine think of the eager pursuit of anything conjoined with pride; and how worthless everything is after which men violently strain; and how much more philosophical it is for a man in the opportunities presented to him to show himself just, temperate, obedient to the gods, and to do this with all simplicity: for the pride which is proud of its want of pride is the most intolerable of all.

28

To those who ask, Where hast thou seen the gods or how dost thou comprehend that they exist and so worshippest them, I answer, in the first place, they may be seen even with the eyes; in the second place neither have I seen even my own soul and yet I honour it. Thus then with respect to the gods, from what I constantly experience of their power, from this I comprehend that they exist and I venerate them.

29

The safety of life is this, to examine everything all through, what it is itself, what is its material, what its formal part; with all thy soul to do justice and to say the truth. What remains except to enjoy life by joining one good thing to another so as not to leave even the smallest intervals between?

30

There is one light of the sun, though it is distributed over walls, mountains, and other things infinite. There is one common substance, though it is distributed among countless bodies which have their several qualities. There is one soul, though it is distributed among infinite natures and circumspections [or individuals]. There is one intelligent soul, though it seems to be divided. Now in the things which have been mentioned all the other parts, such as those which are air and substance, are without sensation and have no fellowship: and yet even these parts the intelligent principle holds together and the gravitatuin towards the same. But intellect in a peculiar manner tends to that which is of the same kin, and combines with it, and the feeling for communion is not interrupted.

31

What dost thou wish? to continue to exist? Well, dost thou wish to have sensation? movement? growth? and then again to cease to grow? to use thy speech? to think? What is there of all these things which seems to thee worth desiring? But if it is easy to set little value on all these things, turn to that which remains, which is to follow reason and god. But it is inconsistent with honouring reason and god to be troubled because by death a man will be deprived of the other things.

32

How small a part of the boundless and unfathomable time is assigned to every man? for it is very soon swallowed up in the eternal. And how small a part of the whole substance? and how small a part of the universal soul? and on what a small clod of the whole earth thou creepest? Reflecting on all this consider nothing to be great, except to act as thy nature leads thee, and to endure that which the common nature brings.

33

How does the ruling faculty make use of itself? for all lies in this. But everything else, whether it is in the power of thy will or not, is only lifeless ashes and smoke.

34

This reflection is most adapted to move us to contempt of death, that even those who think pleasure to be good and pain an evil still have despised it.

35

The man to whom that only is good which comes in due season, and to whom it is the same thing whether he has done more or fewer acts conformable to right reason, and to whom it makes no difference whether he contemplates the world for a longer or a shorter time—for this man neither is death a terrible thing.

36

Man, thou hast been a citizen in this great state [the world]: what difference does it make to thee whether for five years [or three]? for that which is conformable to the laws is just for all. Where is the hardship then, if no tyrant nor yet an unjust judge sends the away from the state, but nature who brought thee into it? the same as if a praetor who has employed an actor dismisses him from the stage—"But I have not finished the five acts, but only three of them"—Thou sayest well, but in life the three acts are the whole drama; for what shall be a complete drama is determined by him who was once the cause of its composition, and now of its dissolution: but thou art the cause of neither. Depart then satisfied, for he also who releases thee is satisfied.

GLOSSARY

AGRIPPA, M. Vipsanius (63-12 B.C.), a distinguished soldier under Augustus.

Alexander the Great, King of Macedonia, and Conqueror of the East, 356-323 B.C.

Antisthenes of Athens, founder of the sect of Cynic philosophers, and an opponent of Plato, 5th century B.C Antoninus Pius, 15th Roman Emperor, 138-161 A.D. one of the best princes that ever mounted a throne.

Apollonius of Alexandria, called Dyscolus, or the 'ill-tempered,' a great grammarian.

Archimedes of Syracuse 287-212 B.C., the most famous mathematician of antiquity.

Athos, a mountain promontory at the N. of the Aegean Sea.

Augustus, first Roman Emperor (ruled 31 B.C.-14 A.D.).

Avoid, void.

BACCHIUS: there Were several persons of this name, and the one meant is perhaps the musician.

Both names were household words.

Brutus (1) the liberator of the Roman people from their kings, and (2) the murderer of Caesar.

CAESAR, Caius, Julius, the Dictator and Conqueror.

Camillus, a famous dictator in the early days of the Roman Republic.

Carnuntum, a town on the Danube in Upper Pannonia.

Cato, called of Utica, a Stoic who died by his own hand after the battle of Thapsus, 46 B.C. His name was proverbial for virtue and courage.

Cecrops, first legendary King of Athens.

Charax, perhaps the priestly historian of that name, whose date is unknown, except that it must be later than Nero.

Chrysippus, 280-207 B.C., a Stoic philosopher, and the founder of Stoicism as a systematic philosophy.

Circus, the Circus Maximus at Rome, where games were held. There were four companies who contracted to provide horses, drivers, etc. These were called Factiones, and each had its distinguishing colour: russata (red), albata (white), veneta (blue), prasina (green). There was high rivalry between them, and riots and bloodshed not infrequently.

Cithaeron, a mountain range N. of Attica.

Comedy, ancient; a term applied to the Attic comedy of Aristophanes and his time, which criticised persons and politics, like a modern comic journal, such as Punck. See New Comedy.

Conceit, opinion.

Crates, a Cynic philosopher of the 4th century B.C.

Croesus, King of Lydia, proverbial for wealth; he reigned 560-546 B.C.

DEMETRIUS of Phalerum, an Athenian orator, statesman, philosopher, and poet. Born 345 B.C.

Democritus of Abdera (460-361 B.C.), celebrated as the 'laughing philosopher,' whose constant thought was 'What fools these mortals be.' He invented the Atomic Theory.

Diogenes, the Cynic, born about 412 B.C., renowned for his rudeness and hardihood.

EMPEDOCLES of Agrigentum, fl. 5th century B.C., a philosopher, who first laid down that there were "four elements." He believed in the transmigration of souls, and the indestructibility of matter.

Epictetus, a famous Stoic philosopher. He was of Phrygia, at first a slave, then freedman, lame, poor, and contented. The work called Encheiridion was compiled by a pupil from his discourses.

Epicurus of Samos, 342-270 B.C.

Lived at Athens in his "gardens," an urbane and kindly, if somewhat useless, life. His character was simple and temperate, and had none of the vice or indulgence which was afterwards associated with the name of Epicurean.

Eudoxus of Cnidus, a famous astronomer and physician of the 4th century B.C.

FATAL, fated.

Fronto, M. Cornelius, a rhetorician and pleader, made consul in 143 A.D. A number of his letters to M, Aur. and others are extant.

GRANUA, a tributary of the Danube.

HELICE, ancient capital city of Achaia, swallowed up by an earthquake, 373 B.C.

Helvidius Priscus, son-in-law of Thrasea Paetus, a noble man and a lover of liberty. He was banished by Nero, and put to death by Vespasian.

Heraclitus of Ephesus, who lived in the 6th century B.C. He wrote on philosophy and natural science.

Herculaneum, near Mount Vesuvius, buried by the eruption of 79 A.D.

Hipparchus of Bithynia, an astronomer of the 2nd century B.C., "The true father of astronomy."

Hippocrates of Cos, about 460-357 B.C. One of the most famous physicians of antiquity.

LEONNATUS, a distinguished general under Alexander the Great.

Lucilla, daughter of M. Aurelius, and wife of Verus, whom she survived.

M. AURELIUS carried on war against them, and part of this book was written in the field.

Maecenas, a trusted adviser of Augustus, and a munificent patron of wits and literary men.

Maximus, Claudius, a Stoic philosopher.

Menippus, a Cynic philosopher.

Middle Comedy, something midway between the Old and New Comedy. See Comedy, Ancient, and New Comedy.

Middle things, Book 7, XXV. The Stoics divided all things into virtue, vice, and indifferent things; but as "indifferent" they regarded most of those things which the world regards as good or bad, such as wealth or poverty. Of these, some were "to be desired," some "to be rejected."

Muses, the nine deities who presided over various kinds of poesy, music, etc. Their leader was Apollo, one of whose titles is Musegetes, the Leader of the Muses.

NERVES, strings.

New Comedy, the Attic Comedy of Menander and his school, which criticised not persons but manners, like a modern comic opera. See Comedy, Ancient.

PANCRATIAST, competitor in the pancratium, a combined contest which comprised boxing and wrestling.

Phocion, an Athenian general and statesman, a noble and high-minded man, 4th century B.C.

He was called by Demosthenes, "the pruner of my periods."

He was put to death by the State in 317, on a false suspicion, and left a message for his son "to bear no grudge against the Athenians."

Plato of Athens, 429-347 B.C. He used the dialectic method invented by his master Socrates.

He was, perhaps, as much poet as philosopher. He is generally identified with the Theory of Ideas, that things are what they are by participation with our eternal Idea. His "Commonwealth" was a kind of Utopia.

Pompeii, near Mount Vesuvius, buried in the eruption of 79 A.D.

Pompeius, C. Pompeius Magnus, a very successful general at the end of the Roman Republic (106-48 B.C.).

Pythagoras of Samos, a philosopher, scientist, and moralist of the 6th century B.C.

QUADI, a tribe of S. Germany.

RUSTICUS, Q. Junius, or Stoic philosopher, twice made consul by M. Aurelius.

SCIPIO, the name of two great soldiers, P. Corn. Scipio Africanus, conqueror of Hannibal, and P.

Corn. Sc. Afr. Minor, who came into the family by adoption, who destroyed Carthage.

Sextus of Chaeronea, a Stoic philosopher, nephew of Plutarch.

Sinuessa, a town in Latium.

Socrates, an Athenian philosopher (469-399 B.C.), founder of the dialectic method. Put to death on a trumped-up charge by his countrymen.

Stint, limit (without implying niggardliness).

Stoics, a philosophic system founded by Zeno (4th century B.C.), and systematised by Chrysippus (3rd century B.C.). Their physical theory was a pantheistic materialism, their summum bonum "to live according to nature." Their wise man needs nothing, he is sufficient to himself; virtue is good, vice bad, external things indifferent.

THEOPHRASTUS, a philosopher, pupil of Aristotle, and his successor as president of the Lyceum. He wrote a large number of works on philosophy and natural history. Died 287 B.C.

Thrasea, P. Thrasea Pactus, a senator and Stoic philosopher, a noble and courageous man. He was condemned to death by Nero.

Tiberius, 2nd Roman Emperor (14-31 A.D.). He spent the latter part of his life at Capreae (Capri), off Naples, in luxury or debauchery, neglecting his imperial duties.

Trajan, 13th Roman Emperor, 52-117 A.D.

VERUS, Lucius Aurelius, colleague of M. Aurelius in the Empire. He married Lucilla, daughter of M. A., and died 169 A.D.

Vespasian, 9th Roman Emperor XENOCRATES of Chalcedon, 396-314 B.C., a philosopher, and president of the Academy.